Franz Heinrich Reusch

Nature and the Bible - Lectures on the Mosaic History of Creation in its Relation to Natural Science

Volume I

Franz Heinrich Reusch

Nature and the Bible - Lectures on the Mosaic History of Creation in its Relation to Natural Science
Volume I

ISBN/EAN: 9783337030667

Printed in Europe, USA, Canada, Australia, Japan

Cover: Foto ©Lupo / pixelio.de

More available books at **www.hansebooks.com**

NATURE AND THE BIBLE:

LECTURES

ON THE

MOSAIC HISTORY OF CREATION IN ITS RELATION
TO NATURAL SCIENCE.

BY

DR. FR. H. REUSCH,
PROFESSOR OF CATHOLIC THEOLOGY IN THE UNIVERSITY OF BONN.

Revised and Corrected by the Author.

Translated from the Fourth Edition
BY
KATHLEEN LYTTELTON.

VOLUME I.

EDINBURGH:
T. & T. CLARK, 38 GEORGE STREET.
1886.

TRANSLATOR'S PREFACE.

THIS translation has been made from the fourth edition, published in 1876, of Dr. F. Reusch's *Bibel und Natur*. In consequence of the rapid progress of science, some portions of the book required alteration; and the whole work has accordingly been revised by the author, and several additions and corrections have been made. Nevertheless the translator does not wish to be thought to agree entirely with all the details of the work, especially with regard to some of the arguments employed in that portion of the second part which deals with the Theory of Descent. In spite, however, of a few shortcomings, the book will, it is believed, be found to be an extremely valuable and learned summary of the teaching of the Church on the relations between Science and Religion.

The translation would be more faulty than it is, but for the kind help of several friends, and especially of Baron Anatole von Hügel, Curator of the Cambridge Museum of Archæology, who revised pp. 289–313, and has made many valuable suggestions.

K. LYTTELTON.

FEBRUARY 25, 1886.

CONTENTS.

CHAP.		PAGE
I.	INTRODUCTION,	1
II.	AUTHORITY OF THE BIBLICAL STATEMENT—THE BIBLE AND THE BOOK OF NATURE,	14
III.	HOW FAR DOES THE BIBLE TREAT OF NATURAL PHENOMENA?	29
IV.	THE TASK OF NATURAL SCIENCE,	48
V.	NATURAL SCIENCE AND FAITH ARE NOT OPPOSED,	69
VI.	GENERAL EXPLANATION OF THE MOSAIC HEXÆMERON,	89
VII.	EXPLANATION OF GENESIS I. 1, 2,	103
VIII.	EXPLANATION OF GENESIS I. 3-31,	123
IX.	EXPLANATION OF THE SECOND CHAPTER OF GENESIS,	147
X.	THE SIX DAYS,	165
XI.	ASTRONOMY AND THE BIBLE,	189
XII.	GEOLOGY. NEPTUNISM, AND PLUTONISM,	207
XIII.	THE THEORIES AS TO THE FORMATION OF THE EARTH,	229
XIV.	FOSSILS,	254
XV.	THE PALÆONTOLOGICAL HISTORY OF THE EARTH,	277
XVI.	GEOLOGY AND THE BIBLE ACCORDING TO THE LITERAL INTERPRETATION OF THE SIX DAYS,	294
XVII.	GEOLOGY AND THE BIBLE ACCORDING TO THE THEORY OF RESTITUTION,	311

CHAP.		PAGE
XVIII.	GEOLOGY AND THE BIBLE: THE CONCORDISTIC THEORY,	330
XIX.	GEOLOGY AND THE BIBLE ACCORDING TO THE IDEAL INTERPRETATION OF THE SIX DAYS,	343
XX.	THE BOUNDARY BETWEEN THE PRIMÆVAL AND THE PRESENT WORLD. THE DILUVIUM,	376
XXI.	THE DELUGE,	403
XXII.	THE DELUGE—*continued*,	426
XXIII.	THE DELUGE—*Conclusion*,	445

I.

INTRODUCTION.

The accounts of the creation, the earliest history of the world which we find in the first chapters of the Bible, and the relation which these short ancient narratives bear to the results of man's investigations into the realm of nature, have, as is well known, caused manifold discussions in this century, and have called forth an almost boundless literature. This is very easily explained. Even if the student of nature disregards or even denies the supernatural character of the Bible, and would treat it like any other human book, he cannot well ignore its narratives. They are at all events the earliest notices of this sort that he can find, and their whole form, their precision and tone of certainty, their shortness and primitive style, oblige him to consider in what relation his conclusions stand to the accounts given by the earliest writers of one of the earliest literatures. These questions become of far greater importance as soon as they are looked at from the theological point of view. In the Christian Church the Bible has always been regarded as a book written with divine assistance, and its contents should be held to be true by all who recognise it as such. And therefore the question, how far the statements of the Bible agree with what are believed to be the incontestable truths and facts discovered by natural science, becomes a vital one. The ordinary Christian may perhaps be able to rest content without comparing the two, he may hold fast simply and in faith to the teaching and narratives of the Bible, and will not suffer himself to be shaken in this belief by all the objections of human science; but such a resolution would be sinful in the theologian, and blameworthy in any one who wishes to be considered an educated person.

It is impossible for theology to maintain her rank as queen among the sciences, if she proudly or timidly isolates herself. She may still indeed keep her royal rank, but what avails a royalty which is acknowledged by no subject? The commentator must take into consideration every new discovery in the province of Hebrew, Greek and Latin philology, and every newly-discovered codex of any Biblical book; the Church historian, theologian, and historian of dogma must notice and make use of every discovery in the sphere of patristic learning, every newly-discovered historical or patristic document, and every improved edition of any of the Fathers; speculative dogma must follow the development of philosophy, and either use or reject the propositions advanced by philosophers. In the same way the theologian when writing on the doctrine of the creation, and the earliest history of created things, and the exegete in interpreting Genesis, must reckon with the conclusions which science has won, or believes it has won, by observations and discoveries in the sphere of the creation.

And it is especially in interpreting Holy Writ that the theologian can no longer avoid considering the results of scientific inquiries. The following facts should be noticed. Eminent natural philosophers have expressed in the strongest terms their conviction that the account of the creation given in the Scriptures finds a striking confirmation in the conclusions of natural science. Cuvier says, "Moses has left us a cosmogony, the accuracy of which is being confirmed every day in a marvellous manner. The books of Moses show that he perfectly understood all the most important questions of natural science. His cosmogony in particular, considered from a purely scientific point of view, is extremely remarkable, because the order in which he places the different epochs of creation is exactly the same as that which is deduced from geological investigations." So also a more recent French savant, Ampère, "Either Moses possessed just as thorough a knowledge of natural science as we have in our century, or he was inspired;" and Marcel de Serres says, "The relations between the narrative of Genesis and the recent discoveries of natural science are most remarkable. They impart a new lustre to the genius of the Hebrew lawgiver, and one cannot help recognising that he possessed either a revelation from above, or at least that penetrating genius which foresees the secrets of nature, pierces the darkness enveloping her, and constitutes the true imagination which conveys to man a gleam of the eternal truth."[1] It is triumphantly maintained, on the other side, that "astronomy takes the roof from over the head, and geology the ground from

[1] See Nicolas, *Philos. Studien*, i. 360, 423, and Debreyne, *Théorie Biblique*, p. x.

under the feet of the old faith;" the discoveries in the sphere of natural science in particular are described as "the knell of the Mosaic cosmogony," and in the name of natural science it is demanded that the Biblical narrative of the creation, the deluge, etc., shall no longer be taught to the young, because it is "senseless" and a "lie."[1] In face of such assertions it is necessary to undertake a conscientious examination of the matter. If the discoveries of natural science should really help to confirm the Mosaic narrative to such an extent as is asserted by the French savants I have mentioned, we ought not to leave unemployed such a useful instrument for the defence of the Bible. If, on the other hand, we find that the incompatibility of science and the Bible is just as explicitly asserted, and that not only by thoughtless and superficial talkers, but also by esteemed savants, the theologian must at least seek to prove that such incompatibility does not in reality exist, but that the propositions of the Bible, rightly understood, are in no way opposed to the assured results of scientific investigations.

We are indeed attempting nothing new in instituting a comparison between the results of scientific inquiry and the Biblical statements. Such a comparison has often been made, and it belongs to the recognised province of theological science in our century. But great and deep-rooted differences of opinion prevail on individual points, among those who have tried to prove that science is in harmony with the Bible. Some believe,

[1] Schleiden, *Ueber den Materialismus*, p. 8.

for instance, that the six days which are mentioned in the first chapter of Genesis must be taken to mean longer periods; while others think that we must hold them to be only periods of twenty-four hours. The events of which geology finds unmistakeable signs in the condition of the earth, are placed by some after, by others before, by others during the period of those days. Every one who lays claim to be considered as a theologian in these days, and indeed every layman who wishes to have a scientific justification for his Christian faith, should inquire carefully into the principal attempts which have been made to reconcile scientific discoveries with the Bible narrative. Under the present circumstances, however, we have more reason than ever for dealing with these questions. In our time science has emerged from the lecture-room, the study, and the laboratory into the streets; it is made popular in lectures, pamphlets, and newspapers; and every one who wishes to be considered an educated person, will not fail now-a-days to hear these lectures and read these pamphlets. The greatest savants and the most earnest inquirers do not think it beneath them to give lectures on their particular branch of science, or their favourite studies, to very mixed audiences; they compile popular handbooks of astronomy, geology, etc., and become contributors to periodicals in which, side by side with poems, novels, and adventurous travels, there are papers on the spectrum analysis and the origin of coal, on infusoria and petrifactions, on lake dwellings and flint implements, on the struggle for existence, and the relation of man to the ape. This extension of knowledge is certainly good in the abstract, for it is the right and the duty of every man to advance in the knowledge of truth according to his powers and circumstances. But at the same time there is this great drawback, that by far the greater number of so-called educated persons do not, and in the nature of things cannot, get beyond a very superficial and inadequate knowledge; nevertheless, by reason of a natural human weakness, they do not perceive its inadequacy, and therefore judge and argue on the strength of that defective knowledge; and usually the less thoroughly educated they are, the more positive and self-satisfied are their judgments and reasonings. Considering these unavoidable results, the popularization of science must be regarded as a doubtful good, and occasionally even as an evil. This is especially so when, as is unfortunately too often the case, increase in the most important of all knowledge, that of religion, and the moral formation of character which is connected with it, does not accompany the diffusion of all kinds of scientific knowledge; or when a superficial statement of such scientific knowledge is used in order to undermine faith and reverence for holy things. But the popularization of science, whatever be its value, is part of the tendency of the age. We cannot stem the tide, we must therefore take the world as it is, and consult the taste of the so-called educated public, at least so far as not to shut our minds to the sciences and the studies which now-a-days have so great an influence.

It is, however, a well-known fact that by far the

greater part of our popular scientific literature contains both direct and indirect attacks on the doctrines of the Christian faith and the direct statements of Holy Writ. Hardly a year goes by without producing a number of more or less important books, written in a popular and often attractive style, which expressly aim at combating the doctrines of Christianity and the authority of the Bible. We may take as an example the form of literature which is most characteristic of our century, the periodical press. Scarcely any well known and widely read scientific or literary periodical appears which does not occasionally contain essays on questions directly or indirectly touching the Bible; and in these essays it is for the most part either openly or covertly assumed that faith in the Scriptures, especially in the Old Testament, is quite irreconcilable with the discoveries of natural science in the nineteenth century. We cannot disguise this from ourselves; it were folly to deny that the ruling current and tendency of our popular scientific literature is decidedly hostile to revelation, and especially to Biblical revelation.

What ought we to do under these circumstances? As matters at present stand, very little is accomplished by applying preventive and prohibitory measures to intellectual subjects; by ecclesiastical interdiction of bad books, and warnings against reading them. It may be lamented, but it cannot be altered. We must therefore make up our minds to fight these, the intellectual evils and dangers of our time, with intellectual weapons. We must oppose that misuse of science by which it is employed against revelation; and we must oppose it by cultivating science ourselves, and by proving that the results of all thorough scientific investigation are compatible with revelation; that they never come into real contradiction with it, and often serve to confirm it; and that so-called educated people are deceived and imposed upon when they are persuaded that they must either give up faith in the truths of the Bible, or belief in the conclusions of the most eminent scientific men.[1]

All who value their Christian faith, and who have greater opportunities of becoming better and more thoroughly acquainted with the state of the case than have the mass of the so-called educated people, should strive by this means to save the honour both of revelation and of science, and to show that a man may have a competent and thorough knowledge of science, and at the same time be a believing Christian and Catholic. It is especially the duty of the clergyman to do this. In a time when scientific education is becoming more and more general, when not only scholars but other classes also are interested in questions which were formerly only discussed in the lecture-rooms of universities, in the studies of savants, and in folios and quartos; in such a time science makes wider if not higher claims on clergymen than it did in past centuries. Clergymen cannot be expected to be as thoroughly acquainted with the natural sciences and other branches of profane knowledge as with theology, but they may and must be required not to cut themselves off from these studies, and clearly to understand what conclusions have been arrived at, and what opinions prevail in this

[1] Cf. Deutinger, *Renan und das Wunder*, p. 19 ff.

branch of research, together with their relation to the doctrine of revelation; and they ought also to know how the assertions which are oftenest heard and read as to these matters are to be examined, corrected, and refuted.

We should be acting in opposition to the spirit of our Church if we were to cut ourselves off from the movements and aims of profane knowledge. Unchangeable as are her doctrines, and uninfluenced as her teaching has been by all the spiritual movements and struggles of centuries, yet the Church would not have her dogmas treated as cold rigid formulas, or her teaching looked upon as a simple repetition of settled unalterable propositions. The Church desires to take into consideration the progress which is made in the cognate sciences, to utilize for sacred science all the good and true results which are attained by profane science, and to help to combat all error which in its further development and in its consequences may also affect the sphere of theology.

The great teachers of the Church in the past have also held these principles. The most eminent fathers of the Greek and Latin Churches expressed their opinion that the theologian should not neglect the profane sciences which come into contact with theology, but that he should get to see clearly on what points they differ and on what points they agree; and this they carried out practically in their own writings.[1] The greatest theologians of the Middle Ages acted on the same principle, and in their exposition of

[1] Wiseman, *Twelve Lectures on the Connection between Science and Revealed Religion.*

theology they paid such regard to philosophy in its widest sense, that, as is well known, they have been blamed, and that not quite unjustly, for going too far in this respect. It is true that in centuries gone by theologians paid less attention to natural science than to philosophy, but this is because natural science was not formerly so important a part of profane knowledge as it is now. Natural science has only latterly attained to true scientific importance, but it has become one of the strongest characteristics of the intellectual movement of this century. We shall therefore be treading exactly in the footsteps of our great predecessors in theology if we follow the discussions of the present day as attentively as they followed the prevailing philosophic struggles of their time, and would most certainly have followed the inquiries of natural science had it occupied the minds of men in the same measure as it does now.

Theologians, indeed, have not failed to turn their attention to natural science, since it has become so much more prominent; and this has been done not only with the permission but also with the express approval and encouragement of the representatives of ecclesiastical authority.[1] In the last decades especially, numberless essays and pamphlets have appeared, written by theologians of all persuasions and denominations, on the relation of the Bible to the results of scientific inquiry. But I may take it for granted that you are convinced of the interest and importance of the subject which I propose to discuss. Perhaps it is more necessary to explain whether and how far I may

[1] Wiseman, *Op. cit.*

believe and pronounce myself qualified to satisfy your wish for knowledge on this question. In order rightly to explain the relation of two sciences to each other, one must of course be acquainted with both. Whoever, therefore, would compare the teaching of natural science and the teaching of the Bible about the origin and earliest history of the world, must be acquainted with the natural sciences and with exegesis; and the opinion of the man who could be both a thorough natural philosopher and a thorough exegete, would have the greatest claim on our attention. But such men are rare. Our geologists either never attempt to compare their geological conclusions with the statements in Genesis, or they assume that the Bible need not be appealed to on this question, and that a historical interest at most can be attached by science to the opinions of a Jewish writer 1500 years B.C.; and if in good faith they do institute a comparison, or if, starting with the belief that the Bible is divine, they try to prove that science is compatible with the narrative of Genesis, they are as a rule wanting in the necessary exegetical knowledge and in theological tact.

On the other hand, the exegete cannot be expected to be as well acquainted with the nature and succession of the strata, with comparative anatomy and such things, as with the Hebrew grammar, Biblical language, and the rules of Biblical interpretation. It is usually only possible for the theologian to accept in faith the conclusions which have been arrived at by the leaders in scientific inquiry. But then there is the danger of his accepting as an assured result something which, according to the judgment of savants, still requires proof, and of his not understanding, or misapplying, the proper meaning and extent of single parts of the scientific system; and further, the theologian is especially tempted too hastily to accept concessions which are made by natural science *at present*, but which may be again called in question by the progress of inquiry; or to sign an agreement between natural science and the Bible, which at first sight seems just to both parties, but which in the end turns out to be one in which both parties have sacrificed too much.

But in this respect those who are only amateurs come off worst; that is, those who, not being really well versed either in natural science or in theology, but knowing a little of both, think they can make up for what is wanting by an undoubted goodwill, a sincere faith, and zeal for the cause of the Bible.

'I am very far from ascribing to myself any wide or thorough knowledge of natural science. I have never carried on any researches personally, nor am I in a position to do so. I must content myself with studying the scientific conclusions embodied by savants in a form in which they are accessible to every educated man. But that will suffice for our purpose, and although, as I have observed, the great number of treatises on this subject has by no means led to a unanimity of views, and thus to a lasting dismissal of the subject, it seems ungrateful not to acknowledge that so much preparatory labour has materially lightened our task.

The merit which I think I may claim for my lectures on the Mosaic history consists principally in this: I hope to put you in possession of the state of the case as completely as is necessary, and as clearly and widely as possible. We must first determine the relation of theology and the Bible to the natural sciences in general, and then ascertain where we may look for teaching from the Bible and where from natural science, which questions revelation and which natural science shall decide. It will then be necessary to examine and explain the first chapters of the Bible, and to ascertain what things the Bible asserts to be matters of faith and what it has left to human discovery; which passages and expressions have, according to the rules of hermeneutics, a distinct meaning which may not be departed from, and which passages and expressions on the other hand are capable of divers interpretations, and so leave room for human inquiry. In addition to this, we must ascertain in what way and with what success men have tried to bring the results of scientific inquiry into harmony with the Mosaic history. We shall then treat the following chapters of Genesis in the same way.

II.

AUTHORITY OF THE BIBLICAL STATEMENT—THE BIBLE AND THE BOOK OF NATURE.

BEFORE entering on the discussion of the relation of divine revelation to human inquiry in general, I must explain how far the primæval history which we find in the first chapters of Genesis is to be looked upon as a divine revelation. In investigating this point we need not enter into the question of the Mosaic authorship of Genesis. The book may be by Moses or by a later writer, but at all events from our ecclesiastical standpoint we must acknowledge it to be an inspired book. Now, when the Church asserts that any books of the Old or New Testament are inspired, she means at least to imply (apart from theological controversies about the exact definition of inspiration) that the authors have received special assistance from the Holy Spirit, in consequence of which they have been enabled to communicate either the results of supernatural knowledge and revelation, or of their own natural personal knowledge, experience, and observation, in such a manner that their communications bear the stamp of a divine confirmation: they must therefore be accepted with faith as the word of God in a more or less strict sense. The prophet—I use the word in its widest sense—was supernaturally enlightened about future events, or other things which are hidden from the unassisted human intellect; and then he was moved by the Spirit of God, and enabled, for the edification of contemporaries and posterity, so to write down his inspirations or his prophecies that his book gives us a faithful and trustworthy account of the divine truths which were revealed to him. On the other hand, the primary function of the Biblical historian was to collect and write down those things which he had either himself experienced, seen, or heard, or which he had received from trustworthy witnesses, or which had been handed down by a credible tradition, or, lastly, which he had obtained from older literary sources. But although in this respect the Biblical historian practically resembles other trustworthy historians in all essential points, yet a historical book to which the quality of inspiration is ascribed, that is, a historical book in the Bible, differs substantially from other histories. First, we must assume that the literary activity of the Biblical historian was the result, not of human free choice, but of a divine ordinance, that therefore this activity must be ascribed to a divine impulse, an inspiration, by which these writers, either knowingly or unknowingly, felt themselves impelled to write. Further, we must assume that the Biblical writers were supported in their work in a special way by divine assistance, and were guided according to the divine will, and that this divine help preserved them in a special manner from every error which would counteract the divine object; so that the writings composed in consequence of that higher stimulus, and by the divine assistance, are not to be regarded as mere human productions, like other literary works. Such is the theory of inspiration as it is now practically unanimously held by the most eminent of those theologians who believe in the doctrine at all. This is not the place for discussing the scientific confirmation of this doctrine, or for investigating the theological controversies which are attached to it. I will only add that many theologians, and some of them Roman Catholics, admit that it is allowable to believe that the assistance of the Divine Spirit, by which error was averted, only extended to such things as stood in immediate and necessary connection with the religious truths of the Bible; and that with regard to other things, which are unimportant from a religious point of view, the Biblical writers had no further divine assistance than is vouchsafed to other honest, pious, or holy writers;[1] and that therefore this divine assistance assures us, not that every word is true, but that nothing in the Bible, rightly understood, can mislead us with respect to religion, faith, or moral conduct.[2] According to this, therefore, we might assume that the Biblical writers may have erred on such points of history, chronology, and archæology, etc., as are not important to the religious contents of the Bible. It is not necessary to examine this opinion here, as I do not mean to make it a starting-point for my inquiries.

I will now proceed to apply what has been said about the inspiration of the Bible to the Biblical narrative of the creation and the earliest history of the world. The author of the first chapters of Genesis might have

---

[1] H. Holden, *Divinæ fidei analysis*, i. 1, chap. 5, sec. 1 (*Bibliotheca regularum fidei*, ed. I. Braun. Bonn 1844. I. p. 39; cf. p. 271).

[2] Walworth, Brownsons, *Quarterly Review*, 1863, p. 337.

acquired the knowledge of what is stated in those chapters concerning the fate of the first man, and the earliest history of mankind, by verbal tradition, or by older writings; and therefore in a purely natural manner. If we admit this possibility, we are not justified in assuming that he acquired his knowledge in any other way; for instance, by an immediate divine revelation. We have therefore in these chapters an account of the traditions of the forefathers of the Jewish people, but an account which is the result of a divine impulse, and has been brought about by divine assistance. It is different, however, with the first chapters of Genesis, which treat of the creation of the world, and of the development, improvement, and history of the earth and its inhabitants before the first appearance of man. No man witnessed these events; and therefore the account given of them cannot be ascribed to human tradition, as with the contents of the following chapters. To what source, then, must we ascribe this first section?

It has been supposed that Moses may have obtained the knowledge of the origin of things, which he displays in the first chapters of Genesis, through observation and thought,—as we should say, through philosophic speculation and scientific inquiry. But this theory, although theologically admissible, seems to me less consistent with the facts than the other, namely, that the contents of the Hexæmeron must be ascribed to a divine revelation. The whole form of the Mosaic account of creation certainly does not strike the unprejudiced reader as an expression of the results of human thought and inquiry; and such short, decided, and apodictical sentences would not be written by one

B

who had arrived at a conclusion or an opinion after laborious thought and search, but rather by one who *knows* something, and whose knowledge is founded either on his own observation or on undoubted information. The division of the work of creation into six parts, and the manner in which the hallowing of the seventh day by the Creator is connected with them, plainly points to a divine revelation as the source of the account of the creation. For instance, later, in the giving of the Ten Commandments, it is God Himself who says, " Six days shalt thou labour and do all thy work : but the seventh day is the Sabbath of the Lord thy God : in it thou shalt not do any work, thou, nor thy son, nor thy daughter, thy man-servant, nor thy maid-servant, thy cattle, nor thy stranger that is within thy gates. For in six days the Lord made heaven and earth, the sea and all that in them is, and rested the seventh day; wherefore the Lord blessed the Sabbath day, and hallowed it."[1]

But to whom did God reveal this knowledge of the creation ? The obvious answer appears to be, to Moses, so that the first chapters of Genesis must be added to those portions of the Pentateuch which, as has been said above, must be ranked with the writings of the prophets. But there are many grave reasons against this opinion, and in favour of the other, namely, that the first revelation of the history of creation was given long before Moses, probably to our first parents ; that Moses knew of this revelation by tradition, and with divine assistance truly reproduced this tradition.

First, Moses prefaces revelations which he himself

[1] Ex. xx. 9-11.

had received with words which we do not find here; such as "And Jehovah said unto Moses."

Secondly, The Sabbath is apparently not a Mosaic institution, in the sense that the hallowing of the seventh day was first prescribed by Moses; on the contrary, Biblical archæology supplies us with reasons, which need not be enumerated here, but which amount almost to proof, for believing that Moses found that his people already kept the Sabbath, and that it was only more decidedly regulated by his legislation. But the hallowing of the seventh day presupposes the Hexæmeron.

Thirdly, The following fact is pointed out by various modern savants, especially by Kurtz.[1] The legends of all other peoples—north and south, east and west—agree so remarkably and minutely with the statement of our Mosaic record, however different the religious spirit which runs through them may be, that we cannot help tracing back all the accounts to a common origin; for it is impossible to believe that every nation could have obtained the same details from Israel. Therefore the independent author of the first record cannot have been the writer of Genesis, nor, indeed, can he have been any Israelite. There must have been a common source from which Israel and also the other nations drew, and this source must belong to a time when the human race was still in its primæval unity, not yet separated in habitation and language by sharp distinctions of race, and by differences of culture and religion. The nations who became isolated must have derived their similar recollections and legends from

[1] *Bibel und Astronomie*, p. 57.

this primæval age. According to the different intellectual developments after the separation, this inheritance of their ancestors took different shapes in the mouths of the people or in the traditions of the priests, but always in such a manner that the mark of the common ancestry, the unity of origin, was unmistakeably stamped on it. But if we are thus obliged to go back to the time when the peoples and tribes of the human race were still united, why should we not go a few steps farther back to the time of Noah, and thence to the time of Adam? I will mention only a few of the points in which the cosmogonies of the different, most widely separated peoples so resemble one another and the Mosaic record of creation, that the assumption of a common source for these traditions is forced upon us. The Thohuwabohu of the Bible has its counterpart in all heathen mythologies, and appears under different names, from the Athor of the Egyptians to Chaos, the *rudis indigestaque moles* of the author of the *Metamorphoses*. The darkness and the mass of waters are everywhere principal features in the description. The six days, or six periods of creation, are found in several cosmogonies—from China in the East to the Etruscans in the West; and they occur mainly in the same order as in Genesis. Man is held by all peoples, without exception, to be the final creation; most heathen mythologies know of his formation from the dust of the earth, and some also of the formation of the woman from a limb of the man.[1]

Besides these great resemblances, there are also very

---

[1] Cf. Lücken, *Die Traditionen des Menschen geschlechts*, p. 28 ff. Stiefelhagen, *Theologie des Heidenthums*, p. 506 ff. Dillmann, *Genesis*, p. 5.

important differences between the heathen cosmogonies on the one hand, and the Mosaic cosmogony on the other. The idea of actual creation is entirely unknown to the heathen. Delitzsch says:[1] "The Biblical cosmogony alone presents the pure idea of creation from nothing, without eternal substance, without the assistance of an intermediate Being or Demiurgos; this idea appears among the heathen, but it is obscured; the heathen cosmogonies either presuppose an existing substance and are therefore dualistic, or they substitute emanation for creation and are therefore pantheistic. Then they are all of a national and limited character, they have been formed by the influence of the particular mythological ideas of the separate peoples, and have been affected by their local and climatic circumstances. There is nothing narrow of this kind in the Biblical account of creation. And how wonderfully the Biblical cosmogony stands out from all the others by its plain and noble historic form! Manu's *Book of Laws* teaches that the seed of the primæval waters developed into a golden egg, in which Brahma remained at rest for a whole year of creation, till at length he split it, and from its two halves formed the heavens and the earth; the Babylonians say that Bel cut the mermaid Homoraka in two, and made from one half the earth, and from the other the heavens; that he then cut off his own head, and that the gods mixed the falling drops of blood with earth and made men out of them; according to the Egyptians, Num-Ra, the great divine creator, made gods and goddesses with his

[1] *Genesis*, 3rd ed. p. 83 (4th ed. p. 71).

hands, and formed the son of Isis on a potter's wheel; while the Biblical account of creation shows in its first verses the grand simplicity which is the stamp of truth. The whole narrative is sober, decided, clear, concrete. The history as it is related is suggestive of much profound thought and poetical beauty; but in itself it is free from the influence of human poetry and human philosophizing." A. Dillmann, another expounder of Genesis, expresses himself in a similar way: "As here the just and clear division between God and the world is accomplished, and God is conceived in His full sublimity, spirituality, and goodness, so the account of the manner of creation is sublimer, worthier, and more exact than anywhere else; without intermixture of the grotesque and fantastic, simple, sober, clear, and true. There is nothing which could seem unworthy even of the purest idea of God, and if an attempt must be made to describe in human fashion the secret of the creation, which yet must always remain a secret for man, it could not have been made more sublimely or worthily."[1]

If, among the different cosmogonies, any one has reproduced truly the original divine revelation concerning the order of the creation, it is without doubt the Mosaic. But to us the Mosaic account of

[1] *Genesis*, p. 10. Dillmann does not trace the Hexæmeron back to an actual revelation, but to the popular ideas about the origin of the world which obtained among the Israelites, and the great family of nations with which they were connected. These old-established ideas were purified and transformed by the Mosaic writer (p. 9). The Hexæmeron may be said to be a revelation, for "only where God had revealed Himself in His true form could this history have been composed: it is a work of the spirit of revelation," p. 10.

creation has more than a merely relative truth, if we believe in the inspiration of the Bible. I trust that the above discussion has at least shown you clearly, that if we take up the theological position, we must accept the following propositions: (1) God gave in ancient times, probably to the first man, a revelation concerning the creation of the world. (2) This revelation was handed down by tradition to Moses, and Moses, with the assistance of the Divine Spirit, so transcribed it, that his transcription reproduces truly the original revelation. We have therefore (3) in the Mosaic account of creation a divine and thus an undoubtedly true account of the creation of all things.

God has, however, revealed Himself to man not only in the Bible, not only in a supernatural way, but also through nature. "The heavens declare the glory of God, and the firmament showeth His handiwork. There is no speech nor language where their voice is not heard. Their line is gone out through all the earth, and their words to the end of the world."[1] And according to the unanimous teaching of the Old and New Testaments, as given in the first chapter of Romans and the thirteenth chapter of Wisdom, the contemplation of visible things is a means of attaining to a knowledge of God and His greatness, even for those who stand outside the sphere of supernatural revelation.

But if the Bible and nature are both a means of revelation, if God speaks to man through both, if both are alike books written by the hand of God, so that

[1] Ps. xix. 1, 3, 4.

man should read the truth therein, it is impossible that the teaching of the Bible and the teaching of nature should contradict each other. Cardinal Wiseman says: If we are firmly convinced "that God is as much the author of our religion as He is of nature, we must be also thoroughly assured that the comparison of His works, in both these orders, must necessarily give a uniform result."[1]

"For," adds another English savant, "an Allwise and Almighty God can have revealed nothing which could be proved afterwards by natural science to be false."[2] We must go farther, and say that nature can teach man nothing which would contradict what God has certainly revealed. "The Bible and nature," says Kurtz,[3] "in so far as they are both the word of God, must agree. When this appears not to be the case, either the interpretation of the theologian or that of the natural philosopher is at fault."

If we hold fast to this simple but weighty statement, it will be a help and a comfort to us in the difficulties and hindrances which we shall find on our way. The revelation of God given us in the Bible can contain no error, but neither can nature teach us anything erroneous, for it is the work of the same God whose word is the Bible; one and the same God speaks to the spirit of man in the language of the Bible and in the dumb signs of nature. But the spirit of man may err. The words of the Bible and the words of nature are undoubtedly

---

[1] *Op. cit.* i. 8.
[2] *Geology in its Relation to Revealed Religion*, by C. B., p. 1.
[3] *Bibel und Astronomie*, p. 6.

true, but we must not forget that we may possibly hear and interpret wrongly these undoubtedly true words, and that we certainly have heard or interpreted them wrongly if it seems that the words of the Bible and the words of nature contradict one another. If, then, it happens that a statement obtained from the Bible by the help of exegesis contradicts a statement which men of science, relying on their observations and inquiries, believe to be an assured truth, we may assume beforehand that it is not the teaching of the Bible or nature, or both, which is wrong, because contradictory, but that the supposed contradiction has been caused through the error either of the theologian or of the natural philosopher; and that a more minute exegetical examination of the Bible, or a more complete and thorough inquiry into nature, would certainly lead to a different result.[1]

This certainty is especially calculated to preserve for the theologian that freedom and honesty which every inquirer, but above all the theological

---

[1] "A theologian may err by drawing a mistaken conclusion from a dogma or a passage in the Bible, and by opposing it to the well-founded assertions of natural science; or he may interpret wrongly a scientific statement, and may mark this wrong interpretation of the statement as contradicting a point of religious belief. A natural philosopher may advance false theories, or draw false conclusions from true theories, and may then use these errors of his to attack religion. But in every case science when it has become more exact and impartial, and theology when it has become better instructed and has abstained from interference outside its own sphere, have reconciled contradictions which were caused, not by the nature of things, but either by a misunderstanding which might be cleared up, or an error which might be corrected, or an interference with each other's province which might be set right. It is fortunate that there are many different ways by which human reason can attain to a conclusion, and that these different ways control each

inquirer, must regard not only as necessary, but as his greatest distinction. Let us suppose that we have before us a contradiction of the kind just described, between what we believe to be the right interpretation of a passage in the Bible and a truth of geological or of some other analogous science which is regarded by the natural philosopher as indisputable : we cannot succeed in discovering where the fault lies, the rules of exegesis forbid us to give any other interpretation to the passage, and the natural philosopher maintains that the facts as they are, and the laws as he knows them, necessarily lead him to the conclusion opposed to the Bible; what is to be done then? Before all things and under all circumstances we must be honest, and not stain our pure and holy cause with sophisms and special pleading; on no account must we conceal and slur over the contradiction, try to explain away the words of the Bible, or minimize the conclusions of the natural philosopher, which he has reached in a true, scientific manner. The greatest savant need not be ashamed to confess with the wise men of the olden time that there is much he does not know.

other. Theoretically, each of these ways is sure and sufficing, but the men who follow them are subject to error, and it is fortunate that the error which can be set right is shown by the want of harmony between the results attained by the different ways of search. Arithmetic is an undoubtedly sure science, but it is well that the faults in the calculations should be discovered by proving the result. If false and injurious doctrines are preached in the name of natural science, these will sooner or later be directly refuted, because the faults in the method or the conclusions through which these errors arose will be pointed out; but it is well that philosophy or religion should be able to confront these errors, even before they are directly refuted, with truths which are supported by sure conclusions of another kind, or by an authority whose infallibility in its own province is proved."—Th. H. Martin, *Les sciences et la philosophie*, p. 62.

In such a case, then, we need not fear to say that we cannot succeed in reconciling the apparent contradiction, but that we are nevertheless persuaded that it is only apparent, and that it will be explained, although in the present state of science that is not yet possible.[1] It is all the easier for us to make such an admission because the natural sciences are continually developing, indeed several branches have hardly got beyond the beginning. The reconciliation of the statements in the Bible with the conclusions of natural science has, as we shall see, made steady progress for a century past; every decade has made their relation clearer, so that if some obscure points still remain, we may conclude from past experience that the further progress of inquiry will throw light on these also.[2]

[1] "To dig deeper, to examine more and more actively and restlessly, and not to draw back timidly should inquiry lead to unwelcome conclusions—that is the mark of the true theologian. He will not at once draw back his foot, timidly and cautiously, as if he had stepped on an adder, and take to flight, if by chance a statement which had been held to be incontrovertible seems to fail under the dialectical process of his investigation, or if a supposed truth threatens to prove an error. He will not wish to resemble the savages who cannot see an eclipse without being anxious about the fate of the sun."—Döllinger, *Die Vergangenheit und Gegenwart der kath. Theologie*, Regensburg 1863, p. 27.

[2] "He who is as sure as he is of his own existence that the God of truth is at once the God of nature and the God of revelation, cannot believe it to be possible that His voice in either, rightly understood, can differ, or deceive His creatures. To oppose facts in the natural world because they seem to oppose revelation, or to humour them so as to compel them to speak its voice, is, he knows, but another form of the ever-ready feeble-minded dishonesty of lying for God, and trying by fraud or falsehood to do the work of the God of truth. It is with another and a nobler spirit that the true believer walks amongst the works of nature. The words graven on the everlasting rocks are the words of God, and they are graven by His hand. No more can they contradict His word written in His Book, than could the words of the Old Covenant graven by His hand or the stony tables contradict the

But do not forget that I have been speaking only of a possible case. I do not know that there is any important point on which we must be satisfied with a "non liquet;" but if in my lectures the harmony between the Bible and science should not seem clear on any particular point, do not let the good cause suffer, but remember that the harmony must exist, although either the savants have not succeeded in proving it, or the knowledge and descriptive power of the lecturer, whom you are honouring with your attention, do not equal his goodwill.

writings of His hand in the volume of the new dispensation. There may be to man difficulty in reconciling all the utterances of the two voices. But what of that? He has learned already that here he knows only in part, and that the day of reconciling all apparent contradictions between what must agree is nigh at hand. He rests his mind in perfect quietness on this assurance, and rejoices in the gift of light without a misgiving as to what it may discover. 'A man of deep thought and great practical wisdom,' says Sedgwick (*Discourse on the Studies of the University*, p. 153), 'one whose piety and benevolence have for many years been shining before the world, and of whose sincerity no scoffer (of whatever school) will dare to start a doubt (Dr. Chalmers), recorded his opinion in the great assembly of the men of science who during the past year were gathered from every corner of the empire within the walls of this university, "that Christianity had everything to hope, and nothing to fear, from the advancement of philosophy." This is as truly the spirit of Christianity as it is that of philosophy.'"—*Quarterly Review*, vol. cviii. (July 1860) p. 256.

III.

HOW FAR DOES THE BIBLE TREAT OF NATURAL PHENOMENA?

IN the foregoing lecture I have explained the statement made by Kurtz in the following words : "The Bible and nature, in so far as they are both the word of God, must agree; where this appears not to be the case, either the interpretation of the theologian or that of the natural philosopher is at fault. For not only the latter," adds Kurtz quite rightly, "but also the former, happens only too often; and it has caused unspeakable confusion in the question as to the harmony of the Scriptures and nature." In order to be secure against such mistakes in our examination of this question, we must next define the limits of the two provinces of knowledge which God conveys to man by means of the Bible on the one hand and nature on the other.

With reference to this, the following simple but important statement must be kept in mind. The object of supernatural divine revelation is never the extension of our profane knowledge, and therefore the Bible is nowhere intended to give us strictly scientific information. This statement is by no means new, and cannot be regarded as a concession wrung by natural science from theology in modern times; on the contrary, we find it in the book which was used as a compendium in all theological schools throughout the scholastic period, and which itself only claims to be an outline of the theology of the fathers of the Church. Peter Lombard says in the second book of the *Sentences* (Dist. 23), "Man did not by sinning lose the knowledge of natural things, nor that by which his bodily wants are satisfied; and therefore in Scripture man is not taught these things; but the knowledge of the soul, which by sinning he lost. Hanc scientiam homo peccando non perdidit, nec illam qua carnis necessaria providerentur. Et idcirco in scriptura homo de huiusmodi non eruditur, sed de scientia animæ, quam peccando amisit."

To illustrate, not to confirm this statement, I will add a few quotations from eminent authors, theologians, and natural philosophers, both Catholic and Protestant. Xaverius Patrizi, one of the ablest Italian exegetes of the present time, says,[1] "In order to shield ourselves from the error of supposing that natural science could come into conflict with the Bible, we must remember that the Biblical writers do not intend to discuss scientific questions, or to enlighten our ignorance on scientific subjects."

One of the most intellectual of English theologians, J. H. Newman, says,[2] "Theology and physical science, on the whole, do most surely occupy distinct fields, in which each may teach without expecting any interposition from the other. It might indeed have pleased the Almighty to have superseded physical inquiry by

---

[1] *De interpretatione scripturarum sacrarum.* Rome 1844, ii. 80.
[2] *Lectures and Essays on University Subjects.* London 1859.

revealing the truths which are its object, but he has not done so."

"The disappointment of those," says the English geologist Buckland, "who look for a detailed account of geological phenomena in the Bible, rests on a gratuitous expectation of finding therein historical information respecting all the operations of the Creator in times and places with which the human race has no concern; as reasonably might we object that the Mosaic history is imperfect, because it makes no specific mention of the satellites of Jupiter or the ring of Saturn, as feel disappointment at not finding in it the history of geological phenomena, the details of which may be fit matter for an encyclopædia of science, but are foreign to the objects of a volume intended only to be a guide of religious belief and moral conduct."[1]

"The Bible," says Kurtz, "preserves its religious character, in that it in no case anticipates human science, in no case treats of problems, the solution of which belongs to empirical inquiry. Therefore none of the conclusions of the latter can contradict the Bible, or come into conflict with revealed truth. Revelation gives *carte blanche* for the conclusions of natural science. It favours neither Plutonism nor Neptunism, it only judges matters which concern religion. It no more decides between Neptunists and Plutonists, than between homœopaths and allopaths."

You see from what has been said that to attempt to extract a system of astronomy, geology, or any natural science from the Bible, and point it out as being

[1] *Geology and Mineralogy cons. with ref. to Natural Theology.* London 1836.

vouched for by revelation, would be vain and indeed blameworthy.[1] The Bible gives us a system of faith and morality; in order to draw up a system of natural philosophy, man must have recourse to nature and to his natural reasoning powers.

To this first truth, that it is not the object of the Bible to enlighten us on scientific as well as on religious subjects, must be added another. The Biblical writers received supernatural enlightenment from God, but the object of this enlightenment and of the divine revelation altogether was only to impart *religious* truths, not profane knowledge; and we may therefore, without diminishing from the respect due to the holy writers, or in any way weakening the doctrine of inspiration, safely allow that the Biblical writers were not in advance of their age in the matter of profane knowledge, and consequently of natural science. The praises given by certain French savants to the genius or the scientific knowledge of the Jewish lawgiver, because of the supposed anticipation in Genesis of modern scientific discoveries, are therefore not to the purpose. As regards profane knowledge Moses was not raised above his contemporaries by divine revelation, and there is no proof whatever of his being in a position to raise himself above them by his own thought and inquiry.

How far the physical views of Moses were right or wrong is, however, a matter of tolerable indifference to

---

[1] Even in recent times some theologians have made this mistake, or at least they have attempted to find far too many scientific truths and doctrines in the Bible. See an American clergyman in *Creation a Recent Work of God* (cf. *Theol. Lit.-Bl.* 1870, 747), and Abbé Choyer, *La Théorie géogonique*, p. 79 (cf. *Theol. Lit.-Bl.* 1872, 357).

us; it is only important to discover what physical views are expressed in the Book of Genesis which are not to be ascribed to Moses, but bear both a divine and human character.

Although the teaching of divine things in the widest sense of the word is the sole object of revelation in the Bible, it is impossible to speak much of the things of God without also touching on the things of nature; and it is especially in the first chapters of Genesis that physical elements of all kinds are in this way interwoven with dogmatic truths of the creation of the world. It is true that the Bible *directly* imparts only religious truths, but it cannot do this without touching indirectly and incidentally on the things of nature. How does the matter stand in this case?

First of all, we have no ground for assuming that in such indirect or casual references to natural things, the Biblical writers intended to give their readers more accurate views, or more complete explanations of these natural things, than they could obtain or had already obtained in a merely human way; nor could this have been the result of their writings. When the preacher says, "All the rivers run into the sea, yet the sea is not full; unto the place from which the rivers come, thither they return again,"[1] he does not mean to explain to us how the mists rise out of the sea and form the rain by which the springs are fed; his sole object is to show in the course of his book the constant change and circulation of earthly things, and he illustrates them by a comparison with one of the phenomena of nature which he had himself observed, and which he

[1] Eccles. i. 7.

assumed that his readers would know or at any rate understand.

Secondly, it is immaterial if a Biblical writer, especially a poetical writer, states or assumes a view of natural things and phenomena which is pronounced by science to be erroneous, but which may be in a measure justified as not being out of place where it is a question of the apparent and popular expression, and not of the real and scientific fact. Few people doubt now-a-days that the earth revolves round the sun, and round its own axis, and think that the sun revolves round the earth ; and yet in everyday life, and indeed on every occasion when it is not important, no one would think of using the scientifically correct expression instead of the common and apparent one ; or would say anything but, "The sun rises and sets," "The sun has run a third of its course," etc. Why should the poet of the Old Testament express himself differently? Why should he not say, "The sun is as a bridegroom coming out of his chamber, and rejoiceth as a strong man to run a race. His going forth is from the end of the heaven, and his circuit unto the ends of it."[1] And what reasonable man would take exception to the words in which Joshua expresses the wish that the daylight might last till the enemy was completely conquered : "Sun, stand thou still upon Gibeon, and thou moon in the valley of Ajalon;" or to those in which the author of the Book of Joshua describes the fulfilling of this wish through the Almighty Power of God : "And the sun stood still, and the moon stayed until the people had avenged themselves upon their

[1] Ps. xix. 5, 6.

enemies."[1] It matters very little to us what the personal views of Joshua and the Biblical writers were as to the relation of the sun and the earth to each other, and as to their respective revolutions; probably they never thought about the subject when they used the words, and if they did think about it, no doubt they held the opinions which obtained up to the time of Copernicus and Galileo. The Holy Spirit, Who inspired the Biblical writer, knew the true conditions; but, if you will permit the somewhat profane expression, it would have been acting out of character to have at this juncture revealed to the Biblical historian the error of the prevailing opinion as to the motion of the sun, and to have caused him to make use of expressions which Galileo would have allowed to be correct. The Bible wishes to make known to us that the daylight that day was unusually prolonged in consequence of a divine miracle, every one may learn this from the account given; there was no intention of imparting further astronomical information, therefore that account was clothed in words which could be understood at every period, and which are so far, if only so far, correct, that in the opinion of the natural and uneducated man the sun does move daily from east to west.

In consequence of this same popular belief, Moses mentions the sun and moon in the first chapters of Genesis as the two great lights of heaven, beside the other stars. They are so to the eye of man, although astronomers know that it is not the case; and although it would be absurd on the strength of Gen. i. 10 to state as the teaching of the Bible that the sun is the

[1] Josh. x. 12, 13.

largest, and the moon the second largest star of the heavens, it would be just as absurd to blame Moses, or the Spirit which inspired him, because he let pass unused the splendid opportunity of improving the astronomical ideas of the Jews. It is quite immaterial whether the readers of the Bible believe this or that star to be the greater, if only they learn and believe that it is God who has created the stars both great and small, and made them shine for the use and delight of man. When, therefore, the Bible speaks of the things of nature as they appear to the eye of man, these conceptions, although they are, as has been said, relatively justifiable, are in no way to be considered as absolutely correct, and we must take care not to treat them as scriptural; they are the conceptions of the natural man as distinguished from the man of science, and the Bible, although placing itself in this respect in the position of the natural man, gives them no more authority than they intrinsically possess. Nor, however, do such popular superficial expressions involve a contradiction between nature and the Bible; the latter does not profess to be scientifically correct in such things, it professes only to be easily understood by the natural man.

So much may be conceded by the exegete to the man of science, and the following quotations from one or two older theologians of undoubted orthodoxy will prove that such concessions are neither new nor hazardous. S. Jerome, who is honoured by the Church as "the greatest commentator on the Bible," may speak for the Fathers. He says, "Many things are expressed in Scripture according to the opinion of the times in which they were written, and not according to the truth — Multa in scripturis sanctis dicuntur juxtâ opinionem illius temporis, quo gesta referuntur, et non juxta quod rei veritas continebat."[1] S. Thomas Aquinas may stand as the representative of the Middle Ages. In his *Summa* he briefly dismisses an objection which might be based on the literal interpretation of a Biblical passage in these words, "Secundum opinionem populi loquitur scriptura,—Scripture here makes use of a popular expression, which must not be strained."[2] S. Thomas observes repeatedly, and especially when explaining the history of creation, that the Scriptures adapt themselves to the reader's power of comprehension.[3]

[1] Jer. xxviii. 10, 11 ; cf. in Matt. xiv. 8.
[2] 1. 2. q. 98, a. 3 ad 2.
[3] *e.g.* 1. q. 68, a. 3 c. ; q. 70, a. 1 ad 3. The astronomer Kepler observes on this point, " Astronomy discloses the causes of natural things ; it examines optical illusions *ex professo*. Holy Scripture, which teaches higher things, makes use of the ordinary forms of speech in order to be understood, and speaks quite incidentally about natural things as they appear, as in that way ordinary language has been formed. Scripture would express itself in the same way, even if all men understood the optical illusions. For we astronomers do not cultivate astronomy in order to change the ordinary form of speech, but we wish to open the doors of truth without affecting language. We say with the multitude, the planets stand still, go back, . . . the sun rises and sets, it mounts to the middle of the sky, etc. We say this with the multitude, just as it appears to our eyes, although, as all astronomers agree, it is not in the least true. Much less can we require that the divinely-inspired Scripture should neglect ordinary language, and model its words according to natural science, confusing the simple people of God with dark and unsuitable expressions about things beyond the comprehension of the uneducated, and thereby itself shutting out its own much more lofty aim."—*Epitome Astronomiæ Copernicanæ*, p. 138. " Supposing that the founder of a faith like Moses possessed all the modern knowledge of astronomy and geology, what use would it have been, or rather what harm would it not have done, if he had spoken in the language of Copernicus, Newton, Laplace, Werner, L. von Buch, or Sir Charles Lyell? He would certainly have been misunderstood and despised for 2000 years,

The supernatural religious teaching which is the task of Scripture, is not often closely connected in the Bible with the occasional and indirect allusions to natural things; and after what has been said, such passages are of no great difficulty compared to the Hexæmeron. But here we find a whole chapter in which the Bible treats of a subject on which it usually only touches occasionally and slightly. Certainly here also the first object is religious dogmatic instruction, but it is in this case completely interwoven with an account of events in the realm of nature. The foregoing general discussion will enable us in some measure to decide beforehand what quantity of information concerning natural things we may expect to find in the Hexæmeron, and what its character will be.

I have already quoted an instance from the first chapter of Genesis, in which the Bible adapts its expression to the ordinary popular idea; it speaks of two great lights in the heavens, apart from the other stars; and this not because the sun and moon are in reality the largest stars, but because they appear so to us, and when we are not speaking astronomically we call them so. We shall find other similar expressions, and during our explanation of the Hexæmeron we shall be justified in applying the standard by which we judge a popular account of the events and appearances in nature, and not that by which we judge the account given us by a savant.

Further, with reference to the Hexæmeron, we must,

and all this only to give some satisfaction in the nineteenth century; for by the twentieth much of the satisfaction of the nineteenth would have been lost."—*Ausland*, 1861, p. 410.

with S. Thomas Aquinas,[1] make the following distinction. Some of the things which are therein related to us belong *ad substantiam fidei*, they are essentially of a theological and dogmatic character, especially those statements which occur in the first verse of Genesis, that the world has a beginning, and has been created. Other things which are related in the Hexæmeron are not in themselves of a theological or dogmatic character, and therefore do not belong *per se ad fidem*; but because they are combined with the dogmatic statements in the Biblical account, they belong *per accidens ad fidem*. Genesis does not only say that the world was created by God,—which, properly speaking, if taken strictly, constitutes dogma,—but it also describes the manner and order in which the world was created; and if this description is not in itself of a dogmatic or theological character, it yet partakes of it because it is combined in Holy Writ with statements which are purely theological. Now, with reference to the first and strictly theological statements, proceeds S. Thomas, no one must have any opinion concerning them but the established, traditional, ecclesiastical one. The Bible here treats of its own special subject, that of the truths of faith, and therefore its expressions are clear and decided; the meaning of its words in this respect is clear to every impartial reader; they have always been understood in one certain sense both by the Jews in olden time and by the Christians later; there is a *unanimis consensus patrum* with reference to their meaning, and there is a traditional interpretation which, according to the rules of Catholic hermeneutics,

[1] In 1. 2. Sent. dist. 12. art. 2.

is binding on the exegete. It is otherwise with the other elements of the Hexæmeron, with the statements and expressions which do not refer actually to dogma, but to the natural things connected with it. With reference to these things, says S. Thomas, the account given in the Bible is differently explained by the Fathers. This observation is somewhat superficial but quite accurate. The separation of light from darkness, of water from land, and similar things which are related in the Hexæmeron, have no dogmatic importance *per se*, but only *per accidens*, in so far as they are combined with the dogmatic statement that the world was created by God. Holy Writ need therefore only express itself clearly and unequivocally about these things when they are connected with dogma. But it is not the aim of Holy Writ to teach things that are of interest only to the natural philosopher, and not to the theologian, and therefore it is not necessary that it should express itself clearly and completely about them, as its teaching is to be altogether theological and not scientific. Now things which by their nature are not the objects of Biblical revelation, cannot either be the objects of ecclesiastical tradition; therefore a *consensus patrum* or an ecclesiastical decision can no more exist about questions of science than about questions of medicine or grammar. The Church is the infallible interpreter of Holy Writ, but only in *rebus fidei et morum*. Savants may discuss the meaning of the Hebrew word Kikajon, and decide what kind of tree or shrub it was, under which Jonah, according to the Biblical account, awaited the fall of Nineveh; a council will never decide these questions, and even if the Fathers were to agree on the subject as completely as in fact they differ, if a *unanimis consensus patrum* were to exist about it, the Catholic exegete would yet be free to hold another opinion; for this question has nothing to do with the *rebus fidei et morum*. But a *consensus patrum* never could exist about such questions, and therefore if, as S. Thomas observes, we find in the first chapter of Genesis much which has been variously explained by the holy Fathers and other expounders, this only proves, first, that these passages and expressions are capable of divers interpretations; and secondly, that in explaining these passages and expressions we are left on the whole unfettered by theology.

S. Thomas therefore teaches this. Whatever is of dogmatic importance in the Hexæmeron is declared clearly and decidedly; whatever is not of dogmatic importance is mentioned by the Bible correctly no doubt, because it is inspired, but obscurely and ambiguously, so that its words allow of several interpretations, and this because it is not intended to instruct us on non-religious questions. By reason of the *inspired* character of the Bible, therefore, we may expect to find no errors even in natural science; by reason of the *religious* character of the Bible, we must not expect to find in the Hexæmeron anything which is new and cannot be discerned by the ordinary man respecting the sciences of astronomy, geology, etc.; because the Bible is not intended to instruct us about science, and its expressions on the subject are not so clear and unequivocal as those which concern theology.

You will see at once after what I have said, that the opinions of Kurtz as expressed in the following quotation completely agree with those of the prince of schoolmen which I have just described to you :—

"A physical element may no doubt be conceivably interwoven with the revelation of religious truth, either as the necessary means through which the latter is revealed, or as the more accidental foil and background of these truths. The subject of revelation is the religious and ethical bearing of the natural things whose physical condition is the subject of science. Now the relation of the two may be such, that a false account of the latter would pervert and disturb the former. So, for example, the physical condition of the universe, the different functions of the separate heavenly bodies, their relation to each other, and so on, has undoubtedly a religious importance, which as such might very well be itself the object of revelation, in so far as this knowledge would give us a deeper, wider, or clearer insight into the Divine Cosmos. But even in such cases revelation would neither convey nor wish to convey physical teaching; it would never induce the faithful believer to give up any error in physical science which he might hold, nor would it enable him on any occasion to anticipate the discoveries of human science. Revelation abstains from any teaching in such cases, for it is not its object to reveal at once everything which is of religious importance. It is more like a teacher who does not impart to the child at once everything which he knows himself, but each time only so much as is necessary for its further education, and for which it has been prepared by former teaching. In Holy Scripture all future science can find a place; it has made no mistake, no new science can cry out to it 'si tacuisses.' It is by this means that it shows its *divine* character in dealing with questions of natural science. But we are assured that at some time, in the life eternal, a far higher and more comprehensive revelation will correct the errors of our scientific knowledge, will supply its defects, and will unfold to us its higher religious signification."[1]

We may therefore expect that the explanation of that part of the Hexæmeron which is not purely dogmatic cannot in one respect produce a perfectly satisfactory result. While we can with certainty point out the religious truths that are taught in the Hexæmeron, we cannot with equal certainty say what scientific truths there are in it; for it is not the aim of the Bible to teach us about such things; indeed, it only mentions them in so far as they are necessary for its object, *i.e.* the imparting of religious truths.

The statements about natural things are therefore uncertain, partial, and ambiguous; nor do the usual exegetical methods enable us to make them more decided, complete, and unequivocal; for exegesis can only explain what Scripture says, and cannot add what it does not say. If, therefore, we wish for a certain and complete history of the development of Creation, the Bible alone cannot give us this, because it is neither its vocation nor its object to do so. It only remains for us, therefore, to fill in and correct the uncertain, partial, and ambiguous notices in the Bible by the results of scientific inquiry. Now, if we do this, we obtain a combined statement which is drawn from two sources. But here also there are difficulties; for while

[1] *Bibel und Astronomie,* p. 10.

we have God's warrant for the truth of that which is taken from Scripture, the conclusions of natural science, which are not taken from the Bible, can only claim human certainty or probability; and it might possibly happen that in the further course of scientific inquiry, we might find that what we have accepted as a certain conclusion is doubtful or erroneous, and that therefore the above-mentioned combined statement must be given up again. The theologian, therefore, cannot insist too strongly on the necessity of separating theology from natural science, in order that its doctrines should not be mixed up with scientific truths, and especially that the character of theological truths should not be given to the latter, however probable they may seem. S. Augustine and S. Thomas warn us very urgently to be careful in this matter. The latter says,[1] "We must steadily hold the doctrines which are plainly taught in Holy Writ. But where the words of Scripture are capable of various interpretations, we must consider well before we accept *one* explanation as being correct, and put aside all the others as quite inadmissible; for it is possible that the explanation of the passage in question which we believe to be correct, might on further investigation turn out to be false; and then the authority of Holy Scripture might be compromised by the caprice of the commentator." In another place S. Thomas says, "It is also very unwise to decide from a theological point of view things which do not belong to dogma; that is to say, to assert that one opinion is theologically right and another theologically wrong. We may make use of any facts

[1] 1. q. 68, a. 1 c.

won by non-theological inquiry which do not contradict the truths of our faith, but we should neither set up facts so obtained as theological truths, nor brand them as opposed to dogma."[1] S. Augustine says,[2] if a Christian teach erroneous scientific views, he may be laughed at; but if he say that these erroneous opinions are supported by the Bible, he is much to blame; for many a one who knows no better might suppose that the Bible really teaches such things. The exegete must therefore firmly insist on all the dogmatic elements in the Hexæmeron, but he must not pronounce more decidedly than does Holy Scripture on all that is only connected with dogma *per accidens*. He will therefore have to content himself with saying: the words of Scripture, looked at exegetically, allow of the following interpretations—which of these interpretations is right, I, as an exegete, do not know, and human inquiry must ascertain in another way. So long as the limits of human inquiry are not reached,— and they have unfortunately not yet been attained,—I must hold myself so far neutral as not to confirm any of the conclusions of geology, etc., by means of the Bible. I can only say and prove this—the Bible leaves room for the results so far arrived at, it has many blank leaves which natural science may fill in, it says so little about natural things that up to this time natural science has never been able to say: Si tacuisses!

---

[1] *Opusc.* X. And Aug. *de gen. ad lit.* 2. 18, 38 : Nihil credere de re obscura temere debemus, ne forte, quod postea veritas patefecerit, quamvis libris sanctis sive Testamenti V. sive N. nullo modo esse possit adversum, tamen propter amorem nostri erroris oderimus.

[2] *De gen. ad lit.* 1. 19, 39.

You will have observed that in my present lecture I have been endeavouring to decide how much we, as theologians, must hold fast and insist upon in the interpretation of the Hexæmeron, and, on the other hand, how much we may concede. When two parties wish to arrive at a clear understanding, it is always best that both should name the points on which under any circumstances they will think it necessary to insist, and also mention those on which they are ready to give way. With these preliminaries it is easy to see whether an understanding is possible or not.

In re Theology *versus* Natural Science, therefore, the following propositions may, after the previous discussions, be made on the part of theology:—

1. Religious truths are imparted to us in the Bible; they are stated decidedly, and we believe them as decidedly; in the interpretation of Scripture on these points, *in rebus fidei et morum*, we can consent to be guided only by the rules of hermeneutics; and we must refuse to admit any suggestion from any kind of profane science whatsoever.

2. It is not the object of the Bible to give us information about natural or any other profane science; and it was not the object of inspiration to place the Biblical historian in a better scientific position.

3. The Bible speaks of the events, phenomena, and laws of nature in the same way as the ordinary man, whose language is formed by what he sees; the Bible, therefore, does not claim to speak scientifically and correctly of these things, but only to express itself intelligibly.

4. In the Hexæmeron, dogmatic truths are mixed up

with physical elements—(1) holds good with reference to the dogmatic; (2) with reference to the physical elements. The dogmatic statements are unequivocal and decided; the non-dogmatic statements are there, not for their own sake, but because of the dogma; their meaning is clear so long as it is of importance to the dogma, after that it becomes vague and ambiguous. With reference to these things, exegesis insists on nothing, and is willing to consider any of the conclusions of natural science with tolerance and goodwill.

5. Speaking in behalf of theology in general, and exegesis in particular, we are firmly persuaded that an honest and lasting union with natural science will surely be attained if the followers of the latter will, for their part, meet us with equal candour and placability.

IV.

THE TASK OF NATURAL SCIENCE.

IN the third lecture I have shown how far we are justified in expecting teaching on scientific subjects from the Bible, and in this way I have prepared the ground for a general settlement of the relation between Biblical revelation and natural science; we must now consider the other side of the question, and ascertain how far profane knowledge, putting aside religion, is able to give us an explanation of natural facts. In this discussion I am treading on strange ground, and I therefore do not feel myself so much at home as in theological questions. But this disadvantage will not, I hope, have any bad results. What we have now to do is to define the limits of each science, and on that point we shall, I trust, be able to agree. Those who are learned in natural science can tell us how much they claim for themselves; and we know how much we theologians may concede, and how far we may allow them to go. Considering the placable and yielding spirit which animates theology, as was shown in the last lecture, and the wide concessions which it can make without giving up any of its principles, the demands made by science must indeed be immoderate if an agreement is found to be impossible.

In deciding what things belong entirely to natural science, you will admit that I am warranted in quoting principally, although not exclusively, from those savants who either betray no wish to defend the Bible or revelation in their writings, or are hostile to them.

The aim of natural science, as Humboldt [1] expresses it, is to comprehend the general relations of material phenomena, and to contemplate nature as a whole moved and animated by internal forces. It is therefore concerned with the visible world, with the phenomena which we see, hear, or perceive in any way, and with material things as they appear to us. These things and phenomena are verified, ordered, and, as it were, catalogued, by natural science; it compares them with one another, combines them, and then uses them in order to find out the laws by which they are governed and from which they come; and it is thus enabled to trace back the complicated phenomena to simple elements and principles.[2] Humboldt describes the discovery of laws as "the final object of human inquiry in empirical science," and he defines the "physical description of the world" as "thought contem-

---

[1] *Kosmos*, i. p. 81.

[2] "The method of induction consists of *perception*, *i.e.* the accidental apprehension of accidentally presented facts; *observation*, *i.e.* intentional apprehension of accidentally presented facts; *experiment*, *i.e.* observation of purposely produced facts; and lastly, *experience*, *i.e.* synthesis of the facts as they appear in regular forms (the simple fact is not yet an experience). By the help of these, the laws of nature which govern the facts may be deduced by arrangement, analysis, conclusion, and other logical means, by employing mathematics and the formulæ, *i.e.* the metaphysical principles which have been laid down, mostly by Newton, as axioms of natural science."—Schleiden, *Der Materialismus*, p. 20. "Conscientiously to ascertain facts by observation is all-important to accurate scientific investigation. The true scientific investigator does not indeed hesitate to recognise the single facts in their connection; on the contrary, his endeavour is to bring individual phenomena under the law, and for this purpose he makes use of hypothesis, which,

plating as a natural whole the phenomena given by experience."[1] There is no doubt that in our century natural science has made immense progress towards the solution of this problem. "It is a well-known fact that, from the days of Newton to our times, there have been more scientific discoveries, there has been produced, for mankind in general, a more accurate and extensive acquaintance with the system of nature, than centuries had before produced; nay, I may say, than had been obtained from the very commencement of civilisation. Indeed, if we except his great discoveries, especially those that relate to astronomy and light, we may even see that in the course of little more than our lifetime there have been greater discoveries made, and the field of science has been more enlarged, than it had been—certainly since the revival of letters—perhaps even during many and many ages before."[2] But no one who is well acquainted with the natural sciences would assert that they have as yet either reached their limit or attained their object. They have not yet been able entirely to solve their first problem, the investigation of the actual facts.

However wonderful are the discoveries which have

however, only signify for him a universal point of view under which many single cases of observation may be brought, and is valuable only as such. But he never adopts an explanation of the fact which is not founded on observation; he never makes a subjective hypothesis explain objective facts. This is much more the way of the so-called natural philosophy, which is as hostile as possible to strict natural science."—Michelis, *Der Materialismus*, p. 21. Cf. F. Bessell, *Die Beweise für die Bewegung der Erde*. Berlin 1871. Pp. 6–15.

[1] *Kosmos*, i. 31, 32; Eng. tr. p. 33.

[2] *Sermons, Lectures, and Speeches delivered during his Tour in Ireland.* Cardinal Wiseman. Dublin 1859. P. 247.

been made in astronomy by the help of the telescope, and lately by that of the spectrum analysis,[1] we must still say with Burmeister, "The discoveries that have been made as to the nature of the separate heavenly bodies are unimportant; and as our power of observation is defective, being only possible at too great distances with insufficient means, it is hardly calculated to enlighten us in full even as to the physical condition of those bodies, much less can it give us a definite idea of their history, the stages of their development, or their inhabitants.[2] As regards the earth, we have certainly—thanks to the untiring and careful examination of the strata which lie under the surface—obtained a mass of most important information; but it is both in a high degree possible and very desirable that this should be completed." Huxley says, "Water covers three-fifths of the whole surface of the globe, and has covered it in the same manner ever since man has kept any record of his own observations, to say nothing of the minute period during which he has cultivated geological inquiry. So that three-fifths of the surface of the earth is shut out from us, because it is under the sea. Let us look at the other two-fifths, and see what are the countries in which anything that may be termed searching geological inquiry has been carried out,—a good deal of France, Germany, Great Britain and Ireland, bits of Spain, of Italy, and of Russia have been examined; but of the whole great mass of Africa, except parts of the southern extremity, we

---

[1] Cf. *Natur und Off.* 1868, p. 154. Pfaff, *Die neuesten Forschungen*, etc., p. 1.

[2] *Geschichte der Schöpfung*, p. 1.

know next to nothing; little bits of India, but of the greater part of the Asiatic continent, nothing; bits of the Northern American States and of Canada, but of the greater part of the continent of North America, and in still larger proportion, South America, nothing. Under these circumstances, it follows that even with reference to that kind of imperfect information which we can possess, it is only about the ten-thousandth part of the accessible parts of the earth that have been examined properly."[1] The greatest depth to which the earth has been penetrated is about 4000 feet, not quite two-tenths of a geographical mile,[2] about the 4700th part therefore of the diameter of the earth. According to a striking saying of Nöggerath's, the deepest mines and borings are only as the stings of a gnat in comparison to the diameter of the earth.[3] If you imagine the earth to be represented by a globe 16 inches in diameter, the thickness of the paper which is pasted over it will represent the portion of the earth's crust which has as yet been examined. The scratch made by a needle on the varnish of the globe is comparatively as deep as the deepest mine. Lyell estimates the extent of the ground which has been examined, and from which we may draw conclusions, to be about the 400th part of

---

[1] Huxley, *On our Knowledge of the Causes of the Phenomena of Organic Nature*, p. 37. Hæckel, *Nat. Schöpfungsgesch.*, p. 345, "If, according to Sir John Herschel's latest calculations, the proportion of land to sea is as 57 : 146, the proportion of that which has been geognostically investigated is at most 12 : 51. More than half of the twelfth part of the earth has been cursorily observed by one or two men of science. Detailed investigations, such as are described in English, German, and French books, exist at most in a twelfth part of the twelfth part." Fraas, *Vor der Sündfluth*, p. 42.

[2] Pfaff, *Schöpfungsgeschichte*, 2nd ed. p. 213.

[3] *Ges. Naturwiss.*, iii. 138.

the earth from the surface to the centre.[1] "All that lies under this," says Humboldt, " . . . is even as much unknown to us as is the interior of other planets belonging to our system. . . . Where all knowledge of the chemical and mineralogical natural constitution of the interior of the earth fails us," he adds, "we are again thrown upon conjecture, just as we are with reference to the farthest bodies which revolve round the sun." "Who shall guarantee us," he says in another place, "that the entire number of the vital forces efficient in the universe has been fathomed?"[2]

The book of nature then is still in great measure closed to man, and although many leaves now lie open before us, which were unread half a century ago, no one will deny that there is still much which we cannot understand; and that although the progress of inquiry may give us data which are now unknown to us, much will probably always remain unfathomed by us on earth; natural science in this age cannot even claim to know its own province thoroughly, and an absolute completeness of observation must, humanly speaking, remain for ever an unattainable ideal. "The sciences of experiment," says Humboldt, "are never complete; the realm of the impressions of sense is not to be exhausted; no generation of men will ever have it in their power to boast that they have surveyed the whole of the world of phenomena."[3]

But the branch of natural science with which we shall be principally concerned, geology, does not con-

---

[1] *Elements of Geology*, i. 2.
[2] *Kosmos*, i. 166, 167, 31 ; Eng. tr. 170, 33.
[3] *Kosmos*, i. 65 ; Eng. tr. 67.

fine itself to the scientific examination of the earth in its present condition. It endeavours by help of the knowledge of its present condition, and of the forces and laws of nature now at work, to ascertain what were its earlier stages, and to discover what changes have taken place since the beginning. Science has undoubtedly made surprising advances in this direction also in this century. The theories which were formerly propounded in the name of geology, or geogony, were in many cases only arbitrary speculations and pictures of the imagination, which could have no claim to scientific truth, because it was unhesitatingly assumed that forces and laws had been at work of whose existence there is no proof. But this has now been entirely given up. Burmeister says, "We must explain the signs of past change entirely from the condition in which we find the earth at the present time. For all scientific experience proves that the same forces are still at work in the earth which have developed and altered its surface since it first existed in space as a distinct body. A close study of its present condition must therefore be the foundation of all knowledge of its history, and armed with the results of these inquiries, we may endeavour to explain and represent the earlier periods." [1]

Now if, as we have seen, our information concerning the present condition of the earth is so imperfect, it is impossible that geology, whose knowledge is entirely based upon this information, should fulfil its task. But further, in geology the question is not what are the facts, but what are the conclusions from these facts.

[1] *Geschichte der Schöpfung*, p. 2.

"Those statements," continues Burmeister, "which we call hypotheses, must always play a great part in our history of creation: the further the time we are considering is from the present, and the less an event can be investigated and understood by the help of present facts, the more we must have recourse to hypotheses."[1]

Now no doubt many scientific hypotheses are based on facts which are so completely proved, and on conclusions which are so undeniable, that their probability borders on certainty,[2] and they may therefore be the foundation of a scientific theory. But, on the other hand, there are many points in which such probability has up to this time not been attained, and in the course of our inquiries we shall find more than one case in which a hypothesis has been universally acknowledged as scientifically certain, and yet has been proved later to be erroneous. Finally, from the differences of opinion which prevail among the most eminent savants, we may infer that on many points of geology there are no certain conclusions.

"The most confident men of science," says Deutinger with truth, "will not deny that in natural science error is even now in many cases not only possible, but up to a certain point even inevitable."[3] Really thorough inquirers are very modest in their estimate of what geology and natural science can declare to be perfectly assured results, and they are very strict in their criticism of hypotheses about the earlier periods of the earth's history. After Huxley has enumerated

[1] *Op. cit.* p. 3.
[2] Huxley on *Our Knowledge*, etc., p. 54 seq.
[3] *Renan und das Wunder*, p. 91.

those parts of the earth which have been thoroughly examined by geologists, as I have quoted above, he goes on to say, "Therefore it is with justice that the most thoughtful of those who are concerned in these inquiries insist continually upon the imperfection of the geological record; for I repeat it is absolutely necessary from the nature of things that that record should be of the most fragmentary and imperfect character. Unfortunately this circumstance has been constantly forgotten. Men of science, like young colts in a fresh pasture, are apt to be exhilarated on being turned into a new field of inquiry, and to go off at a hand gallop in total disregard of hedges or ditches, losing sight of the real limitation of their inquiries, and to forget the extreme imperfection of what is really known. Geologists have imagined that they could tell us what was going on at all parts of the earth's surface during a given epoch: they have . . . constructed a universal history of the globe, as full of wonders and portents as any other story of antiquity."[1]

"True geognosy," says Humboldt, "describes the exterior crust of our globe as it exists *at present*. This science has no less certainty than the physical descriptive science in general; on the other hand, whatever relates to the ancient state of our planet . . . is as uncertain as the formation of the atmosphere of the planets; yet the time is still not very remote when geologists were occupied from choice in the solution of problems whose solution is *almost impossible*, and with this fabulous period of the physical history

[1] Huxley, *Op. cit.* p. 38.

of the globe."[1]   J. Bischof says, "Geology in its essential parts will always remain hypothetical."[2]

A French geologist, A. Brongniart, concludes a book on the mountain ranges of the earth with these words, "If there are any who claim to possess sufficient knowledge of geological phenomena, and a spirit bold and penetrating enough to be able to deduce the mode of the earth's creation from the few materials we possess, we will willingly resign to them this noble enterprise; *we* feel that we have neither means nor power sufficient for so bold but perhaps so transitory a construction."[3] The English savant Whewell expresses himself in a like manner, "We have accumulated a vast store of facts of observation, and have laboured with intense curiosity, but hitherto with very imperfect success, to extract from these facts a clear and connected knowledge of the history of the earth's change."[4]

And to return to Germany, Quenstedt says,[5] "It is true that the natural sciences may boast that they know with certainty some few superficial facts, but even this knowledge is only attained through a system of errors. For if one generation announces as an undoubted fact what by the previous generation was declared to be superstition, the ordinary observer cannot fail to be persuaded that it is all a question of human convictions, which appear under different aspects, as soon as the further progress of science has opened up new

---

[1] *Essai geognostique sur le gisement des roches*, p. 5.

[2] *Lehrb. der chem. u. phys. Geol.* (1st ed.) i. 2.

[3] *Tableau des terrains qui composent l'écorce du globe.* Alex. Brongniart. Paris 1829. 8.

[4] J. Trimmer, *Practical Geology and Mineralogy*, p. 478.

[5] *Sonst und Zetzt*, p. 281.

points of view. We do not weary of inquiring, but we long for light, of which, however, there seems but little chance in this life even as regards the most ordinary course of earthly things. Whether we shall ever receive this light the man of science cannot discover, but it would be hard for man to be forced to believe that this strong desire of his soul should never find satisfaction."

The prospects of an understanding between science and theology are most favourable when the position assumed by the former is so modest. Theology acknowledges that the desire of the soul for more perfect knowledge is fully justified, and will not remain for ever unsatisfied. It is true that in this life our knowledge can only be imperfect. Scientific men themselves admit that the astronomical, geological, in short, all the scientific knowledge of our time, is imperfect, and this for two reasons: first, because the observations and discovered facts are anything but complete; and secondly, because in many cases the conclusions drawn by savants from these facts do not agree, and are consequently uncertain. In our inquiries as to the relation of the conclusions of natural science to the doctrines of the Bible, we shall accept without question whatever natural science recognises as a fact, or has inductively proved to be a law of nature; we shall estimate hypotheses according to the degrees in which science has confirmed them, we shall treat probabilities as probabilities, possibilities as possibilities, and we shall find that the doctrines of the Bible, rightly understood, are in harmony with all the assured results of natural science. With respect to one point, however, we can decide definitely upon the relation between the Bible and science, by accurately defining the limits of the latter.[1]

In all its endeavours to follow up as far as possible the history of the changes and developments of the earth, or the universe (we shall see later what these endeavours are), natural science can never get beyond a certain first substance, from which under the influence of certain forces, and under the dominion of certain laws, things have taken their present shape after passing through a series of changes. And however much these forces and this substance may be simplified, the existence of something must be presupposed. Natural science cannot determine whence this primary matter and these forces come. It cannot say that they come into existence from nothing; for manifold as are the changes which natural science observes and explains, it can bring forward no example of the self-evolution of a thing from nothing. Therefore at the end of the inquiry the dilemma remains, that either primary matter and certain forces have existed from all eternity, or they have been created through some cause which existed before and apart from them. Natural science cannot decide which of these two suppositions is the right one; for if in the course of her inquiry she does not find it necessary to postulate any creative force, it is all the more impossible for her to prove either the reality or the

---

[1] For what follows, cf. Newman, *Lectures and Essays on University Subjects*. Deutinger, *Renan und das Wunder*, p. 90. Pfaff, *Ueber die Entstehung der Welt und die Naturgetze*, 1876. Pfaff, *Kraft und Stoff*, 1879.

impossibility of the creation of the primary substance at which her inquiry ends.

These questions then, — What is the origin of matter, and is this its first condition? Has it always existed, or has it been called into being by an external force? Have the laws of nature always existed, or whence do they arise?—are for the man of science *extra artem*, his science is here at fault.[1] Each one may have definite opinions and beliefs on the subject; but he has these as a philosopher, or as the follower of some religion, not as a man of science. We may say that this primary matter obliges us to believe in a Being through whom it exists, but if we come to this conclusion we have left the realms of science and entered those of philosophy and religion. Natural science tells, and can tell us, nothing on the subject. The man of science may say, Give me this primary matter and these forces, and I will construct the world as it at present stands; or, The world as it is may have been developed from this substance, and through the agency of these forces, but whether this substance and these forces have always existed, whether they evolved themselves from

[1] "The first rule for the strict scientific man is to have nothing to do with things which do not and cannot come within the circle of his observation or experience; neither to deny nor to affirm them. Spirit, freedom, God, are not among the possible experiences of the follower of natural science; why should he then speak of them? Whether he affirms or denies them, he is alike inconsistent and confused. But if the man of science speaks of these things as a *man*, he should remember that the second rule for the strict investigator is never to judge or condemn anything till he has thoroughly examined it; that in order to judge astronomy one must have studied astronomy; in order to judge chemistry one must have studied chemistry; and that in the same way in order to judge philosophy, that is to say the above-named ideas, one must have studied philosophy *thoroughly*, in order not to be ridiculous in one's own eyes."— Schleiden, *Der Materialismus*, p. 52.

nothing, whether a Being distinct from this substance and these forces has created them, as a man of science I do not know, and it does not interest me; whoever is interested in it—and who is not?—may seek elsewhere the answer to these questions; he may seek it from philosophy, and if this does not suffice, from theology.

When Burmeister[1] says, "The earth and the world are eternal, for this quality is part of the essence of matter," or, "That which has neither beginning nor end is eternal, and matter is said neither to have beginning nor end;" or when Hæckel[2] asserts that the proposition, "All matter is eternal," is "one of the first and highest laws of nature," and is besides "one which is generally acknowledged," you must not take these for the statements of natural science because they are pronounced by scientific men. It is said[3] that "chemistry teaches that no substance can perish or be destroyed, and that none can come into existence, and physics teaches us that no force perishes and that none comes into existence; the existing quantity of matter and force cannot be increased or diminished in the smallest degree by any event," and this may be true of the chemical and physical processes in the present condition of things; but it does not even follow from this that the present condition of things may not be altered or destroyed in the future by an external force, and still less may we conclude that it could not have had a beginning. It may be added, "The laws of thought

---

[1] *Geolog. Bilder*, i. 243, 60.
[2] *Generelle Morphologie*, i. 171.
[3] Fr. Mohr, *Geschichte der Erde*, Bonn 1866, p. 5; Hæckel, *Nat. Schöpfungsgesch.* p. 8.

require that that which cannot be destroyed in time cannot either have originated in time;" but this, as is shown by the appeal to the "Laws of Thought," is a philosophical not a scientific conclusion; further, it is philosophically false, and violates the laws of thought. At all events the refutation of such statements, which are not scientific but philosophical, or rather unphilosophical and opposed to the idea of creation, does not form part of my task.

Those savants who know the problems and limits of their science have expressed in the most decided manner their conviction that these questions as to the origin of things do not belong to natural science. "It cannot be the object of geology," says G. Bischof, "to go farther back than to the original condition of the world during the period of the creation. Geology takes the earth as existing, without troubling itself as to how it came into existence. It is satisfied if it can discover whether the earth was originally a fiery or a fluid ball."[1] "Cosmogony," says Humboldt, "assumes the existence of all the matter now dispersed throughout the universe, and occupies itself only with the manifold conditions which this matter has undergone before it attained its present form and combination. All that lies outside this belongs to the province of philosophizing reason,"[2] rather let us say to that of other sciences. "We follow matter," says O. Fraas, "from the moment of its appearance in space and time, through all its formation and change, and we never lose it again in the great cycle of the earth's

---

[1] *Lehrb. der chem. u. phys. Geologie*, 1st ed. i. 3.
[2] In Moll's *Jahrb. der Berg. und Hüttenkunde*, iii. 6 (Tholuck's *Lit. Anz.*, 1833, 537).

existence, during which it changes its shape and form thousands of times, but never perishes. Geology requires only the bodies of the planets, that is Archimedes' fixed point, from which it can begin its work. As to the first beginning of things, it can say no more and certainly nothing better than what every one has known long since : " In the beginning God created the heavens and the earth." [1]

The newest discoveries of natural science have not shaken the doctrine that all things were created by God, nor have they rendered its philosophical or theological confirmation more difficult. On the contrary, many esteemed philosophical writers of the present day, Hermann Ulrici, S. C. Cornelius, Johannes Huber, Zürgen Bona Meyer, and others, have proved that modern natural science is far from playing into the hands of pantheism, materialism, and atheism ; it rather leads in results as in its principles to the exactly opposite idea, to the recognition of a creative author of nature.[2]

[1] *Vor der Sündfluth*, p. 8.
[2] Ulrici, *Gott und die Natur ;* Cornelius, *Ueber die Entstehung der Welt ;* Huber, *Die Lehre Darwins*, p. 184 ; Meyer, *Philosophische Zeitfragen*, p. 15 ; cf. A. Fick, *Die Naturkräfte in ihrer Wechselbezïehung*, Würzburg, 1869, p. 70 ; Pfaff, *Schöpfungsgeschichte*, 2nd ed. p. 131 ; Pfaff, *Entstehung der Welt*, 1876 ; Schaarschmidt, *Der Atheismus*, 1879. "Too commonly it is supposed, or taken for granted, that in proportion as it is in our power to trace things to their causes, to connect them one with the other, to systematize them, to tabulate them in geometrical and average conditions and proportions, so much the more we are removed from the necessity of admitting a higher and more final cause. One has often heard or read such reasoning as this : ' We can account for this phenomenon, we know the laws by which it is regulated, and we need not have recourse to the interference of a higher power, because it is in connection with the whole system of the universe, and could not be altered without in some way deranging other portions.' Consequently by every new discovery which brings before us the more immediate or the more remote cause of anything, it is supposed that we are departing a step more from the necessity of admitting the great and final cause. Then, consequently, the

We need not therefore come to any agreement with natural science concerning the origin of the visible world, but only concerning the development of that which God created. But before I turn to this, let me remind you of the full significance of the Christian dogma, God has created the world; it will avoid all possible misunderstanding in our future examination of the natural sciences. When we declare our belief that God is the creator of the world, and, as has been said, we may hold this belief without even coming into contact with natural science, we are not thinking of the God of pantheism, who does not exist apart from the world, but

---

mind begins to be involved more and more in its own speculations and thoughts, comes to look at its own conclusions as final, and almost to think that there is a sort of greatness in not taking the old short road of at once inviting God to take part in the phenomena of nature, or of going through a very few steps to find Him as the ultimate cause; but rather it seeks to spin a network of causes, which shall be so interwoven one with another that we can easily escape, when hard pressed, by following some divergences of science, and so being satisfied with those immediate causes which conceal from us the remote and final one. It would really appear that common reasoning should take us exactly in the opposite direction. If one discovered on the ground a ring, or a piece of metal, which had been twisted into a circular form, he might exclaim, What can this be? He looks at it, examines it, and perhaps concludes and says, it may have been formed by some accident and have fallen there. But if he take it up, and find that to it is attached another made in a similar manner, and that both are connected together, would our natural reason say that this was a stronger evidence of chance; or, on the contrary, would it not suggest that this proved it the more to be the work of the hand of an artificer? And if, bringing it still nearer, he found attached another link, and another, and another, and others going from them in different directions, and saw in all the same exactness of workmanship, the same symmetry of proportion, the same perfect finish, would every step thus made in observation suggest the idea that more and more we should conclude all this only to arise from a fortuitous combination of different chance productions, and not rather that there was an invisible hand here at work which alone could have produced this beautiful complication?"—*Sermons, Lectures, and Speeches*, etc., Wiseman, p. 252; cf. Deutinger, *Renan und das Wunder*, p. 92.

who is in the world, in the laws of nature, and in the spirit of man, so that He has no being except in these. Nor are we thinking of the God of deism, who merely exists apart from the world, who has no doubt created it as well as the laws of nature, but from that moment has left the world to itself and to the working of these laws without being able in any way to interfere with its course. Theism stands exactly between pantheism and deism, and finds its clearest and most perfect expression in the Christian doctrine of God. In a word, we believe in a God who lives and governs, He is the most perfect Being, exempt from all the imperfections which belong to the creature, endowed with all the perfections which it is possible to possess. He exists from eternity and through Himself alone, depending in His essence and action on no other being, limited by nothing which exists beside Himself. He is a personal Being, endowed with intelligence and will, but with an infinite intelligence, and a will that only wills what accords with His perfectness, and He can realize what He wills, so that His power is only bounded by His volition. He is of necessity eternal, but beside Him nothing need of necessity exist. He is self-sufficing, and all-blessed in Himself, and needs no other being existing but Himself. That other beings do exist, is in consequence of an act of His freewill. There was no necessity for creation apart from Him, for there is nothing apart from Him save through Him; nor were there such necessity in Himself, for from eternity He was self-sufficing. He could have not created, and as He did create through a free act of His will, He might have created differently, a differently organized, differently framed world. But what He has created is a monument of His might, wisdom, and goodness. All has been created as He willed it should be created; each separate thing, whether great or small, every sun and every blade of grass came into existence when, and where, and as He willed, and for His omnipotence the creation of a sun or a blade of grass is equally easy. He could therefore have caused the world to come into existence from nothing completely ordered, organized, and developed as we see it now; or He could also have created simple elements, and have given them the power of developing gradually to their appointed form. The one was as easy for His omnipotence as the other, and which of the two He did depended on His wisdom and His freewill. The laws which are in force in the visible world are His laws; He might have given others had He so willed, they are in force so long as it pleases Him; if He so willed He might at any moment change, suspend, or annul them, and His wisdom alone will decide whether He shall change or interfere with them, or allow them to continue in uninterrupted and constant operation. He sees everything, He guides everything, He provides for everything: it is His might and wisdom which uphold the stars in their courses, which clothe the lilies of the field and feed the fowls of the air, and without His knowledge and will there falls no sparrow from the roof and no hair from our head.

Such, feebly delineated, for not even the tongue of an angel could describe Him worthily, is the God who according to the words of the Bible has created heaven and earth. We must believe in this God if we would understand the account given in Holy Writ of His working, and if we would read aright the book of nature which He has created. To the man who believes in this God, His action as shown in the pages of the Bible will fully harmonize with that which is shown in the pages of the book of nature. But where this belief in the true God is wanting, or only exists in a stunted and perverse form, the endeavour to bring the Bible and nature into harmony will succeed only partially or not at all.[1]

When you hear very well-meaning people express their doubts of the possibility, or even their conviction of the impossibility of an agreement between the Bible and science, you will find on closer examination that this is often caused by their misconceiving either what the Bible or what science really says; but sometimes there is a more serious reason, namely, that such people, although without knowing or wishing it, have no clear idea, and no firm conviction, of the Christian doctrine of creation; either, leaning towards pantheism, they conceive of God as existing only in the world, and acting in the laws of nature, and they forget His supermundane existence; or, leaning towards deism, they reduce to a minimum the relation between God and the world, and the influence of God on the world. Subjectively a man may be an excellent Christian and Catholic, and yet objectively, " in theologicis " he may be anything but definite and firm. If we would come to a clear understanding with such people, we must go

---

[1] "The man who brings God with him will find Him in nature, and he who does not bring Him will not find Him."—Quenstedt, *Klar und Wahr*, p. 24.

back to the fundamental cause of the difference of opinion. To argue about the Mosaic Hexæmeron with one who had no clear and definite idea of what the Christian means by "God created the world," would be as mistaken as to endeavour to prove the doctrine of the real presence of Christ in the sacrament to one who does not acknowledge Christ as God and man.

V.

NATURAL SCIENCE AND FAITH ARE NOT OPPOSED.

IT was in consequence of an inconceivable misunderstanding of the real facts, that forty years ago a famous German thinker, Schleiermacher, wrote to a younger friend, the theologian Lücke, in the following terms: "Looking at the present state of natural science, which is becoming more and more an all-embracing cosmogony, what do you forbode in the future, not only for our theology, but for our evangelical Christianity? . . . I fear that we shall have to learn to give up many things which many are accustomed to think of as inseparably bound up with the essence of Christianity. I will not speak of the six days, but how long will the idea of the creation as it is usually believed hold out against the power of a cosmogony constructed from irrefragable scientific combinations? What is to happen then? As for me I shall not see that time, but shall have gone to my rest; but you, and the men of your age, what will you do?"[1]

The words in which the spies sent by Moses into the promised land reported what they had seen have been quoted as a parallel to this timid speech. "Nevertheless the people be strong that dwell in the land, and the cities are walled, and very great. . . . We be not

---
[1] *Theologische Studien und Kritiken* von Ullmann and Umbreit, 1829, p. 489.

able to go up against the people; for they are stronger than we. And they brought up an evil report of the land which they had searched unto the children of Israel, saying, The land through which we have gone to search it is a land that eateth up the inhabitants thereof; and all the people we saw in it are men of great stature. And there we saw the giants, the sons of Anak, which come out of the giants; and we were in our own sight as grasshoppers, and so we were in their sight."[1]

Nevertheless the children of Israel conquered the land which God had given them for a possession, for God was with them. If we are sure that God is with us also, and that His Church is built on an immoveable rock, we need not fear lest her doctrine should not stand before the giants of natural science, and besides there need be no conflict between them; hitherto we have every reason to assume that theologians and men of science can exist peaceably beside one another. Natural science *cannot* call in question the theological view of the creation, about which Schleiermacher was apprehensive. Whatever may be the objections to the theological doctrines that the visible world is not from all eternity, and that it came into existence through the will of God, these objections, as I have shown in my last lecture, *cannot* proceed from natural science. Kurtz says with truth, "The man of science who imagines, or would persuade others, that the result of his scientific inquiries has been to make him disbelieve the Biblical account of creation, is deceiving himself.

[1] Num. xiii. 28 seq. See Hengstenberg's *Ev. Kirchen u. Ztg.* 1830, p. 394.

It is not his science which is in fault, but his philosophy." The astronomer Lalande says that he has searched the whole heaven but has not found God; but that is not the fault of astronomy. "Astronomy may observe the heavenly bodies and their separate phases and developments, and by this means may possibly be able to explain their origin and the successive stages through which they have passed till they reached their present state, but it will never venture to decide whether the primary matter and forces with which it starts are eternal or were created in time; whether the combination of this matter and these forces which formed the heavenly bodies was fortuitous, or if it was governed and guided by a higher personal will."[1] No doubt the man of science is in great danger of losing sight of the first and highest cause in his examination and observation of secondary causes; just as the anatomist may be tempted to forget the soul in his examination of the organism of the human body. But if the man of science becomes a disbeliever in revelation, and the anatomist becomes a materialist, it is not their science which leads to this, but false speculations in other branches of knowledge; and their appeal to scientific conclusions to prove their philosophical errors is just as explicable, but also just as wrong, as the doubt which disbelievers in miracles and prophecy cast upon the authenticity and credibility of the Biblical books.

"If the attitude of science towards religion is indifferent, or even hostile," says Deutinger, "it is so, not because science and religion are incompatible, but

---

[1] *Bibel und Astronomie*, pp. 12, 298.

because science has abandoned her own true principles, or has not yet recognised them. There is a great error involved in saying that the two cannot exist together. He who says, In order to know we must give up belief, in order to believe we must give up knowledge, has an equally erroneous idea of both belief and knowledge. If science contradicts religion, it is not owing to scientific accuracy, but to the want of it. It is not science which contends against religion, but ignorance, an unscientific spirit."[1] This holds good of natural science. Our inquiries will show that we may believe not only the fact of creation, but everything which the Bible teaches concerning the creation and primæval history, and this without ever controverting any of the assured results of natural science.

We may express this conviction the more confidently because we know by experience that it is possible to be a very thorough and zealous man of science, and also a believing Christian. Noble examples of this are not wanting either in ancient or modern times among Protestants and Catholics.[2]

The Franciscan Roger Bacon, in the 13th century, one of the most eminent representatives of science in the Middle Ages, was at all events a faithful Christian, whatever we may think of his philosophical and theological system. His namesake in the 16th century, Francis Bacon, Lord Verulam, is not quite so blameless; but natural science had not made him an unbeliever, as is clear from his well-known saying that a superficial

---

[1] *Renan und das Wunder*, pp. 53, 54.
[2] Cf. Hettinger, *Apologie*, i. 1, p. 202. Berger, *Naturwissenschaft, Glaube, Schule*. Frankf. 1864.

acquaintance with natural science, or, as he calls it, philosophy, might possibly lead to atheism, but that a deeper study of it would lead back to religion. "Leves gustus in philosophia movere fortasse ad atheismum, sed pleniores haustus ad religionem reducere," or as he says in another passage: "Verum est, parum philosophiæ naturalis homines inclinare in atheismum, ad altiorem scientiam eos ad religionem circumagere."[1] For if the human understanding observes secondary causes scattered and unconnected, it may see nothing beyond them, and thus remain in atheism; but if it goes on to recognise their concatenation and their connection with one another, it must necessarily take refuge in the thought of God, or of a Divine Providence. On the whole,—you will allow me to add what follows, which, strictly speaking, does not belong to the subject,—on the whole, atheism is more on men's lips than in their hearts. This is proved by the vigour with which atheists spread and defend their opinion, and endeavour to gain disciples,—the latter only because they mistrust themselves, and would willingly strengthen their wavering convictions by the assent of others. Those alone, he concludes, do not believe in God whose interest it is that God should not exist. "Deum non esse non credit nisi cui Deum non esse expedit."[2] In the introduction to the *Novum Organon,* Bacon asks of God that the brighter burning of the natural light and the progress of science should not cause unbelief in the divine mysteries, but that, on the contrary, the understanding cleansed from vanity and superstition, and submitting

---

[1] Cf. *Freiburger Kirchenlexicon,* xii. 95.
[2] Hettinger, *Apologie,* i. 1, p. 117.

itself to revelation, might yield to faith those things which are of faith.

It is known that the three fathers of modern astronomy, Copernicus, Newton, and Kepler, were faithful and pious Christians. The fact that the Canon of Frauenberg dedicated his account of his astronomical system to Pope Paul III., proves that his conscience was clear in matters of theology.[1] Isaac Newton, as is well known, occupied himself with exegetical as well as with astronomical and mathematical studies.

The following passages from his book about the prophet Daniel, prove his belief in the Bible: "We have Moses, the prophets and apostles, and the words of Jesus Christ Himself, and if we will not hear them, we shall be more inexcusable than the Jews. And the giving ear to the prophets is a fundamental character of the true Christian," etc. "The authority of the prophets is divine, which name is also deserved by Moses and the apostles," etc.[2]

The following words with which Kepler closes one of his books on astronomy will show his religious opinions: "It only remains for me to lift up my hands and eyes from the work table to heaven, and to pray devoutly and humbly to the Father of lights: O Thou who awakenest in us through the light of nature the longing for the light of grace, in order that Thou mightest transport us into the light of glory, I give Thee thanks, my Lord and Creator, that Thou hast gladdened me with Thy creation when I was enraptured with the works

---

[1] Cf. Beckmann, *Zur Gesch. des Copernic. Systems* (Braunsberg), 1862, ii. p. 12.

[2] Zöckler, *Gesch. der Beziehungen zwischen Theologie und Naturwissenschaft*, 1879, ii. p. 13.

of Thy hands. Look on this work of my calling which I have finished by the help of the faculties which Thou hast given me; I have revealed the glory of Thy works, in so much of their infinity as my finite spirit could conceive, to men who will read these proofs. My soul has striven to be as true as possible in its philosophizing; if I have uttered anything unworthy of Thee, teach me to make it better. If I have been led into too great boldness by the wonderful beauty of Thy works, or if I have sought my own honour at the hands of men in creating a work which was meant for Thy glory, forgive me in Thy mercy and pity. Lastly, grant me Thy grace, that this work may lead to Thy glory and the good of souls, and may never harm them."[1]

In spite of Galileo's melancholy contest with the Roman authorities, there is no doubt that he remained a sincere Catholic to his death, and believed that his scientific conclusions were perfectly compatible with his faith.[2]

---

[1] Cf. Hengstenberg's *Ev. Kirchen Ztg.* 1830, p. 411. Raumer, *Kreuzzüge*, ii. pp. 43–45. For another expression of Kepler's on this subject, see above, p. 37, note.

[2] "We maintain that Galileo was a sincere Christian and Catholic. Proof of this may be found in his writings, even in those which have been incriminated and condemned; but especially in his most confidential correspondence, which was never intended for publication. No doubt his life was not spotless . . . but never, either before or after his condemnation, in his books, or in his notes, or his correspondence, whether with Protestants or with Catholics, with Fra Paola Sarpi, the Venetian theologian of very doubtful orthodoxy, or with those who were indifferent to religion, did he utter one word which would justify a doubt of his sincere faith—often and clearly expressed—in the Catholic religion. But both before and after his condemnation he invariably believed that his faith was in no way contradicted by the Copernican system, because, as he had said . . . and as Father Campanella, making use of the very terms used by the Lateran Council, had repeated in his eloquent apology for Galileo, two truths cannot contradict one another."— Th. H. Martin, *Galilée*. Paris 1868. P. 200.

Euler, one of the greatest mathematicians of the last century, has left us a book entitled, *Divine Revelation saved from the Objections of Freethinkers,* in which he says, "As to the difficulties brought forward by freethinkers, and the apparent contradictions which they profess to find in the Bible, it will be useful to observe, first, that there is no science which rests on a foundation so sure that it is not open to equally and even more important objections. We can find in each apparent contradictions, which at first sight appear to be insoluble. But as these sciences can be sifted to their first elements, it is possible entirely to remove these apparent difficulties. And even if we were not in a position to do this, these sciences would yet lose nothing of their certainty. Why then should Holy Writ lose all its authority because of such objections? Geometry is held to be the science in which nothing is assumed which cannot be plainly deduced from the first principles of our knowledge. And yet there have been people of no mean understanding who imagined they had discovered great and insoluble difficulties in geometry by means of which the science would be deprived of all certainty. The objections which they made are so subtle that no slight trouble and discernment are required in order to refute them thoroughly. But still in the minds of all reasonable people geometry has lost none of its value, although they may not be able themselves to refute all these subtle objections. Therefore, what right have freethinkers to require that we should at once reject Holy Scripture because of a few objections which are often not nearly so serious as those which are made to geometry?" Albrecht von Haller, Linnæus, and others express themselves in a similar manner.[1]

In modern times also we find that, besides those scientific men who profess unbelieving and irreligious opinions, there are many savants of the first rank who publicly and gladly own their belief in Biblical revelation, and endeavour to prove scientifically the compatibility of the results of natural science with the testimony of the Bible; there are others who show a religious bias in their scientific works, or who do not at any rate mingle attacks on religion with their scientific discussions, but expressly disapprove of the materialistic and atheistic utterances of their fellows.[2] Among German savants I may mention — without saying to which class they severally belong—Heinrich Steffens, Heinrich von Schubert, Karl von Raumer, Joh. Nep. von Fuchs, Andreas und Rudolf Wagner,[3] Friedrich Pfaff, J. Mädler,[4] Joh. Müller, Christian Gottfried Ehrenberg, J. Hyrtl, Gustav Bischof,[5] Hermann von

[1] Zöckler, *Gesch. der Beziehungen zwischen Theologie und Naturwissenschaften*, ii. 37. Cf. Reusch, *Der Process Galilei's*, 1879, p. 34.

[2] Zöckler, *Gesch.* etc., ii. 330.

[3] "I have never wavered in my belief in the truths of Scripture, or in the ultimate interpretation of natural things; and this belief becomes daily stronger and more decided."—R. Wagner, *Jahrb. für deutsche Theol.* 1862, p. 168.

[4] "The heavens declare the glory of God, so said the Psalmist, and if astronomy springs from heaven, let her show herself worthy of her origin. Let her promote the knowledge of God by discovering truths which make His great works known to us, and by developing laws called, and rightly called, the laws of nature; not because nature herself has made them, but because God has ordained them for her."—Mädler, *Ges. Naturwiss.* iii. 551.

[5] *Populäre Vorlesungen*, p. 46: "The immortal authors of these chapters have derived nothing from strict inquiry, nothing from observation or experiment. They have been led to truth by another source of knowledge, by divine inspiration. But truth will remain truth throughout all ages."

Meyer, E. von Leonhard, Fr. August Quenstedt, K. E. von Bäer, Oscar Fraas, Oswald Heer,[1] Johannes von Hanstein.

Many most eminent Christians are and were to be found amongst modern French savants:[2] Deluc, Hauy, Cuvier,[3] Alexandre Brongniart, Binet, Biot, Elie de Beaumont, Ampère,[4] Aug. Cauchy,[5] Armand de Quatrefages, Th. H. Martin, and others. Marcel de Serres, De Blainville, and others, as also the

[1] *Die Urwelt der Schweig.* p. 604 : " A sheet of paper with a symphony of Beethoven written on it has no meaning save for the musician. For him every note has a meaning, and when he translates these signs into sounds, there results a whole world of harmonies. It is exactly so with nature. Like the single notes, the single phenomena have no meaning except when we are able to combine them, and to understand their connection. Then they are united into one grand whole, and a world of harmony arises in our soul, which, like her sister, the harmony of sound, lifts us above the sensuous world, and fills us with the presentiment of a divine ordering of the universe. Every one would no doubt think that man very simple who asserted that the notes of this symphony consisted of points which had come together by chance on the paper. But it seems to me that those who look upon the infinitely grander harmony of the creation as the work of chance do not judge less foolishly. The deeper we penetrate into nature, the more fervent becomes our conviction that only the belief in an Almighty and All-wise Creator, who has made heaven and earth according to an eternally premeditated plan, can avail to solve the problems of nature and of human life : it is not only the heart of man which shows us God, but also nature."

[2] Zöckler, *Gottes Zeugen im Reich der Natur.* Gütersloh 1881.

[3] The Paris newspaper, *National,* in its obituary notice of the great savant Cuvier, tried to excuse his belief in the Bible by the fact of his having, as a Protestant, been acquainted with the Bible from his earliest youth, whereby he had acquired an affection for it which, when grown to manhood, he could not shake off.

[4] " Ampère had strong religious convictions, and often spoke of them to the writer of these lines. In the year 1836, when he was on his deathbed, a friend wished to read to him a passage from the Acts of the Apostles. He replied that he knew the book by heart. These were his last words. Arago relates this in his posthumous works."—Passavant in the *Katholiken,* 1862, i. p. 261.

[5] The *Athenæum* (1857, 695) said in an obituary notice (23rd May 1857), " He was a Roman Catholic of the strictest kind." Cf. *Contemporain,* N. S. t. 9 (1868), 1084.

Belgian Waterkeyn, have themselves tried to reconcile their scientific conclusions with the Bible.[1]

Geology, it is well known, has of late years been most diligently cultivated in England and North America. In England, Chalmers, speaking in the year 1833 in an assembly of scientific men, went so far as solemnly to assert his conviction that Christianity had everything to hope and nothing to fear from the progress of scientific inquiry; and what is more, this utterance was received with great applause.[2] Among the most eminent Englishmen of science, there have been many most orthodox Anglican clergymen, as W. Buckland, Whewell, Sedgwick, John Fleming, and W. D. Conybeare; and in America Edward Hitchcock. Many esteemed savants, in their discussions on natural science, have had the defence of the Bible very much at heart, for instance, besides Buckland, the Scotchmen Hugh Miller[3] and John M'Culloch, and the American Benjamin Silliman. Others express in strong terms their wish to guard their science from all suspicion of leading to conclusions out of harmony with reve-

[1] The Swiss Louis Agassiz, formerly an inhabitant of Neuchatel, afterwards of North America, opposes the Bible on many points (*e.g.* with respect to the unity of mankind), but he is a decided opponent of materialism and deism. Cf. *Jahrb. für deutsche Theol.* 1861, p. 668. Valroger, *La Genèse*, etc., pp. 61, 228, 253. (P. 77: "He has not devoted any of his writings to a defence of the principles of natural religion, but when, in the course of his investigations, he came across those principles, he did not turn away, and was not afraid to say what he saw. The absurdity of materialistic atheism filled his strong understanding with repugnance, and he betrays no cowardly yielding whenever he comes across it. The animals lower than man were constantly the principal objects of his attention and of his writings, but he found in them countless proofs of the almighty activity of the Creator, and he often did homage to the endless wisdom of the Divine Providence.")

[2] See above, p. 27, note.

[3] *Correspondant*, N. S. t. 39 (1868), p. 230.

lation. The English handbooks of geology sometimes contain a separate chapter on this subject.[1] In one of them, written by Gideon Mantell, the following passage occurs:[2] "There was a time when every geologist was called upon to defend himself against imputations of this kind, but a more enlightened era has arrived, and it is unnecessary to allude to the circumstance except to assure those who for the first time are called upon to follow the researches of the astronomer and the geologist, that in proportion as their minds become acquainted with the principles of scientific investigation, their apprehensions of any collision between the discoveries in the natural world and the inspired records will disappear." In purely scientific works written by the most eminent English and American savants, we often find remarks which show that the religious opinions of the authors have not been affected by their scientific studies, as in the case of Sir Humphrey Davy, Richard Owen, Sir Roderick Murchison,[3] James Prichard, Sir David Brewster, R. Jameson, Edward Turner, Faraday,[4] and others[5] whose writings will often be

[1] Cf. Trimmer, *Practical Geology and Mineralogy*. London 1841. P. 34.
[2] *Wonders of Geology*, i. 4.
[3] He ends his classical work *Siluria* (London 1854, p. 483) with these words: "From the effects produced upon my own mind through the study of these imperishable records, I am indeed led to hope that my readers will adhere to the views which, in common with many contemporaries, I entertain of the succession of life. For he who looks to a beginning, and traces thenceforward a rise in the scale of being until that period is reached when man appeared on the earth, must acknowledge in such works repeated manifestations of design, and unanswerable proofs of the superintendence of a Creator."
[4] Cf. *Contemporain*, t. 26 (3 S. t. 11, 1876), p. 244.
[5] For many of those named here, see amongst others, J. Pye Smith, *The Relation*, etc., pp. 28, 31, 101, 299, 311, 328. Also Zöckler, *Gesch.*

quoted in these lectures. A geologist writing in an American periodical says,[1] "We can assure him that there are very many among them (geologists), both in Europe and this country, who do not merely give their assent to the truth of revelation, but whose whole hope rests upon it; whose attachment to it is stronger than death, and who count it their chief glory and happiness to defend and enforce its glorious truths: men who rejoice to see in every rock formation the marks of a creating and upholding God."

Charles Daubeny, president of the British Association at Cheltenham in August 1856, has well expressed this sentiment. I cannot refrain from quoting part of his address: "At any rate I trust the time has now passed away when such studies as those we recommend lie under the imputation of fostering sentiments inimical to religion. In countries and in an age in which men of letters were generally tinctured with infidelity, it is not to be supposed that natural philosophers would altogether escape the contagion, but the contemplation of the works of creation is surely in itself far more calculated to induce the humility that paves the way to belief, than the presumption which disdains to lean upon the supernatural. We are told that in a future and higher state of existence the chief occupation of the blessed is that of praising and worshipping the Almighty. But is not the contemplation of the works of the Creator, and the study of the ordinances of the great Lawgiver of the universe, in itself an act of praise and adoration? And if so, may not one at least of the

[1] *American Journal of Science*, viii. 155 (cf. *Ev. K. Z.* 1827, p. 108).

sources of happiness which we are promised in a future state of existence, one of the rewards for a single-minded and reverential pursuit after truth in our present state of trial, consist in a development of our faculties, and in the power of comprehending those laws and provisions of nature with which our finite reason does not enable us at present to become cognizant. Such are a few of the reflections which the study of physical science, cultivated in a right spirit, naturally suggests, and I ask you whether they are not more calculated to inspire humility than to induce conceit? to render us more deeply conscious how much of the vast field of knowledge must ever be concealed from our view, and how small a portion of the veil of Isis it is given to us to lift up, and therefore to dispose us to accept with a more unhesitating faith the knowledge vouchsafed from on high on subjects which our own unassisted reason is incapable of fathoming? 'Let us not therefore,' to use the language of a living prelate, 'think scorn of the pleasant land.' Every part of it may be cultivated with advantage, as the Land of Canaan when bestowed upon God's peculiar people. They were not commanded to let it lie waste, as incurably polluted by the abominations of its first inhabitants, but to cultivate it and dwell in it, living in obedience to the divine laws, and dedicating its choicest fruits to the Lord their God."[1] I do not wish to lay more stress on the fact that many great savants are believing Christians than it deserves. But after all, Claudius is not quite wrong when he says in his simple-hearted

[1] *Athenæum*, 1856, p. 999.

way:[1] "I do not deny that I take great delight in these men; not so much because of religion, for that, of course, can neither gain nor lose anything from savants, be they great or small. But it is pleasant to see, for example, some of the most industrious and indefatigable savants, who have grown grey in the service of science, and have experienced and learnt more about her than has fallen to the lot of most, to see such men, not priding themselves on their knowledge, but after they have penetrated more deeply than others into the secrets of nature, waiting, as is fitting, with bared heads, and eager to learn, before the altar, and the deeper secrets of God. It is pleasant, and one turns with fresh courage to learning, which, while giving greater knowledge to its disciples, lets them remain reasonable people, and does not make them fools and scoffers. And it has a remarkable effect when we see, on the other hand, the light troops marching by with their hats on, turning up their conceited noses." No doubt many of the savants who have taken up a position antagonistic to religion do not by any means belong to what Claudius calls the "light troops." Many of them are men who are famous in their profession. But here, as everywhere, the second-rate people and amateurs make most noise.

This at least follows from what has been said. Just as it is wrong to say that theology and science are opposed to each other, it is also wrong to say that theologians and men of science are opposed to each other, as if all the savants were on one side and all

[1] Claudius, *Werke*, vi. 122.

theologians on the other. The names which I have mentioned show that many men of science are on the side of theology, and as you know, there are writers calling themselves theologians who are more resolute and vehement in their attacks on the Bible than ever men of science have been.

It is only fair to admit that if many men of science have been wrong in attacking divine revelation on the authority of their science, some theologians have also committed the fault of unjustly attacking and casting suspicion on natural science on the authority of the Biblical revelation. We need not notice former errors of this kind, for they may be excused by the indefiniteness of the boundary between science and religion which I have described. But it is inconceivable that in our day theologians should treat natural science as an enemy to revelation. We can assert with some satisfaction that among Catholic theologians this is seldom the case. In Germany it is very rare; but English writers who seek to prove the harmony of the Bible and science think it necessary to attack not only those men of science who are assailants of the Bible, but also the "anti-geologists" among the theologians, and in answer to the latter they lay stress on the fact, that not all the interpretations of passages in the Bible brought forward by theologians, and not all the scientific theories propounded by them on the authority of the Bible, can claim to be regarded by men of science as unassailable facts. Hugh Miller and John Pye Smith, two of the most zealous defenders of the harmony between the Bible and nature, the former a man of science, the latter a theologian, enter into long discussions with a series of theological writers who would make the Bible, as explained by them, the arbitrator in purely scientific questions, who further maintain that all the geological statements which contradict their own exegetical views are irreligious, and occasionally declare geology itself to be "an invention of the enemy of God and man."[1]

It is only necessary to mention these things. Reasonable theologians will not dispute the justice of the following observations of Whewell's:[2] "In the first place, the meaning which any generation puts upon the phrases of Scripture depends more than is at first sight supposed upon the received philosophy of the time. Hence, while men imagine they are contending for revelation, they are in fact contending for their own interpretation of revelation, unconsciously adapted to what they believe to be rationally probable. And the new interpretation which the new philosophy requires, and which appears to the older school to be a fatal violence done to the authority of religion, is accepted by their successors without the dangerous results that were apprehended. When the language of Scripture, invested with its new meaning, has become familiar to man, it is found that the ideas which it calls up are quite as reconcilable as the former ones were with the soundest religious views."[3]

[1] Hugh Miller, *Test. of the Rocks*, p. 342 ; J. P. Smith, *The Relation*, etc., pp. 8, 26, 155 ; Brownson's *Quarterly Review*, 1863, p. 23.

[2] *History of the Inductive Sciences*, 3rd ed., London 1847, 1. 403.

[3] Pianciani, *Erläuterungen zur Mosaischen Schöpfungsgeschichte*, p. 8. He says of the interpretation of the six days in Gen. i.: "We cannot reject an entirely new explanation of some Mosaic passages and words in our text. There is no question here of doctrines of faith or morality, but only

I will conclude this lecture by mentioning an incident which caused some sensation at the time, and which has often been somewhat misrepresented. In the autumn of 1864 a great number of English men of science were requested to sign a paper to the effect that no contradiction could exist between the divine revelations in the Bible and those in nature; that it was to be regretted that certain people had made use of natural science in order to dispute the truth of Holy Writ, etc. It is strange that over 200 people, among whom were some eminent men of science, should have signed this paper; for it is awkwardly drawn up in parts, it proceeded from a perfectly unknown person, and there is a strong suspicion that it was intended to be used for a demonstration against certain eminent geologists; besides which there was no reason why the savants should make such a *professio fidei*, still less was the author of the paper in any way entitled to require it of them. For this reason Sir F. Herschel and many others refused to sign, expressly stating, however, that they did not believe that there was any contradiction between the Bible and science. I should certainly not have signed, first of all because the form did not seem to me to be correctly drawn up. The *Athenæum* tried to revenge itself on the theologians by proposing another declaration, a kind of parody on the first, which should be signed by theologians and men of science alike. Of course the invitation to sign was not seriously meant, the newspaper only wished to defend

of the reckoning of time. The result of the progress of natural science is sometimes to make us understand more clearly some passages in the profane writers; much more then is this progress likely to throw light on the word of God when the latter treats of created things."

the rights of men of science against theologians, and to oppose one demonstration to the other. Probably the author of the second declaration thought that theologians would be much embarrassed by it. That was not the case; in my opinion, apart from its intention and object, any theologian might sign the declaration. The two forms are as follows :—

We, the undersigned students of the natural sciences, desire to express our sincere regret, that researches into scientific truth are perverted by some in our own times into occasion for casting doubt upon the truth and authenticity of the Holy Scriptures.	We, the undersigned students of theology, and of nature, desire to express our sincere regret, that common notions of religious truth are perverted by some in our own times into occasion for casting reproach upon the advocates of demonstrated or highly probable scientific theories.
We conceive that it is impossible for the word of God, as written in the book of nature, and God's word written in Holy Scripture, to contradict one another, however much they may appear to differ.	We conceive that it is impossible for the word of God, as correctly read in the book of nature, and the word of God as truly interpreted out of the Holy Scripture, to contradict one another, however much they may appear to differ.
We are not forgetful that physical science is not complete, but is only in a condition of progress, and that at present our finite reason enables us only to see through a glass darkly ; and we confidently believe that a time will come when the two records will be seen to agree in every particular.	We are not forgetful that neither theological interpretation nor physical knowledge is yet complete, but that both are in a condition of progress; and that at present our finite reason enables us only to see both one and the other as through a glass darkly ; and we confidently believe that a time will come when the two records will be seen to agree in every particular.
We cannot but deplore that natural science should be looked upon with suspicion by many who do not make a study of it, merely on account of the unadvised manner in which some are placing it in opposition to Holy Writ.	We cannot but deplore that religion should be looked upon with suspicion by some, and science by others, by the students of either who do not make a study of the other, merely on account of the unadvised manner in which some are placing religion in opposition to science, and some are placing science in opposition to religion.

We believe that it is the duty of every scientific student to investigate nature simply for the purpose of elucidating truth, and that if he finds that some of his results appear to be in contradiction to the written word, or rather to his own *interpretations* of it, which may be erroneous, he should not presumptuously affirm that his own conclusions must be right, and the statements of Scripture wrong; rather leave the two side by side till it shall please God to allow us to see the manner in which they may be reconciled.	We believe that it is the duty of every theological student to investigate the Scriptures, and of every scientific student to investigate nature, simply for the purpose of elucidating truth. And if either should find that some of his results appear to be in contradiction, whether to Scripture or to nature, or rather to his own *interpretation* of one or the other, which may be erroneous, he should not affirm as with certainty that his own conclusion must be right, and the other interpretation wrong; but should leave the two side by side for further inquiry into both, until it shall please God to allow us to arrive at the manner in which they may be reconciled.
Instead of insisting upon the seeming differences between science and the Scriptures, it would be as well to rest in faith upon the points in which they agree.[1]	In the meanwhile, instead of insisting, and least of all with acrimony or injurious statements about others, upon the seeming differences between science and the Scriptures, it would be a thousand times better to rest in faith as to our future state, in hope as to our coming knowledge, in charity as to our present differences.

---

[1] The first declaration was published in the *Athenæum* of Sept. 17, 1864, p. 375. The second in that of Oct. 8, 1864, p. 464.

VI.

GENERAL EXPLANATION OF THE MOSAIC HEXÆMERON.

I HAVE already proved at length that the object of the Bible is not to give us scientific teaching, but only to impart to us religious and moral truths. That God created the world is apparently such a religious truth; the Bible, therefore, is quite on its own ground when it tells us this in the first verses of Genesis. But why does it not confine itself to this simple, uncontested theological statement? why does it give in the rest of the chapter that which seems to belong more to science than to dogma or morality, a history of the development of the kosmos?

If Moses says more than "In the beginning God created the heavens and the earth," or if God has revealed anything further than this, this further revelation must be of religious, moral, and theological importance, and it must have been revealed because of this theological importance, and not because of its scientific interest. It is in fact only necessary to read the first chapters attentively in order to find out the theological truths, which are plainly enough expressed in it, although they are not formulated as dogmatic statements. I will just enumerate these before I proceed to explain the chapter, because, as you will perceive, it will materially facilitate further inquiries.

1. The general statement, "God created the heavens

and the earth," is made more distinct, although not more complete, if we add to the general idea of heaven and earth an enumeration of the principal things which are contained in this idea, *e.g.* the stars, plants, animals, etc. It was not absolutely necessary that Moses should add this enumeration, but he might have had reasons for it, and we shall see later what these reasons were. His first statement is therefore illustrated and explained by the further relation given in this chapter. We see the heavens bright with the sun, moon, and stars, and covered with clouds from which the rain pours down upon the earth. Moses teaches us that it is God who has created the firmament, and the waters of the firmament, and it is God who has made the two great lights and the stars, and set them in the firmament of the heavens to give light upon the earth. On the earth we see the land covered with various kinds of herbs and trees, we see air, water, and land inhabited by all kinds of animals; Moses teaches us that it is God who has caused the waters to be gathered together into one place, and the dry land to appear; it is God who has commanded that the earth should bring forth herbs and trees after their kind, that is, of different kinds; and that there should be fruit-bearing trees, which could therefore reproduce themselves, and from which the herbs and trees which we now see have sprung. It is God who has made the animals in the water, in the air, and on the land, and He has blessed them, and said, "Be fruitful and multiply." He has therefore given them the power of propagating their species, so that although the animals now living have not been created directly by God, they are descended from those first created by God in the manner He willed and ordered, and therefore they must be called the creatures of God. And man, the highest and noblest of visible living beings, was created by God; male and female created He them, and He blessed them, and said, "Be fruitful and multiply, and replenish the earth." So we all who now live on the earth, and all who have lived before us and have inhabited the earth, are the creatures of God, for we are descended from the man and woman whom God created and endowed with the power of reproduction. You must admit that to the simple childlike mind of man — and it is to this that the Bible first appeals — the doctrine of the creation of the world by God is represented in this detailed and concrete manner much more impressively and effectively than if Moses had confined himself to the simple statement, "In the beginning God created the heavens and the earth," although that would be quite sufficient for a dogmatic compendium. Even from this point of view, therefore, we must admit that Moses was justified in amplifying this general statement; at any rate we cannot reproach him with having in the following verses forgotten the object of Holy Scripture —the religious teaching of mankind. And apart from their form in the Mosaic Hexæmeron, which will be discussed later on, natural science can make no objection to the above statements, for as it cannot dispute the assertion that God created all things, there can be no objection to our tracing back these things to the divine cause, though as to the mode in which this is done we shall come to an understanding later on.

2. When we say God created the world, it follows

as a matter of course that the world coming into being through the will of God, was created as God willed, that the work of the divine creative activity was adequate to the divine idea and plan. But it is often well to repeat a thing which appears to be a matter of course, and Moses had reasons no doubt for insisting on the truth just mentioned. He does this by concluding his account of the separate divine works with the words "and God saw that it was good," that is, that His will had been adequately realized in His works, for God calls that good which corresponds to His idea and to the divine will. Moses repeats this phrase several times, and I cannot help pointing out shortly the peculiarly striking and appropriate way in which he applies the expression. On the first day God creates the light, and divides the light from the darkness, "and God saw the light that it was good,"—not the darkness also, for that is not created by God, it is no Ens, but only the negation of light. On the second day God made the firmament, and divided the waters that were under the firmament from the waters that were above the firmament. The phrase, "and God saw that it was good," is only in the Greek translation here, and it is evidently an unfortunate addition to the text, for the work of the second day is still unfinished and imperfect, and cannot be described as good, because the divine idea has not as yet been realized. It is not till the fourth day that the lights are set in the firmament, and then "God saw that it was good;" the waters under the heavens were all gathered together in one place, and the dry land appeared, and it is only after this separation has taken place and the final condition has been reached that it is said, " and God saw that it was good." The phrase, " and God saw that it was good," is added after each separate perfected divine work, and it is therefore quite right that after the whole divine creation has been finished, and the divine world plan stands realized, not only in its separate details, but as a systematic whole, the observation should follow, " and God saw everything that He had made, and behold it was very good."

The first meaning then which Moses would convey to us by this often repeated observation is that God's creative will has been completely realized in the creation. But there is another meaning. In the chapters immediately following Moses has to mention creatures which are not good; the serpent, the seducer of man, occurs in the third chapter, and later on many things are described in Genesis which are either morally or physically bad. It is plain that it is partly with reference to this that Moses here lays stress on the fact that in the beginning all was good; the world as God created it was good, and what of evil there may be found in it later is not the work of God. You see here again we come upon theological truths which find their expression in the Hexæmeron.

3. According to the account in Genesis, man is not only the last creature in the visible creation, but also evidently the goal of the whole visible creation. The animals were made immediately before him; it is the task and the right of man to rule over them. Before the animals the plants were created; it is expressly said that they were given for food to man and to his subjects the animals. The dry land appears from the

waters, in order to bring forth vegetation, and to be a dwelling-place for the animals and men. The heaven itself is brought into relation with man, for the lights which God has set therein are meant to give light upon the earth, and to serve as signs, especially for signs of the succession of time, for days and for years, of course for the use of man. So that in the Hexæmeron the Bible remains true to its task, to teach us about religious things. The subject throughout Genesis is man and his relation to God, and this involves religion. It is with reference to man that the dwelling-place prepared by God for man is described in the beginning of Genesis, and the truth that for man's sake God has created the unreasoning creatures is uttered.

4. Lastly, Moses had a special religious or theological reason for not confining himself to the general statement, "God created the world," but for describing the work of creation in detail, and he gives this reason plainly enough. He divides the whole work of creation into six days; in these six days, as it is said in the first verse of the second chapter, the heavens and the earth were finished; and after God had ended in six days His work, He rested on the seventh day from all His work which He had made, *i.e.* He ceases to create, *cessat ab opere suo*, as the Vulgate translates it. And although, as is stated in the New Testament,[1] and in Holy Scriptute repeatedly, God is working even now, and will always continue to work, yet the work of the first creation of things has long since been finished, and it

---

[2] John v. 17. "Quia nihil additum est creaturæ, requievisse dictus est ab omnibus operibus suis; quia vero, quod fecit, gubernare non cessat, recte dixit Dominus; Pater meus usque nunc operatur."—Aug. *Sermo* 125. 4; cf. c. Adim, c. 2: *de gen. ad lit.* 4. 12.

lasted only a certain time, which for the present we will call, according to the expression in Genesis, six days, reserving the discussion of the meaning of this expression until later. The third verse of the second chapter explains why this was insisted on: "And God blessed the seventh day, and sanctified it, because that in it He had rested from all His work which God created and made,"—or in other words, that on this day His work of creation was ended. The readers of the Pentateuch knew that a divine law commanded them to observe the seventh day as a holy day, to restrict their work and labour to six days, and on the seventh day, in obedience to Jehovah, for His honour, in acknowledgment of His sovereignty, and in gratitude for the divine benefit of the creation, to rest from all earthly work, and devote themselves to religious exercises. And why, they might ask, did God hallow the seventh day? Why not the tenth or any other? Because the Sabbath is specially dedicated to the worship of God as the Creator, and the whole work of the creation is divided into six parts; and it is therefore fitting that human work and occupation should fill six days, and that a regularly returning festival in honour of the Creator should take place after the lapse of six days, and not of ten.

No doubt there are many scientific objections to the six days, and these shall be considered and noticed in due course. The point now is to show that in giving us such details about the creation, and in speaking of the six periods of creation, Moses has not abandoned religious in order to trench upon scientific ground; on the contrary, there is in these very details a religious element, and therefore he could pass from the opening of Genesis to the Hexæmeron without in any way departing from his principle of never giving us purely scientific teaching. Or, to express myself more correctly, the general principle which I have already established holds good in the Hexæmeron. The object of the divine revelation is not to correct or extend our scientific knowledge, but to convey to us divine truths; and when revelation includes scientific elements, these are touched upon because of the religious elements which they contain, and not for their own sake. If, then, God has revealed to man in the Bible, not only the simple truth that He is the creator of the world, but has added to it other revelations, which make up the rest of the Hexæmeron, He has not done this in order to teach us about the separate part of creation, about the order of its development and the time in which it was accomplished. For those are things which in themselves only interest men of science, or man as a thinking being, but do not touch the moral and religious side of man; and God can therefore leave them to the intellect of man to discover. Such things can only become objects of divine revelation when religious truths are involved in them, the knowledge of which is necessary or useful to man from a religious point of view, and when such truths can only be conveyed to man through the medium of these natural things. Religious truths are the end of divine revelation, the other things are only the means to that end.

Having examined the theological truths conveyed to us in the Hexæmeron, we come now to the form in which the Bible clothes these truths, and here the connection between revelation and natural science begins. I shall begin the explanation of the separate parts of the Hexæmeron in my next lecture. I will now only make a few more general remarks.

Of the four theological statements which, as I have just shown, are contained in the Hexæmeron, the third has had great influence on the whole composition. If Moses desired to show that it was man for whom God had created all things, we may expect that in treating of the created things he would specially mention and lay stress on those which stand in the most direct relation to man; and also that he would consider these things themselves from the point of view of their relation to man. And accordingly we find that after he has briefly mentioned the creation of the heavens and the earth, that is, the whole world, in the first verse of Genesis, he turns first of all in the following verses to the earth. The second verse begins, "And the earth was without form, and void." There is no mention of the heaven; and when it is alluded to in the following verses, it is only with reference to its relation to the earth. God makes the firmament in order to take up part of the waters that covered the earth, and He creates the stars to give light upon the earth, and to be signs of the succession of time to man. The condition of the heavens apart from this, the relations of the stars to each other, whether they also have vegetation and are inhabited, these questions Moses never alludes to at all; and that because he would not tell us of every separate thing which God has created, but after saying generally that God had created all things, he would tell us only of the separate things which God has created for man.

Therefore it is not quite correct to speak of the cosmogony of Moses; his first object is rather a geogony, and it is only when they in any way affect the earth that he alludes to the things in the kosmos outside the earth. The Mosaic account of creation must therefore be called one-sided and incomplete; this, however, is no fault, but a necessary quality. It would be very remarkable were the Bible to say more than it does, for it would then be departing from the rule of only giving us religious teaching, and mentioning natural things only as much as is necessary for the religious teaching. This incompleteness and one-sidedness characterizes the further account of the earth's development. Moses only mentions the separation of water and land, the creation of plants and animals, for that was all that was necessary to describe the position of man in the visible world. Moses does not mention the interior of the earth, the formation of the mountain ranges, the extent of the water and the land, the rational classification of plants and animals and such things; not because his scientific knowledge was too limited, although this may be unhesitatingly admitted, but because these things were of no real importance to what he wished to represent.

The first characteristic of the Mosaic account of the origin of the visible world is then a one-sidedness and incompleteness which is intentional and natural. The second characteristic is the popular, and if you will, unscientific mode of statement. As it is never the object of the Bible to give us scientific teaching, it never speaks the language of science,—as I have already explained at length,—but the language of the ordinary man. It is to be read for the sake of religious teaching, not for the sake of geological, astronomical, geographical, or any other scientific studies, and therefore it chooses those expressions which are intelligible to the ordinary men, not those which will be considered correct by science; and when it speaks of the things of nature, it makes use of the conceptions and ideas which men derive from the natural, superficial, and childlike observations of nature. The man of science knows that the atmosphere of the earth is impregnated with watery vapours, which under certain conditions form themselves into clouds, and fall down to the earth as rain; the ordinary man believes that there is a provision of waters above the *R'kia haschamajim*, the "firmament of heaven," as the Vulgate translates the word, or more accurately, the canopy of heaven, and accordingly this is the way in which the Bible describes it. Man believes that the heaven has two great lights, the sun and moon, and beside them the host of stars; and this is what the Bible describes. Astronomy may say what it likes to this division. The botanist and zoologist may laugh, or be horrified, at the classes into which the animals and plants are divided in the Hexæmeron; the divisions are not meant to be scientific, for the Bible would not give us a system of botany or zoology, but only an enumeration of animals, and its division is quite fitted for this object. In ver. 12 the vegetable world is divided into trees and herbs; the word "green" probably does not mean a third class, grass, etc., but it is applied to all the plants in the first stage of their creation.[1] Nothing can be more unscientific

---

[1] Dillmann, *Genesis*, p. 28. [This refers to the word translated "grass" in our version.—Tr.]

than this division, but it is quite sufficient if all we are to be told is that God created all the plants, both great and small. The zoological system of the Hexæmeron is of the same description: 1st, water animals; 2nd, air animals; 3rd, land animals. The water animals are divided into (*a*) *tanninim gedolim, cete grandia,* the large water animals, to which of course whales belong; and (*b*) the small water animals. The air animals are not further particularized, but of course they include, besides the birds, bats, flies, midges, and in general *col oph canaph,* omne volatile, everything which has wings. The land animals are divided into (*a*) *b'hemah,* jumenta, domestic animals; (*b*) *chajjath haarez,* bestiæ terræ, wild animals; (*c*) *haremes,* reptilia, little creeping things, that is, in the Hebrew language, whatever moves immediately on the earth: rats and mice, serpents, worms, wingless insects, etc. And this enumeration, quite inadequate from a scientific point of view, is quite sufficient to convey to us the truth that all animals, whether moving in the waters, in the air, or on the land, both large and small, were created by God.

Thirdly, this popular, objective mode of representation is apparent in the manner in which the activity of God Himself is described. It is not possible to have a worthy conception of the Divine Being and of His working; if we would obtain an idea of it, or give an adequate description of it, the materials, as it were the colours of the picture, must come from what is accessible to our observation and knowledge, that is, from created things; and among created things, especially from the creature which has been made after the likeness and image of God, from man. This is the cause of the so-called anthropomorphisms in Holy Scripture, the transference of expressions which apply first to human actions, to analogous divine actions.[1] This anthropomorphic mode of expression obtains throughout the whole account of creation, and it is just for this reason that it is such a vivid picture. The writer of the account speaks as if he had been present at the divine work of creation as an eye-witness; he was not that, but the circumstances of the creation have, as I have shown above, been revealed to man, and thus he who received that revelation was supernaturally made, as it were, an eye-witness of the divine working, and therefore he can speak as such. For scientific exposition the separate statements must, of course, be translated from the language of intuition into that of understanding.

In this language we say: Light came into being by the will of God; but as *we* make our will known by speaking, by commanding, so the author of Genesis says: "God *said*, Let there be light, and there was light," etc. God then brings about that that light and darkness should regularly alternate; the present regular sequence of light and darkness rests on a divine ordinance; man calls this alternation day and night. The author of the Hexæmeron expresses it in this way: "God divided the light from the darkness; and God called the light day, and the darkness He called night." Similarly in the following verses God makes the firmament, and divides the waters under the firmament from those above the firmament, and calls the firma-

[1] Habent enim consuetudinem divinæ Scripturæ de rebus humanis ad divinas res verba transferre.—Aug. *de Gen. c. Man.* i 14 20

ment heaven; and He gathers the waters under the firmament into one place, and causes the dry land to appear; and He calls the gathering together of the waters, sea, and the dry land, earth; that is to say, the division between the watery elements on the earth and those in the atmosphere, the creation of what we call the heavens, the division of the earth's surface into what we call land and sea; all this rests—as we see now that we have brought out the real facts which are contained in the language of the Bible—on a divine ordinance.[1]

The expression which we have just discussed at length, "And God saw that it was good," is also an anthropomorphism. The human artist looks back on the work which he has created after he has completed it, and he calls it good; he is satisfied if the work corresponds to the idea which he had of it beforehand. God does not need so to try to compare His work, therefore if it is said, " He saw that it was good," it is simply in order to acknowledge the fact that the divine idea has been adequately realized in the divine work.

[1] "Vocavit" autem dictum est vocari fecit; quia sic distinxit omnia et ordinavit, ut et discerni possent et nomina accipere.—Aug. *de Gen. c. Man.* i. 9. 13. Intelligitur ubique per hoc quod dicetur "vocavit;" dedit naturam vel· proprietatem, ut possit sic vocari. — Thom. i. 9. 69, a. 1 extr. "In dividing the things, God divided also the notions and the names of the things. That is the meaning of the divine naming. Human division is only the echo of the divinely ordained distinction between things."—Delitzsch, *Genesis*, p. 91.

VII.

EXPLANATION OF GENESIS I. 1, 2.

THE first verse of the Bible runs thus: "In the beginning God created the heaven and the earth." The Hebrew word which we have translated "create" means, especially in conjunction with "b'reschith," "in the beginning," the creatio ex nihilo, creation proper, the bringing forth from nothing, to bring forth something according to its being and substance.

The most common Hebrew word for bringing forth is "asah," which answers to our "make," the Greek ποιεῖν, the Latin *facere*. The words "jazar" and "bara" have a more special meaning than "asah." Jazar answers to our "form," Greek πλασσειν, Latin *formare* or *fingere*, and is therefore frequently combined with the so-called accusative of the subject; this is also possible with "asah," because this more general word does not exclude the idea of the special word. In Gen. ii. 7, *e.g.*, it is said: "And the Lord God formed man"—as the context shows, the body of man—"of the dust of the ground." Where we have formed, the Hebrew has jazar, with "dust" in the accusative, the Septuagint ἔπλασεν, the Vulgate formavit. Unlike asah and jazar, bara never has the subject in the accusative, and it is never used for human productions, but only for divine productions.

The fundamental meaning of the word is certainly "to create," and although it may be occasionally found when there is no question of actual creation, it is only employed for divine actions, and for those divine actions which are marvellous, so that they are to a certain degree equal to creation. You will find proofs of this use of the words in every Hebrew dictionary, and in every thorough commentary on this passage. And here the addition "in the beginning" excludes any other idea.

The expression is explained in this way by every exegete who is worthy of the name, although their theological bias may be as different as, among the modern expounders of Genesis, that of Keil and Knobel.[1]

I need not now enter into the question as to whether God is here intentionally called Elohim and not Jehovah, or whether the name Elohim contains a reference to the Trinity.[2] It is sufficient for our object to know that God is described as the creative framer of the world. On the other hand, I cannot overlook the exegetical controversy as to whether the visible material world is here meant by "heaven

---

[1] "How and from what did God create matter? According to the narrator, certainly entirely through His own will, and therefore from nothing."—Knobel, *Gen.* i. 1. Cf. Tuch, *Genesis*, 2nd ed. p. 14. I omit the answer contained in the 1st ed. to Bunsen's assertion "that the question of the schoolmen, whether God created the world out of nothing, is left quite unnoticed in Gen. i. 1, and generally in the Bible," in order to leave room for more necessary discussions. For the translation, "In the beginning, when God created the heaven and the earth,—and the earth was without form and void . . . ,—and God created" (Dillmann, *Genesis*, p. 17, etc.), see Delitzsch, *Genesis*, p. 75.

[2] "We cannot, without destroying the differences between the Old and New Testaments, say that Elohim is *pluralis trinitatis;* but we may perfectly well say the *trinitas* is the revelation in the New Testament of the *pluralitas* of Elohim."—Delitzsch, *Genesis*, 3rd ed. p. 67.

and earth," or whether heaven means the spiritual immaterial creation, the angel world, and earth the material creation.[1]

There is no doubt that in the Hebrew Old Testament generally, "heaven and earth" express one idea, and mean the universe, the same which the Greek books of the Old Testament call ὁ κόσμος.[2] Look at the passage in the Psalms (cii. 25, 26): "Of old hast Thou laid the foundations of the earth; and the heavens are the work of Thy hands. They (heavens and earth) shall perish, but Thou shalt endure."[3] It is impossible to quote a passage in the Bible in which heaven and earth mean two separate conceptions, the spiritual and material creation: and it is the less allowable to take that as the meaning here, because in the following verses heaven certainly does not mean the spiritual (vers. 9, 10) and earth the material world (vers. 2, 10). If, therefore, the angels are meant to be included in the first verse as the creatures of God, it is only in so far as they belong to the world; but it does not mean that they are specially denoted by the word "heaven."

[1] Amongst the modern writers, specially Michelis, *Entwicklung*, etc., p. 7. *Kath. Lit. Zeitung*, 1859, No. 44. *Natur u. Offenbarung*, 1862, 473; 1869, 83. C. M. Mayrhofer, *Das dreieine Leben in Gott und jedem Geschöpfe*, Regensburg 1851, i. 93. Westermayer, *Das alte Test.* i. 6. Baltzer, *Biblische Schöpfungsgesch.* p. 184 seq. Cf. *Theol. Lit. Blatt.* 1867, 236.

[2] Wisd. xi. 18: ἡ παντοδύναμός σου χεὶρ καὶ κτίσασα τὸν κόσμον ἐξ ἀμόρφου ὕλης. 2 Macc. vii. 9: ὁ τοῦ κόσμου βασιλεύς. vii. 13 and xiii. 14: ὁ τοῦ κόσμου κτιστής. viii. 18: τῷ παντοκράτορι θεῷ, δυναμένῳ τὸν ὅλον κόσμον ἐν ἑνὶ νεύματι καταβαλεῖν. Aug. *Qu. in Hept.* v. 5: Assidue quippe Scriptura his duabus partibus (coelum et terra) commemoratis universum mundum vult intelligi.

[3] For other passages, see Reinke, *Die Schöpfung der Welt*, Münster 1859, p. 143.

We find no unanimity among the Fathers with respect to the meaning of this verse. St. Augustine even gives us several different explanations of it at the same time,[1] and it is plain that he did not firmly believe that by "heaven" the angels were meant, because he sometimes lays down the certainly erroneous opinion — that the angels are meant by the light which was created on the first day;[2] and repeatedly says that we may understand by "heaven and earth" in ver. 1 the matter which God formed in the manner described in the following verses.[3]

It would be going too far to say[4] that *all* the Fathers believe that the creation of the spirit world is intimated in the first verse, and that they are only uncertain as to the manner in which it is done; but even if we were to admit this, it would evidently not imply that the idea that heaven means the angels is more favoured by ecclesiastical tradition than the other, for the assumption that the creation of the spirit world is referred to in this verse is quite compatible with the other idea. But above all things I must protest against the assertion that the Church

[1] *Conf.* 12, 17 seq.

[2] *De gen. ad lit.* i. 3, 9 seq.

[3] *Contra adv. legis et proph.* i. 10 : Sive ergo prius nomine cœli et terræ . . . materies ipsa informis significata est . . . sive per cœlum et terram generaliter prius insinuata sit spiritualis corporalis-que creatura, sive aliquid aliud, quod hic salva fidei regula intelligi potest : Deum tamen . . . fecisse cuncta, quæ cernimus et quæ meliora non cernimus . . . dubitare fas non est. Cf. *De actis c. Fel. Man.* i. 17.

[4] Chrysostomus, *e.g.* (*Hom. in Gen.* ii. 2 : *Sermo* 1 in *Gen.* n. 2), and Theodoret expressly say that Moses does not mention the creation of the angels ; see also the author of the *Quæst. ad Ant.* 4 (Migne, 28, 601), wrongly ascribed to Athanasius. Cf. also *Zts. der D. M. G.* 1870, 283. Theophilus of Antioch (*ad Autol.* ii. 13, p. 92 B), Basil (in *Hex. hom.* 1, n. 8. 11), and others think that by heaven the material heaven is meant.

has given an interpretation of this passage which is in a manner authoritative, according to which heaven signifies the spiritual, and earth the material creation. No doubt this passage (and others in which the same expression is found) is the authority for the assertion made by the Church in the Apostles' Creed, that God the Father is the Creator of heaven and earth. In the Nicene Creed this appellation is amplified (referring to Col. i. 16): Maker of heaven and earth, and of all things visible and invisible. But this in no way involves a declaration on the part of the Church that by heaven we are to understand all invisible, and by earth all visible creatures. It follows only that when the Church makes use of the expression "heaven and earth," she means to allude to all visible and invisible things.[1] Nothing in it throws any light on the explanation of the first verse of Genesis, for by adopting a Biblical expression the Church does not mean to declare that when this expression occurs in the Bible it must only be understood in the sense in which she has used it.[2] There can only be an authoritative explanation of a passage in the Bible—an explanation which is "as good as authoritative" conveys nothing to my mind—when it is the Church's object to decide on the meaning of such

[1] When we find the question asked in *Cat. rom.* p. 1, c. ii. q. 16, 17: Quid per cœlum et terram hoc loco intelligitur? and Quid peculiariter cœli nomine significatur? hoc loco does not refer to Gen. i. 1, which is not even mentioned, but to the first article of the Creed. Or are we to suppose that "earth" in Gen. i. 1 means only man, because in c. 18 we find: Quæ creatura terræ vocabulo potissimum hic intelligitur?

[2] In all catechisms the fourth [fifth] commandment runs thus, "Honour thy father and thy mother, that thy days may be long on *the earth*," but all Roman Catholic commentators translate Ex. xx. 22, "that thy days may be long in the land which the Lord thy God giveth thee." [This refers to the Vulgate translation, which is adopted in Roman Catholic catechisms, ut sit longævus super terram.]

a passage, and there is no proof of her having had any intention of deciding what is the meaning of Gen. i. 1 in making use of the expression "heaven and earth."

Again, appeal has been made in this controversy to a decree of the Fourth Lateran Council in the year 1215. But this decree was not intended to define the meaning of Gen. i. 1. In it God is described as "the One Principle of all things, the Creator of all invisible and visible, spiritual and corporeal beings, Who by His almighty power has in the beginning of time brought forth both creations from nothing, the spiritual and corporeal, the angelic and the earthly, and then the human," etc.[1] This declaration was directed principally against the heresy of the Kathari and Waldenses, who held that the visible world was not created by God, but traced its origin to a second, essentially evil Principle.[2] Against this error the Church urges the revealed doctrine that God is the One Principle of all things, and has created the material as well as the spiritual world. There was no occasion for declaring that this revealed doctrine is "plainly taught" or "purposely hinted at" in the first verse of Genesis; or that the spiritual world was meant by the word "heaven" in this verse; and I can see no justification for finding this in the Decree of the Council.[3] Contemporaries found no such declara-

[1] Cap. i.: Unum universorum principium, creator omnium invisibilium et visibilium, spiritualium et corporalium, qui sua omnipotenti virtute simul ab initio temporis utramque de nihilo condidit creaturam, spiritualem et corporalem, angelicam videlicet et mundanam, ac deinde humanam quasi communem ex spiritu et corpore constitutam. Diabolus enim et dæmones alii a Deo quidem creati sunt boni, sed ipsi per se facti sunt mali, homo vero diaboli suggestione peccavit.

[2] Hefele, *Conciliengeschichte*, v. 734, 783.

[3] The Council did not even assert the *simultaneous* creation of the angels and of matter; and therefore did not reject the opinion held by

tion in the Decree; for some decades after the Council S. Thomas Aquinas unhesitatingly states it as his opinion that this verse refers, at any rate directly, only to the creation of the material world.[1] And eminent theologians of a later time, who knew the Lateran Decree, as Petavius, Suarez, and others, unhesitatingly say that the theory that Moses does not mention the creation of the

many of the Fathers, and especially by most of the Greek Fathers, that the angels were created a long time before the material world. Klee, *Dogmatik*, ii. p. 220. Michelis, *Entwicklung*, etc., p. 10. The *simul* in the Lateran Decree no doubt comes from the phrase, Sir. xviii. 1: Qui manet in æternum, creavit omnia simul, *i.e.* The Eternal created all things at once, all things without exception, ἔκτιος τὰ πάντα κοινῇ.

[1] *Summa Theol.* i. q. 61, a. 1 : Ad primum ("De his, quæ sunt a Deo creata, agitur Gen. i.; sed nulla mentio fit ibi de angelis, ergo angeli non sunt creati a Deo") dicendum, quod Aug. dicit, quod angeli non sunt prætermissi in illa prima rerum creatione, sed significantur nomine cœli aut etiam lucis. Ideo autem vel prætermissi sunt vel nominibus rerum corporalium significati, quia, etc.—q. 65, a. 3 : Dicitur Gen. i. 1 : In principio creavit Deus cœlum et terram, per quæ creatura corporalis intelligitur. . . . Ut Moyses ostenderet corpora omnia immediate a Deo creata, dixit : In princ. etc.—q. 66, a. 1 : Cum præmisisset duas naturas creatas, sc. cœlum et terram, informitatem cœli expressit per hoc quod dixit "Tenebræ erant super faciem abyssi," secundum quod sub cœlo etiam aer includitur: informitatem vero terræ per hoc quod dixit "Terra erat inanis et vacua."—q. 67, a. 4: Aug. videtur dicere, quod non fuerit conveniens, Moysen prætermisisse spiritualis creaturæ productionem. Aliis autem videtur quod sit prætermissa a Moyse productio spiritualis creaturæ. S. Thomas wrote a treatise on the Lateran Decree Firmiter credimus (*Opusc.* 23, in the Antwerp ed. of his works of 1612, t. 17. p. 197); but he does not in any way imply that it was of any importance to the above controversies. In the *Theol. Summa*, in discussing the question whether the angels were created before the material world (i. q. 61, a. 3), he takes no notice of the Decree, and only says that he thinks the theory that the angels were created at the same time as the material world is the more probable, but that the other, which has been adopted by all the Greek Fathers, must not be considered as erroneous. The statement that the latter theory has been held by *all* the Greek Fathers is, however, incorrect We find it in many of them (*e.g.* Bas. in *Hex. hom.* 2. 5, and in some of the Syrian Fathers, see *Zts. der D. M. G.* 1870, 288); but Theodoret, for instance (in *Gen.* ix. 3), does not adopt it ; on the other hand, amongst the Latin Fathers, Cassian, for instance, holds it (*Coll.* 8. 7). In support of this theory Job xxxviii. 6, 7 has been quoted. See Delitzsch on the passage, p. 460.

angels in Gen. i. 1 is right, or at least admissible.[1] In explaining the expression "heaven and earth" in the first verse of Genesis, we are then in no way fettered by the authority and tradition of the Church; and from a purely exegetical point of view the theory is to be preferred according to which the first verse, at least directly, only expresses the truth that the whole visible world came into being through God. It does not determine whether God created the world with its present or with any definite organization, or whether He created the simple elements of the world from

[1] Petavius, *Theol. Dogm.* t. iii. de opif. sex dierum. i. 1, proœm. § 4: Rerum a Deo creaturam solas illas, quæ sub sensus cadunt, a Mose descriptas esse, quamquam nonnulli secus judicant, verior est opinio. § 5: Nullam in tota illa narratione nisi corporatarum rerum mentionem putamus fieri, de angelis vero ceterisque corpore carentibus Mosen omnino tacuisse. c. 2. § 9: Superest, ut cœlum hoc loco non aliud sit, quam quod videtur a nobis et cœlum proprie nuncupatur.—*Suarez* de opere sex dierum. i. 1, c. 6: Est opinio satis antiqua et recepta, Moysem in eo capite nullam de creatione angelorum mentionem fecisse. . . . Secunda sententia huic extreme contraria est, Moysem in illis verbis per se ac immediate locutum esse de angelis illosque solos nomine cœli significasse. . . . Verum tamen sine ulla dubitatione dicendum est primo, Moysem nomine cœli non significasse solos angelos. . . . Secundo dico, quamvis expresse Moyses non narraverit per illa verba angelorum creationem, nihilominus non omnino eam prætermisisse, sed implicite sub nomine cœli . . . comprehendisse totum cœli ornatum, qui magna ex parte in habitatoribus ejus sui cœlicolis, qui sunt angeli, consistit.—B. Pererius in *Gen.* i. 1, § 51, thinks that cœlum means only universorum corpus cœleste cunctos orbes complectens, and, § 192, discusses at length the question, cur Moses hoc loco creationem angelorum non exposuerit. Bonfrerius (in *Gen.* i. 1, p. 96) says: Angelorum creationem Moyses omisit, quod tantum suscepisset describendam creationem rerum sensibilium. Similarly W. Smits, *Genesis*, t. i. p. 500. Cf. Pianciani, *Erläuterungen*, etc., p. 242 (*Cosmogonia*, p. 478). He says, p. 251: "Although the Pope and the Synod did not decide on the meaning to be attached to the beginning of Genesis, yet those who drew up the formula must have had those first words of Moses in their minds, for the whole formula is simply a paraphrase of those words." We might, however, say more accurately: "Although those who drew up the formula certainly had the first words of Moses in their minds, yet the Pope and the Synod did not decide on the meaning to be attached to the beginning of Genesis."

nothing, and implanted in them the forces and laws of their development; the words "God created the heaven and the earth" will suit either case.

As the object of Moses was a geogony, and not a cosmogony, he continues without further mention of the heavens, "And the earth was without form and void." These words are in contrast with the account which follows. When man was established as the ruler of the earth, it was ready for him as a dwelling-place; the land was divided from the sea, and the latter was confined within strict limits. It was clothed with vegetation, and land, water, and air were peopled with animals; it was surrounded by the atmosphere, and illuminated by the stars. It was not so from the beginning; on the contrary, this state was preceded by another in which as yet no sign could be seen of this separation of the elements, and of the existence of individual creatures. Moses describes this condition in these words: the earth was "without form and void," thohu wabohu; and either God formed the present organized condition of the earth in succession to this chaotic condition, or the earth developed from this chaotic state into its later condition, according to the will and under the influence of God. This is the only certain conclusion which can be drawn by exegesis from ver. 2. Whether this chaotic condition which preceded the present was the original one, the condition in which the earth first existed; or whether this chaotic state was preceded by another state; or in other words, Did the earth exist only as chaos before the work of the six days? or did yet another organized condition precede chaos, so that chaos was formed by the ruins of a preceding world? these questions cannot be answered by exegesis. The chaotic condition out of which the later state of order was developed is the first of which the Hexæmeron speaks, but it does not necessarily follow that it was the first in which the world existed.

The contents and the connection of the first verses can then be understood in two ways. First, In the beginning God created the heavens and the earth; and the earth, when it was first created by God, was without form and void, and it received its form and development only through the further operation of God. Or, secondly, In the beginning God created the heavens and the earth;—that is an independent statement, and what follows is not to be closely connected with it, but to be considered as a new paragraph;—but before the earth attained to its present condition it was without form and void, and this condition began to give way to the present one with the creation of light, ver. 3. If we adopt the first of these we find that there is a connection between the second verse and the first, and a good progress of thought from ver. 1 to 3; but the second is not exegetically inadmissible.

How long did the condition of thohu wabohu last? To this question the exegete can only answer that he does not know. Genesis only says that the earth was in this condition when God began to form it, but there is no mention of how long it lasted. Nor could we answer the question if we knew anything about the duration of the six days. For the beginning of the first day must be dated from the time of the creation of light, so that the period of the thohu wabohu must have been before the first of the six days. There is therefore nothing in the Bible to interfere with science if it should determine what length of time elapsed between the first beginning of the universe and the beginning of the present condition of the earth.

The condition of thohu wabohu is thus described in the second verse of Genesis: "And the earth was without form and void, and darkness was upon the face of the deep. And the Spirit of God moved upon the face of the waters."

In explaining these expressions we must pay attention to the following facts: The earth is said to be without form and void because the plants and animals did not as yet exist to adorn and inhabit it; the waters are spoken of because the dry land appeared through the gathering together of the waters on the third day only; Genesis describes these waters as covered with darkness because the light was only created on the first day.

This description of the condition of chaos is therefore essentially a negative one; we are only told what was not yet there, but was to come in the course of the six days. And further, we may say that the description is essentially superficial; it only mentions those things in reference to the earth which are quite evident; there is water on its surface, and above it darkness. Genesis does not say what the condition of the interior of the earth was, whether the solid elements had already come together under the water, and were only covered by it, or whether the whole earth was still in a fluid condition. The most mighty fermentings and revolutions may have been taking place in the interior of the earth, chemical and mechanical forces at work, fire and volcanoes glowing; the spiritual eye of man, to which God reveals the history of creation, sees nothing of all this, it only knows that the earth did not present that beautiful aspect which we see now, that it was all enveloped in water and darkness. You see that even the description which the Bible gives us of the state of chaos is very poor and incomplete. If science can tell us more about it, if it has discovered anything about the condition of the interior of the earth, and about the forces in action there, we may welcome these discoveries, for Genesis tells us less about this period than we should like to know, and it tells us too little for us to fear that anything which may be discovered by natural science could not be brought into harmony with the Bible.

The description which Genesis does give of the thohu wabohu is not attractive, for it consists only of the words: without form and void, waters and darkness. The last part of the second verse gives a lighter touch to the picture, adds a joyous or at least hopeful element to it: "and the Spirit of God moved upon the face of the waters," or as the Hebrew word is more correctly translated, having regard to the related dialects, and as it has been translated by some of the Fathers:[1] "The Spirit of God *brooded* upon the face of the waters." Chaos is therefore under the influence of the Divine Spirit, and it is intended that life shall come forth from it, as from the egg on which the bird is brooding. The chaotic mass, as it is, is a creature unworthy of God, it has not been produced in order to remain as it is, but that it may supply the raw material for more perfect forms; and by the words, "the Spirit

[1] Cf. Bas. in *Hex. hom.* ii. 6.

of God moved or brooded upon the face of the waters," Moses declares that chaos contains the germ of these more perfect forms; or that the divine purpose and the divine power are ruling over this inorganic matter, in order to form it into something organic and complete.

Another interpretation of this passage has been given by both ancient and modern, rationalistic and believing writers. It is this, "and a wind of God hovered or passed over the waters." This translation is exegetically inadmissible. No doubt the first meaning of *Ruach* is "breath," and so of course "wind," and the expressions "mountains of God," "cedars of God," may be quoted as parallels to that of "wind of God;" as these expressions denote mighty mountains and mighty cedars, so "wind of God" would mean a mighty storm. But these expressions are strictly poetical, and *Ruach Elohim* never has this meaning in the Old Testament, although it very often has that of "Spirit of God." And besides this, the word *rachaph*, whether it is translated hovered or brooded, does not apply to a storm. Very few competent interpreters, however, are in favour of this translation; almost all hold to the ordinary one, "Spirit of God." I need not therefore consider it further, neither is it necessary to consider the question whether or how far the expression the "Spirit of God" here means what we from the point of view of Christian theology mean by the Holy Ghost, the third person of the Trinity. The Old Testament gives the name of the Spirit of God to the indwelling divine force which forms, preserves, animates, and perfects, and we from our point of view may retain this conception. The following exegetical results then may be obtained from the first two verses :—

1. God has created all things; or, all things, except God, have their source in the creating will and creating power of God.

2. The earth has not always existed in the condition of order in which it was when man first appeared upon it; on the contrary, a condition of formlessness and desolation preceded the state of order.

3. In this time there was no light on the earth, and the surface presented the appearance of a mass of waters.

4. But even in this condition the earth, or the matter from which the earth proceeded, was under the influence of the divine power, and was intended to be fashioned by the action of God. The verses following ver. 2 give an account of this fashioning.

I cannot yet, however, leave ver. 2, although we have arrived at these conclusions. I have said that we could not discover from the words of Holy Scripture whether the state of chaos, which is described in ver. 2, was the first condition of the earth, or whether yet another condition, one of order, had preceded it, so that the chaos mentioned in ver. 2 was caused by the destruction of an earlier world. I have already observed that this last theory is exegetically and theologically admissible, and I might confine myself to this observation were it not for the construction often put upon this admission, which obliges me to explain it a little further.

Certain supporters of this theory are not satisfied with its being recognised as exegetically admissible, but seek to prove that it is the only correct theory. This we must protest against. First of all the assertion that the second verse might or should be translated, "and the earth *became* without form and void,"—that is, after having been previously formed,—is incorrect. According to the rules of Hebrew grammar, the translation must be, "the earth was without form and void."[1] Further, it has been said that the expression "God created the heaven and the earth" in the first verse, cannot be reconciled with the theory that God created first only the substance of the world without its later order and form, because this formless matter could not be described as heaven and earth. But S. Augustine observes that this name could be given to chaos by anticipation, because it was intended to be formed into heaven and earth.[2]

Again it is said that other passages in which the expression occurs prove that thohu wabohu means desolation after a condition of order.[3] It occurs in this combination once in Isaiah and once in Jeremiah,[4] and in both instances in the description of a country desolated by a divine punishment. No doubt in their description both prophets were thinking of the passage in Genesis; and how could they describe a waste and desolate land in stronger and briefer terms than by comparing it with the chaos of Mosaic history? The *tertium comparationis* does not lie in the fact that the

---

[1] Cf. Kurtz, *Bibel und Astronomie*, p. 90.

[2] Cœlum et terra potuit dici materia, unde nondum erat factum cœlum et terra, sed tamen non erat aliunde faciendum. Aug. *de Gen. c. Man.* i. 7, 11; cf. *de actis c. Fel. Man.* i. 17.

[3] Vosen, *Das Christenthum*, p. 742, and many others, especially W. Fr. Hezel; see Diestel, *Gesch. des alt. Test.* p. 640.

[4] Isa. xxxiv. 11; Jer. iv. 23.

condition described in these words followed a condition of order, but in the fact that it presents an abrupt contrast to a condition of order; with the prophets it is a contrast to the preceding, in Genesis to the succeeding, state of order.[1]

Further, it may be said that it is impossible that God should have created desolation and darkness,[2] that a chaotic creation is unworthy of God, and so on, and that therefore the state of chaos mentioned in the second verse must be looked upon as a later condition; but I would recall to your mind what I have just said, namely, that although the chaotic mass in itself is not worthy of creation by God, it was not created in order to remain as it was, but to serve as material for more perfect forms. And it cannot be said to be unworthy of God that the world should be first brought forth as unformed matter, in order to be fashioned by a series of further creative acts.[3]

Other supporters of the theory in question rightly give up all these and other groundless arguments, and are content to say with Kurtz, "The theory that a

---

[1] Cf. Isa. xlv. 18: "God Himself that formed the earth and made it, He hath established it, He created it not in vain (void, thohu; Vulg. in vanum), He formed it to be inhabited;" that is, that it should not remain void, but should be inhabited. See Delitzsch on this passage, p. 450.

[2] Westermayer, *Das alte Test.* i. 12; Raumer, *Kreuzzüge*, ii. 7, and others.

[3] Quid autem inconveniens, si mundanæ materiæ fuerant tenebrosa primordia, ut accendente luce melius, quod factum est, redderetur. Nec mala est putanda (materia), quia informis, sed bona est intelligenda, quia formabilis, *i.e.* formationis capax. Aug. *c. adv. legis et proph.* i. 8; cf. *De nat. boni*, c. 18. Si informitas tempore præcessit formationem materiæ non fuit hoc ex impotentia Dei, sed ex ejus sapientia, ut ordo servaretur in rerum conditione, dum ex imperfecto ad perfectum adducerentur. Thom. i. q. 66, a. 1, ad 1.

devastation of the earth took place between the primary creation of heaven and earth and the fashioning of the earth during the six days, which devastation made a restitution and new creation necessary, cannot be proved from Gen. i.; but neither does the whole chapter contain anything which would exclude it."[1] With this view I have already said that I agree.

There is, however, another hypothesis which is usually connected with that of a restitution of the originally and perfectly created and then devastated earth. To the question, "Why then was the earth in its original form devastated, so that it needed the restitution and new creation which is described in the first chapter of Genesis?" it is answered that some of the angels created by God fell, as we know: and that this fall took place certainly before the fall of man,—for a fallen angel is his tempter,—and according to the general opinion of theologians soon after their creation, and thus certainly before the end, and perhaps before the beginning of the six days mentioned in the first chapter of Genesis. So far all is well; but they go on to say that this fall of the angels caused the desolation of the earth, and that the condition which occurred after this desolation is described by Moses in ver. 2. As it has been lately said, "Because the prince of the angels would not continue in the truth, the world was consumed with wrath, and the thohu wabohu is the rudis indigestaque moles into which God shrunk up and struck down that spiritual world, now inflamed against Him, by materializing it, in order to make it the substratum of a new creation; and this was begun by submerging the chaos of the original

[1] *Bibel und Astronomie*, p. 91.

world, which had become fire.[1] This was the first, but unluckily not the only time when the flame of his ambitious self-confident pride, striving after dominion and destruction, was quenched."[2]

Those who hold this theory—with many individual modifications—are men of no little authority; they are, among men of science and philosophers, Jakob Böhme, Friedrich Schlegel, Julius Hamberger, Heinrich von Schubert, Karl von Raumer, Andreas Wagner; among theologians, Kurtz, Baumgarten, Drechsler, Delitzsch, and others among the Protestants; Leopold Schmid, Mayrhofer, and Westermayer among the Roman Catholics.[3] There is nothing in Holy Scripture or ecclesiastical tradition which could support such a theory; its supporters themselves admit this, and Westermayer only tries to explain the silence of the Fathers by their fear of Gnostics and Manichæans, in the face of whose dualistic systems it would have been more than unwise "to pour oil into the flames by promulgating such a doctrine." The earliest trace of such

[1] Delitzsch, *Genesis*, 3rd ed. p. 103.
[2] Schubert on Delitzsch, *Genesis*, 3rd ed. p. 613. The play upon words in the original, "zu Wasser wurde," can hardly be reproduced.
[3] Cf. Kurtz, *Bibel und Astr.* p. 539. Delitzsch, *Genesis*, p. 137 (cf. 3rd ed. p. 166). Drechsler on *Delitzsch*, p. 539. Keerl, *Schöpfungsgesch.* p. 537. Raumer, *Kreuzzüge*, ii. p. 7. Hamberger in the *Jahrb. für Deutsche Theol.* xii. 466. Wolf, *Die Bedeutung der Weltschöpfung*, p. 29. Mayrhofer, *Das dreieine Leben*, i. 95. Westermayer, *Das alte Test.* i. 37. Michelis thinks (*Erläuterungen*, p. 43) that in consequence of the fall of the spirits, the full development of the corporeal creature was hindered; which hindrance necessarily appears as disturbance and confusion. "The provisional, transient, and one-sided development of nature in the six days' creation, is explained by the fall of the angels, just as in like manner the *Incarnation* of the Son of God was conditioned by the fall of man." *Natur und Off.*, 1862, p. 473. He declares in *Natur und Off.*, 1864, p. 46, that this theory has no more in common with that of Kurtz than the dogma of the Trinity with the Indian Trimurti.

a theory is an utterance of the English king Edgar in the 10th century, to the effect, that as God had driven the angels from the earth after their fall, whereupon the earth had been changed into chaos, He had now placed kings on the earth so that justice might reign.[1] But a theological theory is not to be rejected because it is new, it only has to be proved that the new theory is in harmony with the old assured propositions. For my part I believe the opinion in question to be theologically admissible if it is thus formulated: "It is possible that the destruction of the original form of the earth is connected with the fall of the angels."

But how we are to conceive this causal connection I do not know. I cannot reconcile myself to the ordinary idea of it. If the devastation was a consequence of the fall of the angels, we must not think of the angels as purely spiritual beings. They must have a bodily form by which they are connected with the material world; the fallen angels must have been inhabitants of the earth just as men are, and the angels who have not fallen must now inhabit the fixed stars, as Kurtz, Zöckler,[2] and others imagine; the earth was destroyed through their fall, restored again through the work of the six days, and made into a dwell-

[1] Tholuck, *Vermischte Schriften*, ii. 230. Delitzsch's quotation from the Anglo-Saxon poet Caedmon (*Genesis*, 3rd ed. pp. 106, 613, cf. 4th ed. p. 530) contains nothing but the opinion, found also among the Fathers and mediæval theologians, that man was created in order to replace the fallen angels. (Klee, *Dogmengeschichte*, i. 275 ; Joh. Delitzsch, *Ein altkirchliches Theologumenon*, *Zts. für luth. Theol.*, 1872, p. 427.) The passage which Delitzsch quotes from the *Quæstiones ex V. et N. T.*, q. 2 (in the Migne ed. of Aug. iii. 2216), which is ascribed to St. Augustine, is also inapplicable.

[2] *Die Urgeschichte*, p. 12.

ing-place for man. There is no doubt about the consistency of all the suppositions in this theory, as it is circumstantially detailed by Kurtz, and as it has been, without any important modifications, adopted by Westermayer. But the last supposition is rather hazardous. According to the ordinary theory, the angels are incorporeal beings, and although some of the Fathers and some theologians have not thought it necessary to deny that they possessed *any* bodily form, but only that which resembled man, it seems to me that the bodily form of the angels must at any rate be supposed to resemble *very nearly* that of man, if the causal connection between the fall of the angels and the chaotic condition of the earth is to be explained by it.

VIII.

EXPLANATION OF GENESIS I. 3–31.

THE earth, we are told in the second verse of Genesis, did not always exist in the condition of order which prevailed when man first appeared upon it. It had been waste and desolate, there was no light, and its surface presented the appearance of a great mass of waters. The forming of this chaotic mass is described from ver. 3 onwards, it is what theologians call the creatio secunda. Moses begins with a sentence which has been often since ancient times justly quoted as an example of sublime language:[1] "And God said, Let there be light, and there was light." He continues, "And God saw the light that it was good, and God divided the light from the darkness. And God called the light day, and the darkness called He night. And the evening and the morning were the first day."

We shall discuss these statements at greater length later, especially the peculiar circumstance, which has been often pointed out with triumphant scorn, that light was created on the first day, and the stars only on the fourth. At present I shall only remark that nothing is said in the words of Genesis about the nature and essence of light; the questions whether

---

[1] Spengel and Creuzer, however, doubt the authenticity of the passage in Longinus, in which this sentence is quoted as an example of sublime language testifying to a sublime spirit. Cf. Delitzsch, *Genesis*, p. 529.

light is matter, or only a condition or motion of matter, are not answered here. The third verse only says that it became light in consequence of an act of the divine will; that is, that one quality of chaos, darkness, was removed. Darkness, however, is not quite removed, but it is no longer absolute; it loses its sole supremacy, it is kept within certain limits, and its relation to light is fixed. God divided the light from the darkness. This relation is that of regular change; and this alternation between light and darkness is called day and night, so that when Moses says God called the light day, and the darkness called He night, he means that the alternation between light and darkness, called by men day and night, rests on a divine ordinance. This alternation begins at once; God creates light, and so it is day; after a time, about the length of which nothing is said, darkness again sets in and it is night; this again in its turn gives place to light, the second appearance of which is the beginning of the second day. And the evening and the morning were the first day.

In order to explain the fact that here and in all the following passages the evening is mentioned before the morning, it is usual to appeal to the Hebrew custom of beginning the civil day in the evening. This, however, is an unfortunate explanation. Moses could not have expressed himself in any other terms. The first day of creation begins with the appearance of light, with the morning therefore; the natural day ends with the withdrawal of light and the recurrence of night, that is, the evening; the second day begins again with the morning; the night which lies between the evening of the first day and the morning of the second natural day constitutes with the first natural day a single alternation of day and night, that is, a civil day, a νυχθήμερον. Moses declares: "The evening and the morning were the first day," and not: "It became evening and night, and thus one day was ended," because the former is only a short way of expressing that it became evening and night, and this up to the following morning was the first day. Moses chooses this mode of expression in order to lead up to the second morning.[1]

The darkness therefore, which, according to ver. 2, covered the waters, was removed on the first of the six days. The work of the second day is concerned with the waters themselves; ver. 6: "And God said, Let there be a firmament in the midst of the waters; and let it divide" (or be a dividing thing, or that it should divide) "the waters from the waters," *i.e.* as the following verse shows, so that one part of the waters spoken of in ver. 2 should be above, and one part below this firmament. Ver. 7: "And God made the firmament, and divided the waters which were under the firmament from the waters which were above the firmament, and it was so: and God called the firmament heaven. And the evening and the morning were the second day."

I have hitherto translated the Hebrew word "Rakia"

---

[1] Chrysostom in *Gen. hom.* x. 5, and Aug. *de Gen. c. Man.* i. 10, are right as to this: quia etiam nox ad diem suum pertinet, non dicitur transisse dies unus nisi etiam nocte transacta, cum factum est mane: sic deinceps reliqui dies computantur a mane usque in mane. Cf. *Sermo* 220 (*de div.*, 79). The above theory is disputed by Choyer, *La théorie géogenique*, p. 144. See *Th. Lit. Bl.* 1872, 358. Delitzsch, *Genesis*, pp. 82, 106. Dillmann, *Genesis*, p. 23

as firmament, according to the firmamentum of the Vulgate. The word, however, probably means something spread out, a spread out cloth or curtain or carpet, so that the heavens are described not as a fixed vault, but as a curtain spread out above the earth, as the psalmist says (civ. 2): "Who stretchest out the heavens like a curtain." Of course, while retaining this poetical, pictorial expression which is natural to the Hebrew language, we must not conclude that Moses imagined the heavens were a vault or a canopy, although we do not indeed know anything to the contrary, and the question is quite unimportant.

Commentators inquire whether by heaven—for so God calls the canopy—we are here to understand the cœlum sidereum, or the cœlum aëreum, the starry sky or the atmosphere. I think that this question should be answered by another; did Moses distinguish between the starry sky and the atmosphere? I think not; at least there is nothing in the Hexæmeron which obliges us to go beyond the general and vague meaning of the word, which simply signifies what we see stretched out over the earth, in the apparent form of a vault or canopy, in short, the same which we also call by the perfectly vague word heaven.

One part of the great mass of waters mentioned in the description of chaos, in ver. 2, is lifted up on the second day from the earth, while the other part remains; a division is made between heavenly and earthly waters. What are we to understand by the waters above the firmament? Some very weighty authorities hold the theory that the waters of the chaotic state were so divided on the second day, that as on the third day the earth was formed from the lower waters, so the upper waters afforded the substance for the formation of the heavenly bodies which appeared on the fourth day.[1] The other theory is, however, undoubtedly the true one, namely, that the water above the firmament is what forms the clouds; in short, the work of the second day was the formation of the atmosphere. Part of the water which formed the surface of the earth in its chaotic state rises in mists from the earth, and forms the atmosphere which surrounds it.

It will not be necessary to enumerate all the reasons which tell in favour of this theory and against the other, if any one can be found which is sufficient to decide the point in question. Nor will this be difficult. Moses had no occasion to tell us how and of what the stars were formed. For, as he intended to write a geogony, not a cosmogony, as I have already shown, it was not necessary that he should say anything about the stars except in so far as they are connected with the earth; and he does this in describing the fourth day. On the other hand, his account would have been strikingly incomplete if he had not spoken of the atmosphere, and specially of the clouds; because the rain, which, according to the popular view and the Bible, falls from the clouds, is essentially necessary for the growth of vegetation, and in the Hexæmeron the latter is brought into close connection with man. We therefore

---

[1] See Delitzsch in the first editions of his *Commentary on Genesis* (in the 4th ed., p. 38, he explains the "meteoric" water correctly), and Kurtz in the first editions of *Bibel und Astronomie* (in the latter editions he gives up the theory). Similarly Baltzer, *Bibel Schöpfungsgesch.* p. 315. Zollmann, *Bibel und Natur*, p. 94.

maintain that the work of the second day was the creation of the atmosphere.

As I have already observed, there is a good reason for the absence of the remark: "And God saw that it was good," at the close of the second day. The work of this day was not complete in itself, and its result was not perfected, for heaven still wanted the stars, and earth the division between water and land. The divine work, therefore, at the point which it has reached on the second day, is not yet good; *i.e.* the divine idea has not yet been adequately realized—that is, reserved for the next day.

I now come to the third day. Its work is divided into two parts. First of all the water and land are separated; vers. 9 and 10: "And God said, Let the water under the heaven be gathered together into one place, and let the dry land appear, and it was so. And God called the dry land earth, and the gathering together of the waters called He seas; and God saw that it was good." The fact that the portions of the earth's surface, which now appear as separated into solid and fluid, have names given to them, show, as has been said, that God has now caused to exist the definite condition which man calls "land and sea." As the relation of succession has been definitely appointed for light and darkness, so the relation of juxtaposition has been definitely appointed for water and land. With regard to the translation here "seas," in the Hebrew text we find the plural "jammim," which has been preserved in the Vulgate "maria" [and also in our version "seas"]. But the plural is, as Delitzsch observes, not numerical but intensive: it denotes the ocean, or the idea which we form of the word sea when we use it in contrast to land; while the singular would mean one single sea. It will not surprise you that the streams which flow into the sea, and the lakes and inland seas which are like scattered portions of the ocean, should not be mentioned here. It is only the separation of water and land as a whole which is in question.

If we compare the condition of the earth now with that in which it was before the first day, we shall more clearly understand the description of the earlier condition. The dry land has now appeared, whereas formerly the surface of the earth was described as "Th'hom" and "majim," an immense mass of waters. It is now light; the mass of waters was covered with darkness: these two characteristics of chaos are therefore removed. Only the third remains; the earth was without form and void, it is so still, and this state must be altered. God begins this work on the third day, for the second work of the third day is the bringing forth of vegetation.

Vers. 11–13: "And God said, Let the earth bring forth grass, the herb yielding seed, and the fruit-tree yielding fruit after his kind, whose seed is in itself, upon the earth: and it was so.[1] And the earth brought forth grass, and herb yielding seed after his kind, and the tree yielding fruit, whose seed was in itself, after his kind: and God saw that it was good. And the evening and the morning were the third day."

[1] The words "upon the earth" are a clearer definition of the foregoing: the earth is to bring forth the three classes of plants upon the earth, that is, as clothing for herself. See Delitzsch, *Genesis*, p. 93. Dillmann, *Genesis*, p. 28, explains it differently, "(fruit) whose seed is in itself (is for reproduction) upon the earth."

S. Thomas Aquinas, following S. Augustine, points out that the bringing forth of vegetation is quite rightly mentioned as part of the work of the third day. "The creation of the plants is considered as part of the formation of the earth," he says, "because they are immoveably fixed in the earth."[1] Kurtz expresses the same thought in these words: "The vegetable world, fast rooted in its native soil, and covering its nakedness with a beautiful garment, has no separate or individual existence. Its creation, therefore, belongs to the work of the same day which gave free existence to the land to which it is fast bound." On the other hand, the two connected works of the separation of water and land, and the clothing of the land with vegetation, are marked as separate works in spite of their connection, because in the account of the work of the third day it is twice said "and God said," and twice "and God saw that it was good." "Itaque," says S. Augustine, "et uno die ista junguntur et iteratis verbis Dei distinguuntur ab invicem."[2]

We have already spoken of the division of the plants.[3] The expression "herbs and trees *after their kind*," shows that God caused various kinds of plants to spring forth—that is, different genera and species, not one kind only. It is not without reason that Moses says that God created *seed-bearing* herbs and trees— that is, that He gave the power of reproduction to the plants which He had first created, and that therefore the present vegetable world is to be considered as the

---

[1] i. q. 69, a. 1.
[2] *De Gen.* 1. *imp.* c. 10, § 35.
[3] P. 99.

creation of God, because it is descended from the plants which God created on the third day. Genesis does not say in what manner the plants were brought forth; we are not told whether God had implanted their seeds, or the power to produce them, in the earth, so that these seeds and forces caused the plants to spring forth on the third day according to the divine will; or whether God created the vegetable world from nothing by His word. For God Almighty one is as easy as the other; Moses does not care which method God chose, he is satisfied with declaring that the existence of the plants is to be traced back to the divine causality. This is expressed in these verses plainly enough; for the rest, Moses chooses expressions which describe vividly the external aspect of the event. The earth has been bare and naked; after the creative work of God, it is clothed as now; as we express it, the earth brings forth plants. What more fitting expressions could Moses have chosen when speaking of the appearance of the first plants?

The end of the third day brings us to the middle of the Hexæmeron. What follows not only forms a parallel to the first part in that both are periods of three days, but each single day of the second half of the week of creation corresponds most strikingly with one day of the first half. On the first day light was created, on the fourth the light-giving heavenly bodies; on the second day the earthly waters were divided from the heavenly, and the heavens were formed; on the fifth the waters of the earth are peopled with animals, and birds appear in the air of heaven; on the third day the dry land appears, clothed with vegetation; on the sixth it receives its inhabitants, the land animals, and man, the noblest of the living beings. This fine parallel has been observed not only by modern writers, but also by S. Thomas Aquinas.[1]

The account of the *fourth* day, vers. 14-19, runs thus: "And God said, Let there be lights in the firmament of heaven, to divide the day from the night; and let them be for signs, and for seasons, and for days, and for years: and let them be for lights in the firmament of heaven, to give light upon the earth: and it was so. And God made two great lights; the greater light to rule the day, and the lesser light to rule the night: He made the stars also. And God set them in the firmament of heaven, to give light upon the earth, and to rule over the day and over the night, and to divide the light from the darkness: and God saw that it was good. And the evening and the morning were the fourth day."

The first thing expressly detailed here is the end and object of the stars in relation to the earth. First, they are to be for lights in the firmament of heaven, to give light, or to make it light upon the earth. As it became light on the first day, these words can only mean, that the light which God created on the first day is henceforth to be connected with the stars, as far as the earth is concerned.

Secondly, the stars are to divide the light from the darkness, as it is said in ver. 18, or between day and night, as in ver. 14. The division of light and darkness, that is, the establishment of the alternation of light and darkness, which we call day and night, is also a work of the first day. This work is now therefore

[1] Thom. i. q. 70, a. 1, c.; q. 71, a. 1, c. Delitzsch, *Genesis*, p. 73. Dillmann, *Genesis*, p. 14.

completed by connecting the alternation of day and night with the heavenly bodies, and especially with the sun and moon. This is poetically or figuratively expressed in ver. 16; they are to rule the day and the night; the larger of the two great heavenly lights is specially intended to govern the day, the lesser, with the other stars, to govern the night.[1]

Thirdly, the stars are to be, according to ver. 14, "for signs, and for seasons, and for days and years." We do not gain much, if, to explain this somewhat strange expression, we say that it is a Hendiadys for "for signs of the seasons," etc. We should rather explain it thus. The stars are to serve generally as signs for man, *e.g.* for prognostics and tokens of physical events, as of weather, but especially "for seasons," *i.e.* for signs of time, as the measure and rule for the calculation of time, and for the determining of times in general, therefore of the seasons of the year, and of the seasons for agriculture and navigation, festivals, etc., and particularly for the determining of days and years, and therefore of the calculation of time in the ordinary sense of the word.

You see that these three things only tell us what is the object of the stars for the *earth;* Moses does not say what other objects they might have, and what their condition might be, nor does the general aim of the Hexæmeron oblige him to do so. In a geogony, or to speak more correctly, in a description of the preparation of man's dwelling-place, the stars—and strictly the sun and moon, the other stars only in-

---

[1] Ps. cxxxvi. 7-9 : " To Him that made great lights,—the sun to rule by day, the moon and stars to rule by night."

cidentally—find a place only in so far as the earth receives light from them; and because such a relation exists between them and the earth, that upon the rising and setting, and other regularly recurring changes of the stars, there depends for the earth the alternation of day and night, and above all, time, and everything connected with it.

But as the only importance of the stars in the Mosaic geogony lies in their relation to the earth and to man, Moses could not mention them in the Hexæmeron until this relation began. This occurred on the fourth day. We need not therefore conclude from the words of Genesis that the stars began to exist only on the fourth day, they might have been in existence for a long time, although Moses, from his point of view, did not think it necessary to mention them; *for the earth* they began to exist on the fourth day, for not till then was their relation to the earth fixed by God, and for this reason they are then first mentioned. These preliminary observations must suffice for the present, I shall have to discuss this very point later; I may, however, remark that exegetically it is quite wrong to limit the stars mentioned in ver. 18 to the planets, as some interpreters have done.[1] Evidently Moses here makes no distinction between planets and fixed stars, they both belong to the lights of heaven.

The work of the fifth and sixth days is the creation of living beings; on the fifth day the animals of the water and air are created, corresponding to the formation of the atmosphere, and the separation of the waters

---

[1] Keerl, *Schöpfungsgeschichte*, p. 396. Ebrard, *Der Glaube an die heilig Schrift*, p. 29, etc. Against this view, see Kurtz, *Bibel und Astr.* p. 96.

on the second day; on the sixth day the land animals and man, corresponding to the appearance, and the clothing, of the dry land on the third day. The work of the fifth day is thus described vers. 20-23: "And God said, Let the waters bring forth abundantly the moving creature that hath life, and fowl that may fly above the earth in the open firmament of heaven. And God created great whales, and every living creature that moveth, which the waters brought forth abundantly after their kind, and every winged fowl after his kind: and God saw that it was good. And God blessed them, saying, Be fruitful, and multiply, and fill the waters in the seas, and let fowl multiply in the earth. And the evening and the morning were the fifth day."

I add the two following verses, 24 and 25, which describe the work of the sixth day: "And God said, Let the earth bring forth the living creature after His kind, cattle, and creeping thing, and beast of the earth after his kind: and it was so. And God made the beast of the earth after his kind, and cattle after their kind, and every thing that creepeth upon the earth after his kind: and God saw that it was good."

I have already alluded to the popular and superficial method of classing the animals.[1] As regards the manner of the creation of the animal world, it is probable that the use of the word "bara" in ver. 21 for the first time since ver. 1 is intentional. No doubt this word, which in ver. 1 means creation from nothing, might also be used for the creatio secunda, as with God formation from existing matter might also be called creation, the original matter being in the strictest sense of the

[1] P. 100.

word, created by God. But the use of the word here for the first time since ver. 1 seems to point to the giving of life to the animals, which is certainly a creative act.

Nothing more is said about the way in which the animals were created. We are told in ver. 24: "And God said, Let the earth bring forth the living creatures after his kind;" but in ver. 25 it is said: "And God made the beast of the earth." We can only suppose that the process resembled the making of man's body; from the earth God took the matter which formed the bodies of the beasts, and by His creative will He quickened them. In like manner He may have created the animals of the water and the air. Nothing is said about it in the text. In ver. 20 we are simply told: "And God said, Let the waters bring forth abundantly the moving creature which hath life, and fowl that may fly above the earth;" that is, the waters, which till then were without living beings, were to be filled with them, and winged creatures should fly about the air, which till then had no inhabitants; then comes ver. 21, "And God created great whales," etc.

In the Vulgate the words of ver. 20 are translated "Producant aquæ reptile," etc. This variation from the Hebrew is unimportant. S. Jerome has supposed that the waters were to bring forth the animals or let them appear, just as it is said directly afterwards in the Hebrew text: "Let the earth bring forth the living creature." The Latin translation of the words which follow in ver. 20 is rather more doubtful: "Producant aquæ reptile animæ viventis *et volatile super terram* sub firmamento cœli;" that is, the waters shall bring forth first the water animals, and then the animals of the air. Ancient interpreters and theologians, who only take this verse into consideration, have made many conjectures which are often very acute and ingenious as to why God caused the waters to bring forth not only the water animals, but also the birds and other winged creatures. In one of the hymns of the Roman Breviary also, the subject is thus described: God causes some of the animals which have come forth from the water, ex aqua ortum genus, to remain in the depths of the ocean, partim remittis gurgiti—these are the water animals; and some He raises up into the air, partim levas in aera—these are the birds, etc.[1] But a reference to the Hebrew text will prevent the necessity of such discussions; for it may be translated simply: "Let the waters bring forth abundantly the moving creature that hath life, and let fowl fly above the earth in the firmament of heaven."

If we look at ver. 19 of the following chapter, we find: "And out of the ground (de humo) the Lord God formed every beast of the field, and every fowl of the air." Therefore, as I have said, we may suppose that the creation of the animals resembled that of man in so far as the body was formed out of matter that already existed, and the principle of life was added by a creative act of God.

One thing more with reference to the creation of animals should be remarked. In the account of the creation of plants, stress was laid on the fact that God had created seed-bearing plants, which could propagate themselves, and it was therefore indirectly asserted that

---

[1] Cf. *Theol. Lit.-Bl.* 1870, p. 234. Basil gives the same interpretation. See Weiss, *Die grossen Kappadocier.* Braunsberg, 1872, p. 97.

the present vegetable world, having sprung from that created on the third day, was to be regarded as the creation of God. Similarly we are told in the history of the fifth day that "God blessed them (the animals), saying, Be fruitful, and multiply, and fill the waters in the seas, and let fowl multiply in the earth;" that is, God gave to the animals He had created the desire and the power of propagating and multiplying their species. What holds good for the animals of the water and the air holds good, of course, also for the land animals; they also have received the power and the desire of reproduction. And because this follows as a matter of course, after it has been said of the other animals, it was not necessary that Moses should say in his account of the creation of the land animals: "And God blessed them," etc.

Besides, as Delitzsch quite rightly observes: "Moses does not say that all the animals sprang from one common local centre of creation, nor does he say that one pair of each species was created, which multiplying afterwards spread over their present range of habitation. Older men of science, as Linnæus, and modern ones also, hold this theory, which is not in the least favoured by the Bible. What the Bible says about man may not be applied to the animal world. Any one may imagine, if he pleases, that in the beginning only two ants, bees, buffaloes, and antelopes were created, but the Bible must not be taken as the authority for this. The unity of mankind and the unity of a genus or race of animals are two totally different things. The unity of the latter remains, although it may have begun with many forms. Evidently this is the idea of the author of Genesis ; the animal world called forth by the word of God began to exist everywhere simultaneously, on the fifth day in air and water, on the sixth on land."[1] S. Augustine held the right view on this subject,[2] and Giebel might have spared himself the trouble of detailing the evils which must have arisen if only one pair of each kind of animal had been created.

But besides the creation of land animals, the work of the sixth day includes the *creation of man*.[3] Man also, as S. Augustine observes with reference to this passage,[4] belongs to the terrena animantia, to the living beings which inhabit the earth, and accordingly he is created on the same day as the land animals ; but in consideration of his privilege of reason, and of his likeness to God, he is specially mentioned after the account of the creation of the land animals has been closed with the usual formula : " And God saw that it was good." The description which Moses gives of the creation of man, vers. 26-31, shows at once that man is an essentially different creature from any of those which have hitherto been mentioned. " And God said, Let us make man in our image, after our likeness ; and let them have dominion over the fish of the sea, and over the fowl of the air, and over the cattle, and over all the earth,"—or as the text should

---

[1] *Genesis*, 3rd ed. p. 116 (4th ed. p. 97).

[2] *Sermo* 90. (*ex-Sirm*. 14) 7 ; *Sermo* 268. (*ex-Sirm*. 20) 3 : Numquid Deus de ave una fecit cæteras aves? . . . de uno equo omnes equos? Numquid non multa simul terra produxit et multiplicibus fetibus multa complevit? Ventum est ad hominem faciendum, et factus est unus, de uno genus humanum. According to Theodoret (in *Gen*. ix. 39), Theodore of Mopsuestia held the wrong view.

[3] For Baltzer's theory in the *Bibl. Schöpfungsgeschichte*, p. 376, that man was created on the *seventh* day, see *Theol. Lit.-Bl.* 1867, p. 236.

[4] *De Gen*. 1. *imp*. c. 16, § 55.

probably be amended, " and over all the beasts of the earth "[1]—" and over every creeping thing that creepeth upon the earth. So God created man in His own image : in the image of God created He him ; male and female created He them. And God blessed them : and God said unto them, Be fruitful, and multiply, and replenish the earth, and subdue it ; and have dominion over the fish of the sea, and over the fowl of the air, and over every living thing that moveth upon the earth. And God said, Behold, I have given you every herb bearing seed, which is upon the face of all the earth, and every tree, in which is the fruit of a tree yielding seed ; to you it shall be for meat. And to every beast of the earth, and to every fowl of the air, and to every thing that creepeth upon the earth, wherein there is life, I have given every green herb for meat : and it was so. And God saw everything that He had made, and behold it was very good. And the evening and the morning were the sixth day."[2]

The essentially different and higher nature of man is here implied by the fact, that God announces His resolution of creating him before He does so. "The world and its parts," says S. Gregory of Nyssa, "are as it were at once created by the divine might, in that at the mere command of God, 'Let there be,' they come into existence : but the creation of man is preceded by reflection ; the Creator first describes in words what is to exist. The divine words decide how man shall exist, to what end he shall be made, what he

---

[1] See Delitzsch and Dillmann on this passage.

[2] The sixth day of creation is distinguished from the others as being the last, by the article. It is properly " one day the sixth." See on this passage Keil.

shall do after he has been made, what he shall govern; so that man partakes of his high honours even before his creation, and ere he has come into being he has obtained the dominion of the world."[1]

Man is distinguished from the other animals, which have been mentioned hitherto, principally by the stress laid on his likeness to God. The plural form in the words, "Let us make man," might be supposed to be the pluralis communicativus, so that God in these words would be speaking to the angels; for man might be said to be created in the likeness of the angels, in so far as they also were made in the likeness of God. But as S. Augustine observes,[2] this idea is excluded by the following verse, for Moses says, as if he could not lay sufficient stress upon it: "And so God created man in His own image, in the image of God created He him." Therefore, S. Augustine continues, we must consider the plural here as referring to the Trinity. This is the prevailing opinion among the Fathers, and they lay stress on the manner in which the Trinity is alluded to in the words, "Let us make," and "in *our* likeness," and the unity of the Godhead in the singular "likeness," and in "God created man in His own image." The question as to how far this patristic exegesis is justified, is connected with the far larger question as to how far allusions to the Trinity are to be found in the Old Testament at all. This question has, however, no bearing on our present subject, and I shall not go into it further. I will only quote the words of a most able modern interpreter of Genesis, who

[1] *De opif. hom.* c. 3.   [2] *Civ. Dei*, xvi. 6.

embodies the theory which seems to me the right one in the following short sentence: "From the Old Testament point of view this is the pluralis majestatis, which if we look at it in the light of the New Testament, at least tends to become the pluralis trinitatis."[1]

The questions as to wherein man's likeness to God consists, and how far we are to distinguish between the image of God and the likeness to God, have been differently answered by theologians. If we entirely overlook the dogmatic side of the question, which does not concern us here, we must from the exegetical point of view say first, at all events, that man's likeness to God consists in the sovereign authority which has been given to him. S. Chrysostom observes strikingly that "God does not only say, Let us make man in our image, but He shows in the words which immediately follow in what sense the word image is used. He says, Let them have dominion, etc. Therefore He speaks of the image with reference to the dominion, and to nothing else."[2] But the dominion of man involves the possession of an immortal, reasonable and free soul, so that the other Fathers and theologians are also right when they name this point as the one in which man's likeness to God consists.

The dignity of man as the ruler of the visible world, placed there by God, and made in the likeness of God, is the real cause of his being created last. It may be pointed out that all through the Hexæmeron there is progress from the lower to the higher, from

---

[1] Delitzsch, *Genesis*, 2nd ed. 1, 109 (cf. above, p. 104). Delitzsch himself thinks that the plural is a pluralis communicativus.

[2] *Hom.* 8. *in Gen.*

the imperfect to the more perfect, and that, therefore, the highest and most perfect of the visible creatures would naturally close the series. It may be also pointed out that man, as the Fourth Lateran Council declares, is the link between the purely spiritual beings which were created in the beginning, and the material beings whose creation was finished on the sixth day. But the main point is that on which S. Gregory of Nyssa lays stress in the following words: "It would not have been fitting had the ruler existed before his subjects; on the contrary, the king must appear after his dominion had been prepared for him. And for this reason man was created last, not as if he were insignificant, and therefore created at the end of everything, but because he was to rule as a king over his subjects as soon as he was created."[1]

The existence of the earthly creatures for the sake of man, for his service and use, is, as I have already observed, one of the four religious truths which it is the object of the Mosaic Hexæmeron to convey to us. It is here expressed in the verses in which God names man as the ruler of the whole earth, and specially lays stress on the fact that although the vegetable world is not given to man alone, but to the animals also for food, the animals, on the other hand, are appointed for his service and use.

And here I may remove an objection which has been made against Genesis by some men of science. It is not clearly connected with the other objections which I shall discuss later all together, and as you will shortly see, it can be shown to be a pure mis-

[1] *De opif. hom.* c. 2.

understanding. The Bible teaches, it is said, that death came into the world through the sin of Adam: further, it says expressly that vegetable food was originally assigned to both man and beast. But the remains of primæval animals which we find buried in the geological strata, show that even in the primæval world animals devoured each other; for instance, the great saurians were beasts of prey, they lived principally on fish; their petrified excrements, the so-called coprolites, prove their great voracity, and contain recognisable remains of animal food. Besides this, unmistakeable marks of disease have been found on the bones of primæval animals. "Thus evident are the proofs," says Oersted, "that bodily ills, destruction, disease, and death are older than the fall." "No resistance of faith," says Karl Vogt, addressing theologians, "no pious salto mortale will avail to remove this stumbling-block which lies in your way: death has existed from the beginning."[1] W. E. Hartpole Lecky goes so far as to say that "to more scientific minds the most important effect of geology has been that it has conclusively disproved the belief that death was the result of disobedience in Paradise, and has proved countless congenial beliefs to be erroneous; that it has proved that countless ages before man trod this earth death raged and revelled among its occupants. To deny this," he says, "is now impossible; to admit it is to abandon one of the root doctrines of the past."[2] Frohschammer also lays great stress on this point.[3]

---

[1] Cf. Delitzsch, *Genesis*, p. 104.
[2] *History of the Rise and Influence of Rationalism in Europe*, vol. i. 279.
[3] *Das Christenthum*, p. 104 seq., 238 seq. (cf. *Theol. Lit.-Bl.* 1868, p. 195).

We may fearlessly admit that carnivorous animals existed before the fall, and that animals died and were killed, without thereby contradicting one single passage in the Bible, or being obliged to give up the Christian doctrine of the fall and its consequences. By the doctrine that death came into the world by the sin of Adam, Holy Scripture only means to teach us that through sin man has lost the gift of bodily immortality, which had been granted to him. The teaching of the Bible, therefore, is that man would not have died had Adam not sinned; but nowhere does it teach that immortality and exemption from suffering were originally given to the animals also. But Frohschammer's assertion, that "if the animals were subject to physical evils and death from the beginning, man who bears within him the same matter, the same chemical, physical, and organic forces and laws, cannot be exempt from this legitimate course of nature," and that, "scientifically speaking, there is hardly any alternative but to accept suffering, disease, and death for man from the beginning," is entirely arbitrary; for natural science is not in a position to prove that the body of man, which by nature was liable to disease and death, could not have been preserved from disease and death by a supernatural act of God. No doubt the sayings in Genesis, that God had made man to rule over the animals, and had given him the plants for food, and had also "given every green herb for meat" to all the animals, have been explained by many exegetes as meaning that God had originally assigned vegetable food to both man and

Similarly Pozzy, *La mort et le Péché, Revue théologique* (Montauban 1876), ii. 364.

beast. But so far is this opinion from being universal, that S. Thomas Aquinas does not hesitate to say that it is unreasonable to hold that the beasts which, are now carnivorous had originally lived on vegetable food.[1] We need not enter into the question whether God originally intended man only to eat vegetable food, although the exegete may unhesitatingly deny this also. But with regard to the animals, we may reconcile the opinion of S. Thomas Aquinas with the words, "to every beast," etc., by supposing that God gave the plants and herbs for meat to the animal world in general, but not to each kind of animal. Karl Vogt's stumbling-block does not lie in the way of the Bible, but at most in the way of those exegetes who hold the other opinion.[2] They may remove it; to us it is of no importance.

[1] q. 96, a. 1, ad 2. Cf. Pianciani, *Erläuterungen*, p. 211. *Cosmogonia*, p. 445. Kurtz, p. 404. S. Augustine speaks doubtfully on this point. *Retr.* i. 10. 2. In the *Op. imperf. c. Jul.* i. 3. c. 147, he says of *Paradise* (therefore not of the animal world before the fall in general) : Si beatitudinem loci illius Christiano cogitaretur affectu, nec bestias ibi morituras fuisse crederetis sicut nec sævituras, sed hominibus mirabili mansuetudine subditas, nec pastum de alternis mortibus quæsituras, sed communia, sicut scriptum est, cum hominibus alimenta sumtura. Aut si eas ultima senecta dissolveret, ut sola ibi natura humana vitam possideret æternam, cur non credamus, quod auferrentur de paradiso mortituræ vel inde sensu imminentis mortis exirent, ne mors cuiquam viventi in loco vitæ illius eveniret?

[2] *E.g.* Hengstenberg, *Christologie*, ii. 138 ("Where there was as yet no Cain, there was no lion"), and also apparently Delitzsch, *System der Christlichen Apologetik*, Leipzig 1869, p. 148 seq. For the right view, see Vosen, *Das Christenthum*, p. 747.

IX.

EXPLANATION OF THE SECOND CHAPTER OF GENESIS.

"So God created man in His own image . . . male and female created He them." This is all that is told us in the Hexæmeron about the manner of the creation of man. "Man" here does not mean the individual, but the genus; for after God has said, "Let us make man," He adds at once, "and let *them* have dominion." The words, "male and female created He them," signify that God created mankind in different sexes. The extraordinary theory held by certain Jewish interpreters, and also by a few ancient and modern philosophers,[1] that the first man was originally created by God androgynus, is not only unsupported, but directly contradicted by this verse. If Moses had said, "God created man in His own image . . . male and female created He *him*," this might leave room for the idea that God had created the first man as man and woman in one person; but even this mode of expression would not oblige us to assume it, for in Hebrew the singular "haadam" may have the collective meaning "men," and after such a collective noun the pronoun may be in the singular or the plural. But as Moses did not make use of the singular, which would have been

---

[1] Böhme, Oetinger, Bader, Pabst, Hamberger, Ennemoser, de Paravey (*Annales de philos. chrét.* vi. S. t. 2. 1871, p. 405).

grammatically allowable, but of the plural, as He did not say, " man and woman created He *him*," but " created He *them*,"—every meaning except the one we have stated is shut out. Delitzsch's remark, therefore, that "it seems as if the author had written 'otham,' *them*, instead of 'otho,' *him*, which last expression would have been quite allowable, in order to prevent this androgynus theory,"[1] is quite right; and I need only add that the same remark occurs in a like form in the works of S. Augustine, but this is probably unknown to Delitzsch. S. Augustine says : " In order to prevent the supposition that both sexes were united in the same individual, Moses shows that he only used the singular on account of the unity of conjunction, propter conjunctionis unitatem, because the woman was formed from the man. He therefore adds the plural directly after : He created *them*." [2]

It does not follow from the first chapter of Genesis that God only created one man and one woman ; Moses only tells us this, and also teaches us the manner in which they were created, in the second chapter. In ver. 7 it is said : " And the Lord God formed man of the dust of the ground, and breathed into his nostrils the breath of life, and man became a living soul ; " which means, stripped of anthropomorphic and pictorial expressions, that God forms the body of man from already existing matter, and makes it human by giving or providing for it a soul.[3] The

---

[1] *Genesis*, 2nd ed. p. 112. In the 3rd ed. p. 124 (4th ed. p. 103), Delitzsch himself inclines to the other view.

[2] *De Gen. ad lit.* iii. 22. 34.

[3] Cf. *Theol. Lit.-Bl.* 1869, p. 90.

anthropomorphic term "breathed into" implies that the soul is something incorporeal, and not an emanation from the Godhead. The breath of life is breathed into his nostrils, or as the Vulgate has, it into his face, because the breathing of man conveys to the perception of the senses that he is a living being.[1]

The Hebrew expression which is translated "breath of life," in the Vulgate " spiraculum vitæ," and in the Book of Wisdom in a passage referring to this verse, πνεῦμα ζωτικόν, spiritus vitalis, breathed by God into man,[2]—is used in another place in Genesis[3] for the principle of life in animals.[3] It cannot therefore be said that this expression denotes the reasonable soul of man as such. It is rather the technical name for that which constitutes men and animals living beings.[4] Moses does not assert in this passage that the principle of life in man is essentially different from that in

---

[1] "We must not suppose the formation of man from the dust of the earth, and the inbreathing of the spirit of life, to have been merely mechanical; that God first formed a human figure from the dust of the earth and then made the humanly shaped lump of earth into a human being by breathing into it the breath of life. The words must be understood *διαπριστῶς*. Man was produced from the dust of the earth by an act of divine power, and in the same moment as the dust took by this divine power a human form, he was penetrated by the divine breath of life, and created as a living being, so that it cannot be said that the body was created before the soul. The saying: 'The Lord God ... breathed into his nostrils the breath of life,' evidently refers only to the phenomena of life, the breath which is the outward sign of life. Consequently the breathing into the nostrils can only mean that God by means of His breath brought forth and united with the bodily form that principle of life which then became the origin of all human life, and which shows its existence continuously by the coming out and going in of the breath through the nostrils." See on this passage Keil.

[2] Wisd. xv. 11. [3] Gen. vii. 2.

[4] Et *animam viventem* et *spiritum vitæ* etiam in pecoribus invenimus, sicut loqui divina scriptura consuevit. Aug. *Civ. Dei*, xiii. 24.

animals, but he asserts it plainly enough elsewhere. Man is created in the image of God, and made the ruler over all other visible creatures; according to the further account given in this chapter, God gives him a command; he also names the animals, and recognises the essential difference between himself and them. All this clearly points to the fact that man is endowed with intelligence and freedom, and is therefore animated by a higher principle of life than are the animals. The account of the creation demonstrates this; the animals are created by the word of God, and several of each kind are created; while, on the contrary, God creates first only one man, and the formation of the body and the imparting of the soul are distinguished from one another as a sign that the soul of man is self-existing, and that the soul is separate from the body and can exist without it.

After the creation of the first man God says: "It is not good that the man should be alone; I will make him an helpmeet for him." God created first a human individual, a man, but the divine plan of creation was not yet fully realized, for God wished to create man in separate sexes; the actual condition, in which only one man existed, did not correspond to the divine idea, and was therefore according to the usual expression in Genesis "not good;" for before it can be said, "God saw that it was good," the divine idea must be fully realized, and therefore the man who has been first created must have in woman an adjutorium simile sibi, an adequate helpmeet, the completion which the divine idea considers necessary for him.

After his creation God brings all the animals to

Adam, and Adam names them; but there is no helpmeet found for him, as we are told in ver. 20. The naming of the animals involves a knowledge of their nature, and with this knowledge the man acquires the conviction that he is essentially different from them, and that among them there is no being like him, and consequently no helpmeet for him.

When God has in this manner made man conscious that this help is wanting to him, He completes His plan of creation by forming the body of the woman from a rib which He takes from the man in his sleep, and animates the body by breathing the soul into it, as He had before done with the man. In the woman the man recognises the suitable help for him which he lacked, and a being in all ways resembling him. This he expresses when God brings her to him in the words: "This is now bone of my bones, and flesh of my flesh; she shall be called woman, ischa, because she was taken out of man, isch."

Now follows what has been described in the first chapter of Genesis: "And God blessed them, and God said unto them, Be fruitful, and multiply and replenish the earth," etc.; that is, God has given to man the power and the function of propagating his kind, and has established the marriage state; the first and most important object of which, the generatio et educatio prolis, is implied in these words, while the description of the woman as the helpmeet for man points to the second natural object of marriage, the reciprocal help and support of husband and wife; the creation of a single pair establishes monogamy, and the indissolubility of marriage is shown by the formation of the woman from the man, and by the words: "Therefore shall a man leave his father and his mother, and shall cleave to his wife; and they shall be one flesh."

The creation of man closes the series of divine creations, and the creation as a whole is finished: "And God saw everything that He had made, and behold it was very good." "Singula tantum bona erant, simul autem omnia valde bona," or as Delitzsch, perhaps again unconsciously, repeats S. Augustine's words:[1] "Each separate thing is *good*; as a single harmonious whole, it is *very* good."

"Thus the heavens and the earth were finished, and all the host of them;" or as the Vulgate has it in a rather free but good translation, "et omnis ornatus eorum." Elsewhere we read: "Heaven, the heaven of heavens with all their host, the earth, and all things that are therein."[2] "And on the seventh day God ended His work which He had made, and He rested on the seventh day from all His work which He had made," or as we might render this passage more in accordance with modern idiom: "Since God had ended all His work on the seventh day, He rested." "And God blessed the seventh day, and sanctified it, because that in it He had rested from all His work which God created and made."

The translation "God *rested*" is not quite correct, because the actual meaning of the Hebrew word "schabath" is not to rest, but to cease, and for this reason the Vulgate translates ver. 3 "cessare." The meaning therefore is clear, God had finished His

---

[1] Aug. *Conf.* xiii. 28. Delitzsch, *Genesis*, p. 126. Cf. above, p. 92.
[2] Neh. ix. 6.

work, and created no more; He ceased to bring forth new creatures, and since then, as S. Thomas explains, He has produced nothing entirely new, nothing which did not exist in some form after the six days of creation, either materialiter, as the inorganic objects, which already then existed in substance; or causaliter, as the individual creatures which are now brought forth existed in the first individuals of their species; or lastly, secundum similitudinem, as the souls of men which at their generation are created by God, but only as individuals of a race of beings, which was created in the souls of their first parents in the Hexæmeron.[1]

The formula: " And the evening and the morning were the seventh day," is wanting here, because no new day of creation follows after the seventh day, and with the dawn of the seventh day the Hexæmeron which Moses was describing was at an end. He only adds that God blessed the seventh day, because He had rested on it from the work of the six days; that is, that God—whether immediately after the creation or later, is not said—set apart the seventh day as a day which men were to keep holy, and on which they should rest, in remembrance of the creation.

This fact is important, for it explains, as I have already mentioned, why Moses, or the divine revelation, was not satisfied with saying that God had created all things, but specially mentions that God created all things in six days. In this statement therefore is expressed the fact that the Hexæmeron is intended for religious teaching, which we have

[1] i. q. 73, a. 1. Cf. above, p. 94.

already seen is an essential characteristic of Biblical narratives.

The first portion of Genesis ends with the 3rd verse of the 2nd chapter. Our division of the chapters, which as we know is not earlier than the Middle Ages,[1] is here, as in some other cases, inappropriate. The second portion begins at ver. 4, and only part of it is within the bounds of our discussion. I have already alluded to some of it in my account of the creation of man, and made a few remarks on the relation of the second portion to the first, especially as an erroneous idea of this portion has often caused unnecessary confusion and difficulty in questions with which we are concerned.

The section begins with the heading: "These are"—or the following are—"the generations of the heavens and of the earth," etc.[2] There are many such headings in Genesis; their object is to mark the beginning of a new section, and therefore the end of the preceding one. Having described the creation of the world in the six days, Moses now proceeds to a new subject. If we examine the contents of these sections we find the following: the description of Paradise, the creation of woman, the command not to eat of one tree in the garden, the temptation of man, the fall, and the banishment of man from Paradise. If we put all these things together, we find that Moses tells us in what con-

---

[1] *Theol. Lit.-Bl.* 1867, p. 237.

[2] Many interpreters (see Dillmann, *Genesis*, p. 43. Delitzsch, *Genesis*, p. 111) wrongly hold this passage to be the end of the first portion. See, for the contrary opinion, Keil, and Kurtz, *Einheit der Genesis*, Berlin, 1846, p. lxxiii.

dition man originally found himself, and how he was transferred from this condition to another. How is this described in the heading? It runs in the translation, into the philological justification of which I cannot enter here, "These are the generations of the heavens and of the earth when they were created, in the day that the Lord God made the earth and the heavens."[1] Moses meant to say that the creation of the heaven and the earth had been described in the first section, the history of the visible creation now follows,—first of all indeed only of man; but as the centre of the visible creation, the history of man is the history of the world; and the expression history of the world is here preferred to that of history of man, in order to mark the connection with the previous section, in which the creation of the world is described.

But the account given in the first section is in two points insufficient for the object of the second section, viz. the narrative of man's primæval history; and a supplement is therefore needed. The first scene in which man moves is Paradise, and woman plays a prominent part in the first important, and very sadly important, event in the creation of the world. Now as in the first section Paradise has not been mentioned at all, and woman only indirectly, a more minute account of both must now be given. But why were not all the needful particulars about these two subjects given in the first section? Because it was inconsistent with the object of the first section, which was to announce the truth that God had created everything in six

[1] On this passage see Keil.

days; it would have disturbed the harmony of the whole.

In order to describe the origin of Paradise, Moses is obliged to recur to the creation of the plants on the third day. He does this by first describing in ver. 8 the condition of the earth on the third day before the creation of vegetation: "And every plant of the field before it was in the earth, and every herb of the field before it grew: for the Lord God had not caused it to rain upon the earth, and there was not a man to till the ground." Rain and the care of man are the conditions now wanted to ensure the growth of plants; these conditions did not then exist, therefore plants could not spring up as they do now, and there must have been some other cause for the existence of the first plants.[1]

Ver. 6 goes on: "But there went up a mist from the earth, and watered the whole face of the ground;" that is, by coming down in rain or dew. The ground was thus fitted to bring forth vegetation, and then followed the creation of the plants on the third day, as it is described in the Hexæmeron. This is not specially mentioned here, as that has been already done; only those details are supplied here which could not have been given in the first section without disturbing the narrative, but which are necessary in order to understand the second section. "And the Lord God planted a garden eastward in Eden,"—of course on the third day,—"and out of the ground made the Lord God to grow every tree that is pleasant to the sight and good for food."

[1] Similarly Vosen, *Das Christenthum*, p. 757.

Then follows the second event, which is only just mentioned in the Hexæmeron, but which it was necessary to describe here in detail, the creation of woman. Of this I have already spoken.

In ver. 19, indeed, the creation of the animals is mentioned: "And out of the ground the Lord God formed every beast of the field, and every fowl of the air, and brought them unto Adam to see what he would call them." But the Hebrew may be also translated, "The Lord God had formed," etc. It is also well known that in Hebrew sentences are often grammatically co-ordinated which logically are subordinated. Instead of the above literal translation Jerome gives the following, which is true to the meaning: "When God Almighty had formed all the animals, He brought them to the man;" or it might be even more clearly translated thus: "The Lord brought all the animals which He had created to the man." The creation of the animals is here only mentioned as a preliminary of the account here given of their being brought to the man. The second chapter therefore speaks of the creation of plants with reference to Paradise, of the creation of animals with reference to their naming by man, and also with reference to the connection of the latter incident with the creation of woman.

This, then, is the right connection between the two sections; the second is the continuation of the first, but in some ways it supplements it. No doubt this treatment of the subject-matter is peculiar, and it must seem somewhat remarkable to any one who is not acquainted with the manner in which the subject-matter is usually treated and handled in Genesis. The result, as you may have observed, is that the mode of expression and narration is occasionally strange to us, and it is sometimes obscure and difficult for the reader who is not accustomed to the style of Genesis. But let us compare with this the beginning of the next section. Chap. v. 1 seq.: "This is the book of the generations of Adam. In the day that God created man, in the likeness of God made He him; male and female created He them; and blessed them and called their name Adam in the day when they were created. And Adam lived an hundred and thirty years, and begat a son in his own likeness after his image,"—*i.e.* a man like himself,—"and called his name Seth. And the days of Adam after he had begotten Seth were eight hundred years; and he begat sons and daughters. And all the days that Adam lived were nine hundred and thirty years, and he died," etc. The creation of man in the image of God, male and female, has been described in the first and second chapters together with the divine blessing of reproduction; the birth of Seth and even that of his son Enos has been recounted in the fourth after the history of Cain and Abel; and yet this is all recapitulated again in the fifth chapter, because it is necessary to make this chapter complete, as it is to contain a genealogical and also chronological review of the time between Adam and Noah.

It would have been possible to treat the subject-matter differently; but we must take the narrative of Genesis as we find it, and there can be no doubt that Moses has expressed himself in a manner which is clear to the unprejudiced and thinking reader, whatever we may think of his style and arrangement.[1]

Not only the difficulties in the way of a reconciliation between the Bible and science, but also those of exegesis are rather increased than diminished if we consider (as some have done in spite, or because of this) that the second chapter contains a second account of the creation different from and contradicting the first; or if we suppose that an account is given of a different animal and vegetable creation. I need not criticize this theory; that which I have been explaining to you can be justified exegetically, and in our further inquiries and in comparing the narrative of Genesis with the accounts of natural science, we may leave the second section unnoticed, with the exception of one or two things which supplement the first.

Besides, most of the false interpretations of the second section are connected, as you probably know, with the series of attempts which, since the French physician Astruc first started them one hundred years ago, have been renewed with wonderful perseverance, to dissect Genesis, and to resolve it into a a series of fragments, or into several original records by different authors. It may be admitted by those who hold to the old theory of the Mosaic authorship of Genesis, which is supported by many good reasons, that the writings of many older authors have not only been used, but have also been wholly or in part incorporated in Genesis, without any, or without any material alteration. For instance, we might unhesitatingly admit

---

[1] Cf. Oehler, *Theologie des Alten Testamentes*, Tübingen 1873, i. 77. A. Kohler, *Lehrb. der Bibl. Geschichte A. T.*, Erlangen 1875, i. 23.

that at chap. ii. 4 a second writer, distinct from the author of the Hexæmeron, appears. But there are no imperative reasons for supposing this. The fact that in the Hexæmeron God is always called Elohim, but after chap. ii. 4 consistently Jehovah Elohim, is specially one which only the superficial writer would take to be a mark of double authorship. The two names Elohim and Jehovah, and other rarer names for God, may in many cases be used promiscuously; for instance, the same Hebrew writer might, for the sake of change or for other reasons use, as he liked, sometimes Jehovah and sometimes Elohim, if the two names for God came as easily to the Hebrews as, for instance, the two names Christ and the Saviour to us. But in many cases in Genesis the reason for using sometimes Elohim and sometimes Jehovah is easily seen, and a closer examination can only make us feel more reverence for the penetration and thoughtful description of the old Jewish historian. Elohim denotes a mighty, awful, supernatural Being; Jehovah, on the other hand, means God not exalted above the world, but condescending to the world, and especially to man, revealing Himself to man, and forming relations of alliance or friendship with man. It is therefore Elohim who creates the world by His word in the first chapter, but in the second chapter, when God condescends to man, places him in Paradise, gives him His commandment, and supernaturally guides and educates him, He is called Jehovah. And if the compound name Jehovah Elohim, which occurs but seldom, is used instead of the simple one Jehovah, the author of Genesis probably wishes to intimate that the Jehovah of the second section is identical with the Elohim of the first.

I have now explained the whole Biblical account of creation, with the exception of the statement that the creation took place in six days. This point is of peculiar importance, and it is especially so in the question of the relation between the Bible and natural science. I now turn to the discussion of this point, but I must ask you to remember that I am speaking for the present entirely as an exegete; that is, I do not at present intend to inquire whether the creation took place in six days or in a longer time, but only what Genesis says and what it does not say about the duration of the creative period. When we have ascertained what the Bible teaches concerning the chronology of the creation, we may proceed to inquire what natural science teaches on the same subject, and we can then find out how far the two statements agree or differ.

The subject of my next lecture then will be the question of the duration of the six days spoken of in the first chapter of Genesis. I will now only make one more preliminary remark. We shall have to decide whether the exegete may assume that the six days need not be considered as periods of twenty-four hours each, but may mean periods of uncertain and very long duration. I shall endeavour to prove that this question may be honestly answered in the affirmative, and that this last theory concerning the six days is theologically and exegetically admissible, just as admissible as the other.

You will observe that I do not merely say admissible, but just as admissible as the other theory. For, as I shall show you, it is not a fact that the first and more literal conception of the six days is the one to which theology would cling if possible, and that the other is only a concession forced from her by the attacks of natural science, and for the sake of peace, which she would gladly retract if opposing science would allow. The case is sometimes so represented by ignorant persons, but this is quite erroneous.[1] Even if there were no natural science, an exegete might believe that the six days meant a period of uncertain duration; and before there was any thought of a science of geology as it exists to-day, and without in the least anticipating any of the objections to the Hexæmeron, no less a person than S. Augustine propounded a theory concerning the six days which, as you will see when I mention it in the course of my discussion, will prove to be very different from the literal explanation.

With regard to this question of the meaning of the

---

[1] Bosizio likewise adopts this point of view, and after him B. Jungmann, *Institutiones theologicæ dogmaticæ specialis, Tractatus de Deo creatore*, Regensburg 1871, pp. 30–32. He expressly admits, in "The Hexæmeron," p. 18, "the possibility of an interpretation of the six days of creation in a sense of the word 'day' different from the usual one;" but he thinks that we should depart from the plain and apparent meaning of the sacred text (the literal interpretation of the six days) only when and in so far as the geological statements that seem to be irreconcilable with the clear literal meaning of Scripture are absolutely proved. But, so long as this is not the case, we need and should not depart from the plain sense (207; cf. 216, 255). Bosizio wrongly appeals to Aug. *de Gen. ad lit.* ii. 8, to justify his point of view, as we can easily see if we read the passage connectedly, and add to it the warning given in the same book, c. 18: Nunc autem servata semper moderatione piæ gravitatis nihil credere de re obscura temere debemus, ne forte, quod postea veritas patefecerit, quamvis libris sanctis sive Testamenti Veteris sive Novi nullo modo esse possit adversum, tamen *propter amorem nostri erroris* oderimus. (Cf. above, p. 45.) The history of the exegetical contradiction of the Copernican system should have made Bosizio careful. (*Theol. Lit.-Bl.* 1867, p. 752; 1869, p. 14.)

six days, the Catholic exegete is just as free as the non-Catholic. As you know, the Council of Trent claims for the Church the right of deciding on the true meaning and interpretation of Holy Scripture in questions of faith and morality; and it declares that, in "questions of faith and morality," the interpretation of the Bible must not go against the unanimis consensus patrum, against the doctrines shown by the Fathers unanimously to belong to Christian revelation. I need not discuss whether the explanation of the six days at all affects "questions of faith and morality;" the following quotations from S. Augustine will show that there could be no question of a unanimis consensus patrum concerning it, or of an explanation of the six days handed down from the Fathers through the traditions of the Church. "It is very difficult, arduum et difficillimum est, to understand what Moses meant by these six days."[1] "If any one wishes for any other explanation but that I have stated, let him seek it, and with God's help find it. It is not impossible that I myself may find another which agrees better with the words of Holy Scripture. For I do not confidently bring forward my present explanation, as if no other or no better one could be found."[2] And in another passage of a later work he says: "It is difficult and almost impossible for us to imagine, much more to describe, the nature of these days."[3] S. Thomas also testifies to the fact that there is no consensus patrum with reference to this point. He begins his discussion of the six days with these words: "S. Augustine

---

[1] *De Gen. ad lit.* iv. 1.   [2] *De Gen. ad lit.* iv. 23.
[3] *Civ. Dei*, xi. 6.

does not agree with other interpreters on this point." He then states both theories, and expressly observes that he does not wish to prejudice any one in favour of either, as the difference between them may be important exegetically, but not dogmatically.[1]

I may further remind you with regard to the theological admissibility of the broader view of the six days, that many Roman Catholic savants either have declared that their opinion alone is the right one, or, even while disputing it on other grounds, have allowed that it is admissible from an ecclesiastical point of view; and also that it has been stated in books printed in Rome, with every "imprimatur" required by the rules of the Church. There can be no question of more or less orthodoxy with reference to these theories, for their connection with dogma is so slight that they cannot be the objects of an ecclesiastical decision. And if it is anti-ecclesiastical to advance theories which either directly or indirectly contravene the acknowledged doctrines of the Church, on the other hand it is neither ecclesiastical nor scientific to designate questions which are quite independent of the decision of the Church as "more or less orthodox, favoured by or admitted by the Church," etc. The Church is quite neutral with regard to this question, and we may therefore freely proceed to inquire how far the different theories about the six days may be scientifically and above all exegetically justified.

[1] *Summa Theol.* i. q. 74, a. 2; cf. in 2. 1; Sent. dist. xii. q. 1, a. 2. Schanz, *der h. Thomas und das Hexæmeron, Tübingen Quartalschr.* 1878, p. 3.

X.

THE SIX DAYS.

I PROPOSE to inquire to-day what we are to understand by the six days of the Mosaic account of creation. This inquiry, however, will, as I have explained in my last lecture, be at first purely exegetical; that is, I shall for the present entirely leave aside all the teaching of natural science with reference to the duration of the period of creation, and simply ascertain what Genesis tells us about it. We may therefore put the question in this form: What period of time must the exegete assume to have elapsed during the creation of things, between the first act of creation and its termination? or, What period of time does Genesis suppose to have elapsed between the beginning of God's creative activity and the creation of the last creature, man? or, As time begins with God's first creative act, what length of time was there according to Genesis before the appearance of man on the earth?

The first explanation of the six days which we find in both ancient and modern writers, is that according to which they each signify periods of twenty-four hours. As there are innumerable instances in Holy Scripture where the word day has this meaning, from an exegetical point of view there is nothing to prevent our so understanding it in the first chapter of Genesis. There is a difficulty only in the following circumstance. No doubt God instituted the alternation of light and darkness which we call day and night on the first day; but it was on the fourth day that He placed the sun and moon in the heavens, to give light on the earth, and to rule the day and the night. Therefore the regular alternation of day and night as connected with the rising and setting of the sun began only on the fourth day, and it is only since then that days like the present can have existed. Of what kind then were the three days which preceded the fourth day on which the present relation between the sun and the earth was fixed? Two things are possible. The first three days may have resembled the present days in so far that they consisted of a single alternation of light and darkness, and lasted twenty-four hours, although the alternation of light and darkness was not the result of the rising and setting of the sun, but of some other cause. In this case we should have, as the old commentators say, three natural and three "artificial" days of twenty-four hours each.[1] But it is also possible that the first three days simply meant in a general way that each consisted of one alternation of light and darkness, and that this alternation which now lasts for twenty-fours hours, because it depends on the rising and setting of the sun, was of longer duration before the fourth day. In this case the Hexæmeron would consist of three days of twenty-four hours each, and of three of uncertain duration.

As we have already seen,[2] the first day begins with the creation of light. The period described in ver. 2,

[1] Cf. Aug. *de Gen. c. Man.* i. 14. 20. [2] P. 123.

in which the earth was without form and void, would therefore be before the first day. Genesis does not say how long a period elapsed between the beginning of God's creative activity and the beginning of the first of the six days. God may possibly have created the heaven and earth as a formless mass, thohu wabohu, and have begun at once to produce the kosmos from this chaos, so that only one moment preceded the first day. But it is also possible, as I have already shown,[1] that the beginning of God's creative activity described in ver. 1, and the dawn of the first of the six days described in ver. 3, were separated from one another by a long period of time.

We have therefore two different forms of the literal explanation of the six days. According to the first, the whole period from the beginning of the creation to the appearance of man on the earth consisted of six days of twenty-four hours each.[2] According to the other, this period consisted first of a space of time of uncertain length, preceding the first of the six days, and secondly of six days of which the last three at any rate were each twenty-four hours long.[3] Both theories are exegetically admissible; we must ascertain later whether they can be reconciled with the results of natural science.

To these theories, which are grounded on the literal

[1] P. 112.

[2] "Ver. 2 describes the condition in which the earth was directly after the creation of the universe. We must consider the days of creation as ordinary days, without supposing that there was any important difference between the three first, and the three last, which were defined by sunrise and sunset." Thus Keil, *Genesis*, pp. 16–19. Also *C. B. Geology*, etc.; Sorignet, Vieth, Bosizio, and the author of *Creation a recent Work of God*.

[3] For this theory and other similar ones, see Chalmers, Buckland, Sedgwick, Wiseman, A. Wagner, Hengstenberg, Kurtz, Vosen, Fabre d'Envieu, and others.

conception of the six days, is opposed the other, according to which the week of creation does not consist of six days of twenty-four hours each, but of a period of time of uncertain duration. Different justifications of this theory have been attempted.

1. It has been said: "The word *Jom*, which is used in the Hebrew text, denotes rather an uncertain than a certain, limited period of time.[1] The Arabs call a period of time *Jaumun*, which word is evidently related to the Hebrew *Jom*.[2] The expressions *Ereb* and *Boker* no doubt mean in Hebrew evening and morning, but *Ereb* also means confusion, disorder, and change, and *Boker* order, arrangement. And as every act of creation must have begun with a mighty upheaval of the forces of nature, and ended with the perfecting of the step in creation which was contemplated in the act, what can be more natural than the expression, confusion—order?[3] We should therefore not translate: 'And the evening and the morning were the first day,' but 'And the confusion and the order were the first period.'"

All this is as wrong as possible. It is not necessary to understand more Arabic than I do in order to know that the etymology and meaning of the Arabic word *Jaumun* is the same as that of the Hebrew word *Jom*, and that the first meaning of neither is an uncertain period. The supposition that the Hebrew word *Jom* means an uncertain rather than a limited period of time, is purely imaginary. The words *Ereb* and *Boker*

---

[1] Mutzl, *Die Urgeschichte der Erde*, p. 5.
[2] Pianciani, *Erläuterungen*, p. 18.
[3] Mutzl; cf. Pianciani, *Cosmogonia*, p. 40.

may be derived from a root which means to "confuse and to order," but this does not help us much. Etymology is an uncertain guide in Hebrew as in other languages, if we wish to find out the meaning of a word;—the lucus a non lucendo finds a counterpart in the Semitic language also; the surest way to ascertain the meaning of a Hebrew word always is to examine the custom of the language, and in Biblical language the primary meaning of the words *Ereb* and *Boker* is undoubtedly evening and morning.

We must therefore accept the following statement: *Jom* means primarily day, just as *Ereb* and *Boker* mean evening and morning. No doubt a word may have other derived meanings besides its original meaning, other secondary meanings besides its real meaning; let us see therefore whether *Jom* is used in the Bible to express other periods of time besides a day. This is clearly the case in the plural; "in the days of Noah," means "at the time when Noah lived," and we shall find scores of such instances in the Concordance. "At the end of days" ["am Ende von Tagen," A. V., "in process of time"], means in Gen. iv. 3 and elsewhere, "after a long time," and so on. But in these instances we invariably find the plural. The singular, however, occurs in a similar way. "In that day" often means with the prophets "in that time;" usually it signifies the time of the Messiah. The misfortunes which are to overtake Israel are called "the day of destruction," "the day of God's wrath," and so on. *Col. hajjom* means not only "all the day," but also "always, for ever."

B'jom, literally "in the day-time," invariably becomes a particle when followed by the genitive or infinitive, and should be translated "when, after that." For instance, the divine warning in Paradise should not be translated: "In the day that ye eat thereof ye shall surely die," but "If ye shall eat thereof," etc. Immediately after the Hexæmeron, which describes the creation of the world in six days, we find an expression which, literally translated, would run: "In the day of the creation of the heavens and the earth;" but it really means "when the heavens and the earth had been, or were, created."[1]

Jom does not then always mean literally "day" in Hebrew, it is used for an uncertain period, or for time generally. This further meaning is, however, of course, only derived and secondary; "day" is the original and real meaning. Now the rules of hermeneutik teach us that in explaining any passage we should first take the primary meanings of words, and only proceed to those which are secondary and derived if we have a valid reason for departing from the primary meaning. But in the passages just quoted there is no proof of any reason which would justify us in giving up the meaning "day" in the first chapter of Genesis. These passages show no doubt that "day," *Jom*, is used when there is no question of actual days; but as you will have observed, none of these passages are quite analogous to that which we are discussing.

2. Kurtz justifies the wider theories concerning the six days in another way in his book, *Bibel und*

[1] Gen. ii. 4.

Astronomie.[1] I have already pointed out that the Mosaic Hexæmeron is grounded on a divine revelation, and that that divine revelation was vouchsafed to the first man. In what manner did God instruct man concerning the creation? Kurtz answers: In the same way as the prophets were taught by God what would be the events and developments of the times to come. The source of all *human* history is personal observation and experience, whether that of the writer or that of others which he has obtained by tradition. The only subjects for *human* history are those which a man has himself observed and experienced. *That* history therefore which a man can write unaided can only begin with the beginning of the human race, and it must end with the time at which the historian is writing. But there is a history beyond both the boundaries of human experience; on the one side the past, on the other the future. Both these histories, that of the pre-human age and that of the future, lie outside the limits of human knowledge. Only God, who is exterior and superior to time and space, can see the past and the future; for Him there is no past and no future, but an eternal present. Man can only attain to any authentic knowledge of the pre-human time and of the future by divine revelation. How is this divine revelation conveyed to man? There is only one instance of a divine revelation of the pre-human history in the Bible, that given in the Hexæmeron; on the other hand, there are countless instances of a divine revelation of the future to the prophets. But how is the revelation of the future

[1] P. 73.

given to the prophets? The Spirit of God for whom there are no limits of time, no past and no future, but only eternal present, who therefore sees the future in time as the present, raises the spirit of the prophet momentarily and partially above the bounds of time and space, and enables him to share the divine power of beholding the future as the present. Every reader of their prophecies knows that the prophets foresaw the future by means of a supernatural spiritual vision. What is more natural than to assume that the same kind of divine revelation existed in the opposite but analogous case, when the pre-human past and not the future was the object of divine revelation, and to . suppose that God instructed man concerning the course of the creation by lifting his spirit momentarily and in part above the bounds of space and time, so that he beheld the past as the present?

This theory is confirmed, as Kurtz rightly observes, by the character of the Mosaic record of creation. We find in it a vividness of perception, a distinctness of expression, a picturesqueness of colouring which almost forces us to suppose that the writer is giving an account of what he has seen. I have repeatedly pointed out this pictorial mode of expression in my explanation of the separate details. But if we may assume that man has gained his knowledge of the course of creation from a supernatural and spiritual vision, it is easy to see the importance which must be attached to the division of the whole course of events into the work of six days. The single days are simply prophetic and historic pictures, which unroll themselves before the spiritual eye of the man to whom God vouchsafes this revelation; they are visions of the creative activity of God; each portrays one great scene in the drama of creation, one principal phase of its development. One scene after another is displayed before the eyes of the seer, till at length in the whole seven the full historical sequence of the creation lies open before him.

When the divine revelation begins, the man sees nothing, for all is wrapped in darkness. God says: "Let there be light," and there is light, and he now sees the earth covered with water, and can therefore describe its condition in the words: "And the earth was without form and void, and darkness was upon the face of the deep." Light again gives place to darkness, and the first act of the divine drama of creation of which he is a witness is at an end. Again the curtain rises, there is light, and the man sees God dividing the waters into the waters above and those below the firmament,—the second act. A third time there is light; and God causes the dry land to appear and gathers together the waters in one place; and He clothes the land with vegetation, — the third act. Thus six acts follow each other, each separated from the other by the intervening darkness. How could the narrator describe these more fitly than as days? How depict the succession of light and darkness which answers to the rising and falling of the curtain more fitly than in the words: "And the evening and the morning," etc.?

Kurtz has been blamed for making the whole matter too subjective; it is said that according to his view the days have no objective reality at all, as they only exist in the divine revelation of the course of creation vouchsafed to man, and therefore are only meant for man. This reproach seems to me undeserved; no doubt the days belong only to the form of the revelation concerning the creation, and so far are only subjective, ideal days. But if there is anything real in the course of the creation itself which corresponds to them, they are not *merely* ideal, and this Kurtz does not deny. The creation is divided into a series of six divine acts, and so far these six days are no doubt real, only there is no reality in the name day.[1]

3. I now come to that justification of the wider view of the six days which I believe to be the right one; and to my mind its fundamental thought must be included in Kurtz's theory, if the latter is to become tenable.

We must begin with this question: What interest had Moses in telling us, or better still, what was God's object in revealing to us, not only that the world was created by Him, and created well, and created for the sake of man, but also that it was created in six days? It is clear that this is not mentioned in order to give us a chronological starting-point, or an impulse and guide to geological inquiry; the direct object of the Bible, as I have repeated till I fear you must be weary of it, is, first and foremost, to impart to us religious truths; and Moses would no more have cared to mention whether the world attained its present form

---

[1] This theory of Kurtz's has been adopted in all its essential points by Hugh Miller, *Testimony*, p. 159. The latter also quotes some English savants who hold similar views. Pianciani took the theory from Miller's book, and expresses his general concurrence with it (*Cosmogonia*, p. 477). See also Godet, *Biblical Studies Old Test.* p. 80 [Eng. trans.].

in six or eight days, in one moment or several thousand years, than he would have specified the number of years each of the Pharaohs had reigned; nor would God have revealed it to us had He not given the commandment to the Jews: "Six days shalt thou labour,—but the seventh day is the Sabbath of the Lord thy God; in it thou shalt not do any work," etc. The only object of the enumeration of the days in the first chapter of Genesis, first, second, and so on up to the sixth, is to prepare the way for the statement in the first verse of the second chapter: "And on the seventh day," etc.,—there could have been no question of a seventh day had not six preceding days been mentioned,—"and God blessed the seventh day, and sanctified it." The six days of divine labour and the divine Sabbath which followed them on the one hand, and the week of six working days and the Sabbath on the other, form a parallel which is not arbitrary and casual, but willed and designed by God. The week of creation is the divine original, our week is the human copy. The chronological principle from which we must proceed is not the *day*, but the *week*. Moses only speaks of seven days of which the last is God's day of rest, because seven days of which the last is the day of rest form a week. Therefore it is the idea of a hebdomad which is important, not the idea of a day. It is of importance to religion to acknowledge that the number seven has a distinct place in the course of creation, and therefore it should not be overlooked; whether seven minutes, hours, days, years, or thousands of years are in question is quite immaterial. To say that God created the world in five or in eight days, would be to differ far more widely from the Mosaic record than to say that He had created it in six thousand years; for from a religious point of view it is comparatively immaterial whether God caused the division of the water and the land to take place, and completed the other creative and formative acts, in a moment or in a thousand years, if only it is remembered that God, and only God, can do the one and the other. But the number is not so immaterial. If God has commanded that one, not of six or eight, but of exactly seven days, shall be hallowed by man in honour of the Creator, and in gratitude for the benefit of the creation, it is clear that the time of creation must have been a hebdomad, in which the last monad corresponds to the day of rest commanded by God, while the six preceding monads correspond to the six working days.

The division of the week of creation into seven parts, then, is of importance to the divine revelation only because of the analogy intended by God between the divine week of creation and the human week. This analogy between the divine week of creation and the human week, which must be distinctly emphasized in all explanations of the six days, would no doubt be most perfect if the single parts of one hebdomad corresponded to the single parts of the other; that is to say, if each day of the week of creation consisted of twenty-four hours, as do the days of the week. But the analogy remains even although the separate parts of one hebdomad differ from those of the other, that is, although the week of creation did not consist of seven days of twenty-four hours each, but of other periods of time; the important thing, the number seven, would still exist even in this case.[1] For, of course, the seventh day of the divine week of creation is not a day in the ordinary sense of the word,—God is still said to be resting in the same sense as that in which He is described as resting on the seventh day, that is, He does not now create and work as He created and worked during the six days. Let us assume that the six days also were long periods of time, perhaps periods of unequal length; we have already ascertained that even according to the first literal theory concerning the six days, the first three need not be supposed to consist of twenty-four hours each. Supposing, therefore, that the creation, as Moses describes it, took place during six periods of time of great, perhaps of unequal length, what would Moses call these periods? He might describe them exactly or figuratively. If he wished to use a figurative expression, nothing was more natural than to call them days, considering the analogy between the divine week of creation and the human week; he could not point out this analogy more plainly and shortly than by calling the separate parts of the week of creation by the same name as those of the human week. If he did this he was expressing himself quite as plainly as was necessary; for from his description his readers would understand the relation in which the institution of the Sabbath stands to the accomplishment of the creation, and this was all that Moses wanted. He must have said *as much as this* in order to explain the institution of the Sabbath; nothing more was necessary if he had no further object, and as he

[1] H. Miller, *Testimony*, p. 154; *Footprints*, p. 296. Pianciani, *Cosmogonia*, pp. 42, 469.

had no further object, and certainly not that of conveying to us geological knowledge, he would have been exceeding his task and acting unlike himself had he said anything more, had he told us what the duration of the separate parts of the week of creation was, and, avoiding the expression day, had substituted for it 1000 or several thousand years. In other words, God has instituted the Sabbath; in order to give a reason for its institution, it was necessary for God to reveal to man that the week which ends with the Sabbath is the copy of a divine week consisting of six periods of creative activity and one period of divine rest. It was necessary for God to reveal so much; more was not required if the revelation was to retain strictly its religious character. But if no more was to be revealed, if God only wished to reveal that there were seven periods in the time of creation, without revealing anything concerning the duration of each one of those separate seven periods, He would have called them by the name which they bear in the copy, the human week, namely days.

You see that the rule of hermeneutics which lays down that a word is to be understood in its ordinary meaning unless there are reasons for supposing that it is used in a derived meaning, holds good according to this view; there *was* a reason here for the use of the word day to describe the periods of creation, namely, the connection which exists between the week of creation and the human week. We need not therefore confine ourselves to the literal meaning of the word "day," but we may assume that the name day has been transferred from the separate parts of the week to the separate parts of the prototype of the week, that is, to the periods of creation.[1]

If it be said that the word day must be taken in its literal meaning in the first chapter of Genesis, because the evenings and mornings of six days are mentioned, we may answer that if it is possible to call the whole period of creation figuratively a week, and each separate part figuratively a day, there is nothing more natural than that the beginning and ending of such a figurative day should also be figuratively called morning and evening. It is just as natural as that in the Parable of the Labourers in the Vineyard, our Lord, having described the whole time in which men were to earn for themselves the heavenly reward as one day, should proceed to describe the hour at which each man began his work as the third, sixth, ninth, and eleventh hour of the day.

A great friend has sent me the following objections: "If the orthodox commentator, by interpreting a text, which is evidently not a parable, in a manner so widely different from the literal meaning, silently admits that revelation is in general indefinite in language and ambiguous in meaning, does he not put most dangerous weapons into the hands of the enemies of his faith?"[2] I do not admit either

---

[1] "The succession of six periods of divine creative activity, with a period of rest following on them, is the basis of the later weekly rest. Man works for six days and rests on the seventh. The expression *day* which is employed by the sacred writer for each of his periods explains to us his intention of giving us the model of the week in the seven parts of the creation. He wishes to describe a *divine week*. We cannot say with certainty how long each day of this divine week was, according to our measure of time." Haneberg, *Gesch. der bibl. Offenbarung*, 2nd ed. Regensburg 1852, p. 13.

[2] Dr. Vosen in the *Programm des Katholischen Gymnasium's an Marzellen zu Köln*, 1860-61.

silently or explicitly that revelation is in general indefinite in language. Where revelation is in question the Bible speaks most precisely, and its expressions are so carefully chosen that its statements cannot be misunderstood. The only objects of revelation are religious and moral truths, and those things which are important from a religious point of view; and it only touches on other things in so far as they are necessary for the imparting of religious truths. The religious truth which is in question in the Hexæmeron is the celebration of the Sabbath in honour of the Creator, or the hallowing of the seventh day. This truth is stated in perfectly distinct and intelligible terms; every one can understand from the Mosaic narrative that the divine week of creation is the prototype of the human week, and this is all which it is necessary that every one should understand. It matters nothing whether the divine week comprises seven periods of twenty-four hours, like the human, or seven other periods; and it was not necessary that the Bible should express itself accurately on this point. No doubt when I say that what is here called a day may possibly be a period of several thousand years, I may seem to be adopting an interpretation which "differs widely from the literal meaning;" but the difference seems to be greater than it really is. I believe that the period of creation was a week, for this is essential, otherwise it would not be a prototype of the human week, but that is all which is essential; whether it was a hebdomad of days, years, longer periods, or other intervals of time, is of quite minor importance. If, therefore, as my friend observes further, "the ordinary reader actually understands the expression in the sacred text in another sense," that is, if he believes it to mean days of twenty-four hours, there is not much harm done. Indeed, I would not even call this theory incorrect. Moses means us to understand seven days,—this the "learned commentator" must believe as well as the ordinary reader, —whether these days are to be taken literally or figuratively is a question quite irrelevant to the objects of Biblical revelation. The account given in the Book of Joshua of the sun standing still is understood by the commentator, as by ordinary readers in all times, to mean that that day was prolonged by God. But up to the time of Copernicus probably no reader of the Bible knew that this was not brought about by arresting the movement of the sun, possibly many do not know it now—and this without any harm to their souls. And therefore when I hear it said that "Moses might just as easily have written periods as days, and the divine inspiration surely would have preserved him from such an unfortunate choice of words," I can only answer that it was just as easy for the author of the Book of Joshua to write the day was prolonged, as the sun stood still; and the divine inspiration did not prevent his choosing the words which he has employed. Besides, the choice of the word day for describing the separate parts which together make up the divine week of creation cannot be called unfortunate; rather the contrary, for the parallel between the divine week of creation and the human week could not have been more shortly and plainly expressed than by transferring the name of the separate parts which make up the human week to the separate parts of its prototype. As I have already mentioned, the use of the word "day" in a figurative sense is justified by this circumstance, although we certainly have no "parable" here. I certainly cannot admit that the Biblical expressions "Son of God," "everlasting fire," "heaven," etc., could be understood in the same way. Where matters of theological importance are in question, and the expression "Son of God," for instance, always comes in connection with such, the Bible should speak decidedly and unequivocally, and it does so ; nor can any sufficient reason be found in such cases for departing from the literal meaning. Here, on the contrary, we have first of all found a reason for the use of the word "day" in a figurative sense, and, secondly, we have seen that, according to the custom of Holy Scripture, the matter of theological importance, namely, that the human week is the copy of the divine week of creation, is quite clearly and distinctly expressed, while the only matter which remains uncertain is whether the days of the divine week are twenty-four hours in length, and this is theologically unimportant.

We need not therefore understand the "days" of the first chapter of Genesis to mean periods of twenty-four hours. What then are we to understand them to mean ? Most of the supporters of this theory answer that the six days mean six successive long periods in the history of creation, and that each of the periods of the earth's history which science has revealed corresponds to one day of the Mosaic Hexæmeron. Whether this correspondence is borne out, and if so, how, I cannot discuss till I come to consider the results of geological inquiry; but, as has been said, no objection can be made to this, the "Concordistic theory" as it is usually called, from a theological or exegetical point of view. If the history of the earth, as it is taught us by geology, can in reality be divided into six periods, and if these periods in their development and process of formation successively correspond to the account given by Moses of the creation and formation of the earth, they may be perfectly described as the days of the week of creation.[1]

But, besides the Concordistic theory, there is yet another, proceeding from the wider interpretation of the six days which has been shown above to be admissible. Its fundamental idea is alluded to by S. Augustine.[2] S. Thomas Aquinas mentions

---

[1] The Concordistic theory is supported by Cuvier, Marcel de Serres, Nicolas, Bishop Meignan, Hugh Miller, Pianciani, Bernuzzi, Pfaff, Delitzsch, Ebrard, Stutz, Zöckler, Godet, Dawson. Cf. Zöckler, *Gesch.* etc., ii. 497.

[2] The interpretation which S. Augustine gives of another passage in the Old Testament has had no little influence on this theory. In Sir. xviii. 1 we find, "Qui manet in æternum, creavit omnia simul," that is, "The Eternal has created all things without exception;" see above, p. 108, n. 3. But S. Augustine understood this to mean "the Eternal has created all things at once, in one moment." If this interpretation is right, and S. Augustine erroneously held that it was right, the question arose, "How could Moses have been right in saying that God created in six days?" (*de Gen. ad lit.* iv. 33). S. Thomas, following S. Greg., *M. Mor.* xxxii. 12 (i. 1055), answers that the statement, that God created everything at once, refers to the bringing forth of things according to their substance, of which Moses says, in ver. 1: "In the beginning, God created the heavens and the earth." This does not exclude the fashioning by God during the six days of the material which had been brought forth by one act of creation. But I do not find in S. Augustine's works this really very evident solution of the seeming contradiction. He therefore found himself obliged to explain the temporal succession of the separate creations which is narrated in the Hexæmeron by another interpretation of the six days. Thus he adopts the theory that it is not a question of six successive and separate days, but

it;[1] and it has been adopted by many modern men of science.[2] The supporters of this theory differ considerably from one another in details; and I should probably find something to criticize in each of the different forms which this theory assumes in the hands of different authors, were I to explain them in detail. But no objection can be made to the fundamental idea of this theory, which is called not quite correctly the "Ideal theory;" and it will be sufficient for our object if we describe it generally, and in that form which I hold to be completely admissible.

The creative activity of God is represented by Moses to be the prototype of man's work in the week days, because the Sabbath is to be represented as the earthly

---

of only one day, which, in the narrative of Moses, is six times repeated, idem dies sexies repetitus (*Civ. Dei*, xi. 30). The works of the six days are therefore not to be understood as following each other chronologically, but only as logically distinguished from one another. We are taught that God created all things, that He separated the elements and realms of nature from one another, and that He adorned them, and caused them to bring forth life; but this is only meant as a logical explanation of the creative activity, not as a chronological and historical account of it. According to S. Augustine, in the statement six times repeated, "And the evening and the morning," etc., the word "day" does not represent the time, but the apprehension of the angels; the number six, applied to the days, represents the angelic apprehension of the six logical parts of the plan of creation; and the evening and the morning are figurative representations of the two parts of this apprehension, the apprehension which comes from the contemplation of reality, and the knowledge of the idea of things; the cognitio vespertina et matutina, as the schoolmen, on the strength of this theory of S. Augustine, call these kinds of apprehension. Baltzer gives a detailed account of this theory of S. Augustine, differing from the above notice, in the *Bibl. Schöpfungsgesch.* p. 63 seq.

[1] *Summa Theol.* i. q. 74, a. 2; in 2. 1, Sent. dist. xii. q. 1, a. 2.
[2] Waterkeyn, Michelis (*Natur u. Off.* i. 100, ii. 57, iii. 299, vii. 215), Schutz (*Schöpfungsgesch.* p. 329), Baltzer (*Bibl. Schöpfungsgesch.* p. 304; cf. *Theol. Lit.-Bl.* 1867, p. 234), Zollmann (*Bibel und Natur*, p. 76), Walworth (*Brownson's Review*, 1863, p. 213); cf. Zöckler, *l.c.* ii. 538.

copy of the divine rest after the creation of things. Therefore, because of this analogy, Moses is able to describe the creative activity of God as the work of six days. But this description is not only justified if the creative activity of God is spread over six successive periods,—as is supposed in the Concordistic theory which has just been described,—but also if, contemplated as a whole, it comprises six single moments which can be logically distinguished from one another, six divine thoughts or ideas which were realized in the creation. This can be easily proved. As I have already shown, the Hexæmeron naturally falls into two parts, which are a parallel to each other. S. Thomas Aquinas calls the works of the first three days " opera distinctionis ; " of the last three days " opera ornatus ; "[1]—the first three acts of the Creator are the separation of light from darkness, of the earthly from the heavenly waters, and of the land from the sea ; the three following are the formation of the light-giving heavenly bodies, and the creation of the animals of the air, and the water, and of the land ; and as the creation of plants was added to the work of the third day, so the creation of man is added to that of the sixth. The truth which Moses must have specially wished to bring out in his description of the creative activity of God is this, that the visible creation as it exists at present is a realization of divine ideas brought about by the divine will. If, then, he wished to include the creative activity of God within the limits of a week, he might perfectly represent the realization of the single divine thoughts, or the principal moments [Haupt-momente] of the creative activity

[1] i. q. 70, a. 1. Schanz, *Tüb. Quartalschr.* 1878, p. 16.

of God as the work of six days. The succession of these single acts need not be looked upon as chronological in the sense that one moment of creative activity was completely closed, and one period was thus ended, before the realization of a new moment, and with it a new period, had begun. It would be quite possible to suppose that historically or chronologically the realization of the separate moments took place simultaneously; for instance, the separation of the waters and land might have actually extended over the time of the creation of the first plants and the first animals, and the creation of vegetation over the creation of the first animals. That, in Moses' description, each separate work is represented as being complete in itself, is explained by the fact that each forms a particular moment in the creative activity of God; and the succession in which these separate works are described to us is explained partly by the logical order into which they are brought, and partly by the dependence of each work in turn on those which preceded and conditioned it. It cannot be said that there is anything prejudicial to the historic character of the Mosaic record in this interpretation of the Hexæmeron, although it does, no doubt, put the historical character in the background. If, of two historians, one should describe the life of Charlemagne in strict chronological order, so that family and state affairs, battles, and the founding of churches should follow one another in confused variety; while the other should arrange the events which show forth the work of the great emperor under certain principal heads, and should therefore describe him successively in his private life as a conqueror, a lawgiver, a protector of the Church, and so on, we should not deny historical accuracy to the latter description because the chronological point of view is made subservient to the logical or ideal.[1] As I have said, I do not hesitate to say that this theory of the Hexæmeron also is theologically admissible. There is no more justification here for the objection that the formula "the evening and the morning," etc., does not allow of such an interpretation of the days, than there was in the theory we examined before this one; if the single acts of creation were to be described as days, to speak of morning and evening was only a continuation of the image which had been chosen.[2]

I have now shown that four theories concerning the six days are exegetically admissible; according to two the days are understood literally, and according to the two others figuratively. To recapitulate once more, they are as follows:—

(1.) The whole period treated of in the first chapter of Genesis comprises only six periods of twenty-four hours.

(2.) The six days, at least the last three at any rate, are periods of twenty-four hours each, but an indefinite period preceded the six days, which lies between the first day of creation and the beginning of the first of the six days. To this is attached the "Theory of Restitution."

---

[1] Michelis, *Natur und Offenbarung*, i. 102.

[2] Aug. *de Gen. c. Man.* i. 14. 20: Restat ergo, ut intelligamus, ipsas distinctiones operum sic appellatas, *vesperam* propter transactionem consummati operis et *mane* propter inchoationem futuri operis, de similitudine scilicet humanorum operum, quia plerumque a mane incipiunt et ad vesperam desinunt. Habent enim consuetudinem divinæ scripturæ de rebus humanis ad divinas res verba transferre.

(3.) The six days are six successive periods of indefinite length; this is the "Concordistic theory."

(4.) Taken as a whole, the six days correspond to the whole series of periods which elapsed between the first beginning of things and the creation of man; but they do not mean six successive periods, but only six sides or phases of the creative activity of God; six principal heads under which the creating and forming acts of God can be brought. This is the "Ideal theory."

We shall see later which of these theories can be brought into harmony with the results of natural science, and which agrees with them best; my object to-day was only to point out those explanations of the six days which are *theologically* admissible.[1]

[1] An interpretation of the six days, given according to Pianciani, *Erläuterungen*, p. 28 (*Cosmogonia*, pp. 35, 36), by the Barnabite, Hermenegild Pini, is quite inadmissible. According to this, the six days are to be considered as the principal periods in the world's development; they need not have followed directly on one another, but may have been separated by long spaces of time; on six days the Creator interfered immediately in the development of the earth, between these days the development took its usual course; Moses mentioned the six days of divine creative activity in his narrative, but he passed over the periods of development in silence, because the former were of importance for the history of the redemption, but the latter only for the history of nature. According to this theory, the connection between the human Sabbath and the divine week of creation is put far too much in the background. And the statement, "The evening and the morning," etc., only retains its correct meaning if it is understood that the morning is the morning of the next day. The phrase, "and the morning," etc., carries one on to the next day, as I have shown above, p. 124, and Moses would have had to express himself quite differently, if he had not meant to imply that six directly consecutive days found their close in the divine Sabbath.

XI.

ASTRONOMY AND THE BIBLE.

THE discussion on the six days brings me to the end of the first half of my task, which is to lay down what the Bible teaches us concerning the origin of the visible creation; and it only remains for me now to compare the statements in the Bible with the results of scientific inquiry. It is, of course, neither necessary nor possible for me to collect all the scientific statements concerning the primæval world as thoroughly as I have collected and discussed the statements in the Bible. As I announced in the beginning, my lectures are only intended to prove that the Bible teaches about the primæval world nothing which has been shown to be incorrect by natural science. I need therefore only discuss those results of natural science which have been said to contradict the statements of the Bible. Any one defending the harmony between the Bible and science may adopt one of two ways of meeting such an assertion; he must either prove that what is supposed to be an assured result of scientific inquiry, and as such is opposed to the statements in the Bible, is not an assured result, but an error on the part of the man of science, and he must prove this, of course, on scientific and not on theological grounds;[1] or he must prove

---

[1] "I observe that there are two ways of solving these and similar difficulties. The first is to deny the assumptions of geologists, and to reject them as being false, or at least not very credible. Not a few

that the asserted contradiction between the Bible and the results of scientific inquiry rests on an erroneous interpretation of the words of the Bible; that is, he first assumes that the results of scientific inquiry are true, and then shows either that the Bible asserts the same truth, or that there is nothing in its language to deny such a truth, or lastly, that it does not mention the matter in question at all, and so leaves it entirely to natural science.

You will agree with me in thinking that it would be presumptuous in me to adopt the first of these two ways, that is, to combat the statements which are regarded as assured by men of science, on scientific grounds. I could only dispute the asserted results of scientific inquiry, if men of science themselves put the weapons into my hands, that is, when two scientific opinions are opposed to each other. So long as men of science themselves—I am speaking, of course, of those who are recognised as the leaders—differ widely on any point, there can be no question of any definite scientific result, and we cannot therefore, of course, institute any comparison with the Bible. But in those cases where competent men of science are at one, I shall take care not to throw doubt on facts which they have recognised, and I shall then prove that the words of the Bible are in perfect harmony with these facts, and that the apparent contradiction is caused by an erroneous interpretation of the words of the Bible.

have adopted this way (in recent times Bosizio), but as I think with an unhappy result. It encounters most serious difficulties, which do not rest on suppositions or systems, but on many and carefully examined facts. The wiser and more learned among the theologians and apologists now adopt another course," etc. Pianciani, *Erläuterungen*, etc., p. 7.

Having spoken of the general account in Genesis, it will be best to class the objections which have been raised against it according to the separate sciences on which they are based. I shall therefore discuss the astronomical objections to the Biblical narrative in to-day's lecture, next the geological objections, and so on. But before I proceed to this, you will allow me to make one more observation on a point which can be best decided in discussing the chronology of the first chapter of Genesis.

I have shown that the literal conception of the six days is not the only one which can be justified exegetically, but that, on the contrary, it is allowable to assume that the length of time which elapsed before the creation of man is undefined in Genesis. But the theologian who believes this to be so must not begin to hesitate when scientific men endeavour to estimate the number of years which forms the periods of the development of the earth or of the kosmos. It is well known that astronomers, and still more geologists, are very ready with large figures on this subject; they speak of millions of years or centuries so coolly, that a historian, who is accustomed to be careful even about decades, is inclined to regard such extravagant liberality with some horror. I maintain that a theologian is always wrong if he disagrees with astronomers or geologists about such figures; for *he* only knows that the six days need not necessarily denote periods of twenty-four hours. He has therefore no right to go beyond this purely negative statement; as soon as he asserts that perhaps some thousands of years might be meant, but surely not millions, he shows that he does not know where the boundary lies between theology and natural science. Theology, as I have said, only teaches that the creation of man may have been preceded by a period of more than six times twenty-four hours. Theology has no means of calculating this time exactly; and if astronomers and geologists think that they do possess such means, the theologian has not the slightest right to meddle with their calculations. If, besides being a theologian, he is also versed in natural science, he may then make calculations, and criticize and refute the calculations of others, but in such a case he must never confound his scientific beliefs and opinions with the theological statements which he has to represent. In discussing the pre-human period, therefore, I shall not dispute or cast doubt on geological and astronomical figures. Although personally I may be far from convinced of their correctness, as a theologian I can simply put aside all question of this in discussing the Hexæmeron, and say that the six days of Genesis denote no particular period of time, and may therefore comprise as many millions of years as astronomy and geology can prove to have elapsed.

I now come to the objections which have been made to the Mosaic Hexæmeron from an astronomical point of view. D. Fr. Strauss has thus enumerated them in his so-called *Glaubenslehre:* "Modern astronomy thought it wrong that the earth, the planet, should not only have been created before its central body, the sun, but also that, besides the alternation of day and night, the separation of the elements and the bringing forth of vegetation should have taken place on the earth without the sun; that five whole days should have been spent in the creation and development of the earth, while one single day was sufficient for the creation of the sun, besides all the fixed stars, planets, and moon; and that the heavenly bodies, which have been shown by modern discovery to be spheres in many instances far surpassing the earth in magnitude, should be here represented—according to the belief of the old world, and of ignorant men now-a-days—only as accessories to serve as lights and signs of the seasons to the earth."[1]

Let us consider the last part first. It is doubtless true that Genesis represents the earth as the most important part of creation,—as Strauss says, in accordance with the belief of ignorant men at present,—and that it speaks of the millions of other heavenly bodies only as accessories to the earth, as lights and signs of time, even that it mentions only the sun and moon, and includes the mass of much larger and more brilliant stars in the word "the stars." This is all true,—I have so little hesitation in admitting it, that I go further, and announce it as my firm conviction that if Moses had known as much astronomy as the most learned astronomer of our century,—which I do not think probable,—he would still have expressed himself exactly as he does here.

For astronomers, of course, the earth is simply one of the planets which revolve round the sun, and not even the largest; the sun itself is only one of many

---

[1] Strauss simply repeats these statements in *Der alte und der neue Glaube*, p. 17, with only a slight difference in the wording. I have therefore let the quotation from the *Glaubenslehre* stand.

equally splendid, or more splendid fixed stars, and possibly the suns revolve round one central sun, as our planets revolve round our sun.[1] But Moses neither wished nor was intended to teach us astronomy, and he therefore does not adopt the scientific point of view of astronomers. He wishes to impart religious instruction, both to his contemporaries and to posterity. He therefore only mentions what is of religious importance, and he clothes this in a form which can be universally understood, not therefore in the language of science, but in that of the common man.

The first thing he has to say about the stars is, that they, as well as all visible things, have been created by God. The general words, "In the beginning, God created the heavens and the earth," suffice to express this. After this, Moses' object was to write, at most, a geogony, not a cosmogony; or, rather, having announced the truth that God had created all visible things, he wishes to announce the further truth that God prepared a dwelling-place for man, the last and highest of visible creatures, beforehand; and that everything which man sees around him was created and formed by God for man. But in a geogony such as Moses wished to write, the stars need only be mentioned and noticed in so far as they stand in relation to the earth. Astronomically, no doubt, the earth is not to be looked upon as the central or chief point of the universe, but it is so for Moses, for the earth is the scene of all the series of events which he intends to narrate in his book, the scene of the whole history to which his account of creation is only the introduc-

[1] Pfaff, *Schöpfungsgeschichte*, p. 182.

tion. In Genesis, Moses is not at all concerned with the relation in which the earth stands to the other bodies in the sidereal world; for him, the earth itself possesses interest only as the dwelling-place of man, because his theme is the description of the gesta Dei inter homines, and not the "physical description of the world."[1] Moses therefore necessarily looks at things not from the astronomical, but from the earthly, or rather the human point of view. Astronomy may investigate what the stars are in themselves, what they are with regard to one another, what they are with regard to the heavens; the only question which can concern the Bible is the relation which they bear to man; and in answer to this question, it is enough to say that the stars are, to use Strauss' own words, " to serve as lights and signs of the seasons to the earth," not, as he says in another place,[2] "only kindled lights."[3]

And, further, from this point of view it is just as right as from an astronomical point of view it is wrong, that the sun should be described as the largest, and the moon as the next largest heavenly light; and that, besides these two great lights, the millions of other stars should only be accidentally mentioned. For man—I do not mean for the inquiring man of science, but for man, the

[1] Humboldt.
[2] *Der alte und der neue Glaube*, p. 17.
[1] "For religious contemplation, which alone is here in question, it is enough to know, with reference to the origin and nature of these heavenly bodies, that they are miracles of the almighty creative power of God; for the rest, we may consider them as they appear to us, and as they affect us. According to God's ordinance, they serve us in the manifold ways mentioned in the narrative; and by this service they teach us to believe in the wonderful harmony of the universe, and in the might and wisdom of the Creator." Dillmann, *Genesis*, p. 30.

servant of God, as he is looked upon in the Bible—they are of far less importance than the sun and moon;[1] from his point of view, they exist only in order to illumine the dark nights with their sparkling light, to delight man with their nocturnal shining, to guide wanderers and sailors, to be objects for the intelligence of astronomers, and last, though not least, in order that man, when he contemplates them,—whether simply gazing at the nocturnal starry splendour of the skies, or wandering in spirit hand and hand with science through the vast spaces of the heavens, and measuring the paths of the stars,—should, through the contemplation of their wonders, acknowledge and adore the greatness and wisdom of the Master who has created and who sustains them all.

Palestine occupies a very humble position amongst the countries in the physical description of the earth, and Bethlehem occupies a still humbler one among the towns; but in the history of religion, Palestine is more important than America, and Bethlehem than London. Whatever places may be assigned to the earth, sun, moon, and other stars, in a system of astronomy, no other could have been given to them in the first chapter of the Bible than was given by Moses.

The second objection brought forward by Strauss is connected with this first point; he thinks it is wrong to suppose that "five whole days should have been spent on the creation and development of the earth,

---

[1] As S. Chrysostom says, "The sun and moon are called the two great lights, not with reference to their size, but with reference to their efficacy and power; for although other stars may be larger than the moon, yet the moon produces more effect on the earth, and to our senses she appears to be larger." S. Thomas Aquinas, i. q. 70, a. 1, ad 5.

while one single day was sufficient for the creation of the sun besides all the fixed stars, planets, and moons." To this it may be answered that the account of the fourth day of the Hexæmeron need not be supposed to refer to the *creation* of the sun and the stars, and we need not therefore assume that the stars were only created or formed on the fourth day. The Hexæmeron, as a geogony and not a cosmogony, is no way concerned with the creation of the stars; it simply describes the creation of the earth, and therefore in the account of the fourth day it is not said when and how the stars were created, but only that on this day they were brought into their present relation to the earth, or rather that the earth was brought into its present relation to them. Genesis does not say that the stars first began to exist on the fourth day,—it does not say when they began to exist at all,—but only that they began to exist *for the earth* on the fourth day, and that on this day began the relation between the earth and the stars, in consequence of which the stars are lights and signs for the earth. If a gradual and slow formation of the stars took place, it may have been already accomplished before the creation of the earth, or it may have taken place simultaneously with the development of the earth during the first three days; Moses had no need to speak of it, the stars could only be mentioned in his geogony when their relation to the earth was regulated and fixed, or when the development of the earth had progressed so far that it was incorporated as a single member of the stellar system.[1]

[1] " In the description of the work of the fourth day, the sun and moon and also the stars are spoken of only in their relation to *the earth*, and are

But here another chronological difficulty seems to arise. Supposing that, according to the most recent calculations, light travels about 42,000 geographical miles a second, astronomers tell us that the nearest fixed star would have been visible on the earth only after three and a half years, the polar star after thirty, and stars of the twelfth magnitude only after 4000 years, and that therefore the stars of the milky way and of the nebulæ must have been created many myriad and even million years before their light could

in nowise considered as they are in themselves. It is therefore a non sequitur to insist that the sun and moon as well as all the fixed stars were really *created*, that is, called into being from nothing, only on the fourth day, after the earth had been fully formed as a heavenly body. The record does not tell us what these heavenly bodies are *in themselves*, neither does it say *when* and *how* they were created to be what they are *in themselves*. No doubt the work of the fourth day is introduced like all the others by the creative 'and God said, Let there be,' but we are in addition told what is the purpose of the stars that shine on the earth, viz. to give light. All that the words of the record require is that they should not have fulfilled *that* purpose before, but only *then* for the first time ; for this relation of the stars to the earth, which only then began, which was only then regulated and fixed, is just as much an act and a result of creative activity as the regulation of the relation between light and darkness, between land and sea. Thus it is said quite rightly, 'God set them in the firmament (Rakiah) of the heaven ;' for as Rakiah means the heaven over the earth, which was only created on the second day, the stars, even if they existed before the second day, could not be considered as standing in the Rakiah, but could only take their place in this sky when they began to have some relation to the earth. The explanation of 'God *made*' the sun, moon, and stars in ver. 16 is just as easy and unstrained, for He *then* first fitted them *for the earth*, and they then first began to exist for the earth. But this does not in any way exclude the supposition that, as they are *in themselves*, they were created much earlier. It therefore remains uncertain whether the sun, moon, and stars were first created after the earth, or whether they existed in a completely formed condition before the creation of the earth, but were then first connected with the earth ; or lastly, whether they were formed coincidently with the earth, and in stages so similar that on the fourth day for the first time both they and the earth were in a condition to assume and thenceforth to preserve the ordained relations to each other." Kurtz, *Bibel und Astronomie*, p. 101 ; similarly Vosen, *Das Christenthum*, p. 749.

have reached the earth. And yet not only are they visible to us, but so far as human memory reaches they always have been visible.[1]

Kurtz objects that it is by no means certain that the ray of light, whose velocity is no doubt in the ether of our planetary system limited to 42,000 miles in a whole second, is confined to this snail's pace everywhere in space; but this carries no weight. We must admit the assertions of astronomers that there are stars whose light, according to the laws of nature, would take thousands of years to reach us. But this only throws difficulties in the way of those theologians who hold the literal theory of the six days, and they could always say with an English man of science:[2] "The distinct light of the sun, and each of the fixed stars, was cast to its utmost limit the very instant they were called into existence. . . . Light moves progressively from those luminous bodies to which it is attached, but it moves and radiates only in the track which the first rays which emanated from the hand of the Creator had marked out to those that were to follow." In other words, God may have created the stars in such a manner that even the farthest were at once connected with the earth through their rays of

---

[1] Pfaff, *Schöpfungsgeschichte*, p. 146. Kurtz, p. 307. Cf. Mädler, p. 653: "W. Herschel estimated the time which light would take to travel from the farthest nebula which was just visible through his telescope at two millions of years. His contemporaries thought the computation too bold, but it is not difficult to show that it is considerably under the reality." Mädler's calculations showed that light would take eighty millions of years to travel from the nebulæ to the earth, the minimum would be thirty-two millions; the first computation would make the distance, expressed in miles, reach a number of twenty-one figures.

[2] *C. B. Geology*, etc., p. iii.; cf. Wagner, *Gesch. der Urwelt*, i. § 12.

light, while for the later diffusion of light those laws were given which astronomy has discovered by observation.

However, as I have said, it is only those theologians who hold the literal theory of the six days who are obliged to take refuge in this somewhat hazardous assumption.[1] According to the more liberal theory of the six days, there is time enough for the rays of light from the farthest stars to reach the earth before the creation of man, whatever astronomers may decide as to the measure of the velocity of light and the mode of its diffusion.

Even if the scientific hypothesis be correct, according to which the stars were formed by the gradual cooling and thickening of a gaseous matter, a cosmic vapour,[2] —as we know, it is often supposed that such star matter still exists in space in the shape of the so-called nebulæ,[3]—and if the stars have really undergone a process of formation lasting many thousand years, yet this would not afford any difficulty to the exegete, provided he does not hold the literal theory of the six days.

---

[1] Pianciani, *Cosmogonia*, p. 119, quotes with reference to this assumption the following passage from Suarez (*de op. sex*, d. 1. 2, c. 7): Opera miraculosa vel extraordinaria absque necessitate vel sufficienti testimonio audienda non sunt.

[2] C. Pfaff, *Die neuesten Forschungen*, p. 17. For some objections to this hypothesis, see Ulrici, *Gott und die Natur*, p. 344.

[3] After Lord Rosse and others had succeeded in ascertaining by means of powerful telescopes that many of the so-called nebulæ are masses of stars crowded together, Humboldt (*Kosmos*, iii. 48) and Mädler (*Ges. Naturw*. iii. 649, 652) thought it probable that *all* the nebulæ were in reality groups of stars. But according to more recent investigations by means of the spectrum analysis, it appears that many nebulæ really consist of coherent gaseous matter, which is not yet divided into separate masses. Pfaff, *Schöpfungsgeschichte*, 2nd ed. pp. 185, 188. Le Soleil in *Etudes religieuses*, N. S. t. 13 (1867), 404.

But—and here we come to the most dangerous astronomical objection, and one on which Strauss has not laid sufficient stress in the passage we have quoted—is it not absurd that Moses should have described the sun and moon as being created, or rather as giving light on the earth, on the fourth day only, while the light, which, as every child knows, is caused by the sun, is supposed to have existed on the first day?

Now, first of all, the difficulty here is not that Moses appears to be ignorant of what every child knows, but that he certainly does know it,—he says in ver. 17 as plainly as possible that the sun and moon were intended by God to give light and to shine upon the earth,—and that in spite of knowing this he still says that it was light before the sun existed.[1] By this Moses teaches—if we suppose that the six days mean six successive periods, whether of twenty-four hours or of uncertain duration—that, since the fourth day, the light on the earth has been connected with the heavenly bodies; but that there was light upon the earth before the time when the earth was thus connected with the heavenly bodies, for the words: "God said, Let there be light; and there was light," only signify that it became light in consequence of God's command.

Is it then possible that the light, which, as Moses says himself in ver. 17, is now as it were bound to the sun, can have existed formerly on the earth independently of the sun? I answer with the counter question, What is light? Science has not yet answered this question; this universally known phenomenon is

[1] Kurtz, p. 302.

rather the one of whose cause and nature she is most ignorant.[1] Formerly, as we know, light was supposed to be a fine matter proceeding from a shining body. Instead of this view, the so-called theory of emanation, the theory of vibration or undulation, was adopted later, according to which light proceeds from very slight vibrations of the smallest portions of the shining bodies; these vibrations or oscillations are transmitted, as is sound through the air, through an extremely fine matter which exists everywhere, and which is called ether. Further, modern inquirers lean to the opinion that light, and the other so-called imponderables, warmth, magnetism, electricity, are related to one another, and intimately connected.[2]

However this may be, Genesis does not interfere with these theories. It only says that there was light at God's command. It does not say *how* God caused this light, and although the earth is now regularly illumined by the sun, yet natural science, whose source must necessarily and exclusively be the observation of present phenomena, will never be able to prove that before the present relation between the sun and the earth was fixed, that is, before the fourth day of the Hexæmeron, God could not have produced light by other means.[3]

---

[1] Ulrici, *Gott und die Natur*, p. 92. Eisenlohr simply observes: "Light is the cause of brightness," which only tells us what is the effect of light, but not what light itself is. He adds: "We know nothing certain about its real nature, although we already know many of its qualities. For this reason all attempts to explain the phenomena of light are founded on hypotheses." Cf. Pfaff, *Schöpfungsgeschichte*, 2d ed. p. 746.

[2] Ulrici, pp. 110, 123, 137.

[3] Delitzsch says, see *Genesis*, 3rd ed. p. 97 (cf. 4th ed. p. 81): "It is

Strauss objects that, according to Genesis, the alternation of day and night took place before the creation of the sun, or, more correctly, before the present relation of the earth to the sun was established; but this rests on a pure misconception. God created the sun and moon on the fourth day only, to rule the day and the night, and to be signs of the days and years; that is, translated into our plainer language, on the fourth day began the regular apparent rising and setting of the sun, or the regular rotation of the earth round its own axis and round the sun, by which the days and years are measured. Genesis does not know of this before the fourth day. The first three days of creation are either to be understood figuratively with the three others as long periods of time, or at least all that they have in common with our days is, that they are caused by one alternation of light and darkness. And when we find in the account of the first day, in vers. 4, 5, the words: "And God divided the light from the dark-

---

hardly necessary to remind those who take offence at the existence of light before the creation of the sun, the source of light, that the sunlight does not come from the sun itself, but from a shell which surrounds the body of the sun, and that from the occasional tearing of this shell we sometimes obtain a glimpse of the darkness underneath." Cf. Mädler in the *Ges. Naturw.* iii. 563 : "A shining gaseous envelope is spread round the sun, which is itself a dark body, and this has been called the photosphere (the surrounding light), in contradistinction to our atmosphere." This seemed to be a fact which would justify the expressions of the French savants detailed on p. 2. The theory (which I have adopted in the two previous editions) that the sun's body is dark in itself, and that a photosphere surrounding it is the source of light on the earth, is now contested on the ground of the investigations conducted by means of the spectrum analysis ; and it is supposed that the sun consists of a solid or fluid nucleus, which is in a state of white heat, and of a gaseous and glowing envelope, the photosphere, which has a rather lower temperature than the nucleus. See Secchi, p. 396. Pfaff, *Schöpfungsgeschichte*, 2d ed. pp. 122-127. Cornelius, *Entstehung der Welt*, p. 23.

ness; and God called the light day, and the darkness called He night," they only mean, as I have shown in the exegetical discussions on these verses, that after God had created light He established the relation of light and darkness; and this relation established by God is the regular sequence and alternation of light and darkness, which we call day and night. Again, Genesis does not say that this alternation of day and night immediately took place regularly once every twenty-four hours; it rather seems to wish to point out that this only began with the fourth so-called day of creation.

The difficulty that the plants were brought forth on the third day, that is, before the sun gave light and warmth on the earth, is not insuperable. No doubt the light and warmth of the *sun* are *now* necessary in order that the plants should flourish. But if before the fourth day light and warmth were not, for the earth, connected with the sun in the same way as at present, vegetation was not dependent on the sun in the same way as at present.[1] Further, the establishment of the sun's relation to the earth follows, in the Hexæmeron, immediately on the bringing forth of the plants, so that we need only assume that their first origin took place without the light and warmth of the sun, and not that they existed a long time without them.

In this way the supporters of the literal and concordistic theories of the six days may combine the results of astronomical inquiry with the Biblical narrative. I must postpone a further explanation to another lecture. But I may just point out here that the objec-

[1] Pfaff, *Schöpfungsgeschichte*, 2d ed. p. 747.

tion which is based on the separation of light from the sun in the Mosaic record entirely falls to the ground if, according to the theory discussed fourthly in my last lecture, the six days are considered not as six successive chronological periods, but as six chief moments of the creative activity of God. In this case the establishment of the regular alternation of day and night—according to the Biblical expression, the separation of light from darkness—would be represented as one moment of the divine creative activity, the establishment of the earth's present relation to the sun and the other heavenly bodies as a second; and no one would be justified in concluding from the fact that these two moments are distinguished, and that the one is represented as the first and the other as the fourth among the six, that these two divine works took place chronologically one after the other, and were separated from each other by several other intermediate divine works. On the contrary, it is according to this theory possible that events which Genesis logically distinguishes were chronologically simultaneous; therefore the fact that the alternation of day and night and other phenomena are placed by Genesis in the first half of its narrative, and the connection of the earth with the sun and star system on which those phenomena depend is placed in the second half, need not hinder astronomers and geologists from investigating these things by their own methods, for the account in Genesis is unchronological.

The explanations I have given to-day will, I think, warrant my drawing the following conclusion. There can only, at any rate, be a question of an irreconcilable contradiction between the assured results of astronomical inquiry and the statements in the Mosaic record, if we hold fast to the literal interpretation of the six days. But I have already proved that this interpretation is not the only one which can be justified exegetically; and my next lectures will show that it cannot be brought into harmony with other results of scientific inquiry. No doubt, even if we adopt the other explanations of the Hexæmeron, it cannot be proved that they agree with the results of astronomical inquiry, in the sense that the Bible teaches the same as does astronomy. But there could be no greater mistake than to require such a thing of the Bible. Here, as elsewhere, its task is to teach only that which is of importance to its religious object. By restricting itself to this, it does not forbid man to find out by his own investigations more about the creation than the Bible tells him; and the theologian should recognise with thankful admiration all that astronomy has discovered with respect to the extent of the star system in space and in time, and not criticize these discoveries in a narrow-minded spirit.

Hundreds of years ago, God may have caused the splendid primæval forests to grow, which in our day have been seen with reverential surprise for the first time by the eye of the bold traveller, or the scientific man thirsting for knowledge; what then if it were true, as astronomers say, that many thousand years ago God sent forth the rays from the farthest stars,—those rays which now meet our eye when we look up to heaven, indifferently, inquiringly, or devoutly. "I have loved thee with an everlasting love," saith the Lord.[1]

[1] Jer. xxxi. 3.

XII.

GEOLOGY. NEPTUNISM AND PLUTONISM.

GEOLOGY is the science which investigates the inner structure of the earth. It endeavours to discover the phenomena which occur in consequence of this structure; and from these it deduces the laws according to which these phenomena themselves must occur, either in historical sequence, or in their connection with one another. The groundwork of this science is the investigation of the earth's structure as it at present exists; as it were, the anatomy of the earth, or, rather, of the crust of the earth which is alone accessible to us. Having ascertained these facts, it then endeavours to derive from them a knowledge of the entire earth; to draw conclusions about the condition of its interior, and about its earlier stages up to the time of its first existence. The purely empirical part of the science, which is concerned with the composition and the present condition of the earth, is also called *geognosy;* and by *geology* or *geogony* is thus meant the inferential part of the science which is concerned with the origin and development of our planet. But, practically, these two branches of the science can hardly be distinguished from one another; and accordingly they are now-a-days usually united in the term geology. Mineralogy is distinguished from geology in so far as it is concerned with the knowledge and classification of the separate minerals of which a great part of the earth's crust is composed. Another branch of geology is palæontology, the science which deals with fossils and petrifactions, the knowledge of the organic bodies of the animals and plants which are found in a more or less altered condition embedded in the crust of the earth. This will be specially discussed later.

At present we are concerned with that part of geology which deals with the ancient conditions and earlier developments and changes of the earth. Experience teaches us that the surface and crust of the earth are still subject to important changes, and the nature of the crust obliges us to assume that similar changes must have taken place in former years. The inquiry into the present condition of the earth's crust, into the forces which produce the changes in it, and the laws under which those changes occur, afford us therefore a means of ascertaining what earlier changes have taken place. The history of the earth in this sense is, it may be said, engraven in the earth's crust, and geology deciphers the chronicle.[1] No doubt, as I have already observed, the chronicle to be deciphered is not yet completely before us, because our knowledge of geognostical facts is still incomplete,[2] and we cannot hope ever to know this chronicle thoroughly. And what we do possess of this chronicle resembles in one respect the cuneiform letters of Assyria and Babylon; savants must first find the key to the discovery, must discover the meaning of separate signs, and of the words which they

---

[1] Vogt, *Grundriss der Geologie*, § 2.
[2] The geological record is a history of the earth, imperfectly preserved,

compose, before we can read and understand the writing. But it is an uncontested fact that, up to this time, the chronicle has been read and interpreted by experts in very different and sometimes contradictory ways; and from this laymen may conclude that geologists have not got very much farther in their attempts at deciphering it than have Rawlinson, Offert, and Schrader in theirs. This is the less surprising, because geology is still a comparatively recent science, as it has only been pursued according to a strictly scientific method for about half a century.

In comparing the results of geological inquiry with the Bible, we must therefore distinguish between facts which are ascertained by observation, hypotheses founded on incontestable conclusions, and suppositions which are simply probable or possible; between statements which are recognised as true by all competent authorities, and those which are asserted by some and disputed by others.

All modern geologists, who deserve the name, acknowledge that all hypotheses about the former history of the earth must be based upon its present condition, upon the forces now at work and the laws which now exist; and that all those hypotheses must be rejected which begin by assuming that formerly different laws of nature were in force. The only question on which they do not agree is this: Have the causes which are now at work always existed in

and written in an everchanging dialect. Of this we possess only the last part, which describes but two or three countries. A few chapters only of this part have been preserved, and of each page, only a few lines. Cf. Lyell. Also *Jahrbuch für Deut. Theol.*, 1861, p. 696. Darwin, *Origin of Species*, p. 317.

a like measure, with equal force, and to the same extent as they do now?—this view is supported especially by the English geologist Sir Charles Lyell;— or, as others say, may we assume that such causes have worked differently at different times, and in ancient times much more powerfully than at present? According to the first theory, the course of the earth's history would have been comparatively quiet; according to the second, its development would have often been interrupted in ancient times by great catastrophes, revolutions, and convulsions.[1] The effects which those who hold the latter theory, the Convulsionists, or Catastrophists as they are called by their opponents, believe to have been caused by such events, the "quietists or uniformitarians" explain by assuming a

[1] Leonhardt, *Geologie*, ii. p. 70: "It is extremely arbitrary to assume that all the geological phenomena have been brought about by causes similar to those which are at work in these days, and that those causes have never possessed greater force than they have had since the present order of things. Nature does not now work as she did formerly; for the circumstances are no longer the same. We see the great series of Neptunian deposits divided off into a certain number of groups. This leads us to the thought of a series of sudden violent catastrophes, of which each one was able to change the form of the seas, and the course of rivers over vast tracts, and which were separated from one another by periods of comparative quiet in each region." Sir Roderick Murchison, speaking in the year 1865 (see *Athenæum*, Sept. 16, 1865, p. 376), says: "I adhere" (in opposition to Ramsay, Jukes, and Geikie) "to my long cherished opinion as to the great intensity of power employed in the production of dislocations of the crust of the earth. . . . Admiring the Huttonian theory . . . I maintain that such reasoning is quite inadequate to explain the manifest proofs of convulsive agency which abound all over the crust of the earth. . . . Placing no stint whatever on the time which geologists must invoke to satisfy their minds as to the countless ages which elapsed during the accumulations of sediment, I reject as an assumption which is at variance with the numberless proofs of intense disturbance, that the mechanical disruptions of former periods, and the overthrow of entire formations, as seen in the Alps and many mountain chains, can be accounted for by any length of existing causes."

constant but much longer working of the ordinary forces.[1]

The names *Neptunists* and *Plutonists*, or Vulcanists, denote another deeply-rooted opposition of parties; this depends on the relative influence which is accorded to water and to fire respectively in the formation of the earth.

Water and fire are still active agents in forming and transforming the crust of the earth. The agency of fire shows itself principally in the volcanoes, which cause mountains and islands to rise, cast forth lava, ashes, and other substances; and possibly are the principal causes of earthquakes, and of all their effects on the earth's crust. The agency of water is twofold, chemical and mechanical. From substances which have been chemically dissolved in water are formed precipitations, tufaceous limestone, silicious sinter, stalactites, travertine marble, etc., and solid substances are carried by water, especially by rivers, from place to place, and then deposited. The deltas at the mouths of the Nile, the Ganges, the Rhine, and other rivers were formed in this way; it has been estimated that the Ganges and the Mississippi, for example, carry down yearly several thousand million cubic feet of solid substances, either floating in the water or in a state of solution.

---

[1] Cf. Hæckel, *Nat. Schöpfungsgeschichte*, p. 101; and "Die Entstehung der Erdoberflache," in Burmeister's *Geol. Bildern*, i. p. 1. "The earth, and especially the earth's surface, has been entirely produced (!) by forces which we ourselves still find acting with similar power; it has never been subjected to more violent, or to any other kind of catastrophes of development. On the other hand, the period of time in which the development took place is quite immeasurable; there is nothing prodigious, nothing marvellous in the course of the earth's development, except the immense duration of time." P. 12.

As it appears from these and other facts that water and fire are at present active agents in transforming the surface of the earth, we are justified in assuming that they acted analogously in earlier times. If we go beyond the surface, and investigate the earth's crust, we find throughout, superposed one on another, a series of strata, or of stratified formations,[1] which it is universally supposed were formed by the gradual deposit of water. As a rule they consist of substances which are not soluble in water, and they certainly have all the qualities which we now find in newly formed watery deposits or sediments. Further, many of them contain petrifactions, that is, remains of organic bodies; now organic substances are not fireproof; therefore the strata which contain petrifactions can never have been in a state of igneous fusion, but can only have been dissolved by being mingled with water. All stratified formations which contain petrifactions are therefore supposed by geologists, Plutonists as well as Neptunists, to have a Neptunian origin.

But the crust of the earth does not consist entirely of stratified rocks; a great part of it is of different formation. These unstratified rocks are not found in parallel layers, but they occur without regularity in their stratification and succession, under, among, and above the stratified rocks; they consist of several mixed, completely or incompletely crystallized minerals; they are occasionally rich in precious stones and all

---

[1] A formation, sometimes called system, by the French "terrain," is a collection of rocks which, either through age, origin, or composition, have a common character. Thus we speak of stratified and unstratified, Plutonic and Neptunian, soft water and sea water, metalliferous and non-metalliferous formations.

kinds of metals, but they are without petrifactions. Some of these unstratified rocks, as, *e.g.*, true basalt, are generally acknowledged to have a volcanic origin. But when we come to the great mass of the unstratified rocks, consisting of granite, porphyry, serpentine marble, gneiss, mica slate, etc., the contest between Neptunism and Plutonism begins. The Plutonists assume that these rocks were formerly in a state of igneous fusion. Further, they think they may assume that the interior of the earth is still in a condition of igneous fusion. They found this assumption on the fact that heat increases as we penetrate deeper into the interior of the earth;[1] and further, on the existence of hot springs, and especially of volcanoes, which, according to this theory, are open chimneys connected with the fluid nucleus of the earth. If this theory is admitted to be true so far, it is only logical to assume further that the whole earth was formerly a molten mass of igneous fluid, and from this condition passed by degrees into a solid state through the gradual cooling of its surface. While the earth was cooling, the outermost layer congealed first and formed a solid crust, on which water could gather, and the different stratified systems could by degrees be deposited. The irregularities of the earth's crust, the mountains and valleys, the seas and continents, were caused by the rebellion of the igneous fluid against the increasing mass of strata on the crust; for the outer strata were puffed out, vaulted, rent, dislocated, and occasionally overturned by upheavals, which were caused by the vapours enclosed in the interior. In many places the

---

[1] Pfaff, *Schöpfungsgeschichte*, p. 208.

upheaving masses came to light, and appear in the shape of crystalline rocks, showing their primitive form principally in granite. In other places the convulsion was not great enough to cause the upheaving masses to appear, and here only the lower strata are seen in a more or less vaulted shape. In other places again the fiery masses penetrated into splits and cracks in the stratified formations, and are there found as crystalline rocks. Sometimes the fiery masses and the vapours which caused their upheaval transformed the stratified formations with which they came in contact. In this manner the fiery masses in the interior of the earth acted in ancient days on the formation of the earth's crust; and the present volcanic outbreaks are feeble successors of those ebullitions of force which must have been much mightier and more extended in former times.

This, the Plutonic theory, was defended by Hutton (1726–1797) and by the great German geologist Leopold von Buch; and judging from the most recent handbooks of geology, it may be regarded as the one most generally recognised. As you see, even according to this theory, the authority is divided between Pluto and Neptune; but fire was the first and most mighty agent in the formation of the earth. Water formed and moulded the crust of the earth, but the deeper we penetrate into the earth, and the farther we go back in its history, the more do we find fire as the active agent.

I now come to the second theory, the Neptunian. This does not assert that fire had no part in the formation of the earth's crust; the volcanic phenomena which we still witness would of course not permit of this.

The basaltic rocks, for instance, are regarded by Neptunists as in great part volcanic masses which have sprung forth from the depths of the earth. But in this theory it is supposed that volcanoes are local phenomena, fed by fire which exists in certain places at no great depth, whose outbreaks are conditioned by chemical reactions. According to this view, the earth has no igneous core. Further, it is assumed that the earth never existed in a condition of igneous fusion, but was dissolved in water, or was partly just solid, partly fluid or dissolved, which condition was produced by water. This primæval broth (Ur-brei) gradually assumed a solid form through mechanical forces, pressure, etc., and still more through chemical processes, and by degrees the separate mountain ranges appeared. Most of the rocks which, according to the first theory, were originally in a state of igneous fusion, and in this condition were pressed up from below, according to this theory, were originally watery deposits and sediments, which gradually reached their present condition through chemical changes, metamorphoses and crystallization. Granite, porphyry, and the greenstones were thus formed. The numerous phenomena which, in the first theory, are regarded as the effects of volcanic agency, and of the rebellion of the igneous core against the hard crust of the earth, are here supposed to be the results of this chemical transformation, and of the continual dissolving and crystallization which are going on in the interior of the stratified rocks. The cause of earthquakes, for instance, may often be this: the limestone and other strata in the interior of the earth which are soluble in water, may be washed away and gradually removed by the infiltration of subterranean waters; then the upper strata, being deprived of their support, sink down and fall in, and the concussions thus produced are radiated by shocks, as is the case with waves. In this manner it is supposed that earthquakes can be explained, especially when they occur in regions where no volcanoes are to be found near at hand.

Such are the principal points of the Neptunian theory, which was originated by the founder of scientific geology in Germany, A. J. Verner (1780–1817), and which has been developed and of course considerably modified by more recent writers. In the course of the history of geology it appeared to be gradually losing ground, but latterly the application of chemistry to the history of the earth's formation has afforded it a new support. The theory has been principally developed in this direction by G. Bischof and O. Volger; besides these, Neptunism has been defended by Nepomuk von Fuchs, von Schafhäutl, and especially by Andreas Wagner.[1]

I am neither able, nor have I the inclination, to consider which of these theories is to be preferred. For our object it is only necessary that we should be acquainted with both theories, and know that up to this time neither the one nor the other has been proved to be alone scientifically correct. This is admitted by geologists themselves. "Geology" says Pfaff, himself

---

[1] *Geschichte der Urwelt*, i. 18 seq. "Betrachtungen uber den gegenwärtigen Standpunkt der Theorieen der Erdbildung nach ihrer geschichtlichen Entwicklung in den letzten funfzig Jahren," in the Report of the Royal Bavarian Academy of Science for 1860, p. 375 seq. Cf. Stutz, *Schöpfungsgeschichte*, p. 6. *Allg. Lit. Anz. für das evang. Deutschland*, 1867, p. 17.

a Plutonist, "is at present in a state of transition with reference to these questions; the encroachments of Plutonism have necessarily caused a reaction in favour of Neptunism, and we cannot yet calculate whither it will lead us, and what the end of it will be."[1] And Karl Vogt says in his sketch of geology: "The theories as to the formation of the solid crust of the earth in general, and of the mountains in particular, are at present in an unsettled condition; out of which two diametrically opposed views seem to stand out, which would include all other less divergent opinions." He then sketches these two views, which he calls the physical and the chemical theories; they are the two theories which I have discussed under their usual names of Neptunism and Plutonism, and I have based my description principally on this sketch of Vogt's. "These two opposing theories," he continues, "contradict one another on most points to such an extent that it would be hardly possible to reconcile them." He rightly thinks that such a reconciliation would not be impossible, but it has not been accomplished hitherto, nor does there even seem to be any prospect of it. To use Vogt's own words: "It is necessary here, as in so many branches of scientific observation, to inquire minutely into each particular case, and to make known the causes which produce it; not to fall back on the general application of absolute theories, which might be valid for one case, but would not be justified in another."[2]

I have already said that the Plutonic theory is that preferred by most geologists. I must not omit to add

[1] *Schöpfungsgeschichte*, p. 422.   [2] *Grundriss der Geologie*, p. 340.

that G. Bischof, the very geologist who has most decidedly and successfully opposed the Plutonic theory, in discussing the origin of the separate constituent parts of the earth, has declared himself against the assumption that a watery or paplike substance formed its original condition. He expresses himself as follows: "The condition of igneous fusion in which the earth is supposed to have existed during the period of creation, is not incompatible with any of the phenomena, and it explains some indubitable facts, such as the increase of temperature as we get deeper into the earth, the hot springs and volcanic phenomena, in the simplest and most natural manner."[1]

You see that under these circumstances there would be danger, if, as many commentators have asserted, the Bible really taught that the earth was formed by the action of water. We might no doubt still say in this case that the Bible did not contradict any certain results of geological inquiry; for the contest between Plutonists and Neptunists is not yet decided; but still the situation would be disturbing. It is possible, at all events, and many think it probable, that the Plutonists will at length win a decided victory, and that further geological inquiries will conclusively prove fire to be the original and determining force in the formation of the earth. Nor is it impossible that an entirely new theory should become scientifically important, and that thus both Plutonism and Neptunism may be set aside. Considering the rapid progress made by the natural sciences in our century, it is even possible that before very long, perhaps in our lifetime, Plutonism or some

[1] *Lehrb. der chem. und physik. Geol.*, 2nd ed. i. p. 7 seq. Cf. p. 479.

other theory, which is not Neptunism, may be opposed to the Bible, no longer as a hypothesis, but as a system substantiated by science. What then?

All these fears are groundless. I may say that I am ready to prove this; for the question is exegetical and not geological, and therefore it is one which, unlike those I have till now been discussing, is within my province.

A learned geological writer, a moderate Plutonist, Quenstedt, says briefly: "Moses was a Neptunist."[1] He thinks that he can even explain this circumstance, and excuse it from his point of view by adding: "The home of the patriarchs in the land of Ur (in Chaldæa) and afterwards in Egypt presented so few volcanic phenomena, and the power of the waters in the countries of the great rivers must have been so striking, that the forming agency of the watery element was only too apparent." Against this we may observe first, that assuming, but not admitting, that Moses ever occupied himself in investigating the geological condition of the countries in which he lived and with which he was acquainted, and again assuming, but not admitting, that in consequence of these investigations, or in consequence of the opinions of others which were known to him, Moses held the Neptunian theory, this can be of little interest to the exegete. The latter need only ask whether the Neptunian theory is advanced in the book which Moses wrote with the supernatural aid of the Spirit of God; for the exegete need not assume the opinions of Moses, but only the statements in the Bible, to be true. But we cannot expect that the Bible should

[1] *Sonst und Jetzt*, p. 194.

advance the Neptunian theory; for as the object of the Bible is to convey to us religious truths, but not to teach us scientific things, it clearly cannot mean to decide against Plutonism and in favour of Neptunism. The utmost we can concede as possible is this: in stating religious truths concerning the creation of things by God, the Biblical writers may have occasion to use expressions which indirectly imply that the earth was formed in one or other particular way. We cannot allow that Quenstedt's statement means more than this; that the Biblical description of the formation of the earth appears to rest on the Neptunian theory, or to favour that theory by the way in which it is expressed.

One of the most decided Neptunists, Andreas Wagner, thus sums up the question. He says: "Those who hold the Neptunian theory, believe with Moses, the world's most ancient geologist, and with another unusually gifted wise man of antiquity, the Apostle Peter, that 'by the word of God the heavens were of old, and the earth standing out of the water and in the water,' and they are in a position to justify that assertion scientifically."[1]

Neptunists will do well to confine themselves to science, and not to appeal to Moses or S. Peter. The former cannot with any accuracy be called the world's most ancient geologist, and it is just as incorrect to call S. Peter an unusually gifted wise man of antiquity. His gifts, so far as they interest us, were supernatural, received through the Spirit of God, and therefore his

[1] *Geschichte der Urwelt*, i. 142. K. von Raumer also appeals to 2 Pet. iii. 5 seq. Kreuzzüge, ii. 20: "The words in ver. 5 bear out the Neptunian theory of the formation of mountains; ver. 10 refers Plutonists to a *future* burning up of the earth."

wisdom was limited to supernatural things. It is quite wrong to ascribe great knowledge of geology to Moses and S. Peter, and to quote them as authorities in geological controversies.

As there are still some theologians of the present day, as Keerl[1] and Zöckler[2] in Germany, and the Abbé Choyer[3] in France, who assert that the Bible teaches or favours Neptunism, I cannot avoid examining their arguments. I shall confine myself to the first-named writer, because he defends his opinion in the most decided and circumstantial way. He even says : " We might assert that the Plutonic theory would share the fate of the Copernican system, which was long and violently opposed as being contradictory to the Bible, and now is admitted by the most orthodox. But the acceptance of the Plutonic theory of the earth's origin is quite a different thing from the acceptance of the Copernican system. Holy Scripture has never expressed itself against the latter ; on the other hand, it says clearly and unequivocally that the earth was created out of water" (2 Pet. iii. 5).

If S. Peter really meant in these words to teach clearly and decidedly the Neptunian origin of the earth, it would be a very strange exception to the rule I have just mentioned, namely, that Holy Scripture only touches on things which are the objects of scientific inquiry, when, and in so far as, it is necessary for the teaching of religious truths. But if we look at the passage with the context, we shall find that nothing could be further from S. Peter's intention than to

---

[1] *Schöpfungsgeschichte*, p. 433.   [2] *Die Urgeschichte*, p. 15.
[3] *La théorie géojénique*, p. 41 ; cf. *Theol. Lit.-Bl.* 1872, 357.

enlighten the readers of his Epistle, even indirectly, on any geological question. In the third chapter of his second Epistle, he is speaking of those who do not believe in the coming of our Lord in the Last Judgment, and he says that the day of the Lord will come as a thief in the night; in the which the heavens shall pass away with a great noise, and the elements shall melt with fervent heat; the earth also, and the works that are therein, shall be burned up. The apostle adds that *one* such judgment of destruction has already passed over the earth, the judgment of the Deluge; " by the word of God the heavens were of old, and the earth standing out of the water and in the water, whereby the world that then was, being overflowed with water, perished." There needs no further proof that the apostle does not wish to teach us new doctrines, but that in order to prove and explain what he is teaching concerning the destruction of the world by fire, he refers his readers to what they already know about the former judgment; and how should they know this except from the account in Genesis? This teaches us, the apostle would say, that originally a mass of waters existed, from which the heavens were formed, and the earth came forth by the word of God, and that God in the judgment of the Deluge allowed the original condition, in which the earth was without form and void, and covered with the waters, to return. S. Peter is therefore referring to the account given in Genesis of the formation of the earth, and not to the Neptunian origin of the earth, and we are not justified in finding in his words a plainer testimony in favour of Neptunism than is given by Moses in Genesis; and that is none at all, for neither does Moses teach the Neptunian origin of the earth, as I am about to prove to you.

Ver. 2 of the Hexæmeron runs: "And the earth was without form, and void, and darkness was upon the face of the deep. And the Spirit of God moved upon the face of the waters." After God has created the light on the first day, and has thus ended the rule of darkness, He separates, on the second day, the upper and lower, the heavenly and earthly waters; that is, as I have already shown, He forms the atmosphere of the earth. On the third day, He causes the dry land to appear from the waters, and clothes it with vegetation, and on the fifth and sixth days living creatures are added to it. This might be held to mean, as Neptunists say, that in ver. 2 the earth is described as existing only as a great mass of waters, in which its constituent parts were held in a dissolved or softened condition, and that on the third day the formation of the solid ball of the earth from this fluid mass was completed. But the question is not whether the words *may*, but whether they *must* be understood in this sense. And this question must be answered most decidedly in the negative. First of all it must be remembered that Moses is not speaking of the formation of the earth in itself, but of the fashioning of the earth as a dwelling-place for man; he is not therefore concerned with the interior, but only with the surface of the earth, and his geogony is in consequence, in the literal sense of the word, superficial. Further, in explaining ver. 2 it must be remembered that it is contrasted with the following verse. We now see the earth divided into land and sea, both of which are inhabited by animals, the earth is clothed with vegetation, and all is illumined by the stars. All this, says Moses, was brought about by the word of God; it was not so in the beginning; the present condition of the earth was preceded by another, in which all this did not exist. How could Moses describe this original chaotic state otherwise than he does: "The earth was without form and void," that is, without vegetation and living inhabitants; even the water and land were not yet separated, the earth appeared to man as one great mass of waters, and light also was still wanting, so that "darkness was upon the face of the waters." Thus it appears to the gaze of the man whom God is instructing concerning the history of creation; the surface of the earth is water, and above that is the darkness, until at God's command there is light, and the dry land appears from out of the waters which cover it. The mightiest revolutions and convulsions may be taking place in the interior of the earth, chemical and mechanical forces may be at work, fires and volcanoes may be glowing; concerning all this Moses has nothing to say.

Or another condition may have preceded that described in ver. 2. The earth may have been an igneous, glowing, gradually cooling mass, before it appeared as a body covered with water; or, as some believe, the earth may have existed beforehand in a condition of perfection and order, and may have been destroyed by God, in order to be anew created; Moses has nothing to tell us about this; his narrative begins at the time when water formed the surface of the earth.

It was not necessary that Moses should mention all the processes of formation which may have gone on in the interior of the earth, and all the processes of formation which may have occurred before the first day of the Hexæmeron, for he does not aim at giving us a scientifically exact and complete geogony, but only a narrative of how the earth was made into a dwelling-place for man; and for this object it is quite sufficient to say, as he does, that the animal and vegetable worlds were created by God; the light was brought forth by God; the separation of the water from the land was the work of God; and that before all this was created by God, it did not exist; it was dark, and the waters still covered the land.

Keerl is attributing far too much meaning to the words of the Bible in saying that "Holy Scripture everywhere includes the formation of the mountains in the work of the third day."[1] Genesis simply says nothing whatever about the formation of the mountains. It only says that on the third day God caused the waters to be separated from the land. When this occurred, of course the land and the unevennesses of the earth's surface existed, otherwise the separation could not have been accomplished. But whether these unevennesses were caused by the raising of one part of the earth's surface, or the sinking of another, whether the solid parts of the earth were only then separated from the fluid, or whether these solid particles existed before the third day, and the formation of the unevennesses of the earth's surface had begun before the third day, and was already far advanced, concerning all this

[1] P. 478.

Moses says absolutely nothing; his words are true provided the formation of the mountains had progressed so far on the third day as to allow the dry land to come forth from the waters. From an exegetical point of view, therefore, we must refrain from fixing any time for the formation of the mountains, and we have no more right to say that it happened during the third day, than to say that it happened in the period of the thohu wabohu. It is simply not mentioned in the account of the creation given by Moses, and is only indirectly alluded to as being at least partly accomplished, in so far as it is implied by the separation of water and land.

The way in which quotations from the 104th Psalm and other passages from the poetical books of the Old Testament have been adduced in this controversy is still more blameworthy. Evidently the Psalmist is only poetically amplifying the short description given by Moses of the separation of water and land on the third day, when he says: "Thou laidest the foundations of the earth, that it should not be removed for ever. Thou coveredst it with the deep as with a garment: the waters stood above the mountains. At Thy rebuke they fled, at the voice of Thy thunder they hasted away. They go up by the mountains; they go down by the valleys into the place which Thou hast founded for them. Thou hast set a bound that they may not pass over; that they turn not again to cover the earth."[1] Who would think of seeking for information concerning the formation of the mountains from poetical words such as these?

We may judge of the lengths to which Keerl's zeal

[1] Ps. civ. 5 sq.

leads him, from the fact that he even taxes some of the Neptunists with heresy,—those, namely, who believe that the earth may have existed in a partially fluid and partially solid condition. Such a condition as this, Keerl thinks,[1] "would not be consistent with the declaration of Scripture, which says that the whole mass of the earth originated out of water, and in water." The original condition of the earth, therefore, was water, and nothing but water, and all the other substances were "dissolved or swallowed up in water;" for it is written, "the earth standing out of the water, and in the water." I call that straining a passage in the Bible, in questions on which it has no bearing. S. Peter and Moses do not intend to give us information about the scientific process by which the earth was formed, and we therefore have no right to learn more from their words than this: that the earth was formerly covered with water, and that the waters were separated from the land on the surface of the earth by the word of God. But this may be reconciled both with the Neptunian and Plutonic systems, and Delitzsch is therefore quite right in saying that the Biblical account of creation[2] does not in the least oblige us to oppose Plutonism with such apologetic zeal as Keerl thinks necessary. On the other hand, I cannot think Delitzsch is right in adding, that the statement, "the earth was without form, and void," might denote an igneous condition, and the next statement, "and darkness was upon the face of the deep," the condition which followed, in which the earth was either fluid or covered with water, so that after all we might find a Biblical

[1] P. 434.   [2] *Genesis* 3rd ed. p. 611 (4th ed. p. 529).

confirmation of Plutonism.[1] It is clear that in the three statements made in the second verse—"And the earth was without form, and void; and darkness was upon the face of the deep. And the Spirit of God moved upon the face of the waters"—there is no intention of describing two or three consecutive conditions, but one condition of the earth, the condition of ἄμορφος ὕλη, in contrast to the order and the form which was brought about by the work of the six days.

We therefore maintain that Genesis and the Bible generally only say that in the most ancient times water once formed the surface of the earth. No geologist can object to this; for even the Plutonists admit, as we have seen, that at least the so-called stratified rocks were formed by watery deposits. On this point then geologists agree with each other, and with Moses. If some geologists affirm that there were, besides and before these Neptunian processes, other Plutonic processes of formation, while others assert that these also were Neptunian, and if therefore geologists themselves are at variance here, it is clear that this is just the point on which there can be no contradiction between the Bible and geology, because the Bible does not mention the subject. Genesis therefore need fear nothing whether Plutonism, or Neptunism, or yet a third system is victorious, for Genesis takes no part in the contest. The narrative begins at a time concerning which geologists agree, and it confines itself to subjects which even geologists consider to admit of no discussion.

[1] *Genesis*, 3rd ed. p. 611. In the 4th ed. p. 529, he only says that the thohu wabohu leaves room for an igneous condition anterior to the fluid condition.

XIII.

THE THEORIES AS TO THE FORMATION OF THE EARTH.

GEOLOGISTS conclude from the following facts that the earth was originally in a fluid condition :—1. The form of the earth, apart from the unevennesses of the surface, is that of a figure resembling a ball, a spheroid flattened at the poles ; 2. The polar diameter is two and four-fifths of a geographical mile shorter than the equatorial diameter ; 3. It is believed that a fluid mass revolving round its own axis invariably assumes such a spheroidal shape. And, as I have shown in my last lecture, most geologists assume that the earth existed originally in a state of igneous fusion. Many, however, do not stop here, but think it likely that another nebulous or gaseous condition had preceded the fiery state ; and some have even gone farther than this, and have supposed that our whole solar system could be traced back to such a nebulous, gaseous vapour. Kant first suggested this theory.[1] Herschel, Laplace, and others have tried to support it scientifically. Before I inquire what, according to Biblical revelation, we should think of this theory, I must first

---

[1] Kant developed this theory in his book, *Allgemeine Naturgeschichte und Theorie des Himmels*, as early as 1755. Herschel first discussed it in 1784 (in the *Philosophical Transactions*), and Laplace in 1796, (*Exposition du système du monde*). Pfaff, *Die neuesten Forschungen*, p. 35.

shortly explain the history of the earth according to it.[1]

The solar system was originally one enormous ball of gas. In this, through the concentration of substances, a centre was formed which became later a solid nucleus. To this some external force imparted a motion round its own axis, and by degrees the whole of the gaseous matter surrounding it took part in this motion, so that the whole ball of gas rotated round itself. This motion, which was at first slow, grew quicker and quicker in consequence of the increasing density of the mass and the accompanying diminution of its volume; the form of the ball of gas became more and more spheroidal and lentiform, because the centrifugal force increased with the quicker motion. In consequence of the increasing density of the whole, and of the greater tendency in the outside parts to fly off from the centre, it was inevitable that at some period the centrifugal force should prevail over the centripetal, and that a ring-shaped part should be separated from the whole. Later on, this girdle or ring was broken by disturbances which took place in it, it was torn in one or in several places, and rolled itself up into as many balls, which now retained their separate existence. The result of this was either to form one new large spheroid with a double motion, a revolution round its own axis and a revolution round the original gaseous ball, or a number of small spheroids, which rolled on with the same double movement at about an equal distance from the centre. I may say here that in the first way were

---

[1] Burmeister, *Gesch. der Schöpfung.* p. 123 seq., also Nöggerath, *Ges. Naturwiss.* iii. 312 seq.

formed the larger planets, and in the second the asteroids. This process by which rings were thrown off and were formed into separate balls was repeated several times, till the central body had become so small that it could throw off no more rings. And so at last the relation between the central *sun* and the surrounding *planets* was established for ever, and the solar system was in this sense complete. But meanwhile the planets had gone through new stages of development. They also showed a tendency to throw off rings. Separate rings were formed which shaped themselves into balls, and became the moons revolving round the planets. The smaller planets did not form rings, while the larger threw off several, of which perhaps some have not yet rolled themselves up into balls, as the double ring of Saturn seems to show.

Let us now turn to the history of the earth in particular. When it had become a separate body, the numerous elementary substances of which it still consists were mingled with each other in the form of vapour in the same proportions as those in which they are actually the constituent elements of the earth. The heaviest metals first separated from the gaseous compound, and formed a solid or a fluid nucleus, which grew larger by degrees through the gradual attraction of similar parts. In the further stages which gradually came about, the earth was a ball of igneous fluid surrounded by an atmosphere, which, however, contained many more substances than ours, water, chlorides, sulphur, and other substances being then only present in a vapourous or gaseous condition. The temperature in space is very low, and it therefore had a cooling effect on the hot ball of the earth. The steam in the upper regions of the atmosphere cooled, and was precipitated on to the hot earth. The water which had thus bècome fluid was again heated with the other substances which it contained, at first probably before it reached the earth; it was changed into steam and again ascended. This process must have been often repeated. But at last the surface of the ball cooled in consequence of the continued diminution of heat, and the first solid crust was formed out of the molten masses of the earths, alkalis, and metals. The nucleus of the earth cooled continually, and contracted more and more. Vacant spaces were formed in the solid crust, as this had become too large for its contents, and the rocks which lay above these spaces sank in places and became crumpled on the surface, forming splits and cracks. The sunken masses pressed on the fiery core, molten rocks forced their way to the surface through the cracks and fissures; they partially raised the masses of the solid crust, and cemented these schistous masses together in more or less inclined positions. In the places where no disruptions occurred, the schistous rocks became thicker and thicker. The masses which had forced themselves between the portions of the crust, and which had cooled there, formed with these the first mountains and mountain-ranges, which probably were of no great height. After many of these disruptions and cementings, the crust of the earth, which from the continual cooling of the interior had become much thicker, at last obtained a certain amount of firmness; the disruptions occurred more seldom, and the surface became more undisturbed and more solid. The precipitations from the atmosphere, which took place continuously, remained longer and longer upon the earth. By degrees a large ocean was formed, which possibly covered all or nearly all the surface of the earth; so that at most a few islands of granite appeared above it. It was boiling hot, and contained many substances besides water, and had chemically a dissolving, and mechanically a destroying effect on the crust. Those particles which were contained in the water after having been either dissolved or mechanically broken up, were deposited in quiet places in the shape of slate and greywacke, and were the first Neptunian formation. While these deposits were being formed, the crust of the earth cooled so considerably that it became fit to be the habitation of organic beings. The eruptions and the Neptunian deposits which were always elevated by them, increased the quantity of dry land, or rather the number of the islands. At this period the earth received the first vegetation and the first animals; first of all sea and marsh plants and sea animals. We need not now consider the changes which the earth has undergone since that. As to the time which must be supposed to have elapsed according to this history of the earth, it cannot very well be given in figures. But if we consider how great is the difference between an igneous or a gaseous ball and the enormous masses of granite which now constitute the principal part of the earth's crust, and if we look back on the series of formations and revolutions which, from the above description, the earth must have passed through, a few hundred thousand years will hardly be deemed sufficient, and we shall rather be disposed to assume that it is a question of millions. To give an example, G. Bischof says that 353 millions of years must have elapsed, and Pfaff thinks it likely that the solidifying of the earth's crust took place not less than 20 millions and not more than 400 millions of years ago.[1]

Let us suppose now that this theory of the earth's formation was laid before a theologian, and that he was to give judgment upon it; that is, to say, not what his personal opinion was, whether it appeared to him scientifically tenable or admissible, but whether in his opinion this theory could be set up without coming into conflict with the Bible, or with revealed religion generally. To put the matter in a more practical form, we will assume that this theory is laid before a theological censor in order that he should decide whether the Church could give her approval to a book which contained this theory, which as we know does not mean that the contents of the book are true, but only that they are not opposed to the teaching of the Church. What would the censor do? If he is a reasonable man, he will unhesitatingly send back the manuscript after writing on it *Imprimatur*, or at least *Imprimi permittitur*, for, as I have represented the theory, there is not one single statement in it which a theologian could point out as *sententia hæresim sapiens, temeraria*, or such like. The theologian need not be at the trouble to ascertain whether scientific heresies or hazardous assertions are contained in it,— the author must settle that with his fellow-savants. If we may believe the English papers, a treatise

[1] *Grundriss*, p. 219.

appeared some years ago, in a periodical published in Rome, in which it was attempted to prove, of course by scientific, not by theological arguments, that the sun is not nearly so large as is commonly supposed,—if I remember right, it was said to be only seven or twelve yards in diameter.[1] The treatise had no doubt been seen by the ecclesiastical censors; but if an Italian savant chose to make himself ridiculous by writing such a treatise, or if the editors of the periodical in question allowed him a few pages for this object, it was not the business of the Magister Sacri Palatii, or whoever was the censor in this case, to make any objection. There was no question of theological heresy, and it was not the business of the censor to judge of the scientific value of the treatise.

The doctrine of the Bible, and therefore, as I have said, of the Church, with reference to the formation of the earth, is, putting aside for the present the details in the Mosaic Hexæmeron, as follows:—(1) The earth, like all things which exist beside God, is not eternal. (2) God is the cause of its existence, it was created by God's will. (3) Its real mode of existence answers to the divine idea and the divine will; if therefore it has undergone several processes of formation, this has happened in accordance with the divine will. It is

[1] A book written by the Rector of the Gymnasium at Hirschberg, G. Hensel, which was published in 1740, may be mentioned as a pendant to this: "Cosmotheoria biblica restaurata, or new Mosaic world-system, wherein is proved by divine and natural arguments: (1) that the earth is stationary; (2) that the sun moves, . . . (4) that the heavenly bodies are large, but not of such a terrible size as they are now-a-days universally represented to be . . . with plates in praise of the great Creator, for the preservation of the truth, set forth for the useful education of every one, and especially for youthful students."

true that these three dogmatic statements are not expressly mentioned and recognised in the theory of the earth's formation which has been just described; but neither are they there denied; and they can be added to, or inserted in the theory, without altering it scientifically. The following questions must remain unanswered in this theory, because they cannot be answered by natural science. Whence comes the original matter from which the earth has been evolved and developed? Whence comes it that this primæval matter did not remain in its original state? Whence came the first impulse to this series of changes? How was the capacity for such developments, and the impulse towards them, imparted to matter? or whence are the forces which have moved, dissolved, cooled, condensed, stiffened, and hardened matter? and whence are the laws according to which the processes of formation have led exactly to this end? I have already shown that it does not lie with geology to answer these questions, but if they are rightly answered the above theory is perfectly admissible. It would then run thus. God originally created a gaseous compound of substances, which was capable of undergoing different processes of formation under certain conditions: God caused these conditions to take place, and so the primæval matter which God had created was in the course of many ages formed into our earth, through the action of natural forces, which had been created and set in motion by God. In such a form the geological theories which have been mentioned, and other similar ones, are, speaking theologically, perfectly admissible, whatever may be thought of them from a geological point of view. Deluc and Ampere, for example, who propounded such theories, were thoroughly believing Christians; Bishop Meignan speaks very favourably of Laplace's theory;[1] and the learned Roman Jesuit Pianciani has adopted it in all essential particulars, and has only modified one or two things in it on purely physical grounds.[2]

No doubt the theory is not always actually stated in a harmless manner. There is a great temptation to mingle false philosophical and theological ideas with it. For instance, the older French savants, such as Buffon and Lamarck,[3] mention a Creator, but He creates only two things, la matière et la nature, primæval matter and the laws of nature; and after He has accomplished this, He withdraws from all interference; the further processes of formation take place by themselves, and it is either the result of chance, or of a necessity of nature, that primæval matter under the influence of the laws of nature has gradually taken the form which it at present bears. This theory is carried out most consistently in a book which was translated by Vogt from the English, *Vestiges of the Natural History of Creation*. God created matter, and at the same time He gave the laws of nature, so that the history of the world has gone on from that time without any further interference on His part. The author[4] thinks it is inconsistent to confine this natural course of things to the

---

[1] *Le monde*, etc. p. 36.   [2] *Cosmogonia*, p. 63.
[3] Cf. Sorignet, *Cosmogonie*, p. 194.
[4] The book, which appeared anonymously in 1844, is now known to have been written by Robert Chambers. Zöckler, *Gesch. der Beziehungen*, ii. 610.

formation of solar systems, and to the formation of our earth from matter, which is endowed with certain tendencies and forces. The origin of the first organic beings, the gradual development of different plants and animals, and the perfecting of the latter till man was produced, must be explained in the same way. The same system of laws, in which all is ordered from the beginning, and which is so exhaustive that it entirely rules the world, governs the history of mankind. It is obvious that the doctrine of Providence, and of the regular ordering of creation, is so treated in this theory, that the God who lives and reigns is entirely kept in the background; that there can be no idea of God's free sovereignty over the world and its laws; that man loses the relation to God and the world which Christianity assigns to him, and that a supernatural revelation from God to man must be looked upon as an impossibility.

But this *deistic* theory is in itself only half-hearted and commonplace. If, according to this system, a supernatural being is only supposed to exist in order to create matter, and to give laws to nature, it is very easy to go a step farther and to say, as the German translator of the English book in question cynically expresses it, " a personal Being existing apart from the world, who, after creating the world and the laws of nature, becomes perfectly passive, is ridiculous. Matter was not created, neither were the laws of nature given; both are necessary and mutually conditioned, and they have their origin in no third power." Thus the *pantheistic* dogma of force and matter replaces the theistic dogma of a God who lives and reigns, and we have reached the last and deepest contradiction to which the scientific contest between truth and error leads.

It is no doubt much to be lamented that deistic and pantheistic speculations should be thus included in scientific theories, and especially that this should occur in popular writings. The less intelligent and less instructed readers will not always know whether it is the man of science or the philosopher or theologian who is speaking, and he may believe things to be the result of scientific inquiry which are not and never can be so, but which, on the contrary, are borrowed from another branch of knowledge. But as natural science prides itself, and justly so, when it confines itself to its own province, on attaining to its conclusions only by observing facts and by strict scientific induction, and therefore claims that these conclusions should be relied upon and trusted, such a mixture of scientifically proved truths or possible hypotheses and philosophical or theological errors may easily be terribly misused. For this reason I have tried in a previous lecture to define the objects and the limits of scientific inquiry. If you will bear in mind the statements there laid down, you will easily be able to eliminate what has been unjustifiably added to the theories concerning the formation of the earth.

True savants, who know well the objects and the limits of human inquiry, protest most decidedly against the arbitrary extension of this theory in a deistic or pantheistic sense. For instance, Oscar Fraas says: "Honest savants will admit that they simply know nothing about the origin of things. Looked at dispassionately, this modern theory of geologists, which begins with the earth as a ball of glowing sun substance, tells us nothing about its actual beginning; it only puts it a little farther back; and instead of supposing that bodies existed in the condition in which we see them now, it assumes that they were in a gaseous state, perhaps because the uninstructed think that gas is nearer to nothing than is a solid body. But in reality there is nothing gained; the absolute beginning still remains hidden; we are no nearer to it even if we suppose that the earth, in the shape of a ball of gas, originally flew through space like a rocket."[1] The English geologist Gideon Mantell speaks even more decidedly : " You will at once perceive that this theory can in nowise affect the inference that the universe is the work of an Allwise and Omnipotent Creator. Let it be assumed that the point to which this hypothesis guides us is the ultimate boundary of physical science —that the nearest glimpse we can attain of the material universe displays it to us occupied by a boundless abyss of brilliant matter; still we are left to inquire how space became thus occupied, whence matter thus luminous? . . . And if . . . our planetary system was gradually evolved from a primæval condition of matter, and contained within itself the elements of each subsequent change, still we must believe, that every physical phenomenon which has taken place from first to last has emanated from the will of the Deity."[2]

---

[1] *Vor der Sündfluth*, p. 99.

[2] *Wonders of Geology*, ii. 21 and ii. 679. Cf. H. Lotze, *Mikrokosmus*, vol. i. 2nd ed. p. 418 seq. " Now that the theory of the formation of the planetary system from a fiery gas has passed into the region of universal knowledge,—an ingenious view of the events of a period which

We need therefore only say that the nebular hypothesis is incompatible with the belief in a free and conscious creation of the world by God,[1] when it is interwoven with deistic and pantheistic views, and not when it stands by itself. The theory, as I have described it purely scientifically in the beginning of this lecture, is perfectly admissible theologically. A theologian might no doubt make the following objections. He might say: "Geologists tell us that the earth was originally a mass, either partly dissolved in water, or in a state of igneous fusion, or even perhaps in a gaseous condition, and that it underwent a series of developments till it reached the state in which it is now, or in which it was when God made it a dwelling-place for the first man; faith teaches us that God is able to create what and how He wills, and therefore was able at once to create the world in a condition in which it was fitted to be the dwelling-place of man:" so far all is right, but now comes the error, "It is not to be supposed that God would create by a long and useless process what He could have created

is without the range of all experience,—people seem to think that they have discovered a fine evolution of phenomena, not indeed from nothing, but at least from a formless primæval matter. But they forget that the history of this fiery ball, the later developments of which they have so cleverly followed, must necessarily extend backwards also into an endless past. The gradually cooling and solidifying ball must have passed through a period when its temperature was still higher, its extent still greater: what was the first moment of that process of solidifying during which this theory first takes it up? And whence comes the original direction and speed of the revolution, in which we suppose that all its constituent parts were simultaneously moved? All our science merely works up and down this unending scale, apprehending the internal connection of single parts according to general laws, but everywhere unable to see the first origin of the whole, or the goal to which its development is tending."

[1] Zöckler, *Urgeschichte*, p. 34.

immediately. If the earth was created in order to be a dwelling-place for man, why should God have created it so many thousands of years before, and only have fitted it for its object after so many processes of formation had been gone through, when He might have reached the same end in a much shorter time?" Do not let us forget that Holy Scripture says, "How unsearchable are His judgments, and His ways past finding out!"[1] "Where wast thou when I laid the foundations of the earth? declare if thou hast understanding. Who hath laid the measures thereof if thou knowest, or who hath stretched the line upon it? Whereupon are the foundations thereof fastened? or who hath laid the corner-stone thereof: when the morning stars sang together, and all the sons of God shouted for joy?"[2] Revelation only teaches us that God might have created the earth at once, or have brought it to perfection after many processes of formation—whichever He would; it does not teach us which of these two ways God has chosen, whether the shorter, or the so-called circuitous way; but it does teach us that we have no right to judge God's ways according to our standard, and that from our point of view we cannot decide what is or is not fitting for the divine wisdom and might. God may have had reasons for beginning to form the earth and the other heavenly bodies thousands of years before the creation of man; and if God really did this, and if we cannot understand why He should have done it, we must only bow in humility before the incomprehensibility of God, and we must not say, that because we cannot understand why

[1] Rom. xi. 33.   [2] Job xxxviii. 4–7.

God should have done this, therefore He cannot have done it.

But revelation does not tell us whether God did in reality begin to fashion the earth so long before the creation of man, and did cause it to go through such numerous and complicated processes of formation. If geology can find out anything certain on this subject, it will in no way come into conflict with the Bible, and the theologian is therefore very wrong if he thinks he may combat such results of geological inquiry with theological weapons.

Pianciani even attempts to prove that the theory of the earth's formation which we are speaking of is philosophically and theologically probable: "It might appear to our weak reason likely that God's almighty power would have been shown more fully and fittingly if He had created the world, and especially the earth, in a complete and perfect condition by one act of His will. But as God did not do this, even according to the literal interpretation of the Hexæmeron, it seems more befitting His divine wisdom that He should have created matter in its simplest form, and at the same time should have given to it those laws which are still in force, and should have caused these laws to produce the results for which they were intended; so that He only interfered again immediately when the action of the forces and laws of nature was not sufficient to produce what He desired (as in the creation of organic beings and of man). God is consistent in His working, but He acts now in the material world through the laws of nature; it is therefore not likely that He should have acted otherwise in ancient times."[1] To the question how the perfecting of the world, by gradual development, through long periods of time, could tend to the glory of God, man having only been created at the end of these long periods, Pianciani answers with Petavius,[2] that the heavenly spirits witnessed the divine working, and were led through its contemplation step by step to a deeper insight into the wisdom of the Creator. We may add that research into the earth's history, and into the pre-Adamite period, is a means by which man may recognise the working of the Creator's might and wisdom.

Whatever the value of this philosophical and theological speculation may be, we can at any rate say with Deutinger: "If it is seriously asked whether the idea of a primitive completeness of creation, excluding all progress and all gradual development, is so bound up with the Christian doctrine of creation, that if it falls the whole history of creation must fall with it, the answer must be in the negative. It does not lessen our idea of almighty power to say that the almighty power of God acted in the creation in a modified form. Unlimited power does not cease to be unlimited because it limits its actions according to a self-chosen plan. A giant does not cease to possess a giant's strength because he does not make use of his whole power at every moment, and, for instance, touches a captive butterfly very gently. If the divine power is perfect, it is free, and therefore can be completely controlled by the divine will, which limits the working of the power in proportion to the aim which the

---

[1] *Cosmogonia*, p. 68.
[2] Pianciani, *Cosmog.* p. 78; Petavius, *De opif.* i. 1, c. 9, § 1, 2.

wisdom would attain, or in proportion to the subject by means of which it would reveal itself. It was necessary that a creation in space such as God willed, should be conditioned by development in time, because formation in space cannot exist without formation in time. God does not cease to be a creator because He willed and created not only space, but time also. He must indeed have subjected the earth to such a development, because development in time, like form in space, constitutes the difference between the existence of the world and the divine, eternal Being. The fact that the development of the earth took place in a series of periods does not in the least contradict the belief in a power which brings forth the creation; on the contrary, it can itself only be understood by presupposing the original activity of the divine Omnipotence.[1]

I said above when I began to discuss the question of the harmlessness from a theological point of view of this theory of the earth's formation, that I would not then consider the details of the Mosaic Hexæmeron. It therefore remains for me to prove that this theory does not contradict these details. But I will postpone this until we have learnt what was the earth's history after the first appearance of organic beings. The theory of the earth's formation which we are now considering only contradicts completely one view of the Hexæmeron. If only six days of twenty-four hours each elapsed between the beginning of God's creative activity and the creation of man, this theory cannot be correct, this requires no proof; on the contrary, we

[1] *Renan und das Wunder*, p. 98.

must assume that, putting aside the historic strata which may have been formed after the creation of plants and animals, the earth was created essentially in the same condition as that in which it now exists during the three first days of the Hexæmeron. Although I am by no means inclined to adopt this view, I should not like to assert that it is evidently incompatible with the assured results of geological research. The following arguments may be used in its defence.

Geologists conclude from the spheroidal shape of the earth, and from the flattening at the poles, that the earth was originally in a fluid condition; yet it is not in the least necessary to suppose this. The earth may have received this shape by other means, or may have had it from the beginning. In this form, for some reason, it may have been created by God. The theologian need not regard this view as being scientifically inadmissible, for no less a man than the great English geologist Sir Charles Lyell rejects the theory that the earth had originally another form as an unproved hypothesis.[1]

It is supposed that the earth was originally in a state of igneous fusion, because of the existence of the central fire, the igneous nucleus of the earth. But the existence of this central fire is itself only a hypothesis, and it is one which is supposed by eminent geologists, not only by A. Wagner[2] and other Neptunists, but also by Lyell,[3] Greenough,[4] and others, to belong to the

---

[1] *Principles of Geology* (4th ed.), ii. 352, 372.
[2] *Geschichte der Urwelt*, i. 81.   [3] *Principles*, etc., ii. 356.
[4] Address delivered at the Anniversary Meeting of the Geological Society of London. By G. B. Greenough, London 1834, p. 22. Cf. *C. B. Geology*, etc., p. 170.

class of geological myths and fancies. Volcanoes, earthquakes, and hot springs are no doubt geological facts; but as we have seen, they are explained by many geologists without the hypothesis of a fiery centre. The same holds good of the increase of warmth in the interior of the earth.[1] And if the interior of the earth really is in a state of igneous fusion, why should not God have created the earth as a fluid nucleus surrounded by a solid crust? Because the interior of the earth is in a state of igneous fusion, it does not necessarily follow that the whole earth was originally in such a condition.

And as to the idea that the whole solar system was originally in a gaseous condition, from which the earth was developed in the manner that has been described, no geologist would seriously assert that it ought to be considered even as a strictly scientific hypothesis. A series of weighty objections has been made to this hypothesis by many eminent scientific men, and it has been described as scientifically unsatisfactory, or even impossible.[2] Karl Vogt calls this part of the earth's history "the mythical period;"[3] and G. Bischof says

---

[1] A. Wagner, *Gesch. der Urwelt*, i. 81. Those geologists who support the Neptunian theory assume that the warmth of the earth is caused by chemical and physical processes in its crust. Cf. Pfaff, *Grundriss*, p. 16.

[2] Cf. Ulrici, *Gott und die Natur*, p. 344. Huber, *Zur Kritik moderner Schöpfungslehren*, p. 28.

[3] "The geologist who wishes to discover the earth's history must begin his more direct task from the moment when, by the deposit of different strata on the surface of the earth, a solid crust is formed, and fixed epochs are marked out. We find here a relation somewhat similar to that which obtains in the history of the human race (of one people); the real history only begins from the period when chronological information, drawn from documents, gives a more solid foundation; before this everything is lost in the darkness of legend. The documents of geology are stratified rocks

that geology should not go back farther than the time when the earth was either a ball of fire or of water ; it should not venture into a region where all facts cease, as even within its rightful boundaries its explanations are often hypothetical.[1] Even the theory that the earth was originally in a fluid condition must only be considered as an extremely probable hypothesis ;[2] the theory of an originally gaseous condition of the earth is "against the laws of chemistry," and like other similar theories, "it is full of difficulties and contradictions, to remove which fresh arbitrary assumptions are required." "This," he adds, "is the inevitable result if we go beyond the limits of experience. All such theories must therefore be regarded as deviations into the realm of fancy, and are, strictly speaking, out of place in a science which should endeavour more and more to get rid of all that is arbitrary, in order by degrees to obtain the honour of being classed among the exact sciences."[3]

We should therefore be contradicting no assured result of geological inquiry if we were to assume that God in a few days had created the world in a state of general completeness, that is, in the condition in which

---

in their order of superposition. The mythical period of the earth's history is that for which records are still wanting. . . . An exact science, resting on facts, like geology, cannot remain content with brilliant fancies, but must base its conclusions on observation ; it should rather admit its ignorance than eke out the poverty of the facts by groundless assumptions." Vogt, *Lehrb. der Geologie*, ii. 330.

[1] *Lehrb. der chem. und phys. Geologie*, 1st ed. i. p. 3.
[2] *Op. cit.* 2nd ed. i. p. 7.
[3] *Op. cit.* 1st ed. p. 6 seq. Cf. i. p. 584. "Is it not much simpler to suppose the composite, as we find it, has come forth from the hand of the Creator ? To us the creation of the composite seems not less admirable than that of the simple."

it was when man first appeared; and the hypothesis of geologists that granite, gneiss, mica slate, etc., existed in the beginning in a fluid state, and not in their present form, is one which is incapable of proof. All that geologists can prove is that these rocks *may* have reached their present form after passing through a fluid condition; they cannot prove that this has *actually* been the process of formation, that the fluid condition which *may* have preceded the present state *must* have done so. If geologists follow up the history of the earth's formation from its present condition to the most elementary state possible, they can show what series of changes must have taken place under the dominion of the laws of nature, but they cannot prove that the earth must actually have passed through the whole series of changes as they appear in geological theories; or that God, who foresaw the whole series of the different possible conditions of the earth, could not have begun in the middle instead of with the first most elementary condition, and, as it were, omitting the first stages, have created the earth in a latter stage of its existence.

A few examples will make the matter clearer. We see many people of different ages, from childhood to old age; from these empirical observations we derive certain rules by which we judge of the age of men, and by means of these rules we are able to say of any entire stranger we may see, that he is about such an age. We may not always be quite right, but no one will say that a grown-up man is one year old. These rules hold good for all men except for two; Adam and Eve were created as grown-up people; and therefore, according to analogy, any one who had seen them on the day of their creation would have said that they must be at least from fifteen to twenty years of age ; and yet they were not yet one day old. With respect to every other individual who is similarly grown up and developed, we conclude from his present condition that he has passed through a series of changes before growing up to be a man; but this does not hold good of the first man and woman, for they passed through no childhood and youth such as ours.

We can compute the age of a tree from its rings, and even from its size ; from our observations, and according to analogy, we can at least say that an oak which we cannot encircle with our arms has stood for more than ten years. But could we apply these conclusions to the trees of Paradise ? Would it not be at any rate possible that God should have created Paradise, and all the first vegetation of the earth, in a moment, out of nothing ; and with it oaks and cedars which would have appeared to us as giants one hundred years old, whereas in reality they had only existed one day ? Chateaubriand expresses this thought very poetically in the following words : " If the earth was clothed with vegetation by God, and was peopled with living beings, and at last man was created, in the course of a few days, it was part of the perfection and harmony of the nature which was displayed before man's eyes, that the deserted nests of the last year's birds should be seen on the trees, and that the sea-shore should be covered with shells which had been the abode of fish. And yet the world was quite new, and nests and shells had never been inhabited.[1]

Of course this is fantastic;[2] but we are only giving utterance to sober truth when we say that human empirical inquiry can only draw conclusions from analogy, but that the series of conclusions must be interrupted somewhere. Unless the man of science starts from the belief in the eternity of matter, he must admit that matter in some form came into existence through the creative will of God.[3] If the geologist were to pursue his argument from analogy, he would derive this first form of existence from another still earlier one, for it would probably bear signs of a previous form of being, and yet it had no previous existence except in the thought of God.

Let us go a little farther still. If any one who was unacquainted with modern discoveries were shown a photograph which represented a great many figures, and he were asked how long he thought the artist had worked at the picture, which in spite of its small size was so strikingly like, he would certainly suppose that it had taken some weeks or months, and yet it is the work of a few minutes.[4] When a geologist contemplates

---

[1] *Génie du Christianisme*, p. 1. 1. 4, ch. 5.

[2] Cf. Brownson's *Quarterly Review*, 1863, p. 54.

[3] "However far we go back in the Becoming, even if to the nebulæ, we must always start from a Being. The whole difference consists in this, that the bolder man starts from an earlier, the less bold man from a later condition." G. Bischof, *Lehrb.* 1st ed. ii. p. 12. Cf. Lotze's observation above, p. 240, note 2.

[4] Schubert, *Weltgebünde*, p. 565. Cf. Delitzsch, *Genesis*, p. 87. Moses says, Ps. xc. 4, that a thousand years are as one day for God; but it is not the less true, as S. Peter says, that one day is for Him as a thousand years; that is, He can bring forth in one day what would naturally seem to require a thousand years.

the granite mountains in the belief that they are the result of the gradual cooling and hardening of fluid matter, he will conclude that at least several hundred thousand years have passed during the process, if their formation is to be explained by any known natural laws. But is it impossible that God's omnipotence should have created in a moment that which, according to the present condition of things, would have required so long a time to come into being?

In this way, as I have said, those who support the literal interpretation of the six days may reconcile their view with the geological theories of the earth's formation. Those who hold any of the other views, in which the time which elapsed between the beginning of God's creative activity and the creation of man, is not limited to a period of six days of twenty-four hours each, but is left uncertain, although they may not perhaps accept these geological theories, and acknowledge their truth, —for that is not the business of the theologian,—may yet fearlessly leave them to be discussed by men of science, and need only show how the details of these theories can be brought into harmony with the Mosaic narrative of the creation. But before I proceed to this, we must examine more closely those portions of the earth's crust which are believed by geologists to have been formed at later periods of the earth's history; and especially the so-called stratified rocks, in which we find the remains of organic beings, of plants and animals; and which therefore we must conclude did not exist in their present situation and condition from the beginning, but were formed when the organic creation was already in existence. No doubt, as geologists themselves maintain,[1] these stratified formations are not new productions, in the sense that they were added from outside to the parts of the earth which already existed; they have existed as portions of the earth ever since the beginning of the creation, but in different places, and sometimes under different forms, and have only been displaced and transformed by various agents, of which water was one of the principal. Lime, sand, clay, etc., were carried by water from one place to another just as they are now; many minerals were dissolved in water, and were then deposited in various places and in various combinations, when they again hardened. The bulk of the earth has therefore not increased, nor has its crust become thicker on the whole by the formation of these strata, but there has been a removal of matter from one place to another, and a partial transformation of the same from one condition to another.

At this period of the earth's history, for which geologists rightly claim a greater amount of certainty than for the "mythical period," with which we have been occupied to-day,[2] that science, which is a branch of geology and a help to it, and which, under the name of *Palæontology*, has been cultivated in our day with special zeal and success, comes into prominence.

[1] Burmeister, *Gesch. der Schöpfung.* p. 271.
[2] See above, p. 247, note 3.

XIV.

FOSSILS.

The name of *Fossils* is given to those organic bodies of animals and plants, or to separate portions of them, which are found buried in the strata of the earth's crust, generally in a more or less altered condition.[1] The name *Petrifactions*, which was formerly in use, does not apply to those organic bodies which have been preserved entire, with the original proportions of their elementary parts, such as the insects and parts of plants which we find enclosed in amber or rock-salt, and the bodies of mammoths, which have been dug out of the ice in Siberia in a perfectly undecayed condition.[2] But these cases are rare; generally the softer parts of the bodies of the animals and plants which were enclosed in the hardening masses of the strata were dissolved or destroyed, or else they decayed, and as a rule only the firmer and harder portions of the organisms have been well preserved; especially the stems, branches, and hard fruits of plants; the bones, scales, teeth, horns, and shells of animals.

---

[1] The following observations are principally taken from Nöggerath, *Ges. Naturwiss*, iii. p. 166; and Leonhard, *Geol.* i. p. 342. Fraas, *Vor der Sündfluth*, p. 56. Cf. Zittel, *Aus der Urzeit*, and his treatise, "Beitrage zur Geschichte der Palaontologie," in the *Historischer Taschenbuch*, 5 Jahrg. (1875) pp. 139–180.

[2] *Bulletin de l'Académie de St. Petersbourg*, xvi. 147.

Many organic bodies, especially those of plants, have become carbonized, and changed into peat or coal. Others, especially the bodies of animals, have been lixiviated and disintegrated; that is, they have lost their gelatinous and other animal substances by gradual destruction and lixiviation, and in this altered and calcined state their colour, hardness, and weight have more or less disappeared. Other organic bodies again have been covered or surrounded, or encrusted as it is technically called, by mineral substances, as, for instance, calcareous tufa, which were originally fluid, and then hardened. But the real petrifaction occurs when an organic body is entirely changed into a mineral substance and still retains its original form. The solid parts of an organic body are, as is well known, porous; the pores are filled up by the minerals which are dissolved in water, and the substance of the organic body is by degrees chemically removed; the mineral substance replaces it, and gradually hardens; so that at last the organic substances have made way for mineral substances without producing any important change in the original form.

Sometimes an organic body, which after being entirely dissolved has been washed away and has disappeared, has left the impression of its outward form on the surrounding mineral rocks. Stems of trees, for instance, enclosed in some rock, have decayed in this manner, and their component parts have been entirely carried away; in their place a hollow space has been left, which has been filled up by some mineral substance, and this has taken the form of the original tree.[1]

[1] "Some years ago I had to make an inquiry into the nature of some

The fossil impressions or footprints of animals, "Ichnites or Ichnolites," belong to this class. An animal passing over the surface of a bed of clay which had not yet hardened, left the impression of its feet marked in it. After the bed of clay had hardened, with the marks of these impressions, a new layer was formed above it which filled up the impressions, so that we now find the imprints of the feet engraven in the lower layer and in relief in the upper. These fossil footprints were first observed about fifty years ago by a Scotch clergyman, Dr. Duncan;[1] and since then they have frequently been found. The animal to which these footprints have been ascribed has been named Cheirotherium or hand animal, because the impressions distantly resemble the stamp of a man's hand. It seems certain that these impressions were really made by animals, and did not originate in any other way. As I have said, many impressions have been found, and they have been found in rows, one behind the other, so that the size of the step can

---

very curious fossils sent to me from the north of Scotland; a series of holes in some pieces of rock, and nothing more. These holes, however, had a certain definite shape about them, and when I got a skilful workman to make castings of the interior of these holes, I found that they were the impression of the joints of a backbone, and of the armour of a great reptile, twelve or more feet long. This great beast had died, and got buried in the sand; the sand had gradually hardened over the bones, but remained porous. Water had trickled through it, and that water being probably charged with a superfluity of carbonic acid, had dissolved all the phosphate and carbonate of lime, and the bones themselves had thus decayed and entirely disappeared; but as the sandstone happened to have consolidated by that time, the precise shape of the bones was retained."—Huxley, *On our Knowlege of the Causes of the Phenomena of Organic Nature*, p. 45.

[1] Cf. *Quarterly Review*, vol. cx. p. 109. Lyell, *Geology*, ii. 86, 100, 173. Fraas, *Vor der Sündfluth*, p. 224. Pfaff, *Grundriss*, pp. 293, 305.

be ascertained; and in four-footed animals, the print of the hind feet can be distinguished from that of the fore feet.[1]

This, and much more, is now to be found in every handbook of natural science which treats of fossils. But on this, as on other points, science has only arrived at clear and certain knowledge after long search and many errors; and now that our knowledge of fossils is complete, at least in its principal parts, it will not be uninteresting to look back on the road which, not always in a straight direction, but with many zigzags, has led to this knowledge.

We find even among the ancients occasional allusions to fossils.[2] It is said that in the year 540 B.C. the philosopher Xenophanes of Colophon inferred from the remains of fish and other sea animals which were found in quarries near Syracuse, that the surface of the earth must at one time have been in a slime-like condition,

---

[1] On the other hand, another class of such impressions, the so-called fossil raindrops, do not seem to be authentic. (Fraas, *Op. cit.* p. 169; Zittel, *Aus der Urzeit*, p. 258.) Small rounded impressions are sometimes found in sandstone strata, and, on the overlying stratum, corresponding rounded formations in relief. It has been thought that these impressions were produced by falling raindrops, from rain which fell in primæval times when the sandstone was beginning to harden. In one case it was thought that it could be discovered from which direction the rain came, because the sides of the impressions are rather elevated on one side, just as would be the case if rain driving sideways were to fall on one of our sandy shores. But Vogt says (in one of the notes to the *Vestiges of the Natural History of Creation*, p. 74; cf. H. V. Meyer, *Ueber die Reptilien*, p. 142), "The impressions have been recently much more probably explained, by the action of the atmosphere on the cement of the sandstone, or by air bubbles left on the surface of the sand which was covered with the waves. This superficial change takes place sooner or later in most sandstones, according to the quality of the cement."

[2] Quenstedt, *Sonst und Jetzt*, p. 195. E. V. Lasaulx, *Die Geologie der Griechen und Römer*, Munich 1851, p. 4.

and have formed a sea-bed. The sea-shells found on mountains, or in other places far from the sea, were especially noticed by the ancients; they connected them, as we know from Ovid,[1] with the traditions of an ancient flooding of the earth, and it was very natural therefore that Tertullian should have supposed that they were left by the Deluge.[2]

The ancients were no doubt right in imagining that the fossils come from organic beings, and that they were caused and deposited by the agency of water. It is strange that these two simple truths should have been neglected by so many, when people first began to turn their attention to mineralogy and geology a few centuries ago. Many scientific men in the 16th and 17th centuries thought that fossils had no connection with the remains of plants and animals, but were pure mineral forms, like crystals and stalactites. Their resemblance to shells, bones, and stems of trees was supposed to be accidental, just as stalactites, pebbles which have been rubbed together by the action of water, and the weather-beaten points of rocks often assume all kinds of curious shapes. Fossils were usually called *lusus naturæ* by this class of scientific men. One of them, the famous Athanasius Kircher, says: "As sportive nature cannot give the power of vegetation and sensation to the mineral world, she has done what she could; for as she could not give life and

[1] *Metam.* xv. 262.
[2] Tert. *de pallio*, c. 2 : Mutavit et totus orbis aliquando aquis omnibus obsitus ; adhuc maris conchæ et buccinæ peregrinantur in montibus, cupientibus Platoni probare etiam ardua fluitasse. Isid. *Etymol.* xiii. 22 : Cujus (diluvii) hactenus indicium videmus in lapidibus, quæ in remotis montibus conchis et ostreis concretos, sæpe etiam cavatos aquis visere solemus. Cf. Lasaulx, *Op. cit.* p. 14.

feeling to the stones, she has at any rate given to them the form of animals and plants."[1]

The most adventurous, and sometimes superstitious, conjectures were then made in order further to explain the existence of the fossils: these shapes of stones had sometimes been caused by the influence of the planets; sometimes by an *aura seminalis*, a seed vapour; sometimes by a demon working in the depths of the earth; the more reasonable restricted themselves to the supposition that they were simply the result of a *vis plastica*, a creative force of nature.[2] Many went so far in this theory as to apply it in the most ridiculous way. An Italian doctor declared the potsherds which are found heaped up in the Monte Testaccio in Rome, and which are undoubtedly of human fabrication, to be *lusus naturæ*. The Stuttgard doctor Lentilius, in the year 1709, insisted on it that shells hardly differing from those now washed up on the shores of the Lake of Constance were *lusus naturæ*. In 1696 the skeleton of a mammoth was found at Burgtonna; the Collegium medicum, when they were asked their opinion on it by the Duke of Gotha, declared it to be a *lusus naturæ;* no one but the ducal librarian Tentzel was unprejudiced enough to believe that the bones were real.[3]

This theory had its supporters in all countries during the 16th and 17th centuries. One of the last and

---

[1] *Mundus subterraneus* (1664), ii. 27; see Quenstedt, *Sonst und Jetzt*, p. 199.

[2] Wiseman, *On the Connection*, etc., p. 249. Quenstedt, *Sonst und Jetzt*, p. 202. Lasaulx, *Op. cit.* p. 8. Fraas, *Vor der Sündfluth*, p. 414. Zittel, see the *Hist. Taschenb.* p. 146.

[3] Wagner, *Gesch. der Urwelt*, ii. 386.

most unhappy was the Würzburg professor of medicine, Dr. Beringer. As dean of his Faculty, he published in the year 1726 a Latin treatise, with numerous drawings of some curious stones which he had found in a hill near Würzburg.[1] In his introduction he expresses a hope that the land of Franconia would in future be as renowned for these unique stones as for its excellent wine. The stones, as drawn by him, no doubt have not their match in nature; they consist not only of shells, crabs, fish, etc., but also of bees and butterflies perched on flowers, cobwebs, honeycombs, pictures of the sun, the moon, and of comets with their tails; and also of Hebrew, Latin, and Arabic characters. Of course these could not be fossils, and, as Beringer proves at great length, they could not be supposed to be the work of the heathen Germans, because they did not understand Hebrew and Arabic; therefore they could only be *lusus naturæ*. The learned man does mention in the last pages of his book that there was some talk in the town, and especially over the bottle, of a trick which had been played him; but this idea he dismisses for several reasons, and he accuses two former colleagues of having spread these malicious reports. The facts were soon explained: some mischievous students had made these remarkable shapes out of plaster and clay, and had buried them in the place where the professor was accustomed to seek for fossils, or *lusus naturæ*. They were cruel enough to carry the jest so far as

[1] Lithographiæ Wirceburgensis ducentis lapidum figuratorum, a potiori insectiformium, prodigiosis imaginibus exornatæ specimen, quod . . . præside, J. B. A. Beringer, . . . publicæ literatorum disquisitioni submittit, G. L. Hueber, Wirceb. 1726, fol.

to allow Beringer not only to write his treatise, but also to have it printed with twenty folio leaves of drawings. Except for this one instance, the theory that fossils were not connected with plants and animals fell more and more into disrepute in the intellectual world during the last half of the 17th century. It was revived in a remarkable manner in 1835 by an Anglican divine,[1] who even asserted that the mammoth found in the Siberian ice had never been a living animal, but had been created as a lifeless mass of bones and flesh under the ice. The beds of coal, he believed, had been created by God as they are now; in one case the trunk of a tree had been found in a coal-bed of which the lower part stood upright to a height of ten feet, while the upper part, which was sixty feet long, was bent horizontally; this could not have been a real tree, it had apparently been created solely for the purpose of "silencing the terrible blasphemies of geologists." These words alone would show you that we have here a theologian, who in his shortsighted zeal thinks it necessary to dispute geological conclusions because they appeared to contradict, not the Bible, but his erroneous interpretation of the Bible. Quenstedt has laid stress on the remarkable fact that the struggle against the theory that fossils are *lusus naturæ* has been terminated not by professional savants, but by the laymen of science, and especially by clergymen.[2]

The untenableness of the theory that fossils are *lusus naturæ*, seems to have been first recognised in

[1] See H. Miller, *Testimony of the Rocks*, p. 389.
[2] *Sonst und Jetzt*, p. 239.

Italy. In 1517, Fracastoro declared the fossils which had been found at Verona in the foundations of the fortifications to be the remains of animals.[1] This theory was, it is true, disputed by other savants, and was said to be irreconcilable with the Mosaic account of creation; and they declared that the fossils were *lusus-naturæ*, which had been caused by the influence of the stars, or had resulted from a condition of fermentation, or a formative power in the earth. Nevertheless Fracastoro's theory found supporters in Italy at that time; the celebrated painter Leonardo da Vinci is said to have been amongst their number.[2] The Italian savant Cesalpino enunciated the same theory in 1596, in a book dedicated to Pope Clement VIII.

After it had been generally acknowledged that fossils were the remains of animals and plants which had formerly existed on the earth, the question arose as to how they had come to be enclosed in the strata. The Deluge was first thought of. The animals had probably been killed in the waters, and the remains of the animals and plants had been enclosed in the deposits made by the waters, which deposits had subsequently hardened. This theory was supported in the last century by an Englishman, Dr. John Woodward (1722), and by Joh. Jak. Scheuchzer[3] of Zurich (1733), a doctor and a mathematician, who was then a highly esteemed savant, and could say of himself: "My lectures were

---

[1] Pianciani, *Cosmogonia*, p. 11.

[2] Zittel in the *Hist. Taschenb.* p. 144. O. Peschel, *Gesch. der Erdkunde*, p. 382.

[3] Quenstedt, *Sonst und Jetzt*, pp. 205, 238; *Klar und Wahr*, p. 209 Zöckler, *Geschichte der Beziehungen*, ii. 164.

attended by persons of position and others; the learned and the unlearned were there, men of mature years and esteemed position; there were but few students, they might have been counted on one's fingers." Scheuchzer defended the theory that the fossils were caused by the Deluge in several learned works, and found many supporters. He was, however, unfortunate in one discovery. A fossil skeleton which was found at Oeningen on the Lake of Constance in 1725 is called by him "Homo diluvii testis," and is said to be "a relic, which is the more remarkable, because it undoubtedly dates from the Deluge ; in form it shows not only a part, but half a skeleton; moreover, there is not only a superficially impressed figure from which a high-flying imagination could evolve a man, but one which shows the nature of the bones, yea, of the flesh and other soft parts, and that in the regular form and proportion of the skeleton of a grown-up man; in short, it is a very rare memorial of that accursed race of men of the first world;" or in the words of Deacon Miller, who, according to the taste of that time, headed every chapter of Scheuchzer's book with edifying doggerel verses—

"Betrübtes Beingerüst von einem alten Sunder
Erweiche Stein und Herz der neuen Bosheit's kinder."

Cuvier afterwards proved without doubt that the bones described by Scheuchzer, which are still in the museum at Zurich, are not those of a man at all, but of a tailed frog of the Salamander species, which is accordingly known to palæontology as Andrias Scheuchzeri.[1]

[1] Leonhard, *Geologie*, i. 391.

The way in which fossils were brought into connection with the Deluge by Woodward, Scheuchzer, and other men of science, was naturally approved of by theologians, and they produced a series of writings on the subject. The theory had one good result at any rate, for attention was widely directed to the study of fossils, and they were sought for, collected, and described by many who were not, strictly speaking, men of science. Quenstedt observes that a series of splendid palæontological discoveries was made by Swabian theologians at the beginning of the 18th century.[1]

But the more the knowledge of palæontology increased, the more untenable did the theory that the fossils were all caused by the Deluge appear. The Berlin councillor Johann Esaias Silberschlag, who in 1870 defended this theory in his book on *Geogenie, oder Erklärung der Mosaischen Erderschaffung*,[2] found that it involved him in such difficulties, that he breaks out into the following angry words: "I could almost wish now that we could attach some meaning to the old answer, fossils are *lusus naturæ*; for then we could extricate ourselves from all difficulties by means of this one phrase."

Voltaire[3] was the most vehement and also the most superficial opponent of the Deluge theory. He ventured to assert that most of the fossil shells were not petrifactions at all, but came from still existing races of animals; that the foreign shells which were found on the mountains had been dropped from the hats of

---

[1] *Sonst und Jetzt*, p. 205.   [2] Zweiter Theil (Berlin 1780), p. 194².
[3] Cf. Hugh Miller, *Testimony*, p. 306.

pilgrims, and that many things which looked like fossils were merely stones of an unusual shape, that is, *lusus naturæ*. If we were told, he said, that the bones of a reindeer and of a hippopotamus—that is, of a northern and a southern animal—had been found at Étampes in France, no one would be likely to conclude from this that the Nile and Lapland had had a rendezvous between Paris and Orleans; they would suppose that probably some collector had the skeletons in his possession, and had lost them in that spot.

It is well known with what righteous indignation Goethe met this frivolity. "Voltaire," he says, "in order to injure the priests, could never sufficiently depreciate religion and the sacred books on which it is founded; and this had often made an unpleasant impression on me. But when I heard that, in order to weaken the tradition of a deluge, he denied the existence of petrified shells, and asserted that they were only *lusus naturæ*, I entirely lost all confidence in him; for it was perfectly evident to me when I was on the Baschberg that I was standing on an ancient sea-bed, and among the exuviæ of its former inhabitants. No doubt these mountains were once covered by waves, whether before or during the Deluge did not matter to me; it was enough that the valley of the Rhine had once been an immense sea, an immeasurable gulf; no one could persuade me that it was not the case."[1]

There was this much truth in the theory that the fossils were caused by the Deluge, namely, that they were found in connection with watery deposits. But as soon as the facts became more fully and completely

[1] *Aus Meinem Leben*, 11 B. (*Sämmtt. Werke*, Ausg. von 1840, xxii. 45).

known, it was found impossible, from a scientific point of view, to believe that the fossils could be traced back to the Deluge, or indeed to any one period. For they are found at a depth which could not have been touched by the flood which took place in the time of Noah, which, according to the Biblical account, only lasted for one year. Sometimes they are several hundred feet below the level of the sea; they are not found mixed up together as we should expect would be the case had they been deposited by the Deluge, but particular classes are usually found in particular strata. In one there are only sea animals and sea plants, in another land animals and land plants, and so on. They are found in strata which do not belong to the same period, but which must have been deposited one above the other at long intervals.[1] For these and other reasons, most of which were brought forward in 1517 by the Italian savant Fracastoro, whom I mentioned above, all men of science now assume that the greater part of the fossils at any rate are antediluvian, and that they were buried when the strata were formed, at a time much earlier than that of the Deluge, and even before the appearance of man. Some few ecclesiastical writers have tried, even in this century, to trace back all fossils to the Deluge;[2] but, in general, theologians agree with men of science in asserting the more

[1] Wiseman, *Connection*, etc., p. 276.
[2] This has been done by an Anglican clergyman, mentioned by H. Miller, *Testimony of the Rocks*, p. 389, and by Père Debrayne, *Theorie biblique*, pp. 231, 283. The latter "congratulates the (French) clergy—excepting some single misguided members, who, under the influence of the Academy, have defended contrary opinions—on having, as it were, instinctively held to the theory that all fossils were caused by the Deluge."

ancient origin of petrifactions, and are of opinion that neither the Biblical narrative of the Deluge nor any other Biblical statement is endangered by it.

But the knowledge of the nature and origin of fossils did not bring with it the recognition of their importance to science. They were generally considered simply as curiosities, as a plaything for idle people, and as a burden to mineralogists, who thought it was their duty to study them.[1] As late as 1763 the Frenchman Elie Bertrand published the following depreciatory remark in his geological dictionary: "There are many things in science which are only fit for amusement and curiosity. Fossils are among such things; they form the luxury of our science, and now-a-days luxury is everywhere. But we must be tolerant in order not to repel people who have money and leisure, and who would not become collectors of objects of natural science if they were not to possess some amusing curiosities among them."[2]

Time has changed all this. Palæontology, as it is now called, that is, the science of the organic beings belonging to the earlier periods of the earth's history, is now-a-days recognised as the most important helpmeet of geology. Fossils are used by geologists as the principal means of ascertaining the age and the order of the different strata in which they occur. I shall explain how and why in my next lecture. The English geologist Gideon Mantell called fossils the medals of creation because of this; for as medals are struck in

---

[1] Cf. "Die gegenwärtige Paleontologie," in Burmeister's *Geol. Bildern,* i. 289.

[2] *Dictionnaire oryctologique,* Discours prélim., p. 29.

order to hand down important events to posterity, so has nature given in the fossils a sign to geologists which enables them to estimate the comparative age of strata whose boundaries and order cannot be calculated with certainty from the condition of the rocks alone, whether they be of clay, chalk, or sand. A German savant—Naumann—has compared fossils to inscriptions, and says that as the Punic, Greek, or Roman inscriptions teach the antiquarian that monuments are Carthaginian, Greek, or Roman, so the geologist may ascertain from the presence of certain fossils at what period in the earth's history the separate strata were deposited. Without this aid, geology would not have been able in our time to ascertain accurately and surely so much about the history of the earth in the early ages, long before the beginning of man's history.

But palæontology has become important to natural science in another way also. It teaches us about plants and animals, which for the most part no longer exist, but which have existed, on the earth. The history of the present animal and vegetable world is supplemented by that of the flora and fauna of the primæval world; and natural history thus becomes complete, because it embraces the two great classes of organic beings, those which still exist and those which are extinct. Of course in many of the fossils, parts only of the plants and animals have been preserved, usually the harder, more solid parts; but science has been able by means of careful and comprehensive comparisons to reconstruct with tolerable accuracy the whole form of the animal or the plant, even from the scanty remains which are found.[1]

[1] Vogt, *Lehrb. der Geol.* ii. 604. Pfaff, *Schöpfungsgesch.* p. 615.

I may mention here [1] that one of the results of the more thorough investigations in this province has been to show how erroneous is the belief that the primæval fauna and flora differed generally from the present fauna and flora, in being of a gigantic and grotesque character. This was much insisted on formerly, and the theory may still be found in the popular expositions of some superficial writers, who prefer what is wonderful to what is true. No doubt primæval plants and animals of this description are found; but it is by no means generally or universally the case. Strange forms occur among the petrified remains; for instance, among the reptiles we find various saurians, or species of flying and swimming lizards, as the plesiosaurus and the pterodactylus; [2] and among the mammalia, the

[1] Cf. Wagner, *Gesch. der Urwelt*, i. 378; *Natur und Offenbarung*, iii. 462. Fraas, *Vor der Sündfluth*, p. 59. Giebel, *Tagesfragen*, p. 107, "Die Wunderthiere der Vorwelt."

[2] "As Cuvier said, the plesiosaurii are perhaps the most striking inhabitants of the earlier world. They possessed the head of a lizard and the teeth of a crocodile, an enormous serpent-like neck, the tail of an ordinary mammal, the ribs of a chameleon, and the webbed feet of a whale. The animal probably swam like a swan with its neck bent in the shape of an S, and lived on fish like the ichthyosaurus. We know this from the examination of the coprolites, which contain the scales and bones of fish which formed the food of these animals." Nöggerath, *Ges. Natura*, iii. 266. Fraas, p. 241. "It was formerly uncertain whether the pterodactylus was a mammal, a bird, or a reptile; now it is known to belong undoubtedly to the last class. The head is large, the mouth filled with long spiky teeth, the neck long and thick, the body short and weak, the shoulder-blades very strong, the forearm short and tolerably thick, the bone of the lower part of the arm more than twice as long as the upper bone. Attached to the former by some small metacarpal bones is the most extraordinary hand in the whole animal world; it consisted of four thin claw-like fingers, to which was added one enormously long, thick, sword-like finger, which alone was about as long as the neck and body put together." Nöggerath, p. 269. Fraas, p. 297. This finger was used for stretching out the bat-like skin, which, however, was not intended for flying, but as a kind of parachute when the animals, like our flying

dinotherium giganteum;[1] but strange forms exist also in the present day,—I may mention the ornithorhynchus, ant-eater, sloth, flying dragons, and as a rule they were just as rare formerly as they are now. The same holds good as to the size of the organisms. The present equisetaceæ or horsetails are usually hardly a foot, and at most four feet high, and they are about the thickness of one's thumb; and our lycopodiaceæ or mosses consist of tendrils with thin branching stems, which wind along the ground between the heather; now we find petrified equisetaceæ which are as thick as one's arm or leg, and lycopodiaceæ which were trees of a considerable size. But then we find nothing in the petrified plants corresponding to our oaks, palms, and other giant trees; there is no instance known in which a fossil tree of more than four feet in diameter has been found. And if we are told of the colossal ichthyosaurus, dinotherium, and others among the fossil animals,—the mammoth, or elephas primogenius, was not materially larger than the present Asiatic elephants,—we can show that our seas hide in their depths gigantic kinds of whales, which exceed

---

dragons, threw themselves from a height on to the ground or low branches of trees. The pterodactyls were *small* animals. Cf. Giebel, *Op. cit.* p. 117.

[1] It had, what is the case with no other animal, in the lower jaw two large teeth, bent downwards and backward. It is supposed that it lived mostly in island seas and rivers, that it dragged out the roots and plants from the bottom of the water with its tusks, and then conveyed the food to its mouth by means of the trunk We need not discuss whether, as some people think, it used the tusks as a weapon and also as an anchor; so that the animal could fasten itself to the shore by them while it floated on the water, and so sleep and breathe without danger, or could draw itself up on to the land with more ease. Cf. Nöggerath, p. 288. Of course the description of these animals given here rests partly on mere conjecture.

in size all the types of fossil fauna.¹ Generally speaking, although many of the giant forms of the primæval world do not exist in the present condition of things, yet their place has been filled by other gigantic shapes, so that the present state of nature is not inferior to the earlier state in respect to the size of the organic forms. On the other hand, animals of middle-sized and small, even microscopic dimensions are not wanting in the fossil fauna.²

[1] The mammoth (according to some the name is corrupted from the Behemoth of the Bible, according to others from the Russian " mammont ") did not exceed the largest living elephant in size; on the contrary, it had a smaller head, weaker chest bones, and shorter, thicker legs. When we are told that fossil tusks of 12 feet long and more are found, it must be remembered that the tusks of elephants grow on till the animal dies, no matter how great its age is; and as the mammoth was neither tamed nor hunted for the sake of ivory, it could grow on, and reach the advanced age which was natural to it much oftener than our elephants do. (Fraas, p. 410.) The body of the northern whale is sometimes 66 feet long, and at the fins reaches the immense size of 40 feet in circumference; the body of the sperm whale is sometimes 75 feet long and 38 feet round; and lastly, the fin-backed whale exceeds all other animals in length, and is 100 feet long by 10 round. We look in vain for these monsters of the deep in the earlier periods of creation. . . . The largest crocodiles are on an average 20 to 30 feet long. This was supposed to be too little for the fantastic giants of the primæval world. When the bones of the iguanodon were first found, its length was immediately reckoned to be 160 feet; R. Owen reduced it to 28 feet, of which 3 were for the head, 12 for the body, and 13 for the tail. The hylæosaurus and megalosaurus are often supposed to reach a length of from 60 to 80 feet; and the size and massive form of their separate bones astound all who are not familiar with their organization; but the massive form of a single bone does not determine the whole size of the body. Owen's trustworthy computation puts the length of the hylæosaurus at most at 25, and the megalosaurus at 30 feet. These are the most colossal land saurians; the longest ichthyosaurus did not attain to more than 30 feet. Giebel, *Op. cit.* p. 128. It is generally supposed that the dinotherium was from 18 to 20 feet long.

[2] I am able to refute the theory that the primæval world only produced gigantic animals, and that no vertebrate as small as the present ones existed, by adducing a species of sorex from the Molosse formation at Mainz, which is smaller than the smallest existing shrew mouse, and that is saying a great deal. H. v. Meyer, *Ueber die Reptilien*, etc., p. 111. Many deposits several hundred feet thick in the chalk strata have been

Yet one more question: Do fossil men, or remains of men, exist? If by fossils we mean the remains of organic beings which are found in a more or less altered condition in the strata of the earth's crust, this question must undoubtedly be answered in the affirmative. For human remains have been repeatedly found in the same place and in the same condition as the fossil bones of animals; for instance, a whole skeleton was found in a limestone stratum on the coast of Guadeloupe.[1] The formation of limestone strata is going on still, so that it does not follow that any deposit found in them is of ancient date; and in fact the fossil man of Guadeloupe has been proved to be at most a few centuries old.

But the word "fossil" often conveys to our minds another idea: the remains of plants and animals belonging to the primæval world are called fossils, in contradistinction to those of the present world, so that the bones of species of animals now existing, as, *e.g.*, the present races of dogs, sheep, and cattle, would not be called fossils, even if they were found petrified or buried in strata.[2] This strict distinction between the primæval and the present world is connected with the theory that the plants and animals which are supposed to belong to the earlier periods of the earth's history all

formed of the smaller shell animals, which are called foraminifera or polythalamaceæ; millions of their bodies were required in order to form one cubic foot of chalk. (Vogt, *Lehrb. der Geol.* i. 560.) In the limestone which is used for building in Paris, there are such enormous masses of foraminifera of the size of a grain of millet, that we may say that Paris is, in great part, built of these crustacea. (Wagner, *Gesch. der Urwelt*, ii. 510. Cf. Lyell, *Geology*, i. 35.)

[1] Leonhard, *Geologie*, iii. p. 520. Fraas, p. 448.

[2] Fraas, p. 450. Marcel de Serres suggests that the name "Humatiliæ" be used instead of fossils for petrifactions of this latter kind.

became extinct, or were destroyed by geological catastrophes, and that after a "*tabula rasa*," as it were, had thus been made on earth, the present vegetable and animal world was created. Thus fossil men would be primæval men, so that if it could be proved that these fossil men exist, it would follow that, in ancient times, the earth was inhabited by men, the so-called Pre-Adamites, who were not our ancestors, but who died out before our ancestors were created. But, as we shall see later, most modern geologists have given up the idea of a strict distinction in the sense that I have spoken of between the present and the primæval world. According to the theory which is gradually becoming established, some kinds of animals which exist now also existed in the earlier periods, and we are therefore not justified in assuming that a geological catastrophe took place, which destroyed the former animal and vegetable world, and preceded the creation of the present flora and fauna. Consequently there is no distinct boundary between the primæval and the present world in the sense that I have spoken of, and the idea of a primæval race of men falls to the ground. If the period before the first appearance of man on the earth is called the primæval age, of course there can be no question of primæval men; they would have been men existing before the first men.

If, therefore, we put aside the secondary meanings which have been attached to the word "fossil," and take it in its proper significance, we may speak quite unhesitatingly of fossil men; and if human remains are found in any deposits, or caverns, or anywhere, the question is not whether these remains are fossils, but whether their age can be ascertained.

I shall have to enter fully into this question later. At present let us put aside human fossils, and let us look back at the history of fossils in general. What a change has taken place in the views of men of science during the course of not quite four centuries! The things which were formerly looked upon as strange *lusûs naturæ*, fit subjects for a collection of curiosities, now take a prominent position in geology as medals of creation; and in scientific zoology and botany, as the remains of extinct organic species. We can hardly understand now how such erroneous ideas can have prevailed on this subject in former times; and yet those who held those views were learned men, of great scientific merit, who were as firmly persuaded of the correctness of the theories which are now recognised as erroneous, as are the scientific men of the present day of the truth of their views. This brings the progress of science vividly before us, but it also shows us how imperfect and uncertain is all human knowledge; for although the scientific views of the past are now corrected, who will guarantee that the further progress of research may not prove that much which we now think that we know concerning the things of nature is false; and that in a hundred years' time, many of the views held by the greatest geologists of the present day will not meet with the pitying smile which we now bestow on the geological theories of the 17th century? Quenstedt's striking words can be again applied here: "No doubt the natural sciences may boast now-a-days of knowing some superficial things with certainty, nevertheless even this knowledge has been obtained only by an erroneous system. For if the beliefs which are held to be undoubted by one generation are immediately put aside by the next as false, the discreet observer will not fail to remark it. They are only human opinions, which appear in a new light as soon as new points of view have been opened out by the progress of science."[1] That all our knowledge is fragmentary is true also of natural science.

The history of palæontology contains an important lesson for theologians also. It was hasty to assert that because all fossils were caused by the Deluge, their existence was to be considered as a proof of the truth of the Biblical narrative, and, like Scheuchzer, to unite theology and natural science in a close alliance; the alliance could not last, for it was founded on an error. Since then theologians have perceived that it is far better to take up a position of reserve as regards natural science, and not to mix up theological and scientific matters, but to content themselves with proving that the results of scientific inquiry do not contradict the Bible and religion; a thing which is easily accomplished, and is quite sufficient for the dignity of revelation.

The immediate points of contact between Biblical theology and palæontology are not—as I shall point out in my next lecture—such as to make a hostile collision between them probable. Indirectly, however, the further development of this science, as of all sciences, has its importance for religion. The great English geologist, Sir Charles Lyell, says: "The proofs now accumulated of the close analogy between extinct

[1] *Sonst und Jetzt*, p. 280.

and recent species are such as to leave no doubt on the mind that the same harmony of parts and beauty of contrivance which we admire in the living creation, has equally characterized the organic world at remote periods. Thus as we increase our knowledge of the inexhaustible variety displayed in living nature, and admire the infinite wisdom and power which it displays, our admiration is multiplied by the reflection that it is only the last of a great series of pre-existing creations, of which we cannot estimate the number or limit in times past."[1]

To this I have only one thing to add. All that we now—thanks to the discoveries of astronomers—know of the wonders of the starry heavens, is much more fitted to give us an idea of His grandeur whose glories the heavens declare, than was the scanty and limited knowledge of our forefathers; and in the same way our knowledge of the animal and vegetable world which clothed and peopled our earth in the primæval age, if it is extended and made definite by the progress of palæontology, will make the might, wisdom, and goodness of the Creator more overpoweringly evident to us than can be done by the existing creation.

[1] *Elements of Geology,* p. 772.

XV.

THE PALÆONTOLOGICAL HISTORY OF THE EARTH

BEFORE I can discuss the relation of those results of geological inquiry which deal principally with palæontology, to the Mosaic account of creation, I must enter more fully into certain points which were only touched upon in my last lecture; and this in order to facilitate the review of the whole subject. The first of these is the use of fossils in determining the limits of the separate formations of the earth's crust, and their relation to each other.

I have already discussed the general division of rocks into stratified and unstratified, and I have told you that no fossils are found in the latter. The great mass of unstratified rocks which underlie the stratified rocks are supposed to be the oldest portions of the earth's surface, and these rocks are therefore called primitive. It is commonly supposed by geologists that the stratified rocks which are found in parallel layers, superposed above them, were gradually deposited by water. Werner called this part of the earth's surface the *sedimentary* rocks, in contradistinction to the primitive rocks which are always found below them, and to the alluvial soil which is always found above them. The lowest rocks, *i.e.* those sedimentary rocks which lie next to the primitive rocks, he called *transition*, and he divided the other sedimentary rocks into the *older, middle,* and *recent* formations. In other countries the rocks lying on the primitive rocks, were divided into three groups; the transition rocks, with one or two of the formations lying nearest to them, were called *primary,* the greater portion of the sedimentary rocks *secondary,* and the strata nearest the surface *tertiary* rocks. For the present I may omit other names and divisions. But each of these principal divisions contains several different sub-divisions or strata, which are called by different names, partly from their constituent parts, as coal formation, chalk formation, etc., Lias, the English name for a kind of limestone, the Triassic formation, because it always consists of three component parts, keuper, muschelkalk, and red sandstone or bunter sandstein; partly from the places in which they are found, as, for instance, the Silurian formation, which is named from the district in the West of England which the Silures are supposed to have inhabited in the time of the Romans, the Devonian formation, so called from Devonshire, Permian formation, from the Russian province Perm, Jurassic formation, from the Swiss and French mountain Jura, and so on.

One of the principal tasks of geology was, first to define the limits of the separate formations, and then to determine their relative age; and also, especially, to discover which different strata are parallel to each other in different regions, that is, probably belong to the same period. In order to accomplish this, it was first necessary to ascertain the materials of which they were composed, and the order in which they were deposited; afterwards the fossils occurring in them were examined, and of late this last point has been specially and almost exclusively considered.[1]

In the course of these researches places were observed in which several strata were found resting on each other, without any evidence that a disturbance of the original order of deposit had taken place. In such cases the lower rocks must of course be considered as the older, and those nearer the surface as the more recent rocks. When the fossils contained in the separate strata were examined, it was found that certain fossils were peculiar to certain strata, that they were found only in one particular stratum, not in one above or below it, not in an older or a newer one. This was observed in several places, where a clear and undisturbed succession of strata existed. A series of such observations proved that certain fossils were characteristic of certain strata, and that the relative ages of the strata in question could be ascertained from the presence of these fossils. In one place, *e.g.*, three strata were found superposed, and each contained certain characteristic fossils; we will call them A B C, beginning from the lowest. In another place the same group was found in the same order; in a third there was one stratum above them, D; in a fourth the lowest stratum was missing, but B C D were found in the same order; in a fifth A C D, etc. Supposing that all the strata

---

[1] Zittel, *Aus der Urzeit*, p. 53. The first person who made use of fossils for this purpose (about 1800) was William Smith, "the father of English geology," also called Stratum-Smith. See H. Miller, *Testimony of the Rocks*, p. 119. J. P. Smith, *The Relation*, p. 55. Cotta, *Geologie der Gegenwart*, p. 37. Peschel, *Gesch. der Erdkunde*, p. 621. Zittel in the *Historischer Taschenb.* p. 162.

which exist, and which are characterized by possessing peculiar fossils, were named after the different letters of the alphabet, we should, no doubt, never find the whole series from A to Z together anywhere; generally there are only a few letters, as, for instance, in one place we find A B E F, with C and D wanting; in another B D E, with A and C wanting, but never A B D C, so that D is found under instead of above C. Those fossils which are common to certain strata in different regions, and are also peculiar to those strata, never occurring in earlier or in later ones, and which are therefore characteristic of the formation in which they are found, are called guiding fossils or shells, because they guide geologists in classing the formations in which they are found.

After this law had been confirmed by numerous observations in places where the succession of the strata is undisturbed, geologists were justified in applying it to those places in which the geognostic conditions were not so simple and clear; and thus in making use of the fossils, as I pointed out in my last lecture, as medals or inscriptions in the strata of the earth's crust. We are enabled thus by the help of the fossils to ascertain with tolerable certainty the simultaneous origin or comparative age of deposits which occur at considerable distances from each other, and which are of different mineral composition. Only, in making these calculations, it must not be forgotten that probably fresh water as well as sea water was always in existence, so that the deposits which contain the remains of animals living on the land, or in fresh water, must be distinguished from contemporary sea deposits; and that therefore formations containing land and fresh water fossils must be compared with one another, and the same with formations containing sea fossils.[1]

The employment of fossils as a means of geological calculation is, as has been observed,[2] quite as justifiable as the mode of proceeding which obtains in other provinces of human knowledge, *e.g.* in the history of architecture. Monuments which are historically well authenticated are the foundation for researches into this branch of knowledge. From these the art historian collects the special characteristics of a particular style or period, round arches, pointed arches, for instance, and so on, and from the presence of these characteristics he draws inferences concerning the date of those monuments, which are not historically authenticated. Surely we may say that a rule drawn from the works of man is less certain than one drawn from the works of nature.

No doubt in many cases great difficulties attend the application of this rule in geology. It is often difficult, sometimes impossible, to define the boundary between two superimposed strata; we find strata which in some localities appear to belong to the lower, in others to the upper formation, and which are therefore sometimes ascribed to one and sometimes to the other.[3] It is often still more difficult to decide which strata in different countries are to be considered as parallel or equivalent to each other, and ought therefore to be ascribed to the same period. It is true that in every

---

[1] Cotta, *Geol. Bilder*, p. 185. Pfaff, *Schöpfungsgesch.* p. 5.
[2] J. Probst in the *Tübingen Quartalschr.* 1866, p. 140.
[3] Vogt, *Lehrb. der Geologie*, ii. p. 390.

case in which the older formations have been examined, the fossils have been found to be practically similar; but in the more recent formations they afford very few points of comparison in the different localities; sometimes the separate strata are even found in quite a different order in different regions.[1] But, on the whole, the following arrangement of the strata may, according to the unanimous opinion of all modern geologists, be considered as correct.

The first class comprises the lowest rocks, those resting immediately on the primitive rocks, gneiss, mica schist, and chlorite slate, in which no fossils are found, and which, it is therefore supposed, were deposited at a time when there were no organic beings on the earth; these formations are therefore called those of the *Azoic* period. The fossiliferous strata are denominated those of the *Palæozoic, Mesozoic,* and *Cainozoic* Ages—that is, formations belonging to the older, middle, and modern periods of organic life on the earth. (These four periods are also called the Archæolithic, Palæolithic, Mesolithic, and Cainolithic.) The formations made from deposits in the historical period may be reckoned as a fifth class, those of the Recent Age; they include coral islands, river deltas, sand hills, deposits of calc-sinter, turf beds, etc.[2]

---

[1] Vogt, *Op. cit.* i. p. 561.
[2] The following list of the stratified formations may be useful in showing the different names :—

I. Azoic Period (1, 2).	Mica Schist. 1. Gneiss (Laurentian System). 2. Chlorite Schist (Huronian System), (Cambrian System).	A. Transition Rocks (1–4).

As the animals and plants whose remains are found in the strata of the separate systems must have lived on the earth before these strata were formed, we can obtain an approximate idea of the fauna and flora which belonged to the separate periods of the earth's history; it can only be approximate, not accurate, first because we do not know all the fossils which exist, and then because it does not follow that traces remain of all the organisms which existed. This much is certain, that the organic life on the earth has not always been the same; no trace is found in the later formations of

II. PALÆOZOIC PERIOD (3-6).	3. Silurian System. 4. Devonian System (Old Red Sandstone). 5. Carboniferous System. 6. Permian System.	B. Sedimentary Rocks (5-9).
III. MESOZOIC PERIOD (7-9).	7. Triassic System (Bunter sandstein, muschelkalk, keuper). 8. Oolitic System. (Jura Limestone, Oolite Lias). 9. Cretaceous System.	
IV. CAINOZOIC PERIOD (10-13).	10. Eocene Series. 11. Miocene Series. 12. Pliocene Series. 13. Pleistocene Series.	C. Tertiary Rocks (10-12).
		D. Diluvium or Quaternary Formations.
V. RECENT PERIOD.		E. Alluvium.

Lyell, by whom the name "Eocene," etc., was introduced, has modified this division in the following way: he includes the eocene, miocene, and pliocene series in the Tertiary or Cainozoic period; and he calls everything more recent than the pliocene, post-tertiary. He then divides these post-tertiary formations into post-pliocene and recent. He calls those strata recent whose fossils, shells as well as mammals, belong to the still existing species; on the other hand, he calls those deposits, in which the shells belong to existing, but the mammals for the most part to extinct species, post-pliocene. Others call the lowest strata of the miocene, "oligocene;" others, everything which lies above the eocene, "neocene," or "neogene."

several of the organisms belonging to the older formations; they must therefore have died out in the earlier period. Again, there is no trace in the earlier formations of several of the organisms belonging to the later formations, therefore they cannot have existed in the earlier period. Geological research will not justify us in assuming anything beyond this general rule. Many of the details are uncertain and disputed. Some geologists say, for instance, that every formation has its separate fauna and flora, and that the same kind of animal or plant is never, or very rarely, found in two succeeding formations; and that it must therefore be assumed that in the course of ages organic life repeatedly became extinct on the earth, and was again restored.[1] Others maintain that since the first appearance of organic beings, single species have now and then become extinct, and others have come into existence, but that such gradual transformation of organic life was caused by the existence and filling up of gaps, and that the thread was never entirely broken.[2] More recently a theory, which we shall discuss at length later on, has been much in favour, namely, that all the later plants and animals, including all at present existing, are descended from those of the earliest period, so that it is not possible to classify the fauna and flora as belonging specially to separate periods.[3]

In comparing with one another the forms of plants and animals belonging to different periods, as we get to

---

[1] Cuvier, A. Brongniart, A. d'Orbigny, Agassiz (cf. *Les animaux et les plantes aux époques géologiques*, in the *Revue des Cours Scientifiques*, Paris 1868, No. 49 seq.), Murchison (*Siluria*, p. 461), and others.

[2] Prevost, de Blainville, Schlotheim, Bronn, and others.

[3] Cf. Zittel in the *Historisch Taschenb.* p. 167.

know them by means of the fossils, we find that the earliest differ most, and the later ones least, from the present fauna and flora. Speaking generally, therefore, we may assume that a development of plants and animals from more imperfect to more perfect forms has taken place, however that development may be explained. The earliest formations contain scarcely any but the remains of creatures of a low organization; flowerless plants, corals, molluscs, and articulata. There are very few signs of fish and reptiles, and as far as is known at present, no signs of birds or mammals. In the succeeding strata more highly organized plants and animals are found; in the Carboniferous period there are some conifers, many fish, a few reptiles; in the Triassic period, many reptiles, a few birds, and mammals; in the Oolitic period, a few dicotyledon plants and more mammals; and in the Tertiary period, many dicotyledon plants and mammals. In all cases the lower organisms of the great separate divisions of the animal and vegetable worlds appear first, and the higher organisms later. Thus, of the radiata, the crinoideæ appeared first; of the fish, first the tailed ganoid and the placoid; of the reptiles, the saurians; of the birds, first the marsh birds and tufted birds; of the mammals, the opossums and cetacea. The organic forms differ most from those now existing in the earliest strata, and the difference diminishes steadily all through the more recent deposits. Some of the animals and plants in the older formations belong to *classes* which are quite extinct; later they differ from those now existing in *genus* only; later still only in *species*. Some still existing kinds of larger animals appear first as fossils after the chalk formation, and they increase in number gradually during the Tertiary period.[1]

It is no doubt unsafe to draw conclusions as to the nature of the fauna and flora of the separate periods from the fossils which are found in the separate strata; for, on the one hand, as I have already observed, those fossils which have been preserved are not yet thoroughly known; and, on the other hand, many organisms which may have existed were either not of a kind to be petrified,—as fungi, slugs, etc., which are entirely wanting in hardness,—or could not be petrified because they existed on land, on high mountains, or in the air.[2] Many geologists have not noticed these facts, and have hastily set up systems of the history of organic beings which later discoveries have shown to be false. It was formerly thought that land animals and land plants had appeared first in the Carboniferous period; since then they have been found in the earlier Devonian system. Before the year 1824, many persons thought there could be no doubt that reptiles first existed in the Permian period; in the course of ten years it had been proved that they existed in the Carboniferous age, and even before that time. Before the year 1818 every one thought that the earliest remains of warm-blooded animals occurred in strata of the Cainozoic period; since then they have been found in the Oolitic, and

---

[1] See Cotta, *Geol. Bilder*, p. 284. Cf. Pfaff, *Grundriss*, p. 380.

[2] *Vestiges of the Natural History of Creation*. It is supposed that the Telerpeton Elginense—a lizard-like reptile—is a land animal; cf. Murchison, *Siluria*, p. 254. Lyell, *Elements of Geology*, p. 533. Latterly, however, it has been decided that the sandstone in which it was found belongs to the Triassic system (New Red Sandstone), and not to the Devonian system (Old Red Sandstone). *Athenæum*, 1863, Jan. 31, p. 153. Cf. *Ausland*, 1863, pp. 144, 192.

even in the Triassic systems, that is to say, in the Mesozoic period. It is because of this that Lyell asserts[1] his conviction that in some ways science is only on the threshold of discovery as to the order in which the separate classes of organisms appear in the strata; and that in the second half of the century, as in the first, it will repeatedly find itself compelled to modify its previous theories.

We may also derive a good deal of information about the condition of the earth's surface in the earlier periods, about the distribution of land and water, climate, and so on, from the position and nature of the separate strata and from their organic contents; but this information must be very untrustworthy on account of the incompleteness and uncertainty of the materials on which the premises are founded. The maps which have been drawn of different parts of the earth's surface, as it appeared in the earlier periods, must in many cases be considered as merely hypothetical sketches,[2] and fancy has more part than science

[1] Lyell, *Elements of Geology*, ii. Fraas, *Vor der Sündfluth*, pp. 214, 255. The common theory, which rested principally on Murchison's investigations (*Siluria*, pp. 21, 469), that the Silurian system contains the remains of the first existing organisms, has also been attacked in recent years. It was supposed in 1864 that a gigantic extinct species of foraminifera, which was named Eozoon Canadense, had been discovered in Canada in the Laurentian strata, which are thought to be older than the oldest Silurian strata, and also in the gneiss of the Bohemian Forest, in Scotland, and in Sweden. See Lyell, *Athenæum*, 1864, Sept. 17. Murchison, *Athenæum*, 1865, Sept. 16. Dawson, *The Dawn of Life*; cf. his *Nature and the Bible* (Germ. tr. *Gütersloh*, 1877). But the organic nature of this fossil is denied on good grounds by others. Cf. Ferd. Römer, *Ueber die ältesten Formen des organischen Lebens auf der Erde*, Berlin 1869, p. 34. Pfaff, *Grundriss*, p. 224.

[2] See Huxley's remark above, p. 56. Cf. S. Zaddach, *Die ältere Tertiärzeit ein Bild aus der Entwicklungsgeschichte der Erde*, Berlin 1869. G. Berendt, *Geognostische Blicke in alt-Preussen's Urzeit*, Berlin 1872.

in the descriptions and pictures of primæval landscapes which are found in the popular expositions of geology written by Cotta, Fraas, and others.[1] The opposition between the "Quietists" and "Convulsionists," which I mentioned above, is specially marked in the discussion as to the manner in which the fossiliferous strata were formed. Some assume that the strata were all formed just as strata of mud and sand are formed now; while others think that unusual catastrophes produced wide effects. Probably both methods of formation took place; it is not necessary to decide which had the greater result.

The animals which were attached to the ground—banks of shells, for instance—were destroyed by the gradual deposit of the surrounding strata. In other cases, sudden events, such as changes in the sea-level, escapes of gases, etc., seem to have killed masses of animals. A volcanic outburst in the middle of the sea, which was recently observed near Sicily, killed an immense number of sea-animals all round it. Similar events no doubt caused the destruction of the animals which we find petrified in masses, although they were easily able to move away, and thus escape. Buckland observes, speaking of a discovery of fossil fish: "The circumstances under which the fossil fishes are found at Monte Baldo seem to indicate that they perished suddenly on arriving at a part of the then existing seas, which was rendered noxious by the volcanic agency, of which the adjacent basaltic rocks afford abundant evidence. The skeletons of these fish lie parallel to the laminæ of the strata of the calcareous slate; they

[1] Cf. Cotta, *Geol. Bilder*, p. 257.

are always entire, and so closely packed on one another, that many individuals are often contained in a single block. . . . All these fishes must have died suddenly on this fatal spot, and have been speedily buried in the calcareous sediment then in the course of deposition. From the fact that certain individuals have even preserved traces of colour upon their skin, we are certain that they were entombed before decomposition of their soft parts had taken place. . . . In the same manner also we may imagine deposits from muddy water, mixed perhaps with noxious gases, to have formed by their sediments a succession of thick beds of marl and clay, . . . and at the same time to have destroyed, not only the testacea and lower orders of animals inhabiting the bottom, but also the higher orders of marine creatures within the regions thus invaded."[1]

Most of the plants which are found petrified in the coal measures are land plants, especially tree-like ferns, and trees which existed between these and pines. These plants seem to have been partly torn from the then existing woods by floods, and to have been collected together at the bottom of lakes, rivers, and in seas or in narrow gulfs, and then transformed into coal. Probably most of the beds of coal were formed on the spot where the trees and plants had grown; the vegetation first passed into the condition of a peat moss, was then flooded by the sea in consequence of the sinking of the land, and was covered with a layer of mud and sand; by a subsequent elevation the mud was converted into dry land, and was fitted to produce a new forest, which then

[1] *Geology and Mineralogy*, etc., pp. 123, 124.

in process of time again became a peat moss. By the recurrence of this process the alternate layers of coal, sandstone, and slate were formed, which constitute the strata of the Carboniferous period.[1]

Our ideas as to the method in which the formation of the strata took place will influence our estimate of the period of time which elapsed during that formation. Geologists are unanimous—with a few unimportant exceptions—in saying that a very long time must have elapsed before all the strata, many of which are in places several thousand feet thick, attained their present form. I quote a few of the calculations which have been made on points of detail, partly in order to show you in some measure what a "very long time" means, and partly to prove how uncertain any attempt to express this very long time in figures must be. The time which elapsed between the beginning of the carboniferous age, which only constitutes one of the divisions of the Palæozoic period, and the recent period, is supposed by Arago to have been 313,600 years; G. Bischof estimates it at 1,300,000 years in one passage, and in another says it may have been 9 millions of years.[2] Quenstedt makes the following calculation:[3] "In order to form the Saarbrück coal-beds, which are 400 feet thick, a mountain of wood 2400 feet high would have been needed, supposing them to have been formed of vegetable matter. Now we know that our forests hardly produce a layer of

---

[1] Pfaff, *Grundriss*, p. 270 seq. Cotta, *Geol. Bilder*, p. 240 seq. Bischof, *Lehrb*. etc. (1st ed.), ii. 1814 (2nd ed. i. 745).

[2] Burmeister, *Geschichte der Schöpfung*. p. 135.

[3] *Sonst und Jetzt*, p. 170.

wood two inches thick in 100 years; therefore a mass of wood such as I have spoken of would take at least 1½ million years to grow, and a corresponding time to be turned into coal.[1] It is of course probable that the growth of the primæval flora was much quicker than that of the present, and the process of carbonization may have been much more rapid in the primæval ages than is possible under present circumstance; but the intermediate strata in which the coal is imbedded must also be considered. Herodotus had heard from the Egyptian priests that the mud-beds formed by the Nile below Memphis hardly increased by a yard in 100 years; recent investigations have shown that the increase is only from three to four inches. Now as the bed of the coal, slate clay, is one of the finest mud deposits known, the deposit of this stratum seems to require periods of time which it makes us giddy to think of. The time it must have taken to form one single stratum seems to us simply infinite; if we reckon it according to ordinary rules, what then must have been the total of the whole?" And now take the opinions of some other geologists. "It would not be too much to suppose that millions of years must have been required to form the different series of strata which we find in the mountains containing coal. But we must remember that the data on which these calculations are founded are taken from our climate, and that with unusually luxuriant vegetation, such as must necessarily have existed during the coal period, the

[1] Bischof, *Lehrb.* etc., 2nd ed. i. 746, calculates that the vegetation which produced the material for the Saarbrück coal measures must have taken 1,004,177 years in growing, he adds, however, "according to another estimate, 672,788 years would have been required."

production of carbon by means of the carbonic acid in the atmosphere must have been very much greater." [1] But as geologists are always referring to the long periods which must have elapsed during the formation of strata as if they had proved the existence of those periods with mathematical certainty, I may in opposition to their exaggerations quote an observation which Göppert makes when discussing the transformation of vegetable matter into coal by means of damp: "No one can calculate even approximately in how long a period all these formations took place. I have seen vegetable matter changed into peat in a year and three-quarters by immersion in water which was nearly boiling, and cloth which was exposed to steam changed into shiny black coal in six years; and I venture to remind those who think to lend a greater interest to their geological statements by talking of millions or billions of years, of these long since acknowledged facts." [2] "We cannot decide how long a time was required for the deposit of a stratum of a certain thickness. If we would calculate it according to the rate at which strata are now formed at the bottom of the sea, it must have taken thousands of years to form a stratum a foot thick. But this mode of calculation seems to be extremely uncertain, as on the one hand accurate measurements are still wanting, and on the other local circumstances exert the

---

[1] Vogt, *Lehrb. der Geol.* ii. 311.

[2] Wagner, *Geschichte der Urwelt*, ii. 561. According to an account in the *Köln. Zeitung* for Aug. 18, 1874, some pieces of wood which had been nailed together, and were at most 400 years old, were found in a mine near Clausthal completely changed, not only outside, but also inside, into peat, which contained considerably more carbon than do most recent peat beds.

greatest influence on the rate of the formation of strata." [1]

We can therefore only estimate with any certainty the relative, not the absolute age of the separate strata; that is to say, we can ascertain the place of a stratum in the whole series of stratified formations, and decide whether it is older or more recent than another; but we cannot say how much time has elapsed between the beginning or the end of the formation of that stratum and the present time. At any rate we cannot give it in numbers, not even in round numbers; but unless geologists are wholly wrong, we must assume that very long periods of time have elapsed since the first appearance of animals and plants on the earth.

I have thought it necessary to put together so much of the teaching of modern geologists, in order to be able to compare the Biblical narrative with what are, or are said to be, the results of palæontological inquiry; for it will, I hope, be clear to you from the description I have given that all that is asserted is not absolutely proved.

[1] Vogt, *Lehrb. der Geol.* ii. 337.

XVI.

GEOLOGY AND THE BIBLE ACCORDING TO THE LITERAL INTERPRETATION OF THE SIX DAYS.

I HAVE already observed in a former lecture[1] that it is not necessary in the present day to refute the theory that all fossils were caused by the Deluge. But still I must examine thoroughly an attempted reconciliation, which rests more than any other on that theory, between the results of palæontology and the statements of the Bible. In addition to the theory that only six actual days elapsed between the first act of divine creation and the creation of man, the following opinion is held by several modern savants, and in Germany especially by Keil,[2] Veith, and Bosizio. They believe that all kinds of plants were created on the third day, all kinds of animals on the fifth and sixth days of the week of

[1] Lecture XIV.
[2] *Genesis*, p. 9. *Zeitschr. für luth. Theol.* 1861, p. 689. I could not obtain Keil's treatise on *Die biblische Schöpfungsgeschichte und die geologischen Erdbildungstheorieen*, which was published in the *Theol. Zeitschr. Dieckhoff und Kliefoth*, 1860, p. 479. This theory has also been supported by Sorignet and C. B., *Geology*, etc., and others (cf. Zöckler, *Gesch. der Beziehungen*, ii. 470); and by the Capucin P. Laurent, *Etudes géologiques, philologiques et scripturales sur la Cosmogonie de Moïse*, Paris 1863 (cf. *Revue des sciences eccl.* 1864, p. 334), by V. M. Gatti, a Roman Dominican monk (*Institutiones apologetico-polemicæ*, etc., Rome 1867; cf. *Revue cath.* 1870, t. 4, p. 198), and by the Abbe H. Rault, *Cours élémentaire d'écriture sainte*, Paris 1871, i. p. 143; see *Theol. Lit.-Bl.* 1872, p. 545. Baltzer criticizes the arguments put forward by Keil, Bosizio, and Veith in his *Bibl. Schöpfungsgeschichte*, p. 202 seq.

creation. The fossils, therefore, are all remains of the plants and animals which have existed since the creation of man, and the formation of all fossiliferous strata must be traced to geological events and catastrophes which have occurred since the Fall. The Deluge was one of the principal causes, and the theory that the Deluge was the original cause of all the fossils was only incorrect because it did not take into account the catastrophes which occurred before and after the Deluge, and the regular geological developments which have taken place since the time of the creation.[1] All that geologists say about the different flora and fauna of different periods is mere fancy; only one kind of fauna and flora has existed, that created in the week of creation. The fossil plants and animals may be included in the classes and orders of the present creation. No doubt the vegetable and animal world is not quite the same as it was in the beginning; many kinds and species died out in ancient times, and are only known to us by the fossils. The fact that fossil remains of existing species have not been found mingled with the fossil remains of extinct kinds and species in many strata, is due partly to the imperfection of our knowledge of the earth's crust, and partly to accident. Men of science have not yet decided, however, whether the species of plants and animals are capable of change, and how far this is the case; it is at any rate possible that the ancestors of our animals and plants were the very fossil animals and plants which palæontologists believe to have belonged to different species.

[1] Veith, *Die Anfänge*, pp. 101, 351, 353 seq. *Prophezie und Glaube*, p. 33 seq. Bosizio, *Das Hexæmeron*, p. 328.

The formation of species is still a secret to us, and recently Darwin and others have tried to prove that species are not created and unchangeable, but derived and changeable.[1] The fact that no fossil remains of human beings have been found in the older strata does not prove that when those strata were formed no human beings existed; for the crust of the earth has not been by any means thoroughly examined, and the interior of Asia, man's first dwelling-place, has not been touched. Thirty years ago Cuvier laid stress on the fact that no fossil apes had been found; since then apes belonging to still existing species have been found in the tertiary formation. It is therefore very possible that remains of men, which have been already found in the so-called Cainozoic period, may be discovered in strata which geologists assign to the Mesozoic and Palæozoic periods, and this would furnish a proof that these strata also were deposited at a time when the whole creation was completed and the race of Adam walked on earth.[2]

There is, from the exegetical point of view, just as little objection to be made to this theory as to that of the literal interpretation of the six days. Nor would it be right to oppose to this theory the fact that in its account of the earlier history of mankind the Bible mentions no geological catastrophe but the Deluge. There was no reason why such catastrophes should be mentioned unless they had stood in the same

---

[1] This Darwinian argument of Keil's was first adopted by Veith (*Die Anfänge*, etc., p. 364), but he gave it up again afterwards (*Prophezie und Glaube*, p. 20).

[2] Keil, see *Zeitschr. f. luth. Theol.* 1861. Veith, *Die Anfänge*, etc., p. 364. Bosizio, pp. 94, 453.

direct relation to man as did the flood in the days of Noah. The only question which must be considered in examining this theory is the following, Can it be brought into harmony with the assured results of geological, and especially of palæontological inquiry? And I may at once state my conviction that this question must be answered decidedly in the negative. I need not show you at length that it hopelessly contradicts all that I have described in my last lecture as the teaching of modern geologists; the only question is, which of the two is erroneous and must be given up, the interpretation of the first chapter of Genesis as given by those theologians, or the history of the palæontological periods as it is represented by nearly all modern geologists. Of course, if one of the doctrines of divine revelation were in question, there could be no doubt that a true Christian must believe it under any circumstances, but this is not a question of revealed doctrine, but only of the interpretation of a passage in Holy Scripture which some theologians believe to be correct, but which is only one of several interpretations, all, as I have already proved, theologically admissible. Theologically, therefore, we are quite unfettered in the question which is now before us; we need not say, nay we must not say, that the teaching of palæontology is false because it contradicts the first chapter in Genesis, we must say rather, that if the teaching of palæontology is right in the main, the literal interpretation of the six days is wrong; it must therefore be given up, and one of the other interpretations which have been shown to be exegetically admissible must be adopted. This no doubt is the point at which we must decide whether the literal theory is tenable or not, for hitherto our comparison of the Hexæmeron with the results of scientific inquiry has not shown that it is untenable.

I have intentionally once more laid stress on the fact that as exegetes or theologians we are not compelled to insist on this interpretation. We must remember this in order that we may remain quite unprejudiced in our examination of the question before us. As theologians we are not obliged to prove that the palæontological theories are untenable in order to defend the truth of the Biblical statements, but we are obliged to prove that the Biblical statements, rightly understood, do not contradict the assured results of palæontological inquiry; in order to attain this object we must first ascertain what the Biblical narrative, which is undoubtedly true, really does mean, and as we have recognised several interpretations as admissible from a theological point of view, we must inquire in the second place which of these interpretations are found to be tenable, and which untenable, when they are compared with the assured results of palæontological inquiry. We shall therefore have done all that is necessary apologetically, if we can prove that at least one of the interpretations of the Hexæmeron which are theologically admissible, is compatible with the approved teaching of palæontology.

The most decided supporter of the theory which has just been mentioned above, the Jesuit Bosizio, has himself, although without intending it, pronounced its severest condemnation as a justification of the Mosaic account of creation. He says quite rightly, that nothing is gained in the endeavour to smooth away the apparent contradiction between theology and geology, unless the theory set up by theologians is acknowledged to be admissible by all geologists, or at least by all the leaders in this science.[1] It is true that he only sets up this rule in order to prove that its conditions are not fulfilled in the case of another attempt to reconcile the Bible and science. But what is true of one is true of the other; "nothing is gained" by Bosizio's attempt at reconciliation, if it is not recognised as admissible by all, or at any rate by the most eminent geologists. And he must admit that this is not the case. He mentions the following savants who support his theory; first Leibnitz, then Nikolaus Steno and Scheuchzer, who both lived in the 17th century (I have already spoken of the latter); and in order to meet the objection that "these learned men lived and wrote in a time when there was very little geognostical or palæontological knowledge," he brings forward "one of our most modern men, of great merit in all geognostical and palæontological inquiry," in the person of the Petersburg professor, Stephen Kutorga.[2] But the fact that this geologist—for Bosizio mentions no other—supports his theory does not justify him in asserting that "the theory has been recognised by learned savants in modern times;" and although Kutorga propounded

---

[1] *Das Hexæmeron*, p. 129.

[2] The work so often and so emphatically quoted by Bosizio (see pp. 264 seq., 277 seq., 327, 332 seq., 408, 453) is a little pamphlet of 25 pages 8vo: *Einige Worte gegen die Theorie der stufenwiese Entstehung der organischen Wesen auf der Erde*, by Dr. Stephen Kutorga, Prof., etc., Bonn, Konig 1839.

his theory in an assembly of savants (at Bern in 1839), and assured them "that it was not the desire of novelty, but an earnest and continuous study of nature, which had gradually called forth this idea in him," yet again Bosizio is not justified in laying stress on the fact that his theory "was not rejected by an assembly of savants, but, on the contrary, was propounded and justified as the result of continuous and earnest geological study, free from preconceived theories." I do not indeed know what judgment the assembly in question passed on Kutorga's theory; he himself declared his belief that savants would rather oppose than support it; and as far as I can judge from my knowledge of modern scientific literature, he stands pretty well alone in his opinion.[1]

If, then, we wished to retain the theory in question, we should have to say that although the geological conclusions which are believed to be certain by the most eminent geologists of the present time contradict our interpretation of the Hexæmeron, yet we may expect that the further progress of geological inquiry will prove that what is now regarded as correct is erroneous, and will lead to conclusions which are in harmony with our interpretation of the Hexæmeron. But, as you will easily see, this is rather a dangerous position for the Biblical apologist, and he should only have recourse to it in cases when the expressions in

---

[1] Bosizio might also have quoted Count Franz v. Marenzi, who expresses himself to the same effect about palæontology in his book, *Zwölf Fragmente über Geologie* (3rd ed., Trieste 1865); but this writer calls himself an unlearned person, and in a supplement to his book he calculates that the "age of the earth" is 8, 10, or 12,000 years; "of which figures everybody is free to choose the one he likes best."

the Bible are so unequivocal that it is not possible to explain the words so as to bring them into harmony with the prevailing scientific opinions.

It would only be possible to prove that the literal theory of the Hexæmeron is in harmony with geological conclusions by showing that the views which now prevail among geologists are not certain scientific conclusions, but arbitrary theories; and this proof must, of course, be supported by scientific arguments. Accordingly this method has been adopted by the supporters of this theory; Bosizio in particular has devoted a great part of his book to the refutation of what I have shown in my last lecture to be the prevailing views amongst modern geologists. Any one who thinks that this refutation is valid may therefore believe that the Biblical statements as interpreted by Bosizio, Keil, and others do not indeed harmonize with the prevailing geological theories, but are in accordance with the real results of geological inquiry. But I very much doubt whether many people[1] will consider Bosizio's explanations to be an "evident proof" that "in our day geognosy has, in a perfectly shameful manner, propounded hypotheses as facts, and fancies as conclusions. I have only seen one review of his book which is written by a man apparently well versed in the subject, and that ends with the declaration that Bosizio has *not* succeeded in proving that the fundamental theories of modern geologists are entirely erroneous."[2] At any rate there is no reason to expect that, in consequence of the objections raised

---

[1] With Hoffner, *Der moderne Materialismus*, Frankf. 1865, p. 30.
[2] J. Probst in the *Tübingen Quartalschrift*, 1866, pp. 130–147.

by the theologians I have named, geology will "return from its wanderings into the region of untenable geognostical theories"[1]—that is, will give up the fundamental theories which I have developed in my last lecture. The fact that, as we have seen, geologists themselves expect that the progress of research will very much modify our conception of the *details* of the earth's palæontological history, no more prevents the confirmation of the fundamental principles than the countless differences of opinion on many single points among inquirers prevents their being at one as to the main idea.

Under these circumstances I do not think it necessary to inquire in detail whether any of the palæontological theories now prevailing, or how many of them, may be regarded as scientifically certain, after such objections as these. It will be enough if I lay stress on one point, which, as I believe, would alone wreck the whole theory in question.

If the fossiliferous strata have all been deposited since the creation of man, we can only allow a few thousand years for their formation. For according to the ordinary and most obvious computation of the chronological statements in the Bible, man was created about 6000 years ago, and the period between the creation of man and the Deluge, in which is included the formation of the greater part of the strata, would be about 2000 years. Is this time—let us say between 2000 and 3000 years[2]—sufficient for the formation of the fossiliferous strata? If we are to believe the geologists, it is certainly not sufficient; for you will remember that in a former lecture I told you what

[1] Bosizio, *Op. cit.* p. 337.   [2] Bosizio gives this period, p. 239.

immense periods they say were required. Now, Bosizio has no doubt collected—partly from my book and partly from other sources—a series of quotations from separate men of science, in which they express themselves very strikingly on the uncertainty and exaggeration of these geological figures. But the conclusion which he draws from these remarks is quite unjustifiable; for he says that as it is admitted that geologists are only able to set up uncertain suppositions as to the time necessary for the formation of such strata, these "merely hypothetical" figures cannot be compared with the chronological figures given us in sacred and profane history, for which we have documentary evidence. Certainly not; but this is begging the question. I do not know how many volumes our University Library contains, or how much they are worth; and if several experts were to look round the rooms once, and were then to estimate the number of volumes and the value of the whole collection, they would probably not agree exactly in their estimates, and they would themselves call their figures uncertain and "merely hypothetical;" but it is none the less indisputable that there are more volumes in the University Library than in my own, and that I could not afford to purchase it. However much geologists may be at variance with one another in their estimation of the period of time in question, and however readily they may admit the uncertainty of their figures, they are, with a few unimportant exceptions, unanimous in asserting that 2000 or 3000 years are not enough; and this they will maintain with the greatest possible determination.

"Besides," adds Bosizio, "if we inquire how these geological assumptions of enormously long periods of time first arose in the books of geologists, we find that these exaggerated estimates are greatest, and occur most frequently, in the works of those authors who incline to materialism and pantheism. Geologists whose philosophy is more sound, and who are certainly not less trustworthy, do not speak of millions of years, but of thousands." Let us put aside the charge of materialism and pantheism with which, as with other accusations, Bosizio is always very liberal, and listen only to those authors who in this respect are quite above suspicion, and we shall find that they all, even if they only speak of thousands of years, with one accord deny that 3000 years is sufficient, which is the point in question. I appeal—to mention a few only— to Buckland, A. Wagner, H. Miller, and Marcel de Serres among geologists, to Cardinal Wiseman and Bosizio's fellow-Jesuit Pianciani among theologians. The latter says simply that the literal interpretation of the six days meets with difficulties which rest not on geological theories and systems, but on numerous carefully examined facts, that for this reason the "wiser and more learned theologians and defenders of religion" are trying to prove that the long periods of time assumed by geologists are not at variance with the Mosaic narrative.[1]

As an example of the time required for the formation of a fossiliferous stratum, let us take the coal-beds, which have been referred to by Bosizio and Veith. Bosizio thinks that they were most frequently formed

[1] *Erläuterungen*, etc., p. 7. See above, p. 187.

in the same way as the peat mosses; and as at the present time a peat moss fathoms deep can be formed in forty or fifty years, it is fair to assume that, taking into consideration the luxuriant vegetation of the marsh plants from which the coal was formed, probably only the seventh or eighth part of that time was required, that is, from five to seven years, and therefore the time necessary for the formation of the present coal measures need not be of such enormous extent.[1] Further, Professor Göppert has made several attempts to produce peat and coal artificially, and he has succeeded in doing this in the space of one year with some kinds of plants, and in two years with others. From this Councillor Haidinger concludes that the enormously long periods of time assumed by geologists were not necessary for the formation of the coal measures.[2] As to the intermediate layers of chalk and sandstone, which are sometimes from 100 to 1000 feet thick, and the greywacke strata, which are some-

[1] Bosizio here quotes from Quenstedt, *Epochen*, etc. p. 401 : "For the most part they were plants of loose fibre and gigantic stalks, which blossomed and faded quickly. As now it takes years, so then it took months to load the flat marshy ground with carbonic acid. If, instead of our present rushy beds, we imagine great bamboos ten times as high and thick, or let us say sigillaria woods of the coal period, the time which this vegetation would take in growing need hardly be considered." But Quenstedt himself says a few pages farther on (p. 404) : "If it was only a question of one stratum, no doubt peat would be the best analogy. But in almost every coal-field we find a succession of strata, recurring in parallel layers one above the other more than a hundred times in perfect order, and imbedded in intermediate strata many thousand feet thick. . . . A coal-bed 400 feet thick, such as we find at Saarbrück, whether it was composed of peat, wood, or vegetable mould, must have taken mountains of plants at least from five to thirty times as large as it is now to compose it. Look where you will, the activity of the earth in our period will not suffice to explain these things."
[2] See above, p. 290.

times from 19,000 to 30,000 feet thick, we must observe that if we are to suppose that they were washed down or deposited very gradually, as is the case now in gardens and streets after severe falls of rain, so that the deposit was made at the rate of about one inch per month, no doubt 30,000 years would be required for a layer 30,000 feet thick; but if we suppose that the deposits took place on a rather grander scale, as may well have been the case, when they were caused by great inundations, and if we assume that the deposits went on at the rate of only 5 feet a month, we have in one year ten fathoms, and in 500 years—supposing that "vast inundations" took place every year for 500 years, that is, that there were 500 deluges—we have 30,000 feet, and this in localities where the deposits proceeded quietly and steadily. In other districts, however, there must have been great eruptions of waters and landslips, in which case deposits several thousand feet thick might have been made in a few hours.

I will not discuss the correctness of these hypotheses, but I will quote a few geological facts.[1] The ordinary thickness of the separate layers of coal varies from a few inches to 20 feet. In a few cases it exceeds 40 feet; for instance, at Dombrowa in Russian Poland there is a seam 48 feet thick, which extends uninterruptedly for a distance of 7000 feet. Peat beds attain to a much greater thickness; at Zittau there is one 180 feet thick. Thick beds of coal are often divided by "intermediate strata" into several seams of greater or lesser thickness, as it were into several layers; and generally the seams of coal are much fewer and less

[1] See Cotta, *Geol. Bilder*, p. 247.

thick than these intermediate strata of sandstone and slate. At Newcastle-on-Tyne there are 40 coal-beds, mostly no doubt of no great thickness, above one another, alternating with slate and sandstones. The entire thickness of the coal-bed on the south side of the Hundsrück is 338 feet, at Colebrooke Dale in the west of England, 500 feet. Some of the English coal-beds may be traced continuously on the surface to the extent of 15-20 geographical miles in length, and 5-10 in breadth, while their subterranean extent is of course much greater, and may probably be estimated at 50 geographical miles. Throughout England about 300,000 people are employed in more than 3000 coal mines, and these afford yearly over 1000 millions of cwts. of coal. The areas of some of the North American coal-beds are much larger.

The enormous mass of plants which was necessary for the formation of these coal-beds must have grown in the localities in question, and then have been turned into coal; the masses of sand, clay, and loam, which were required for the intermediate strata, must have been washed down, deposited, and then have hardened; lastly, the strata must have been formed which cover the coal-beds. I cannot believe that all this took place in the course of 2-3000 years, even though peat may grow quickly under favourable circumstances, even though Professor Göppert has changed a handful of plants into coal or peat in one or two years by keeping them in water which was maintained day and night at a temperature of 50-80 Reaumur; and even though sometimes great masses of sediment are brought together in a short time by great floods. And Professor

Göppert and Councillor Haidinger would be very much surprised if one were seriously to point them out as supporters of the theory which Bosizio upholds. Veith is quite right in saying that the processes necessary for the formation of the coal-beds might have taken place in periods of time which to a Buddhist would not appear worthy of mention; but then 10 and 20 times 2000 or 3000 years is not worthy of mention when compared with the Buddhist periods.[1]

But the coal formation is only one out of the whole series of stratified formations; and therefore 2000 or 3000 years will still less suffice for the formation of the whole series. The thickness of the united palæozoic formations has been estimated at 40,000 feet. Of course this is an uncertain estimate, but I will give you a few data based on measurements. One division of the Permian system, the Rothliegende, is divided at Mansfeld and in Thuringia into three layers which are respectively 500-800, 200, and 80-300 feet thick. The Vosges sandstone, one stratum of one of the three divisions of the Triassic system, is 1200 feet thick in the Vosges; another stratum is 150 thick in some localities, in others above 400 feet thick, and so on.[2]

I think that enough has now been said to show that the theory that the fossiliferous strata have been formed since the creation of man may be set aside as untenable.[3] But if we are to suppose that this forma-

---

[1] *Die Anfänge*, p. 359.   [2] Nöggerath, *Ges. Naturw.* iii. 247 seq.

[3] "There is hardly anything of importance in geology or palæontology which Keil would admit, or would even, as were reasonable, leave to science to decide; and yet there is much which is highly probable, if not completely certain, although many things, of course, are still doubtful. Thus, to mention one thing only, it has doubtless become very apparent that the formation of the enormous coal measures, which evidently con-

tion took place in the pre-human age, the theory that only six days elapsed before the creation of man falls to the ground.

Later on I shall have to discuss more particularly those geological results which must be referred to the Deluge. I close my lecture to-day with a short notice of a theory brought forward by Vosen, who is not a supporter of the theory we have hitherto been discussing.[1] He believes that we may find a reason for the existence of many fossil plants and animals in the curse by which God destroyed the vegetation of Paradise. The expression "Cursed be the ground for thy sake" can, he says, only be understood to mean that in the same moment not the Garden of Eden alone, but also the beautiful paradisaical vegetation of the whole earth was destroyed; that a sudden catastrophe of nature transformed the soil of the earth, and that the vegetation of Paradise forthwith disappeared; whereupon a new stunted vegetation sprang up from its grave. Through this mechanical destruction of the vegetable world many animals were buried in the ground with the plants; other animals, sometimes whole races, were destroyed, because, after the curse on the vegetable world, they could not find the food necessary for them; their organization, like that of man, having been formed to be nourished by the fruits of Paradise.

sist of vegetable matter, and for the most part of small plants, must have taken a much longer time than Keil supposes, even although that time cannot be accurately determined. The impulse simply to turn aside from matters of this kind is wrong in itself, and should certainly be repressed, for in the nature of the case the decision must rest with natural science, and not with the Bible." Schultz, *Schöpfungsgeschichte*, p. 298. Cf. Molley, *Geology*, p. 310.

[1] *Das Christenthum*, p. 715 (3rd ed. p. 750).

So that a great part of the fossils found in later strata, and especially those in the coal formation, may be a portion of the animal and vegetable world of Paradise, which, according to the words of Holy Scripture, existed not only in Eden, but also over the whole earth, and which was then everywhere simultaneously destroyed by the curse.

With reference to this theory, I need, as I have said, make only one short observation. Holy Scripture does not say a word about this, neither does it even indirectly suggest that before the Fall the earth was covered with paradisaical vegetation, and that all or some animals were so organized as to be nourished only by paradisaical food. Nor is there any mention of a sudden catastrophe of nature after the Fall, which would have had the results above described; and had any such taken place, Holy Scripture would hardly be silent on the subject. As to the meaning of the words, "Cursed be the ground," etc., no doubt theologians do not agree about them, but I know no one besides Vosen who would describe the interpretation he brings forward as self-evident, or even, to speak clearly, as admissible.[1] You will see, from the facts I have mentioned, that the coal formation, etc., cannot be explained in this manner.

---

[1] Pianciani (*Cosmogonia*, p. 471) says that "some" think that a catastrophe of this description took place after the Fall, but simply adds that the Bible does not mention it.

XVII.

GEOLOGY AND THE BIBLE ACCORDING TO THE THEORY OF RESTITUTION.

I HAVE shown in my last lecture that the attempt to include those periods of the earth's history to which the fossils bear witness, in the time which has elapsed since the completion of the six days of creation, has failed. I will now examine the theory according to which the geological periods are placed before the six days of creation.

So far as I know, this theory was first brought forward by the Scotch clergyman Dr. Thos. Chalmers;[1] it was first expressly defended by Buckland, and it has since been adopted and developed by many, and has been much modified in detail; in Germany especially by Kurtz and A. Wagner.[2]

In its main outlines the theory is as follows:—Between the first act of creation of which the first verse of Genesis speaks, and the first act of the first

---

[1] Chalmers, writing in 1804, said that it had been asserted by some that geology, by placing the earth's origin at an earlier period than that assigned to it by Moses, had undermined belief in the inspiration of Holy Scripture, and all the comforting truths which it teaches us. But he adds, this is a groundless fear. The books of Moses in *no way* fix the age of the earth. In 1814 he developed this view at greater length in his *Examination of Cuvier's Theory of the Earth.* Cf. H. Miller, *Testimony,* p. 107.

[2] In the second edition of his *Geschichte der Urwelt;* also by Schubert, Raumer, Hengstenberg, Richers, Reinsch, Keerl, Wolf. (In Germany first by Hezel, p. 178; see Zöckler, *Gesch. der Beziehungen,* ii. 513.)—V. de Bonald, Westermayer, Vosen, and others.

day of the Hexæmeron, of which the third verse speaks, there was a long period of time. Even before the Hexæmeron, the earth was formed, and was a dwelling-place for created beings. This earlier form and this earlier animal and vegetable world was annihilated by a catastrophe, the results of which Genesis describes in the second verse. Thereupon the earth received its present form, and its present animal and vegetable world; and this Moses describes from ver. 3 onwards. In other words, the Hexæmeron treats, not of the first formation of the earth, and of the first creation of organized beings, but of a re-formation of the earth and of a re-creation of organized beings; for which reason this has been called the theory of restitution.

There can be no question of any contradiction between geology and palæontology and the Bible, according to this theory, for no direct point of contact is left. The interpreter of the Mosaic Hexæmeron need take no notice of what the geologists say about the formation of the earth from a gaseous mass or from a watery or igneous ball; of their teachings concerning the origin of the Azoic, Palæozoic, Mesozoic, and Cainozoic formations, and about the animal and vegetable world, whose remains are buried in these strata; for all this belongs to a period which preceded the six days of the first chapter of Genesis. The Biblical history of the earth only begins where the palæontological history of the earth leaves off.[1] When

---

[1] "Revelation leaves two large blank leaves between the first and second, and also between the second and third verses of the Biblical account of creation, and on these human science may write what it will in order to

the last fauna and flora of the palæontological period had been destroyed, God created first the plants, then the animals of the water, air, and land; and these still exist in their descendants, and therefore belong to the time unnoticed, or described as the recent period by palæontology, which is the science of the organic beings of the prehistoric or primæval world.

Besides the advantage of harmonizing completely and thoroughly with geology and palæontology, the theory of restitution has the further advantage of making the literal interpretation of the six days admissible. For there is no doubt that after the desolation which closed the earlier history of the earth, the appearance of light, the rising of the vapours, the appearance of dry land, and the creation of the still existing fauna and flora might have succeeded one another quickly, and could have been completed in six periods of twenty-four hours.

If, therefore, we ask first whether this theory is exegetically admissible, I answer unhesitatingly in the affirmative.

fill up those gaps in natural history which revelation has purposely left. Revelation has only given to each of these blank leaves a superscription, a summary of their contents. The first one runs : 'In the beginning God created the heavens and the earth.' It does not say how this happened, how long it took, what followed afterwards, what evolutions and revolutions took place before the state of things was reached which is described in ver. 2. Human science may fill up the blank as it can. On the second blank leaf is written : 'And the earth was without form, and void, and darkness was upon the face of the deep. And the Spirit of God moved upon the face of the waters.' Revelation does not tell us what was the influence of the Spirit of God on the waters, what results and forms it called forth from them. The eye of the seer did not behold what took place in the dread deep so long as it was covered with darkness, he did not know it, and therefore has not described it. It was only when there was light that he could distinguish what occurred, and it is only then that his narrative begins." Kurtz, *Bibel und Astronomie,* p. 397.

I have already shown that we can assume that in the Hexæmeron a re-formation of the earth, and not its first formation, is described; that the thohu wabohu of the second verse was not the first condition of the earth, but the separation between a previous state and that which was established by the six days of creation, and still exists; and that a period of indefinite length elapsed before the first day of creation.[1] From the side of Theology, therefore, there is no objection to be made to the theory in question.

No doubt it might be thought strange that Moses should say nothing of the earlier history of the earth, and of the organisms which according to this theory must have existed on it. If we read the account in Genesis without regard to the results of scientific inquiry, it conveys the idea that organic life first began on the third day, that the plants which were created on the third day, and the animals which were created on the fifth and sixth days, were the first and only ones ever created by God. The author of Genesis does not seem to suspect, certainly the readers of Genesis up to the last century did not suspect, that a number of plants and animals had existed, and had been destroyed, before God said on the third day, "Let the earth bring forth grass." But this objection may be removed. Moses did not intend to write a complete history of the earth's development, but only a history of the preparation of the earth as a dwelling-place for man; he therefore mentions what relates to man, and passes over in silence whatever has no such relation. We have already laid stress on this in noticing what

[1] See p. 111.

Moses says about the stars, and about the separation of water and land.[1] If we keep this stedfastly in mind, we shall see that Moses must have spoken of the creation of plants and animals in so far as they are appointed for the service of man. He implies this himself when he says that God had made man the ruler over the animal world, and had appointed the plants for food for him and his subjects. From this point of view Moses could pass over in silence the plants and animals buried in the strata; for it is a recognised fact that they were not contemporaneous with man, and consequently did not exist directly for his use. They and the minerals stand to man in the same relation, indeed they are organic bodies which have become mineral, and they are therefore no more mentioned than are the minerals.

Moses nowhere says that God had created nothing which was not mentioned in the Hexæmeron. He teaches that everything which exists besides God was created by God, and that everything which man sees around him was created in one week of creation, in a certain order and for a certain purpose, for man. After the truth, that nothing which has existed has come into existence without God, had been expressed with sufficient clearness in the statement, "God created the heavens and the earth," there was no reason for enumerating and describing all the separate parts of creation, and all the separate phases of the creating and forming activity of God, including those which stood in no near relation to man.

But there is still one difficulty left: How does the

[1] See pp. 195 and 223.

matter stand as regards the work of the fourth day, the creation of the stars, or to speak more correctly, the establishment of the present relation between the earth and the sun and the other stars? Those palæontological periods cannot have been without sunlight, or without an atmosphere,—the last is said to have been created only on the second day. The petrified animals had eyes, and in many of the petrified trees we even find the rings, which evidently show that light and even the seasons must have existed, so that probably the alternation of day and night took place.

Geologists conclude from the nature of the primæval plants and animals that in those days the atmospheric, climatic, and other natural conditions of the earth were different from what they are at present; the greater number think that the temperature then was higher, and was more equal over all the earth. But it is impossible to say with certainty what were the conditions of the earth in this respect, still less therefore can we ascertain how they were brought about. Genesis does not exclude the possibility of the existence of light and an atmosphere in that primæval period; for there is nothing to prevent our concluding from the narrative that it was light before the thohu wabohu, that on the first day it became light again at God's command, that from thenceforth the alternation of day and night as it at present exists was established, and that the present atmosphere of the earth was formed on the second day. We need not decide whether in the primæval age the light which illumined the earth was connected with the sun,—we have already seen that we can imagine light even separated from the sun,—or whether, as some believe, the earth was surrounded by a photosphere. Genesis does not contradict the first idea; for, as I have already said, neither the formation of the stars nor the first connection of light with them need be assumed to be the work of the third day, but only their establishment in their present function of giving light upon the earth. The present illumination of the earth by the stars has only existed since the third day; it was not yet the case in the first three days, either because the stars did not yet possess the power of shining, or—and according to this theory this would be the correct view—because the earth with its atmosphere was not susceptible to light on those days, it was only on the fourth day that the formation of the earth and its atmosphere had proceeded so far that thenceforth the light of the sun and the other stars could operate as it still does upon it. Before the thohu wabohu the earth may no doubt have existed in a condition which was analogous to the present one, although not exactly like it; Moses does not say so, because his narrative does not touch upon that period, and precisely for that reason his words do not exclude the idea.

You will not misunderstand the uncertainty with which I speak with reference to many details, and my speaking only of possibilities. As regards the Bible I say quite certainly and clearly, that as these things do not belong to its special province it either does not speak of them at all, or it makes use of such vague and general expressions, that although we can ascertain with complete certainty from its narrative every statement of religious importance, to questions of scientific importance we receive no answer. By this means it leaves a wide field for scientific investigation; and if we can say so little with any certainty about the earliest periods of our planet, and if what we do say is full of hypotheses, that is not the fault of the Bible, which is not called upon to give us information on this subject, but is caused solely by the fact that natural science, to which the Bible entirely abandons the task of searching out these things, has not yet attained, and from the nature of the subject cannot well attain to any certain results.

It is therefore no doubt perfectly allowable, exegetically, to transfer the palæontological periods to the time before the work of the six days. But although I admit that on this the main point I agree with those who support this theory, I must at the same time express myself just as decidedly against several other notions, which have by some been connected with this so-called theory of restitution.

You will remember that by many the destruction of the earlier condition, which brought about the formlessness and desolation described in the second verse, has been connected with the fall of the angels, and that it has been supposed in consequence of this that the fallen angels were before their fall inhabitants of the earth. I have already mentioned my reasons for objecting to this hypothesis [1] in general, but there are other and graver objections to the way in which it is connected with palæontology. On this subject I quote Westermayer,[2] who bases his remarks on the arguments of Kurtz, Delitzsch, and

---

[1] See p. 119. [2] *Das Alte Test.* i. p. 37.

others.[1] He says: The organisms which are found petrified in our rocks probably did not exist on the earth when the latter was the dwelling-place of the angels who afterwards fell. For "the animal and vegetable world could not have been a fitting adornment for a place inhabited by angels, and the monstrous, horrible sanguinary and ugly shapes which come to light in the fossil remains of the primæval animals could not possibly have delighted angelic eyes, for even we men can only look at such specimens with a certain horror mingled with astonishment." The creation and destruction of the primæval animals would therefore have taken place not before the destruction of the original form of the earth, which is designated as the thohu wabohu in the second verse of Genesis, but during the time which comprised the thohu wabohu. God wished to restore the world which had been destroyed in consequence of the fall of the angels. Genesis announces the beginning of this creative activity of God in the words: "The Spirit of God moved (or brooded) upon the face of the water." But when "by the fructifying brooding of the Divine Spirit on the waters of the deep, creative forces began to stir, the devils who inhabited the primæval darkness, and considered it their own abode, saw that they were to be driven from their possessions, or at least that their place of habitation was to be contracted, and they therefore tried to frustrate God's plan of creation, and exerted all that remained to them

---

[1] Kurtz, *Bibel und Astronomie*, p. 539. Delitzsch, *Genesis*, p. 137. Drechsler, see *Delitzsch*, p. 539. Keerl, *Schöpfungsgesch.* p. 537. Cf. Zöckler, *Gesch. der Beziehungen*, ii. p. 516.

of might and power to hinder or at least to mar the new creation." With the permission of the Creator, therefore, "when the Spirit of God began to act creatively on the waters, demoniacal powers interfered with the brooding of the Divine Spirit, not indeed themselves creating, but in such a manner as in some way unknown to us to tamper with the fruitful waters, and to introduce monstrous shapes, unnatural intermixtures, mutual destruction, disease, and death, among the races of animals created by God." In this way arose "the horrible and destructive monsters, these caricatures and distortions of creation." The divine creation was therefore also "a struggle with the powers of wickedness." "Whole generations called into existence by God succumbed to the corruption of these powers, and for that reason had to be destroyed." They were buried in the strata, and "in the work of the six days God caused the devil to feel His power in all earnest, and made his enterprise appear miserable and vain."

I must admit that I cannot well imagine how demoniacal powers could "interfere" with the divine creation, could "spoil and mar the divine efforts of creation," etc. But supposing it to mean that because of the devil God's creations did not succeed according to His idea, or that the devils had corrupted the races of animals created by God, it must be obvious that this view is more in accordance with the dualistic doctrine of a good and a bad god who are equal and opposed to one another, than with the position which the devil occupies in the Christian religion. No doubt dualism is expressly excluded, in that creative power is denied to the devil, and his interference in the creation is made dependent on the permission of God. But what could be the motive and object of this divine permission? Delitzsch and Westermayer say: "The creation of the world was to a certain extent a contest between the Creator and Satan with his powers, just as the redemption was a contest between the Redeemer and Satan with his powers;" but this analogy does not hold good. It is one thing to believe that the devil has power to tempt man, and thus to give him an opportunity of deciding for God by means of his divinely given freewill, and that the Redeemer has freed man from the enemy's power, into which he had fallen through his sin; and it is another to believe that God could have condescended to allow the devil to oppose Him in creating irrational animals. At any rate there must be very strong scientific reasons to induce assent to a theory theologically so unattractive. But this is just what seems to me the weakest point in the whole argument. The primæval flora is very wisely passed over in silence, and in the animal world only the ugly and monstrous shapes are alluded to. Now I have already observed that it is a great mistake to imagine that the primæval animals were universally monstrous and distorted; the most graceful and beautiful forms occur among them. The present fauna is not altogether wanting in shapes which do not please the ordinary taste, and perhaps it is only consistent of Westermayer to connect crocodiles, toads, and spiders with the devil, to call them absolutely ugly under all circumstances, and to explain this by saying that Satan has not been entirely dislodged even from the present creation, so that the forms and instincts of many animals and plants must necessarily exist as they do now in order to symbolize his ugly, horrible, and murderous nature. I fear that this theory is hardly scriptural; at least the crocodile and the hippopotamus, which is not exactly a beautiful animal, are quoted in Jehovah's speech in the Book of Job[1] as evidences of the divine power and greatness. This sentimental and superficial criticism of separate creatures is not at all in place here. S. Thomas Aquinas says that if we wish to judge of the value of anything, we should not look at it in one particular relation only, but should contemplate the thing in itself and in its relation to the world, for every separate thing has its place in the universe.[2]

Kurtz's description of "rapine, war, destruction, and death" as something "positively undivine," which God could not have placed in the primæval world by creation, and which could only have been caused by misuse and the disturbing intervention of an anti-divine freewill,[3] is very strange. The mortality of the animals cannot well be regarded as not originally willed by God, and as regards rapine, war, and destruction in the animal world, it is, as I have already mentioned, quite unnecessary — S. Thomas even says it is unreasonable—to assume that our present beasts of prey were not carnivorous before the fall of man; why then should not God have created voracious beasts of prey in the primæval age?

I must protest against one more error of which the supporters of the theory of restitution have been guilty.

The oldest fossils exhibit, as I have mentioned,

[1] Chap. xl.   [2] i. q. 49, a. 3.   [3] P. 543.

the most imperfect forms of plants and animals; the nearer we approach to the present time, the more specimens do we find of the higher kinds of plants and animals. Now Schubert's designation of these primæval organisms as " the immediate productions of a creative power which, at every beat of its pulse, poured forth on the visible world an abundance of life in the most manifold forms,"¹ seems to be at any rate hazardous. Unless he supposes, which he certainly does not, that the divine creative power worked unconsciously and involuntarily, Schubert has expressed himself very incorrectly. The following observation of Keerl's is just as incorrect, "It is as if in that primæval time the whole of nature had lain in continual labour until she found the centre in which she could rest. No production that she can bring forth satisfies her, she destroys by degrees all the forms that arise, and hides them in a stone grave, till at length she has found the shape which contents her."² Such expressions as these in the mouths of theologians or defenders of the Bible will only provoke ridicule like that of Vogt, who scoffed at the Creator for altering the earth and its organisms twenty-five times or oftener, until at last He had got it right.

The primæval flora and fauna were produced by the activity of God creating freely with wisdom and might, just as were our present animal and vegetable world; if they were different, it is because God wished to create them differently; if they were destroyed, they

¹ *Gesch. der Natur*, i. 487, quoted and approved of by Wagner, *Gesch. der Urwelt*, ii. 343. In another passage (i. 377) Wagner expresses himself more correctly.
² *Schöpfungsgesch.* p. 463.

were destroyed according to the will and wise plan of God. The question as to why God should have created these beings, and then should have caused them to be destroyed and fossilised before the present animal and vegetable world was created, may no doubt very well claim attention. For the present I leave it unanswered; but at any rate the answers I have discussed hitherto are wrong, whether they suppose that these creations were corrupted by the demons, or designate them as the immediate and unsatisfactory products of the divine creative power.

Freed from the errors I have mentioned, the theory of restitution is, as I have said, theologically admissible. The only question now is whether it contradicts none of the results of scientific inquiry. I have already observed that on the whole this theory establishes a relation between geology and the Bible which seems to put far away all possibility of a conflict. The Bible only speaks of the fauna and flora of the present world, it leaves the flora and fauna of the primæval world to palæontology. But where is the line of boundary between the primæval and the present world? or to put the question in its proper shape at once, are the primæval and the present world divided by any such boundary line? If he support the theory of restitution, the exegete must answer Yes, the thohu wabohu is the boundary line; with it the period of the primæval flora and fauna came to an end, and after these had been destroyed the present flora and fauna were created. But can the existence of such a thohu wabohu between the primæval and the present world be proved, or be shown to be geologically admissible? In other words, do the results of geological inquiry confirm this supposition, or at least is it consistent with them to suppose that immediately before the first appearance of man, not only had organic life quite died out on the earth, and been restored by the creation of a new animal and vegetable world, but that besides this, a condition of things had occurred in which the earth was quite covered with water, and enveloped in darkness; so that a new regulation of its relation to the stars, a re-formation of its atmosphere, and a new separation between water and land were necessary. You see that the theory of restitution, from a geological point of view, stands or falls by the answer to this question.

Buckland and other geologists have answered this question decidedly in the affirmative. As I have already briefly mentioned,[1] they draw a sharp distinction between the fossil plants and animals, *i.e.* those belonging to the primæval world, and the present plants and animals; and also between primæval and recent formations of the earth's crust. But other geologists express themselves no less decidedly in the opposite sense. One of the most eloquent defenders of the Mosaic account of creation among British geologists, Hugh Miller, says: "It is a great fact, now fully established in the course of geological discovery, that between the plants which in the present time cover the earth and the animals which inhabit it, and the animals and plants of the later extinct creations, there occurred no break or blank; but that, on the contrary, many of the existing organisms were con-

[1] P. 273.

temporary during the morning of their being with many of the extinct ones during the evening of theirs. We know further, that not a few of the shells which now live on our coasts, and several of even the wild animals which continue to survive amid our tracts of hill and forest, were in existence many ages ere the human age began. Instead of dating their beginning only a single natural day, or at most two natural days, in advance of man, they must have preceded him by many thousands of years. In fine, in consequence of that comparatively recent extension of geologic fact in the direction of the later systems and formations, through which we are led to know that the present creation was not cut off abruptly from the preceding one, but that, on the contrary, it dovetailed into it at a thousand different points, we are led also to know that any scheme of reconciliation which would separate between the recent and the extinct existences by a chaotic gulf of death and darkness, is a scheme which no longer meets the necessities of the case."[1] . . . "From the present time up to the times representing the Eocene formations of the tertiary division, day has succeeded day, and season has followed season, and no chasm or hiatus—no age of general chaos, darkness, and death—has occurred to break the time of succession or check the course of life. All the evidence runs counter to the supposition, that immediately before the appearance of man upon earth there existed a chaotic period which separated the previous from the present creation."[2] If this is true, then the conclusion which H. Miller draws from it is inevitable.

[1] *Testimony of the Rocks*, p. 121.   [2] *Ibid.* p. 129.

... "We are led also to know that any scheme of reconciliation which would separate between the recent and the extinct existences by a chaotic gulf of death and darkness, is a scheme which no longer meets the necessities of the case. Though perfectly adequate forty years ago, it has been greatly outgrown by the progress of geological discovery, and is, as I have said, adequate no longer; and it becomes a not unimportant matter to determine the special scheme that would bring into completest harmony the course of creation as now ascertained by the geologist, and that brief but sublime narrative of its progress which forms a meet introduction in Holy Writ to the history of the human family." [1]

This question must no doubt be left to natural science to decide; and if the decision is unfavourable to the theory of restitution, the latter, although exegetically admissible, must be given up as completely as the theory which was discussed in my last lecture. I intend to return to it later, for to-day let me just say a few words about a curious modification of the theory of restitution which was brought forward by the learned presbyterian divine John Pye Smith in an otherwise in many ways very instructive book, and which has been adopted in England by many writers.[2]

---

[1] *Testimony of the Rocks*, p. 122. Also Walworth in Brownson's *Quarterly Review*, 1863, p. 207.

[2] *The Relation*, etc., p. 250. Also Ed. Hitchcock and others; see Zöckler, *Gesch. der Beziehungen*, ii. S. 32. Cf. on the other side, H. Miller, *Testimony*, pp. 119, 130, and Brownson's *Quarterly Review*, 1863, p. 208. I may mention here another extraordinary modification of the theory of restitution, which is brought forward in a book by the Abbé J. Fabre d'Envieu, *Les Origines de la Terre*. It is as follows: The earlier periods of the earth's history occur before the events spoken of in the first verse of the Hexæmeron; for this verse does not speak

Smith assumes, as do all supporters of the ordinary theory of restitution, that the creation described in Genesis took place about 6000 years ago; that it was completed in six real days, and that it was separated from a previously existing creation by a period of chaos. But whereas, according to the ordinary theory of restitution, both the creation spoken of in the Hexæmeron and the preceding period of chaos extended over the whole earth, according to Smith they were both local, and only extended over a few provinces in Central Asia; in which while light and life continued in other lands, for a time death and darkness reigned, and the waves of a chaotic sea covered everything, until at God's command the light broke through again, and dry land appeared. After this, in the space of a week, certain plants and animals were created, and last of all man appeared.

of the beginning of God's creative activity, but of the beginning of the earth in its present form. The expression "In the beginning" does not refer to the actual beginning of time, but to the beginning of the period which Moses intends to describe; the Hebrew word "bara" does not mean "to create," but "to form." "The sun had become extinct" before the beginning of the six days; it had been the source of light on the earth during the previous geological periods, but had then become a dark body. On the first of the six days, which were all of twenty-four hours' duration, God formed, probably by electricity, a provisional fount of light which was independent of the sun; on the fourth day the sun got back its light-giving power. The moon resumed her functions, with the sun, on the fourth day. As "the stars" are mentioned as well as the sun and moon in the account of the fourth day, we may assume either, that "all the stars became extinct at once, and were reorganized in one day," or we may take "the stars" to mean "the planets." Probably, however, the word "stars" in Gen. i. 16 is a later interpolation. The period of formlessness and void which preceded the Hexæmeron corresponds to the Diluvial age or quarternary period; one of the glacial periods was probably produced by the extinction of the sun; the creation which is described in the Hexæmeron followed one of the two periods which French geologists call Diluvium gris, and Diluvium rouge.

This modification of the theory of restitution would no doubt be free from the objections made by H. Miller in the extract I have quoted, but it will not be necessary for me to prove that the grand description of the creation of things with which the Bible begins, is intended to mean more than a creation which was limited to some hundred square miles and some hundred kinds of plants and animals.

The new pre-Adamite hypothesis, which has been brought forward in recent years by English believers in the Bible,[1] is connected with this extraordinary theory of Smith's; according to this hypothesis the ancestor of the Caucasian race was part of the local creation maintained by Smith; the ancestors of the lower races existed before that creation, and outside the region where it took place. There is nothing too extraordinary to be invented at some time by somebody.

[1] Cf. Zöckler, *Die Urgeschichte*, p. 110; *Gesch. der Beziehungen*, ii. 775.

XVIII.

GEOLOGY AND THE BIBLE: THE CONCORDISTIC THEORY.

In the sixteenth lecture I showed that we cannot prove that the Biblical account of creation and the certain results of geological inquiry are in harmony, if we hold fast to the literal interpretation of the six days, and suppose that only six periods of twenty-four hours elapsed between the beginning of God's creative activity and the creation of man. We are forced to transfer the formation of all the fossiliferous strata to the period which followed the creation of man, and according to the unanimous and well-founded opinion of all modern geologists this is out of the question. In my last lecture I showed that geology will not allow us to suppose that all the history of the earth and its organisms up to the Cainozoic period took place before the Hexæmeron, and during the age which preceded the condition of formlessness and void which is described in the second verse of Genesis; so that the Hexæmeron itself only describes the formation of the earth in the last and still existing period, and the creation of the present or so-called recent animal and vegetable world. If, therefore, we cannot place much of the history of the earth and its organisms, as it is set forth by geology and palæontology, after the Hexæmeron, nor, for the most part, before it, nothing is left but to put the whole of that history up to the first appearance of man into the Hexæmeron ; to which we must therefore ascribe a proportionate duration. I have already shown that this is exegetically admissible, and my next task therefore is to prove in detail that assuming the freer interpretation of the six days, the Mosaic record agrees with the scientific history of the earth in so far as that can be said to be scientifically proved.

But you will recollect that in my tenth lecture I showed that two wider interpretations of the six days were exegetically admissible. According to the first, the six days betoken six consecutive long periods in the history of creation, and each of these periods, the existence of which geologists assert to be proved by their investigations, is denoted by one day in the Mosaic Hexæmeron. According to the second, the six days as a whole correspond to the whole series of periods which have elapsed between the first beginning of things and the creation of man ; but these six separate days do not mean six consecutive periods, but only six moments or phases of the creative activity of God, six great heads under which the creating and forming acts of God as they appear in the earth's history may be ranged. The first interpretation of the six days is called the "concordistic," the second the " ideal."[1] Let us consider to-day the development of the first theory.

According to Genesis, the order of events in the history of creation is as follows : In the beginning the

[1] The principal supporters of both theories were mentioned above, p. 183. Molloy supports both the Concordistic and the Restitution theories.

earth was covered by water, and enveloped in darkness. On the first day God caused the light to appear, and established the regular alternation of day and night. On the second, He formed the atmosphere from a part of the waters which covered the earth. On the third, He separated the water from the land and created the plants. On the fourth, He established the relation which still exists between the earth and the sun, moon, and stars. On the fifth He created the animals of the water and the air; on the sixth, the land animals and man. Let us for the moment put aside the works of the first and fourth days, and confine ourselves to the others, which refer directly and exclusively to the earth; we cannot avoid seeing that the Biblical account of the creation of the earth harmonizes on the whole with the earth's history as described by geologists. Pfaff observes very strikingly with reference to this: " If we look on the earthly creation as being *one* from the beginning of the earth up till now, as forming a *whole* in spite of all changes at different times, it is impossible to describe the events otherwise than is done in Genesis, or to suppose that they occurred in any other order. For in Genesis the separate kingdoms are contemplated separately and apart, without further reference to the changes in the history of each of them, and we are told how they successively made their appearance: the condition of chaos, the mass of waters, the formation of the land, after this the organic world, first the vegetable world, then the animal world represented at first only by inferior water animals, then by land animals, and finally the appearance of man, are represented as occurring in their true sequence, and these separate portions of the history of development are designated as days."[1]

But we must not stop at this general comparison; we must see how the separate days can be compared to the separate geological periods.

With respect to the third, fifth, and sixth days, Ebrard makes the following statement:[2] "The first chapter of Genesis contains no information about the details of the formation of the earth's surface, and the successive appearance of the organisms. Nevertheless, the succession of creations which is here revealed must correspond to the objective reality in such a manner as to describe *in its main outlines* the course of the objective, real history of the formation of the earth and its organisms. Let us for a moment put aside and forget the first chapter of Genesis, and consult palæontology. How would the history of the earth and its organisms be stated, if the results of geology were to be briefly put together *in their main outlines?*

"I think that any savant who meant to undertake this task would consider not only the quality, but also the quantity and number of the organic remains which occur in the separate formations. He would put aside the scanty, very rarely occurring organic remains which are found in the Silurian and Devonian systems, while, on the other hand, the coal formation would appear to him to be of real critical importance. Here there is no question of single sporadic organisms appearing occasionally; on the contrary, so much of

[1] *Schöpfungsgeschichte*, p. 742.
[2] *Der Glaube an die h. Schrift, und die Ergebnisse der Naturforschung*, p. 61.

the earth's surface as rises out of the sea is seen to be covered with a giant vegetation compared to which all the organic remains of the earlier period, including those of animals of the coal formation itself, seem simply of infinitesimal size. If, therefore, we mean to mention the principal among God's creations, we must say that after the tracts of land had first come forth from the sea, the first world of organisms which appeared vast and predominant was a world of plants. And this is just what we are told in Gen. i. 9–13.[1] Now to proceed. The organic remains in the Bunter Sand-

---

[1] Cf. H. Miller, *Testimony*, p. 135 : " In the first or Palæozoic division we find corals, crustaceans, molluscs, fishes, and, in its later formations, a few reptiles. But none of these classes of organisms give its leading character to the Palæozoic; they do not constitute its prominent feature, or render it more remarkable as a scene of life than any of the divisions which followed. That which chiefly distinguished the Palæozoic from the Secondary and Tertiary periods was its gorgeous flora. It was emphatically the period of plants,—' of herbs yielding seed after their kind.' In no other age did the world ever witness such a flora; the youth of the earth was peculiarly a green and umbrageous youth,—a youth of dusk and tangled forests, of huge pines and stately araucarians, of the reed-like calamite, the tall tree-fern, the sculptured sigillaria, and the hirsute lepidodendron. Wherever dry land, or shallow lake, or running stream appeared, from where Melville Island now spreads out its ice wastes under the star of the pole to where the arid plains of Australia lie solitary beneath the bright cross of the south, a rank and luxuriant herbage cumbered every footbreadth of the dank and steaming soil; and even to distant planets our earth must have shone through the enveloping cloud with a green and delicate ray. Of this extraordinary age of plants we have our cheerful remembrances and witnesses in the flames that roar in our chimneys when we pile up the winter fire,—in the brilliant gas that now casts its light on this great assemblage, and that lightens up the streets and lanes of this vast city,—in the glowing furnaces that smelt our metals, and give moving power to our ponderous engines,—in the long dusky trains that, with shriek and snort, speed dart-like athwart our landscapes,—and in the great cloud-enveloped vessels that darken the lower reaches of your noble river, and rush in foam over ocean and sea. The geologic evidence is so complete as to be patent to all, that the first great period of organized being was, as described in the Mosaic record, peculiarly a period of herbs and trees, 'yielding seed after their kind.' "

stein, as also those in the Keuper marls (the Triassic group, therefore the Mezozoic period), are as to quantity almost non-existent, and are really only weak continuations of the already created vegetable world. On the other hand, between the Bunter Sandstein and the Keuper marls in the Muschelkalk (the third division of the Triassic group) a mighty animal world for the first time appears. This includes polypi, corals, radiata, terebrátula, shells, snails, and even saurians (lizards). These remains occur in incredibly large quantities, so that enormous masses of stone often seem to consist entirely of the remains of the scales of these animals. Think what swarms of animals must have existed in the waters which deposited the shelly limestone. The Oolite then appears, similar in kind, but abounding more plentifully in water animals; new species occur, but the principal character of the period remains the same. As then in the coal formation the vegetable world is seen in grandeur and might, so in the Muschelkalk and in the Oolite the world of swimming and creeping water animals appear, from the polypi and corals, through the shell animals up to the fish and saurians. This is exactly what we are told in Gen. i. 20 seq.

"But what of the birds? We can understand that the skeletons of birds cannot be so easily preserved as those of lizards or as shells. The water animals lived in water or in mud, and when they died the mud covered them and filled them up, and they were thus preserved by petrifaction. The birds living on dry land mouldered away. We ought not therefore to expect to find any copious remains of the skeletons of birds, and no false inferences against the existence of a large number of birds should be drawn from their absence.[1] But isolated traces of birds do, as a matter of fact, occur in the same geological period.[2] Isolated traces of mammals occur even in the Jurassic period, but these isolated instances are quite insignificant when compared with the appearance of a whole world of mammals, which we find first in the Molasse (Cainozoic period)."[3]

[1] Leonhard, *Geologie*, i. p. 401.
[2] Hugh Miller, *Op. cit.* p. 136: "The middle great period of the geologist—that of the secondary" (Mezozoic) "division—possessed, like the earlier one, its herbs and plants, but they were of a greatly less luxuriant and conspicuous character than their predecessors, and no longer formed the prominent trait or feature of the creation to which they belonged. The period had also its corals, its crustaceans, its molluscs, its fishes, and in one or two exceptional instances its dwarf mammals. But the grand existences of the age—the existences in which it excelled every other creation, earlier or later—were its huge creeping things,—its enormous monsters of the deep,—and, as shown by the impressions of their footprints stamped upon the rocks, its gigantic birds. It was peculiarly the age of egg-bearing animals, winged and wingless. Its wonderful *whales*, not, however, as now, of the mammalian, but of the reptilian class,—ichthyosaurs, plesiosaurs, and cetiosaurs,—must have tempested the deep; its creeping lizards and crocodiles, such as the teliosaurus, megalosaurus, and iguanodon,—creatures some of which more than rivalled the existing elephant in height, and greatly more than rivalled him in bulk,—must have crowded the plains, or haunted by myriads the rivers of the period; and we know that the footprints of at least one of its many birds are of fully twice the size of those made by the horse or camel. We are thus prepared to demonstrate, that the second period of the geologists was peculiarly and characteristically a period of whale-like reptiles of the sea, of enormous creeping reptiles of the land, and of numerous birds, some of them of gigantic size; and in meet accordance with the fact, we find that the second Mosaic period with which the geologist is called on to deal, was a period in which God created the fowl that flieth above the earth, with moving (or creeping) creatures, both in the waters and on the land, and what our translation renders great whales, but that I find rendered in the margin, sea-monsters." Miller is wrong in making "the moving creature that hath life" (reptile animæ viventis, Vulg.) include what we now call reptiles; it does really mean the smaller water animals, and the *land* reptiles belong to the work of the sixth day. Ebrard is also wrong in putting birds for animals of the air, and mammals for land animals. See above, p. 100.
[3] Miller, *Op. cit.* p. 137: "The Tertiary" (Cainozoic) "period had also

The parallel is similarly worked out by the most recent supporters of the Concordistic theory, Zöckler,[1] and Bishop Meignan.[2] According to Zöckler, the second day corresponds "to that geological epoch which is described as the period of the primitive rocks, or the Azoic period; when, under the surface of the primæval sea which enveloped the whole earth, while the thick covering of atmospheric clouds and vapour was being lifted, the masses were deposited of gneiss, granite, mica schist, and slate, which underlie all existing earth and rock formations. The third day, which includes the two creative acts of the separation

its prominent class of existences. Its flora seems to have been no more conspicuous than that of the present time; its reptiles occupy a very subordinate place; but its beasts of the field were by far the most wonderfully developed, both in size and numbers, that ever appeared upon earth. Its mammoths and its mastodons, its rhinoceri and its hippopotami, its enormous dinotherium and colossal megatherium, greatly more than equalled in bulk the hugest mammals of the present time, and vastly exceeded them in number. . . . The massive cave bear and the large cave hyæna belonged to the same formidable group, with at least two species of great oxen . . . with a horse of smaller size, and an elk . . . that stood ten feet four inches in height. Truly this Tertiary age—this third and last of the great geological periods—was peculiarly the age of great 'beasts of the earth after their kind, and of cattle after their kind.'" P. 146: "As the sun and moon, when they first became visible in the heavens, would have seemed to human eyes — had there been human eyes to see—not only the greatest of the celestial lights, but peculiarly the prominent objects of the epoch in which they appeared, so would these plants, reptiles, and mammals have seemed in succession the prominent objects of the several epochs in which *they* appeared . . . And . . . I ask further whether (of course making due allowance for the laxity of the terms botanic and zoological of a primitive language, unadapted to the niceties of botanic or zoologic science") there is no question of this in the Mosaic division of organic beings, see above, p. 99, "the Mosaic account of creation could be rendered more essentially true than we actually find it, to the history of creation geologically ascertained."

[1] *Die Urgeschichte*, p. 55. Also F. v. Rougemont, *Das Uebernatürliche und die natürl. Wissenschaften*, Gütersloh 1871, p. 45.
[2] *Le Monde*, p. 21. Also Molloy, *Geology*, p. 384.

of water and land, and the first production of vegetation on the latter, denotes the transition to the organic creation in the first stage of its development when it still includes chiefly vegetables. All the transition rocks (the Cambrian, Silurian and Devonian systems), with the lowest of the stratified formations, the coal, that is, the whole Palæozoic group, belong to this period." Zöckler, like Ebrard, identifies the Mezozoic and Cainozoic periods with the fifth and sixth days.

Attractive as is this comparison, I cannot help seeing that there are some objections to it. The third, fifth, and sixth days on the one hand, and the Palæozoic, Mezozoic, and Cainozoic periods on the other, do not, at all events, exactly correspond; for while the Mosaic account of the third day only speaks of plants, the Palæozoic period shows traces of animals; and while Genesis ascribes to the fifth day only the creation of the animals of the water and the air, palæontologists can point to land animals which existed in the Mezozoic period. In addition to this, new kinds of plants appear in the Mezozoic and Cainozoic periods, indeed the Palæozoic flora is almost exclusively composed of Cryptogamia; and the Dicotyledons, that is to say, the very plants which form the principal part of our flora, all the leafy trees, and most kinds of herbaceous plants, are still entirely wanting.[1] In the same way, new kinds of water and air animals appear in the Cainozoic period, so that the creation of plants is not confined to the Palæozoic, and the creation of water and air animals to the Mezozoic period. Further, it cannot be said that the animal world gradually came

[1] Römer, *Die ältesten Formen*, etc., p. 7.

into existence exactly in the order in which Genesis says that the first three groups succeeded one another, viz. water, air, and land animals. Lastly, the results of the examination of the oldest strata seem to show, that the animals appeared, if not before, at least contemporaneously with the plants. No doubt these difficulties may in part be surmounted. But as to the last, I certainly do not think that in order to make the carboniferous system correspond to the second work of the second day, *i.e.* the creation of plants, we ought simply to put aside the organisms which occur in the Silurian and Devonian systems; that is, before the Carboniferous age; the more so as the fossils, especially the petrified sea *animals*, are by no means so "scanty, rare, and isolated" as Ebrard asserts.[1] Nor should I like to say, with Pianciani,[2] that we might admit that the animals in the lowest Palæozoic strata had been created before the fifth day, and were contemporaneous with the plants, because for the most part there were only those kinds of sea animals which were either quite unknown to the ancients, or at any rate were not reckoned as belonging to the animal world by them; organisms, in short, which were of so little account that Moses might have passed them over in silence.

We may sum up the Biblical statement in a form which need not fear any well-founded scientific contradiction: the existence of the vegetable world began before that of the animal world, and therefore the first plants were created before any animals.

[1] Römer, *Die ältesten Formen*, etc., p 10 seq.
[2] *Cosmogonia*, p. 409.

Humboldt no doubt observes: "Nothing seems to prove, as has been inferred from theories about the simplicity of the first forms of life, that vegetable life began on the old earth before animal, that the latter was conditioned by the former."[1] But other men of science bring forward better reasons than "mere theories" for believing that animal life was conditioned by vegetable. The physiologist Johannes Müller says quite decidedly: "The food of animals consists of organically mixed animal and vegetable matter. Plants are necessary to the animals, because they alone possess the power of producing organic from inorganic combinations, and so by means of the plants the new material is brought into the great economy of nature, and is then conveyed from the plants to the graminivorous animals, and from these to the carnivorous animals."[2] S. Bischof expresses himself to the same effect.[3] The following observation of Burmeister's is therefore incontrovertible, "That animals could have originated before any vegetation is impossible, if only because animals require vegetation in order to exist. Although many animals eat other animals, yet we come at last to those who eat plants, and the very notion of an animal is that it takes into its substance nothing which has not already existed in some form as organic matter. For this reason, even in the oldest periods of creation, no animal organisms can have existed before vegetable organisms, although it is conceivable that

---

[1] *Cosmos*, i. 293.   [2] *Handbuch der Physiologie*, i. 36, 44.

[3] *Lehrbuch* (1st ed.), i. p. 1002, with a reference to his observations on the question as to whether vegetable life awoke on earth before animal life, published in the *Munich Gel. Anz.* 1847, No. 75, 76. Cf. Kneg, *Das Pflanzenleben des Meeres*, Berlin 1874, p. 7.

both may have been created at very short intervals, and may have lived very soon after one another."

Palæontology can, no doubt, offer no direct proof of the priority of existence of plants; for the earliest strata which have as yet been discovered do not contain fossil plants exclusively, but rather plants and animals; and, indeed, both sea plants and sea animals.[1] But this does not contradict the supposition that the plants originated earlier than the animals which are petrified with them. Further, according to the opinion of eminent savants, it is very doubtful whether the so-called Azoic formations all belong to that period in which no organic life existed.[2] It is probable that several of the so-called metamorphic rocks, that is, those rocks which are now crystalline, but which were formed from stratified rocks, contained organic remains, which were destroyed after the transition, and these may have been remains of animals.

"In the dark, greyish blue slate," says S. Bischof, "in which no fossils occur, and which occasionally becomes quite black, the colouring proceeds from a pervading alloy of coal. Now, if all coal proceeds from decomposed carbon, a vegetable world must evidently

[1] Römer, *Die ältesten Formen*, etc., p. 9. According to *Murchison*, who has examined the oldest formations more closely than any one else, land plants are only found in the uppermost Silurian strata, but sea plants are found in the lowest (*Siluria*, p. 492). It is said that in some places strata containing sea plants and no animals have been found immediately above the Azoic formations. Cf. Vogt, *Lehrbuch der Geol.* i. 219; *Natürl. Gesch. der Schöpfung.* p. 29. Quenstedt, *Sonst und Jetzt*, p. 111; *Epochen der Natur*, pp. 292, 304, 350. Römer, *Op. cit.* p. 26. There is no question here of the Eozoon Canadense, see above, p. 287, note 1.

[2] Bischof, *Lehrbuch* (1st ed.), i. pp. 44, 97 (2nd ed. i. 628). Vogt even says (*Ausland*, 1863, p. 840) that "*all* the so-called metamorphic slate and gneiss, and most of the granite, porphyry, and greenstone, is formed of rocks which were originally stratified and fossiliferous."

have preceded the formation of this slate, and so the organic kingdom must have come into existence even before the graywacke formation."[1]

We may therefore conclude that the Bible and natural science are in harmony with one another as regards the creation of plants before animals.[2] Nor can there be any doubt that Genesis and palæontology agree on the whole as to the order in which the separate classes of animals appear; and that, even on the showing of those palæontologists who by no means intend to assert that such harmony exists. Giebel, for instance, says, "In the primary formations, zoophytes, trilobites, and fish preponderate; they all inhabit the *water;* they represent the most imperfect stage of development. In the secondary formations the water animals again appear in great numbers, but at the same time crabs and amphibious animals are seen in manifold shapes, giving to the period its special character. They denote the second stage of development, in which the transition from life in the water to life on land and in the air is seen. Lastly, in the tertiary strata, the highest classes of vertebrata and articulata, the insects, birds, and mammals, are found; and in these the development of the animal organism is completed. The preponderance of the determining classes in the series of formations in question is an acknowledged fact. There is an apparent contradiction in the appearance of insects and lizards in the coal measures and Permian system, *i.e.* in the primary period, and in that of mammals and birds in the Oolitic and Cretaceous ages. The wings of moths found at

[1] *Lehrbuch* (1st ed.), i. 97. [2] Stutz, *Schöpfungsgeschichte*, p. 19.

Wettin no doubt represent insect life in the Carboniferous age, and the opossums found at Stonesfield land animals in the period of amphibious life. But these single instances are no more characteristic of the general animal creation of the period than are the apes at Gibraltar of the European fauna."[1]

Of course, all these remarks do not suffice to prove that the third, fifth, and sixth days of Genesis on the one hand, and the Palæozoic, Mezozoic, and Cainozoic periods on the other, correspond as minutely as is required by the Concordistic theory. It seems that the account in Genesis must be understood to mean that the creation of plants was completed on the third day, and that of the water and air animals on the fifth, each time we are told "and God saw that it was good," and that the work of each of the three days was confined to the class of organic beings which is mentioned. From an exegetical point of view it is just as hazardous to depart from this interpretation, as from a scientific point of view it is hazardous, in characterizing the three great palæontological periods, to lay stress solely on the plants in the first, the animals of the water and the air in the second, and the land animals in the third; and to put aside the other classes of organic beings as completely as is done in the above-mentioned explanations of the Concordistic theory.

Nor does this theory encounter less serious difficulties in dealing with the two days which I have hitherto left unnoticed.

Most of its supporters pass over the first day too

[1] *Allgemeine Palæontologie*, p. 18.

easily. If the third day is identified with the period in which the earth was covered by the primæval sea, one might be tempted to interpret the first day to mean the preceding period in which the earth was first a gaseous and then a fiery ball. But here we should come twice into direct conflict with the Mosaic record; first, according to ver. 2, the earth was at the beginning of the first day a ball covered by water, and secondly, the work of the first day is said to have been not only the creation of light, but also the separation of light from darkness which we call day and night. So that the first day must fall chronologically within the geological period, in which the earth had a solid crust which was covered with water,[1] and we should be forced to assume that in this period, in some manner or other, light had appeared, and an alternation of light and darkness, analogous to the alternation of day and night, but not caused by the rising and setting of the sun, had taken place. This supposition, no doubt, is not confirmed by geology, but it cannot be condemned as scientifically untenable, although the fact that the atmosphere was formed on the second day is not in its favour. According to the ordinary form of the Concordistic theory, the fourth day, on which the sun began to affect the earth, and the present relations between the earth and stars were established, must be inserted between the Carboniferous age, which corresponds to the second half of the third day, and the Triassic age, with which the fifth day begins, that is, it must correspond to the Permian age. Accordingly, to

---

H. Miller (*Testimony*, p. 175) identifies the first day with the Azoic, and the second with the Silurian and Devonian periods.

the remarks which have been previously quoted, Ebrard adds, "The species of plants which occur in the coal formation are the same in all parts of the earth; therefore during the Carboniferous age there existed no difference of climate on the earth, and the earth was warmed by its own heat, not by the sun; in the Triassic and Oolitic systems, on the other hand, signs of climatic differences appear. The organization therefore of the present sidereal relations of our earth, which Genesis mentions as being the work of the fourth day, is placed both by natural science and by the Bible between the Carboniferous period (the third day) and the Triassic, Oolitic, and Cretaceous systems (the fifth day)." Similarly Zöckler says,—for the fact that he reckons the Triassic period as part of the fourth day, and begins the fifth day with the Oolitic period, makes no important difference,—" The fourth day of creation evidently takes up no great portion of the whole process of geological development, because during its course no important terrestrial creations take place; but the lights of heaven are established in order to give light on the earth, and to divide terrestrial time, and this is an addition to the earlier acts of creation. It therefore corresponds admirably to those middle strata, following immediately on the strata of the Carboniferous age, which contain on the whole very few new and characteristic types of animals and plants, and which are—according to the description given of them by Edward Forbes and Hugh Miller—the product of a 'comparatively poorly productive epoch,' the result of a pause, as it were, in the primæval organic development. It is an epoch of transition from the Palæozoic period of creation, which reaches its climax in the luxuriant vegetation of the Carboniferous age, to the Mezozoic period; it is marked by the strata of the so-called Permian system, and by the Triassic group, and shows its transitional character mainly by including among the still predominating water animals the first land animals belonging to the classes of the higher Crustacea and Amphibia. But the principal importance of this day of creation consists in the astronomical events with which it deals, and which the Mosaic record describes as its sole work. The great advance made on this day is shown in the establishment of the relation between the stars and the earth, and in the revelation of the sun, with the other heavenly lights, which had been hitherto hidden behind a dull, vaporous, clouded atmosphere. From henceforth the sun begins to operate in its full unveiled strength upon the earth in order to prepare it to be the abode of highly developed organic life, and to call into being a more beautiful and useful kind of vegetation, richer in form and colour than the cryptogamic flora which with its hothouse luxuriance, and absence of fresh soft green leaves, had vegetated up to this time partly under, partly above the surface of the sea; and at the same time to bring forth an increasing variety of more and more highly organized land animals."[1]

I am afraid that this theory will hardly hold good against palæontologists. They will not admit that the sun first began to give light and warmth on the earth after the Carboniferous age, and that up to that

[1] *Die Urgeschichte*, p. 59.

time the earth was only "warmed by its own heat," and was surrounded by such a thick atmosphere that the sun was quite hidden by it. Nor is it correct to assume that up to this time "a flora without fresh green leaves had vegetated, partly under and partly above the surface of the sea;" and if it were correct it would only strengthen an objection previously raised against the ordinary interpretation of the Concordistic theory, viz. that whereas according to the account in Genesis all kinds of plants came into being on the third day, the geological period corresponding to this day only produces the more imperfect kinds, while, on the other hand, the same period produces water animals, that is, organisms which belong to the creations of the fifth day; and the period which corresponds to the fourth day trenches on the creations of the sixth day in that it produces land animals.

I think that after the explanations I have given to-day, we must admit that if we compare the six days of Genesis with the geological periods, it cannot be denied that there is a certain harmony in some of the main features, but that a parallel in detail between the separate six days and six successive geological periods, which is the most important part of the Concordistic theory, cannot be carried out without constraint.

XIX.

GEOLOGY AND THE BIBLE ACCORDING TO THE IDEAL INTERPRETATION OF THE SIX DAYS.

ON a former occasion[1] I numbered myself among the supporters of the Concordistic theory, not, indeed, according to its ordinary interpretation, but in a modified form of the same, which, I thought, was not affected by the objections brought against the ordinary interpretation. I wish to-day first to sketch this modification of the Concordistic theory, although I must, at the same time, confess that a more careful examination has convinced me that it is untenable.

The history of the earth, as traced out by geology, may be divided into two great parts, of which the second begins with the first appearance of organic life. The first part comprises the transformation of the earth from a gaseous, fiery, or watery mass to a solid spheroid, or to a spheroid surrounded by a solid crust; the formation of the primitive rocks, and of the older Azoic strata, and the appearance of the first islands and continents. The narrative in Genesis up to the middle of the third day may be brought into harmony with this portion of the earth's history. The Mosaic record begins at ver. 2 with the period in which the earth was covered with water and shrouded in darkness; on the first day follows the appearance of light, on the second

---

[1] In the 2nd ed. of *Bibel und Natur*, p. 288, cf. p. 260.

the setting aside of part of the waters for the formation of an atmosphere, on the first half of the third the appearance of dry land. The only difficulty here is caused by the existence of light, and of the alternation of day and night without the sun; but it is not inconceivable that in some manner not to be clearly defined, but different from the present conditions, light, with warmth and other imponderable fluids, existed and operated on the earth. We need not fear any substantial objections to this view from geologists, simply because they themselves can give us no more trustworthy information concerning this portion of the earth's history than can historians about the mythical period in the history of an ancient people.[1]

The second part of the earth's history begins in Genesis, as in geology, with the appearance of vegetation. According to Genesis, vegetation appeared on the second half of the third day, and perhaps existed for some time before the earth stood in its present relation to the sun. Genesis does not say how long this condition lasted, but it makes the beginning of the present relation between the earth and the sun follow immediately on the appearance of vegetation. We may therefore assume quite unhesitatingly that vegetation need only have existed a short time—perhaps for a few hours—under other than the present sidereal, atmospheric, and climatic conditions. After these had set in, the animals were created; first (on the fifth day) the water and air animals, and then (on the sixth day) the land animals.

For the reasons given in the last lecture, it is

[1] See above, p. 247.

impossible to identify the second half of the third day and the three following days of the Hexæmeron with the separate periods of the second part, of the geological history of the earth, that is, with the separate palæontological periods; the second part of the Mosaic and the second part of the geological history of the earth only correspond generally. In detail, the history of the earth and its organisms given by palæontology seems very different from that given by Genesis, which I have just quoted. For in the palæontological history, the organic beings do not appear in the same order and grouping as they do in the Hexæmeron; geological events occur in the separate palæontological periods, which entirely or partially changed their fauna and flora, and considerably changed the surface of the earth. In reference to the difference between the Mosaic and the geological records, I added on a former occasion [1] the following remarks to some observations of Delitzsch's: [2]—

"Although it is said that land and sea were separated from one another on the third day, this does not mean that from thenceforth the boundaries of both were unchangeably fixed, and that the raising of the sea-level and the inundations of the land, which, according to the teaching of geologists, affected the formation of the earth's crust even after the creation of organic beings, that is, after the third day, could not have taken place. The separation of land and sea, and God's decree that from thenceforth both

---

[1] In the 2nd ed. of *Bibel und Natur*, p. 248 seq.

[2] *Genesis*, 3rd ed. p. 118 (4th ed. p. 98). Cf. Stutz, *Schöpfungsgeschichte*, p. 40.

should exist together, and that the land should not again for any length of time be submerged by water, was the first work of the third day; the narrative does not say that at the close of the third day the form of the land was absolutely and unchangeably fixed. After Moses had announced the important and fundamental truth that the dry land had come up out of the waters, and that by this means an abode had been provided for plants, land animals, and men, he was not concerned with any further changes which might take place on the dry land, because they would in no way modify that fact. We may therefore say with Delitzsch : 'There is ample space between the third day and the creation of man for the fashioning of the earth's surface (the formation of the fossiliferous strata); and there is no reason against our supposing that this process of fashioning was connected with catastrophes which broke through the (vegetable creation of the third and the) animal creation of the fifth and sixth days, and destroyed whole generations.'

"The Mosaic record, no doubt, seems to say that first the plants, then the water and air animals, and lastly the land animals had each been called into existence by one separate act of creation; and that these were the ancestors of our present flora and fauna, for it is expressly asserted that the plants and animals created by God were intended to reproduce themselves. Nevertheless, we are in no way obliged to limit ourselves to this first and obvious interpretation. The two facts which, as I have shown before, are of religious importance, and which therefore had to be clearly and distinctly stated in the Biblical narrative of the creation, are these, first, that the animal and vegetable world which we see around us was created by God; and second, that the bringing forth of plants and animals had a distinct place in the six acts of the divine drama of creation. Palæontologists may be right in asserting that not only one, but many consecutive creations of plants and animals took place; that catastrophes and developments occurred between these separate creations by which the preceding creations were entirely or partially destroyed or petrified; that whole multitudes of species died out, and were replaced by new species; but yet all these facts do not contradict, but only amplify and carry out the other two facts I have just mentioned. It still remains perfectly true that our present animal and vegetable world is descended from that created by God, that the creation of the first plants is one of the characteristic events of the third day, and the creation of animals one of the characteristic events of the fifth and sixth days of the divine week of creation. The details of the earliest history of the fauna and flora, which palæontology attempts to give us, had not the religious importance of those two facts, and could therefore be omitted from the Biblical record.

"But if we may assume that the formation of the earth's surface, so far as the division of water and land are concerned, began on the third day, as it is said in Genesis, but was continued through different modifications beyond the close of the third day, there is no further difficulty in supposing that the creation of plants does indeed characterize the third day; that is, that it first took place, not before, but during the third day, that it was indeed continued or repeated on the following days also, but that this fact is not specially mentioned by Moses, because the works characterizing the following days were different. In the same way we may suppose that the creation of animals of the water and air, which began on the fifth day, was continued on the sixth. The works of the separate days of creation, only, as Delitzsch says,[1] laid the foundation, the process which they began extends beyond them. The point to be expressed is, not how long, but how often God created."

Having laid down this theory, I then combined the palæontological periods with the periods which are called in Genesis the third, fifth, and sixth days in the following manner. Three kinds of organisms were created, plants, animals of the water and air, and land animals. But more than three creations of organic beings took place; at the first (on the third day), only plants were created; at the second, either only plants again, or plants and water and air animals, the latter on the fifth day; at the third, either one of these three kinds of organisms, that is, either plants, or water, or air animals, or two of these three kinds, or three of these kinds, or together with these three kinds, or with either one or two of them, land animals (the latter on the sixth day). In the creations which followed, all combinations of the classes of organic beings which I have mentioned are, from a Biblical point of view, admissible; palæontologists may choose which they please.[2] The product of these separate

---

[1] *Genesis*, p. 90.
[2] Besides this statement, Bernuzzi (*La div. revelazione*, p. 275) ascribes

creations was then each time wholly or partially destroyed, or partly petrified by the formation of the strata of the earth's crust which occurred in those periods. We leave it to palæontology to decide whether the first process of petrifaction took place after the first creation, which included plants alone (that is, on the third day), or only after animals had been added by further creations (that is, on the fifth or sixth days).

Apart from the fact that this combination appears rather artificial, there are, I think, two points in it which have not been sufficiently considered. First, the beginning of the relations between the sun with the other stars and the earth, of which no notice is taken in the combination I have described, appears in the Hexæmeron as one of the principal events in the history of creation. It is the work of a special day, and that day is placed between the creation of plants and the creation of animals. Secondly, one of the objections which I have raised against the ordinary interpretation of the Concordistic theory, applies still more strongly to this modification of it. At the end of each half of the third day it is said, "And God saw that it was good." Now this sentence means, as I have shown in my explanation of the Hexæmeron,[1] that God's command, "Let the waters under the heaven

to the third day the strata below the Cambrian formation, which contain traces of plants; to the fourth, the Cambrian and Silurian formations; to the fifth, the formations from the Devonian, which contain the first fish, to the lower Oolite, in which the first birds appear; and the sixth day is supposed to begin with the Oolitic strata, in which the first mammals appear. *Land* animals are, however, found in the Devonian system. See above, p. 286.

[1] See above, p. 92.

be gathered together in one place, and let the dry land appear;" and "Let the earth bring forth grass," etc., has been adequately realized. I observed at the time that the formula, "And God saw that it was good," was wanting in the account of the second day, on which the waters which covered the earth were separated, and the firmament was formed, and this because that work was not complete; the lights only appeared in the firmament on the fourth day, and the dry land only came forth from the waters under the firmament on the third day; and it was only after this had happened, after the divine idea had in consequence been quite realized, and the final state reached, that that formula would be in place. Supposing this to be correct, it is clear that this formula should not follow the account given of the two works of the third day if they were not concluded on that day,—if, as is assumed in this modification of the Concordistic theory, the creation of plants was continued on the following days;[1] especially as the first creation of plants, which may have preceded the animal world, did not consist of land plants, but only of fucoides and sea-weed, and the principal classes of the vegetable world, the dicotyledons, the leafy trees, and most of the herbaceous plants, only appear after the Carboniferous period.[2] For these reasons I am compelled entirely to give up my former theory, which occupied a kind of half-way position between the Concordistic and the Ideal interpretation of the six days. What is correct in my argument need not, however, be given up,

---

[1] Schultz, *Schöpfungsgeschichte*, p. 321.
[2] Römer, *Die ältesten Formen*, pp. 8, 9.

it will have great weight in establishing the Ideal theory.

According to this theory, the six days do not signify six consecutive periods, but six chief moments of God's creative activity which can be logically distinguished from one another, six divine thoughts or ideas realized in the creation. That all which has been created has been created by God, and according to the will of God, is a religious truth which must be asserted as decisively and distinctly as possible in the narrative of the creation. This is accomplished by the enumeration of the separate creative and world-forming acts of God. The length of time occupied by the realizing of the separate divine acts and the completion of the whole creation is of no religious importance, and we need not therefore expect to find any information about it in the Biblical account of creation; nor are we justified in asserting that such information is to be found in the designation "six days." Further, the chronological succession of the separate divine acts is in itself of no religious importance, and for this reason we are not justified in expecting to find information concerning this in the Hexæmeron. The distribution of the separate acts into six days, and the consequent connection between them, is caused by the parallel between the divine week of creation and the human week. The separate "days" need not therefore be looked upon as single, separate, consecutive periods. Rather it is possible—and geology and palæontology show us that this was in reality what took place—that the works of the separate days, for instance, the separation of water and land, the formation of the earth's crust, and the creation of plants and of the different kinds of animals, may have occurred to some degree simultaneously. Moses may still represent them as being each the separate work of one day, because each forms a special moment in the creative activity of God, and he may enumerate them in the order in which they are mentioned in the Hexæmeron, first because of the order which prevails in them, and then because the works which follow are dependent on the preceding, and conditioned by them.[1]

I have discussed and proved these statements on a former occasion.[2] In addition to the last I must now proceed to explain the order of the separate works in the Mosaic record. The Hexæmeron consists, as I have shown,[3] of two parts, in which the works of the separate days correspond to one another. The works of the first part we will call, with S. Thomas Aquinas, works of separation; in Genesis itself they are described as the separation of light from darkness, of the waters above from those below the firmament, of the land from the sea. S. Thomas calls the works of the second part works of embellishment or endowment; the heaven receives its shining bodies, water, air, and land receive their living inhabitants. More recent writers have designated the first three works as those by which God founded and separated the different kingdoms, the last three as those by which He filled them with inhabitants;[4] or the first three as separations, the last three as individualizations.[5] Two works are ascribed to the last

---

[1] Schultz, *Die Schöpfungsgeschichte*, pp. 230, 331. Michelis in *Natur und Offenbarung*, i. p. 110.
[2] See above, p. 184.   [3] See above, p. 131.
[4] Schultz, *Op. cit.* 331.
[5] Michelis, see *Natur und Offenbarung*, i. p. 110, vii. p. 215.

day of each part ; " on the third day," as Michelis says, " the establishment of the dry land is followed by the creation of plants, and on the sixth the formation of mammals (land animals) is followed by the creation of man : the dry land is the foundation for the vegetable world, as is the completion of the animal world for man."

You see that in this way the truth that God is the creator of the whole earth, and of all visible creatures, is expressed very distinctly, and in good and easily comprehensible logical order. The chronological order of the works directly referring to the earth is so far preserved, that at any rate geological inquiry shows that they were begun in the same order as they are enumerated in the Hexæmeron : the formation of the atmosphere of the earth, the appearance of dry land, the creation of plants, of water and air animals, and of land animals. Only the Mosaic narrative confines itself to a summary and comprehensive description of each separate work, because, as I have already observed, the details of those works, as given by geology, are not of religious importance. The two works which do not relate directly to the history of the earth itself, are placed at the beginning of each half respectively of the Hexæmeron ; the establishment of the alternation of day and night, or the separation of light from darkness, at the beginning of the separations ; the establishment of the relation of the sun, moon, and stars to the earth, or the appearance of the light-giving bodies, at the head of the works which endowed the different portions of the creation with inhabitants. As I observed in a former lecture,[1] this description does not make

[1] Lecture XI.

it impossible that what is logically distinguished in Genesis may have coincided chronologically, and therefore the influence of the heavenly bodies on the earth may have begun before the creation of plants.

We may, I think, add that in the second part of the Hexæmeron those works are placed together which are of more direct importance to man who is the object of the whole work of creation, than are the works of the first part; the animals are given to him as subjects (Gen. i. 28); and the lights of heaven, according to Gen. i. 14, 15, are not only intended to give light on the earth, and to govern the day and night, but also to be for signs of the time to man.[1]

The ideal theory of the six days cannot be objected to on the ground that if it is true we must give up attempting to prove that the Bible and geology agree in detail, and must not try to make use of scientific conclusions as proofs of the Mosaic narrative; or that this theory as it has just been explained contains very little which, scientifically speaking, could be considered as giving us any important and valuable information about the earth and its inhabitants. On the contrary, all this only confirms the theory. For, as I have repeatedly observed, it is not the object of the Bible to impart to us scientific information, its direct object is rather to impart to us religious information, and we may presume that that interpretation of a Biblical passage is correct which brings out most distinctly the

[1] Zollmann, *Bibel und Natur*, p. 83, assumes that the establishment of the relations between the sun and the earth is mentioned after the vegetable creation and before the animal creation, because the recurrence of day and night in the space of twenty-four hours is important to animal, but not to vegetable life.

religious meaning, and throws into the background the elements of profane science which are connected with it. But as a gifted American theologian has observed,[1] according to the theory just propounded, the Hexæmeron is not a cosmogony which obliges its interpreter to leave the theological platform and dispute in mines, quarries, and observatories with men of science about the priority of plants and animals, of the earth and stars; but it is a grand development and detailed explanation of the important article of Jewish belief which stands at the head of our own creed: *Credo in unum Deum, factorem cœli et terræ.*[2]

Having now discussed in detail the four separate interpretations of the Mosaic account of creation, I will, with your permission, shortly and comprehensively recapitulate them.

Although S. Augustine had propounded another theory which had been treated as admissible by the schoolmen, the literal interpretation of the six days, as being six periods of twenty-four hours, prevailed among theologians until geological investigations threw light on the earth's history, and until the examination of the fossils proved that a long period must have elapsed between the beginning of God's creative activity and the creation of man, during which period those plants and animals must have existed whose remains were found in the different strata of the earth's crust. In consequence of these discoveries, two interpretations of the six days of creation were adopted.

---

[1] See Walworth in Brownson's *Quarterly Review*, 1863, p. 224.

[2] On Baltzer's interpretation of the Hexæmeron, see my remarks in the *Theol. Lit.-Bl.* 1867, p. 232.

First of all, the Biblical account was reconciled with geological conclusions by the supposition that the six days were figurative descriptions of six great periods in the earliest history of the earth. It was Cuvier who more especially obtained a hearing for this, the so-called Concordistic theory. It was thought that by this means a brilliant apology for the Mosaic record could be made, indeed some few, principally French, savants and theologians went so far as to announce triumphantly that it was now evident that the Biblical narrative not only did not contradict the results of scientific inquiry, but that it was remarkably confirmed by them; that Moses had anticipated those results by many centuries, and that if it could not be asserted that he arrived at this complete knowledge by means of scientific inquiries, one might say that the natural science of the present day had furnished a fresh proof of the divine inspiration vouchsafed to Moses.[1]

It is impossible to read these assertions now without a smile. In comparing the six days of Genesis with the periods in the earth's history, we have seen that besides many points of agreement, there are most important differences, so important that the concordistic interpretation of the narrative of creation must be admitted to be untenable. Those assertions rest on a view which is fundamentally incorrect. We have not the smallest right to assume that Moses, or any writer in the Old Testament, could, either by the "penetration of genius" or by scientific inquiry, have attained to more correct or profound knowledge of the questions of

[1] See above, p. 2 ; cf. p. 202, note 3.

natural science than we find was general in his age. Still less are we justified in assuming that by means of supernatural inspiration they were enabled to display a knowledge on questions of natural science which surpassed that of their time, or even to anticipate the results of the inquiries of coming centuries.

If the Concordistic theory is freed from these exaggerated statements of its earliest supporters, and is only made use of to prove that there is no contradiction between the Biblical account of creation on the one hand, provided its six days are looked upon as periods, and the history of the earth as represented by geology on the other, there is no fundamental and exegetical objection to be made to it; but I think I proved in my eighteenth lecture that this course leads to no result.

While this course was being adopted by French savants, English theologians and geologists were the first to adopt another, which should establish the harmony between the Bible and science. It was supposed that in the so-called theory of restitution a radical method of obviating all dissensions between exegetes and geologists had been found. The Bible, it was said, only gives an account of the present formation of the earth, and of the creation of the present animal and vegetable world; and there is nothing to prevent our supposing that this took place in the course of six periods of twenty-four hours. The discoveries of geology about the earlier periods of the earth's history, and about an earlier fauna and flora, lie outside the limits of the Biblical narrative. But if it is necessary to suppose, according to this theory, that the primæval world and the present world were sharply divided from one another in the history of the earth, and that immediately before the first appearance of man, the then existing form of the earth, and the animal and vegetable worlds were destroyed by a great geological catastrophe, whereby a *tabula rasa* was made for the formation of the earth, and the organic creation with which Genesis deals, then this theory is untenable. For I have shown in my seventeenth lecture, and I shall prove in my nineteenth, that this is just the supposition which the geological discoveries of the last few years have shown to be erroneous. The primæval and the present world were not separated in this manner; a catastrophe such as is described did not take place; the present animal and vegetable worlds did not come into existence at the same time as man, but for the most part existed long before him, and organic life when it had once begun, was probably never entirely destroyed and then reproduced by a new creation : at any rate this did not occur shortly before the first appearance of man. For these reasons the theory of restitution is untenable.

It seems to me that in the two theories which I have just shortly recapitulated and discussed, due weight is not given to the principle that the object of Biblical revelation is to give us religious information, and not to impart to us scientific information, that is, in this particular case, geological teaching. This principle is carried out to its full extent in the ideal theory of the six days, described in to-day's lecture, and as this theory does not strain the words of Holy Scripture, and does justice to the results of scientific inquiry, we shall have to consider it as the right one.

In order to avoid any doubts as to the authority of the Bible itself, which might be caused by the manifold and partly contradictory interpretations of the Hexæmeron which have been given by theologians past and present, we must distinguish carefully in the first chapter of Genesis, and also in other parts of the Bible, between the great religious truths which it is the direct object of Biblical revelation to impart to us, and the form given to these truths, together with the other matters which are bound up with them. The former are expressed clearly and unequivocally; no impartial person can read the first chapter of Genesis without seeing that in it God is represented as the Creator of all things; man as the centre of the earthly creation and the Sabbath as the day to be kept holy in honour of the Creator of the world. Any one may learn these things from this chapter; but this is all which any one is intended to learn, for this alone is of religious importance. The rest, the form and development of these truths, is not of religious importance, and if only those facts are borne in mind, the construction of each detail is quite unimportant to religion, and only of scientific interest. Just as, for instance, in the interpretation of the Gospels, if we rightly understand and faithfully believe the teaching of Christ which is given in them, it is not generally, but only exegetically important to decide, whether the public ministry of our Lord lasted three or four years, whether He was present at two or three Passovers, and whether He celebrated the Last Supper at the same time or one day before the Jewish Passover. All these are questions on which exegetes, without any injury to the Christian religion, are just as much at variance as about the six days of Genesis. Here again we recognise the truth of the saying that the Bible is like a sheet of water which an elephant can hardly ford, yet through which a lamb can pass. The fundamental truths of revealed religion are so apparent in Holy Scripture that every educated reader who comes to them willingly and without prejudice may recognise them, but the details which go beyond the religiously important, and therefore essential, contents of Holy Writ, will still, for a long time to come, tax the penetration and erudition of men of science, and will thus furnish matter for their controversies. And if through the progress which has been made in philology, in history, and in archæology, we are now enabled to understand and to value many of these details better than our forefathers could do, why should we not assume that geology and its cognate sciences enable us to understand the Biblical account of creation better than did our forefathers? Those truths which are essential, and which are alone of importance to the Christian, the great truths that God is the Creator of all things, and man the earthly image of God, were known to be doctrines of Biblical revelation by those who preceded us just as well as by ourselves, and in spite of all the progress of science we must cling to those truths no less closely than they did.

But there is still one more point. If plants and animals of various kinds did exist on the earth in great numbers, and were petrified during the formation of the strata, before the creation of man, what was the object of these primæval organisms? For what reason did this whole series of formations and revolutions, of bringings forth and destructions, take place on the earth before it was made fit to be the dwelling-place of man? And why did not God, who is the Almighty, create the earth and its organisms in such a manner as to fit it at once to be the dwelling-place of man? These no doubt are questions which may be asked, and to which answers are much to be desired. And yet I need not hesitate openly to confess that I do not know these answers. Divine revelation has taught us nothing about them, and it was not necessary that it should do so, as it never mentions all these bringings forth and changes, which according to geologists preceded the appearance of man. We know nothing of these events from the Bible; all we know, we know through geology. We may admit that the teaching of geologists is correct, because the Bible tells us nothing which contradicts it; we must only supplement this teaching from the Bible by saying that all these geological events have been brought about by the creative power and providence of God. Natural science can make no objection to this, and by this means peace is established between natural science and theology; nor can this peace be disturbed by the fact that theological speculation, to which alone this question belongs, may perhaps be unable to show why the might and wisdom of God did create the world exactly in this manner.

God is Almighty, and it is just for this reason that

He is able to make use of various methods in His outward working. But the actions of God are incomprehensible to man, and therefore, as I have already said, we have no right to say God should not have done so and so because we do not understand why He should have done it. We must believe that God, if He had so willed it, could, in one single moment, by one single creative act, have made the earth, and fitted it to be at once the dwelling-place of man. But we may not assert that this mode of creation is the only one worthy of God, and that consequently God must have created in this manner, for it is not for us to decide *a priori* how God must have acted, but only to discover *a posteriori* how God has acted. If we have discovered this, we must say that this action of God's is an outcome of His might and wisdom. We may then seek to discover further, *how* God's might and wisdom have manifested themselves in this action. If we succeed in discovering the intentions of God, and the manner in which He has realized them, we shall be able to praise His might and wisdom with full understanding. If we do not succeed in doing so, we must notwithstanding doubt neither God's might nor His wisdom, nor conclude that God must have acted otherwise.

A religious contemplation of history will discover in countless historical events a confirmation of the truth that God is the wise director of the fates of men and nations; but if we come across historical events in which we are unable to recognise proofs of divine guidance, and of which we are unable to discover the divine purpose, we must not therefore suppose that these events have occurred *sine numine*, still less must we deny the facts; we should rather say, that if the facts themselves in their whole connection, and with all their circumstances, causes, and consequences, were more clearly known to us, we might perhaps recognise more distinctly the hand of God in them; and we may also express a hope that the further progress of historical inquiry which investigates the development of the future as well as the events of the present and of the immediate past, and may be called generally, the philosophy of history, will solve for us many of the historical problems of providence.

And it is just the same with what the book of nature tells us about the primæval state of the earth. We must first get a complete survey of the earth's history in the pre-human period, and this geology and palæontology can obtain for us from the chronicles contained in the strata. This must be followed by the contemplation of these historical facts from a religious point of view, that is to say, by the inquiry, "How did God's might and wisdom manifest themselves in the facts of natural history, and with what intentions was God impelled to act in the way in which, according to the evidence of facts, He did act?" That this question is not as yet answered, need neither disturb nor surprise us, because a similar question on a subject which is allied to this one, but is still nearer to us, still awaits a perfectly satisfactory solution. If we contemplate nature in its present shape, we find in its greatness and smallness, in the organization of the universe and of the earth, in the laws which regulate the climatic and other natural conditions of the earth, in the general working together of organic beings, in the structure of separate animals and plants, in the bodily organization of man,—we find, I say, in everything which may become the object of religio-philosophical contemplation, many signs of the might and wisdom of God. But considering the limited nature of our intellectual powers, and the enormous mass and variety of the material, it is not wonderful that the task involved in this mode of contemplating nature, the task of "analyzing the Creator's thoughts as they are revealed in the creation,"[1] is far from being completely fulfilled; that there is still much in the whole of the Cosmos, and in its separate portions, in which we cannot as yet discover the intentions and objects of the Creator. But if this is true of nature in its present condition, it is much less wonderful that we should be unable to assert anything positively concerning the object of those natural conditions and events which belong to the earliest ages, and which are only known to us, as they actually existed and as they occurred, by our observation of the consequences which they entailed, and by scientific inferences and hypothesis.

For what purpose is the splendour of the tropical vegetation; for what purpose the variety of the animal world, which year after year develops its magnificence in the American forests, which lives and dies without having been seen by mortal eyes since the day of creation? Tell me this, and I will tell you for what end the fauna and flora were created, whose petrified

[1] Thus Agassiz; cf. *Jahrbuch für Deutsche Theologie*, vi. (1861) 675.

remains we dig up from the bosom of the earth. Just as the leaves fall from the trees, as millions of blossoms never come to perfection, in the immeasurable store of the divine riches, and yet before they end their short existence fulfil known and unknown ends according to the wise intentions of the Creator, even so by His might and wisdom whole periods of animal and vegetable creations may have lived and died, whose object is known to the Eternal, but is hidden from men.[1]

There are countless stars which no human eye had seen till telescopes were invented, many which have only been discovered in our century, and, as we may conclude with certainty, many which are not yet discovered, and which never will be visible from the earth: these stars also have their end and their meaning in the starry system. The blessed spirits who live above the stars know what this is; we can only conjecture, and for us, therefore, these distant worlds only serve immediately to show us through the vastness of the creation the infinity of the Creator.

Modern savants have discovered, by the help of the microscope, an entirely new world of animal life, of which our forefathers had no idea; according to Ehrenberg's calculations, millions of animalculæ often exist in one cubic inch of water, and the ditches, ponds, and marshes of one single not very extensive tract of country may alone contain a greater number of microscopic animals than is comprised in the whole animal world on the earth's surface. These beings also no doubt have their importance for the whole system of the creation, we may even assume that they are

[1] Vosen, *Das Christenthum*, p. 737.

necessary to it, and that the creation as it is could not exist without them, although we are not, or not yet, able to understand what end they serve.

In the same way, no doubt, the primæval plants and animals have their end and meaning for the whole system of God's creatures, although we do not as yet clearly understand it, and are not able to point out what it is. It has been already shown that some of the organisms of the primæval world bear witness to the wisdom of the Creator,[1] and, as Lyell says: "The proofs now accumulated of the close analogy between extinct and recent species are such as to leave no doubt on the mind that the same harmony of parts and beauty of contrivance which we admire in the living creation, has equally characterized the organic world at remote periods."[2] And we may gather also from the results of scientific inquiry that the different stages of development which the organic creation, and also the inorganic creation, *i.e.* the formation of the earth, have gone through, are so closely connected with one another, and there is so much harmony everywhere, both in their course of development and in their governing principles, that even savants like Burmeister cannot avoid recognising a distinct *design*, with distinct aims and objects in the history of organic nature.[3] Agassiz expresses his enthusiastic belief that the natural science of the future "will point out with growing minuteness, and will describe more and more clearly and suitably, the manifold ties binding together all animals and

---

[1] Especially by Buckland, *Geology and Mineralogy considered with reference to Natural Theology*, vol. i. p. 107. H. Miller, *Testimony*, p. 203.

[2] *Elements of Geology.*

[3] Ulrici, *Gott und die Natur*, p. 417.

plants into the one living expression of the gigantic conception of the Creator, which, like a grand Epic, has, in the course of centuries, attained its fulfilment."[1]

God has created all things for His glory, the unreasoning creatures in order that through them the reasoning creatures should recognise His might, wisdom, and goodness. We may therefore expect that a more perfect knowledge of the earth, of its condition, its fashioning, its organisms, and its history, will show us, with increasing grandeur, how wonderfully the might, wisdom, and goodness of the Creator have acted for the benefit of man in the widest sense of the word. The increased knowledge of the extinct forms of the earth and its organisms, which we shall obtain from the further progress of geological science, will show us more and more plainly the relation of the visible creation to reasoning creatures.

Geologists say, for example, that the luxuriant vegetation of the Carboniferous age served two purposes. First, by absorption, it removed from the air the excess of carbon, and of other substances injurious to animal life, and thus rendered possible the existence of air-breathing animals on the earth; and then it served to hoard up for future ages those mineral masses which provide us with means for warmth, and without which much of the progress of modern civilisation, steamboats, railways and the like, would seem hardly possible. In the same way, the bringing forth of other organic beings, and the formation of the strata in which they found their grave, may either have a direct bearing on

[1] *Jahrbuch für Deutsche Theologie*, vi. 678.

the good of man, or may form a necessary link in the chain of evolutions, through which God brought the earth to the condition in which it was fitted to be man's dwelling-place.[1] The progress of geological inquiry will no doubt show us more and more plainly, that there is a system in the geological developments, that a wise Being has sometimes by creating, sometimes by destroying, worked knowingly for a distinct object, and according to a fixed and clear, although complicated plan. No doubt God could have created any quantity of coal out of nothing, and He could have called forth the earth from nothingness, in the condition in which it was on the day when the first man was created on it. Revelation teaches us that He did not do this. If we read the Bible without any reference to the results of scientific inquiry, and if we take its account quite literally, we find that God did not create the earth in its completed form in one moment,

[1] "We have seen that the infusoria lived and died in countless myriads, and furnished the tripoli and the opal; that river snails and sea shells elaborated the marble for our temples and palaces, and polyparia, the limestone of which our edifices are constructed; and that grass, herb, and tree have been converted either into materials to enrich the soil, or into a mineral which should serve as fuel in future ages when such a substance became indispensable to the necessities and luxuries of civilised man. Thus it is that geology has thrown a new interest around every grain of sand and every blade of grass; and that the pebble rejected by the moralist and the divine, becomes, in the hand of the philosopher, a striking proof of infinite wisdom. But ought we to rest content in the assumption that all these wonderful manifestations of creative intelligence were solely designed to contribute to our physical necessities and gratifications? Say rather that this display of beauty, power, and goodness was designed to fill the soul with high and holy thoughts,—to call forth the exercise of our reasoning powers,—to excite in us those ardent and lofty aspirations after truth and knowledge which elevate the mind above the sordid and petty concerns of life, and give us a foretaste of that high destiny which we are instructed to hope may be our portion hereafter."—G. Mantell, *Wonders of Geology*, pp. 676 and 677.

but fashioned it, in six days, out of the chaotic condition in which He had created it. Therefore, from the Biblical point of view, we must admit that 'it is not unworthy of the Divine Being to choose the way of gradual formation instead of that of immediate creation; and the questions, why did God work in this way, and how did He thereby manifest His wisdom and might, were problems discussed even by the Fathers. They are merely modified, if, in consequence of the results of scientific inquiry, we consider the six days, together with the period of chaos, as a long period, and include the geological developments in the Mosaic record.

By this means a new and wide field is opened out to philosophical and theological speculation, and a new and grateful task is before us. In one of his lectures, Cardinal Wiseman shows very beautifully how the Church has pressed into her service the great spiritual developments of the different centuries, and how, without any change in her own being, she has displayed a wonderful understanding and appreciation of the intellectual tendencies of the separate centuries. But as in other ages philosophy, art, and classical literature were prominent in the intellectual life, so in our age, says the Cardinal, scientific inquiry might be pointed out as the characteristic tendency, and therefore it is unavoidable that this new phase of human endeavour should also leave an evident impression on the Church.[1]

We are now on the threshold of this new development of science. Nature in its details and in its con-

---

[1] *Essays on Religion and Literature, by various Writers*, ed. by H. E. Manning, London 1865, p. 7.

nection, in its phenomena and its laws, has never been known at any time as it is in this century. It was only in our century that an effort could be made "to comprehend the manifold phenomena of the Cosmos in the form of a rational whole,"[1] and the author of the Cosmos who has made this effort, is modest enough to lay stress on the fact that only part of the problem is solved.[2] Still less can we look at present for a complete solution of the higher problem, that of comprehending the manifold phenomena of the Cosmos as a divinely connected whole.

A humbler but a more urgent task is before theologians, that of proving that no contradiction exists between the teaching of the Book of Nature and the teaching of the Book of Revelation. It is to this task that I must confine myself in these lectures.

[1] Humboldt, *Cosmos*, i. 65.   [2] *Ibid.* p. 68.

XX.

THE BOUNDARY BETWEEN THE PRIMÆVAL AND THE PRESENT WORLD. THE DILUVIUM.

THE sharp distinction between the primæval and the present world is connected with the theory discussed in my 17th lecture, namely, that immediately before the creation of man, and of the vegetable and animal world which surrounded him, the earlier form of the earth with its organisms was destroyed by a geological catastrophe. According to the theories developed in my last two lectures, it cannot be supposed that such a clear distinction existed; but the expression "primæval world" may be used in these theories to denote the periods in the world's history which elapsed before the creation of man. There are many reasons, as you will see in the course of my lecture, which will compel me to discuss at what point in the history of the world as it is described by geologists and palæontologists, the primæval world ceases, and the present world, or recent period, begins. The geological formations which certainly belong to the historical period, and are continuing now, *e.g.* the deltas of rivers, coral islands, peat mosses, and such like, must no doubt belong to the latter; while the formations which are ascribed to the Azoic, Palæozoic, and Mezozoic periods must no less undoubtedly belong to the primæval world.[1] The period in which we must undertake to draw the boundary line between the primæval and the present world is the Cainozoic or Tertiary period.[2] Does the beginning of the recent period, or the first appearance of man, occur before the beginning, or after the close of the Cainozoic period, or during this period? The last would be possible, because the Cainozoic period, like the other periods, includes not only one formation, but a whole series of superimposed strata. There are difficulties in the way of minutely defining the boundaries of these strata, and the determination of the boundary between the highest Cainozoic stratum and the lowest recent stratum is especially difficult. It is therefore always possible that formations which are usually ascribed to the Cainozoic period, that is, to the period before man, really belong to the recent period, that is, to the age of man. Geologists say that it is much more difficult to define the limits, to divide and to ascertain the order of the Cainozoic formations, than those of any other period.

Lyell, who has many followers, distinguishes four sub-divisions in this period, to which he gives rather strange names. He calls the oldest strata of the Cainozoic period the *eocene*, from ἠώς and χαινός, thus answering to the dawn of a new period; the two following sub-divisions he calls *miocene* and *pliocene*, from μεῖον and πλεῖον and χαινός, that is, less and more recent. The most recent strata he formerly called *pleistocene*, that is, the most recent. In his later writings, instead of the last name he makes use of the denomination *post-*

[1] See above, p. 283.   [2] See above, p. 312.

pliocene, and includes the post-pliocene and the recent strata under the name *post-tertiary*. I will only mention one of the simplest among the countless other divisions and names ;[1] the *eogene* formation, *neogene* formation (Molasse), and the Diluvium ; this third name brings me to the further remarks which I propose to make.

In a pamphlet which Buckland published in 1823, under the name of *Reliquiæ Diluvianæ*, he put together all the geological phenomena which he ascribed to the flooding of the earth in the time of Noah, the flood which is mentioned in Genesis under the name of the Deluge, Diluvium. Since Buckland, Cardinal Wiseman has been foremost in enumerating in his well-known lectures[2] the "geological proofs of the reality of the Deluge." I must just mention the principal points.

I will begin with the so-called Bone Caves.[3] We find, especially in the limestones of the most different formations, natural cavities, which in places spread out into lofty and enormous vaults, in other places are again contracted, lead through narrow passages into new chambers, and sometimes extend to vast distances

---

[1] See Pfaff, *Grundriss*, p. 346. Cf. Giebel, *Paläontologie*, p. 235 : "The most diverse local strata lie above the chalk rocks; these are all classed together as tertiary formations, and in them, together with the diluvium which is equally spread over the whole surface of the earth, we see the last epochs of the geological formation of the earth's solid crust. It is difficult to divide them into separate systems, corresponding to the primary and secondary (Palæozoic and Mezozoic), because of their small extent, and their peculiarly local characteristics. But still it has been thought necessary to distinguish three formations between the chalk and the diluvium, and these have been called eocene, miocene, and pliocene, or lower, middle, and upper tertiary."

[2] *Twelve Lectures on the Connection between Science and Revealed Religion.*

[3] Burmeister, *Gesch. der Schöpfung*. p. 462. Leonhard, *Geologie*, ii. 315. Vogt, *Lehrbuch der Geologie*, i. 594. Nöggerath, *Ges. Naturwiss.* iii. 290.

underground. Masses of chalk, lime, sand, and all kinds of rolled stones have fallen into these caves through the openings which connect them with the surface of the earth. Under these rolled stones we find in many of the caves great quantities of the bones of animals, usually not exactly petrified, but in their natural condition, often, however, covered with stalagmite, or cemented together. Sometimes it is possible that these bones may have been washed into the caves with the rolled stones. But when the bones are not polished and have not lost their outline, as would be the case had they been washed down and rolled about by water, we must suppose that the animals must have got into the cave, that they there decayed, and that only the skeletons have been preserved, on which a coating which kept them from decomposition has been deposited. Two things are then possible: either the animals lived in the caves, and there died a natural death, or were suffocated and buried by the water which flowed in; or their corpses were washed in. It is supposed that the former occurred in those caves which contain chiefly the bones of one kind of animal, for instance, bears or hyænas. Thus, in a cave at Kirkdale in England, which was explored by Buckland, hyæna bones were principally found. It is supposed that it was inhabited by hyænas, and that the bones of horses, oxen, and deer which were found with them, are those of animals which were dragged in by the hyænas; it is said that whole layers of the excrement of hyænas were found there. Other caves only contain the bones of graminivorous animals, *e.g.* horses, unicorns, sheep, and deer, and as these animals do not usually inhabit caves, it is supposed that they sought a refuge there, flying from the terrors of some convulsion of the earth, or, as is more likely, that the lair of these animals was in some neighbouring place, and that a stream of water washed them into the cave where they were found. The bones of at least 1000 animals have by degrees been extracted from the Gailenreuth cave in Bavaria, of which more than 800 were bears, 130 wolves, hyænas, lions, and wolverenes. These animals cannot all have lived in the cave together; we must therefore suppose that their corpses were washed into it, with all kinds of rolled stones and mud.

Besides the Bone Caves, the Osseous Breccias must be mentioned.[1] These are fissures in the older rocks, which are open from above, and have been filled up with fragments of bones, the teeth of large and small mammals, besides shells, the remains of plants and wood, pieces of limestone and other rubbish; all of which has been cemented into a solid mass by calcareous cement or clay.

The Bone Caves, of which many have been found in very different countries, lie in most cases so high above the neighbouring rivers, that the latter could not reach them when in flood, so that at any rate there must have been very extensive inundations. The fact that the animals whose remains are found in the Bone Caves belong not to the older formations, but to the present animal world, or are very closely related to it, favours the supposition that these floods must be identified with the Deluge in the time of Noah.

To this category belong also the deposits of tufaceous

[1] Nöggerath, *Ges. Naturwiss.* iii. 159.

limestone at Canstatt, in which numerous mammoth bones and teeth are found; the enormous deposits of clay in the Pampas of South America, with their skeletons of gigantic sloths, ant-eaters, armadilloes, and the like; the "loess," a yellowish grey, sandy gravel, produced by the alluvial deposits of several rivers, especially of the Rhine, in which such deposits are found as high as 600 feet above the level of the sea,[1] and so on. Of a similar character are the metalliferous deposits,[2] that is, those masses of conglomerate (gravel, sand, and lime) in which metals, especially gold, platinum, tin, and precious stones are found, which have been carried away from their original beds by flowing streams of water. It is supposed that the metals and precious stones originally formed part of older formations; the rocks surrounding them were crushed and destroyed, the rubbish was dissolved and removed by water washed away with the precious stones and lumps of metal it contained, and deposited in valleys, ravines, and hollows. We conclude that this washing away and intermingling took place in the period of the Deluge, because the gold and platinum ores found in the Ural Mountains contain the remains of the mammoth and rhinoceros; and those found in Australia the bones of extinct species of opossum. The ores found in the beds of rivers are no doubt in most cases probably produced by the uprooting and intermingling of older deposits; but these older deposits must in their turn be traced back to earlier important floods.

Lastly, the so-called *erratic blocks* call for special

[1] Lyell, *Elements of Geology*, i. 119.
[2] Nöggerath, *Ges. Naturwiss.* iii. 292.

attention.[1] These are pieces of rock of various dimensions, reaching to 40,000 cubic feet, which are found scattered about at very great distances from the rocks to which they appear originally to have belonged. These blocks are scattered over the whole North German plain, as far as Poland or Russia; and it is unanimously assumed by geologists that they are not indigenous, but have come there from the mountains of Scandinavia or Finland, inasmuch as they exactly resemble the rocks of these mountains in their conformation. Similarly, blocks of granite, which originally formed part of the opposite Alpine range, are found in the Jura Mountains. The same fact has been noticed in England, Belgium, Holland, and France, in North America, and in the neighbourhood of the Cordilleras.

Buckland traced back all these geological phenomena to the Noachian Deluge. Almost simultaneously, Cuvier was speaking with the greatest certainty of geological proofs of the reality of the Deluge, "I think, with Deluc and Dolomieu, that if there is one thing which is certain in geology, it is that the surface of our earth has undergone a great and sudden convulsion, and that this took place not more than five or six thousand years ago; that, in consequence of this convulsion, those continents which were originally the abode of man, and of animals well known to us in the present day, sank and were overflowed; that, on the other hand, the same convulsion laid bare the bed of the sea, and by this means formed the continents

---

[1] Lyell, *Elements of Geology*, i. 143. Leonhard, *Geologie*, iii. 468, 484. Vogt, *Lehrb. der Geologie*, i. 601. Wagner, *Gesch. der Urwelt*, i. 438, ii. 352. Heer, *Die Urwelt*, p. 509.

which are at present inhabited. This is one of the most conclusively proved, and also least expected results of rational geology."[1]

Buckland's observations were approved of by some English geologists, and were contradicted by others who believed no less firmly in the Bible. Buckland himself withdrew his own theory in later years, and placed the Deluge, of which he had put together the geological proofs, in an earlier age than that of the Noachian Deluge. Speaking of the former, he says:[2] "Hence it seems more probable that the event in question was the last of the many geological revolutions that have been produced by violent irruptions of water, rather than the comparatively tranquil inundation described in the inspired narrative. It has been justly argued, against the attempt to identify these two great historical and natural phenomena, that as the rise and fall of the waters of the Mosaic Deluge are described to have been gradual and of short duration, they would have produced comparatively little change on the surface of the country they overflowed. The large preponderances of extinct animals we find in caves and in superficial deposits of diluvium, and the non-discovery of human bones along with them, afford other strong reason for referring these species to a period anterior to the creation of man."[3]

The Biblical name was, however, retained by geolo-

[1] *Discours sur les révolutions de la surface du globe* (3rd ed. Paris 1826), p. 138. The passage, together with some other observations by French geologists to the same effect, is quoted by Nicolas, *Phil. Studien*, i. 390. Cuvier, however, did not think that the Deluge was universal; see the following lecture.

[2] *Geology and Mineralogy considered with Reference to Natural Theology.*

[3] Jameson and J. Fleming opposed Buckland's theory; the latter in

gists, even after the theory that the Deluge was the same as that in the time of Noah was rejected; and thenceforth the *diluvium* represented the last great pre-human inundation of the earth, with its deposits and its results, while the action of the waters on the earth's surface in the human period, including the Noachian Deluge, was called *alluvium*.

The boundary between the present and the primæval world would therefore be found in this geological diluvium of Buckland's, if we identify it with the covering of the earth by the waters which is described in the second verse of Genesis. Many people have supposed this to be the case, in Germany notably, Kurtz and Andreas Wagner. "Organic life was destroyed on the whole earth by the diluvium," says Wagner. "At the same time, the earth was enveloped in darkness, as we are told in Genesis. It is not unlikely that warmth was withdrawn from the earth with light, and that thus an icy cold supervened which destroyed all the germs of organic life which had been spared by the Flood, and which were buried in the earth. Thus the glacial theory of Agassiz (which must be mentioned here) would to some extent be justified; enormous masses of ice may have been floating on the waters, so that the ground was frozen to such a depth, that the bodies of mammoths and other animals which were buried in it have been preserved up to our day in the Polar regions, where the heat of summer only thaws the surface of the ground. When the time had come for a new order of things to spring

"The Geological Deluge," *Edinburgh Philosophical Journal*, xiv. Cf. Pye Smith, *The Relation*, etc., p. 101.

out of the desolation of the earth, God first caused light to break forth again, and, at the same time, caused the ice-bound crust of the earth to be thawed by the warmth which came from the light; and then there followed the re-formation of the earth which is described in the Hexæmeron."[1]

But in modern times, men have come more and more to doubt whether the geological diluvium was sufficient to produce the condition of the earth which the so-called theory of Restitution presupposes. At least, there are no traces of a desolation so great, that light had to be brought forth anew, and that the atmosphere of the earth had to be re-created. It is not even thought probable by most geologists that a simultaneous inundation of the whole earth took place, whereby organic life was entirely destroyed; on the contrary, they think that the so-called diluvial formations were not caused by one great flood, but by a series of different geological developments and events, which were spread over a long period. Greenough says: "Some fourteen years ago I advanced an opinion, founded altogether upon physical and geological considerations, that the entire earth had, at an unknown period, . . . been covered by one general but temporary deluge. . . . New data have flowed in, and . . . I now read my recantation. . . . If, 5000 years ago, a deluge did sweep over the entire globe, its traces can no longer be distinguished from more modern and local disturbances."[2]

In the same way another English geologist, Sedgwick,

[1] *Gesch. der Urwelt*, ii. 352. Cf. a similar theory held by Fabre d'Envieu, see above, p. 327, note 2.
[2] *Address at the Anniversary Meeting of the Geological Society*, London, 1834, p. 30.

has not only openly recalled his assent to the earlier theory of the Deluge, but has also expressed himself against the other theory I mentioned. He says: "There is, I think, one great negative conclusion now incontestably established—that the vast masses of diluvial gravel, scattered almost over the surface of the earth, do not belong to one violent and transitory period. It was indeed a most unwarranted conclusion, when we assumed the contemporaneity of all the superficial gravel on the earth. We saw the clearest traces of diluvial action, and we had, in our sacred histories, the record of a general Deluge. On this double testimony it was, that we gave a unity to a vast succession of phenomena, not one of which we perfectly comprehended, and, under the name diluvian, classed them all together. . . . Having been myself a believer and . . . a propagator of what I now regard as a philosophic heresy, . . . I think it right . . . thus publicly to read my recantation." The error consisted "in classing together distant unknown formations under one name; in giving them a simultaneous origin, and in determining their date."[1]

We find, then, that the name diluvium is universally given by modern geologists to a whole geological period and formation; the same as that which Lyell calls pleistocene, or post-pliocene. Others have proposed to give the name of quaternary, or *quartary*, to the formations which occur between the tertiary and the recent formations.

---

[1] *Addresses at the Anniversary Meeting of the Geological Society*, 1831, p. 34. Cf. similar opinions expressed by English and American geologists in "*The Relation*," etc., p. 109. T. Pye Smith.

The teaching of geologists about the diluvium in this sense, or about the period of the quarternary formations, is essentially as follows.[1]

It is very difficult to separate this period from the tertiary on the one hand, and from the present period on the other, and it can only be done with some degree of certainty when we observe traces of a phenomenon which appears in this period for the first time in the history of the earth — namely, the Glaciers. These act in two ways—first, by the removal of pieces of rock, and then by rubbing, rounding, smoothing, and grooving the walls of rock and the stones, over and upon which the masses of ice move. If the glacier terminates on dry land, the blocks of stone it carries with it are only transported as far as the ground. But if it terminates in the sea, or in a lake, blocks of the ice are broken off, and float with their load of rocks wherever wind and tide may lead them, until the warmth of the water, the air and the sun, has completely thawed the blocks of ice, so that the rocks sink to the bottom. Now geologists think they have ascertained that, after the pliocene period, glaciers on an immense scale existed in the highlands of Switzerland, Scotland, England, Scandinavia, and North America. In this period the glaciers of Switzerland transported pieces of rock as far as the Jura, beyond the Rhine, and the Lake of Constance, and, on the other side, far into the Italian plain. In Scandinavia the glaciers terminated in the sea, and, by means of the icebergs which were detached from them,

[1] For what follows, see Pfaff, *Grundriss*, p. 371. Cf. *Die neuesten Forschungen*, p. 55. *Schöpfungsgeschichte*, pp. 618, 619, 725. Fraas, *Vor der Sündfluth*, p. 429. Heer, *Die Urwelt*, p. 516. Alex. Braun, *Die Eiszeit der Erde*, Berlin 1870.

the erratic blocks were conveyed to the North German plain,[1] to Holland, and Russia. The finer material of these glaciers—gravel, sand, and clay—is also found in manifold forms in various places, and probably the loess was formed by the waters of the glaciers.

Many of the details are still uncertain, but geologists consider that, after the investigations made in recent years by the Swiss savants Venetz, Charpentier, Agassiz, Studer, Guyot, and others, the great extent of the glaciers in the countries I have named, is a certain and well-assured fact. Most of them think it was extremely probable that, during this glacial period, there were variations; that at one time the glaciers were very large, then became smaller again and contracted, only in order to undergo another vast expansion, after which they shrank into their present limits. For this reason many geologists speak of two glacial periods, divided by an intervening milder period.

But it must not be assumed, as A. Wagner seems to think, in the passage above quoted, that an entire congelation took place, and that all life died out in this age, even in the lands in which it can be proved that there was a Glacial period, as in Northern Europe and America.[2] The animals whose remains are found in the bone caves and other deposits of this time, and which belong partly to extinct and partly to still existing species, lived partly before, partly after, and partly during the Glacial period.

I now return to the question which arose at the be-

---

[1] J. Roth, *Die geologische Bildung der norddeutschen Ebene*, Berlin 1870.
[2] Fraas, *Vor der Sündfluth*, p. 434.

ginning of my lecture, namely, Where is the boundary between the primæval and the present world? or, as I can now more definitely put it, Do these diluvial, pleistocene, or quaternary formations, belong to the present or to the primæval world? The answer to this question will depend upon the answer to the following question, Do we find in these formations traces of the existence of man? Buckland, as you will have noticed, proceeded from the assumption that this was not the case. And this was formerly the general view. This question has been much agitated of late years, and I am the more bound to discuss it thoroughly here, because, as you will see, it is in several ways of great importance in determining the relation between the Bible and geology.

The importance of this question to certain theories is probably the reason that it has often been discussed in a manner which does not give an impression of complete candour. Those who support the theory of a well-defined boundary between the primæval and the present world, are naturally interested in proving that the bones of man are not found in the strata which they believe to be primæval; on the other hand, any one who wished to refer the whole or the greater part of the fossiliferous strata to the period after the creation of man, would equally naturally wish to find traces of man in the earliest possible formations.[1] Of later years the question has usually been discussed in connection with the endeavours to ascertain the antiquity of man by geological means, and as many geologists have come to conclusions which cannot be reconciled

[1] Bosizio, *Das Hexæmeron*, p. 453.

with the customary Biblical chronology, the Biblical apologist is often tempted to doubt the premises of the geological arguments. I must discuss this last point in more detail later; for the present, we will confine ourselves to the question whether the existence of man, in the diluvial age, can be proved, and we will consider the facts which are adduced to prove it without prejudice. If these facts are found to be indubitable, we shall find at most, that not the Bible itself, but only some interpretation of the Bible, is out of harmony with them.

I shall base this inquiry principally on Lyell's book on the *Antiquity of Man*, which treats most minutely of the subject, and also on Karl Vogt's *Lectures on Man*.[1]

Lyell mentions, as one of the palæontological peculiarities of the diluvial or, as he calls them, the post-pliocene deposits, that the shells usually belong to extinct, and the mammalia to still existing species. Was man, then, a contemporary of these extinct species? Lyell answers: "It is already clear that man was contemporary in Europe with two species of elephant now extinct, E. primigenius and E. antiquus; two also of rhinoceros, R. tichorhinus and R. hemitæcus (Falc.); at least one species of hippopotamus, the cave-bear, cave-lion, and cave-hyæna, various bovine, equine, and cervine animals now extinct, and many smaller carnivora, rodentia, and insectivora. While these were slowly passing away, the musk buffalo, reindeer, and other arctic species, which have survived to our

---

[1] I have discussed this subject before, in the year 1864, in "*Briefe über Bibel und Natur*," published in the "*Chilianeum*," iv. 103.

times, were retreating northwards, from the valleys of the Thames and Seine to their present more arctic haunts."[1] The facts on which Lyell bases his theory that man was already in existence before these species of animals had died out, or while they still lived in Central Europe, are, for the most part, well known; but geologists were not unanimous as to the conclusions to be drawn from these facts. As early as 1833, Schmerling had found, in caves near Lüttich, human bones and implements intermingled with bones, not only of still existing species of animals, but also of species which are everywhere extinct,—or, at any rate, no longer inhabit Belgium,—such as the cave-bear, the elephant, and the rhinoceros. Caves with similar contents had also been found in France, England, and Germany. Most geologists, and among them Lyell himself, assumed that it did not follow from this that man had existed simultaneously with these extinct animals. The cave might have served first as a lair for wild beasts, whose bones had remained there; later on, men might have inhabited it, used it as a refuge, or as a burying-place for the dead; and, later still, all these remains belonging to different periods might have been intermingled by floods.[2]

Now Lyell says,[3] that such intermixtures have in reality taken place in some caves, and that sometimes geologists have erroneously assigned fossils to one

---

[1] *The Geological Evidences of the Antiquity of Man.* Sir Charles Lyell. 3rd ed. p. 375. Cf. Vogt, *Vorlesungen,* ii. 15.

[2] See Leonhard, *Geologie,* ii. 334. Mantell, *Wonders of Geology,* i. 148. H. von Meyer, *Die Reptilien,* p. 117. Burmeister, *Gesch. der Schöpfung.* p. 500. Quenstedt, *Sonst und Jetzt,* p. 241.

[3] *Antiquity of Man,* p. 62.

period which in reality had been introduced at successive times; but that, nevertheless, in recent years most convincing proofs had been found that man did exist at the same time as the mammoth and other extinct animals whose bones have been found in several caves together with human bones and implements.

Vogt thus enumerates the facts in question,— "History shows us that in all ages the caves were partly places of refuge, and partly the abode of more or less uncivilised peoples. Ancient writers tell us of the Troglodytes, or dwellers in caves, who inhabited parts of Asia Minor, Greece, and Italy. The assemblies of Pagans and Christians, who were prevented from celebrating the services of their religion by the persecutions of those of a different belief, always took place in woods and caves. Certain caves and ravines were used as places of execution, into which criminals were thrown, and where they were exposed to a lingering death; others were used as burial grounds, in which the bodies were in some cases only laid, in some cases really buried. Most caves and grottoes are used by shepherds and the inhabitants of forests now-a-days, as a place of refuge in bad weather, and for cooking or sleeping purposes while they are dwelling in their neighbourhood for a time. We cannot therefore be surprised at finding in many grottoes and caves great quantities of human bones, remains of the arts and industries of the most various ages, down to modern times. In the cave of Mialet near Anduze in the Cevennes, for instance, there were found fragments of pots, of

Roman lamps, and the statuette of a senator, wrapped in his toga, baked in yellow clay,—that is to say Roman antiquities, mixed with polished flint axes and other flint implements belonging to an earlier period of civilisation. In one part of the cave a burial-place was found; this was dug out of a kind of sandy clay with which were mingled the bones of bears, and it was filled with human bones. In other parts of the cave, objects of art were found in an alluvial deposit, which was evidently more recent than the osseous clay, and which lay above it. At the back of the cave, seven or eight bears' skulls had been laid one above the other in a fissure in the rock, and these had been so surrounded and fenced in with large stones which had fallen from the roof, that they formed a kind of monument. There is no doubt that all these objects belonged to later inhabitants of the cave, especially as it can be historically proved, that during the persecutions in the reign of Louis XIV. the Protestants used to hold their religious services in this cave. I mention this as an example, to show that later deposits such as these may take place either above the original osseous soil, or in its upper strata if there is no covering of stalagmite, or in the soil itself if this had been turned over and dug up by later intruders, and if the covering of stalagmite has been broken through. All these later importations into the caves may doubtless be easily (?) recognised and distinguished, if the research is conducted with some attention and care. But the case is different when the human bones are found in just the same state, and in just the same condition as the other (!) bones of animals, when they are buried in the same clay which shows throughout no signs of change or of upturning, when, together with the bones of extinct animals, they are found lying under a well-preserved cover of stalagmite which nowhere shows a trace of any injury, or are even joined to the other bones by masses of stalagmite, so that the bones of bears and of men are brought out in one and the same block of stone.

"In cases such as these no further doubt can be possible, if the discovery has been made by experienced observers, who have carefully attended to, and minutely investigated, the facts. We can surely no longer doubt that the man who was buried with the bear existed contemporaneously with him on the earth." [1]

Most recent inquirers think with Vogt, that there is sufficient proof in these and other similar facts that man existed at the same time as the extinct animals of the Diluvian (Post-pliocene) age;[2] although there are still a few who dispute this conclusion, and say that the intermixture of human remains with those of extinct animals in the stalagmite incrustations of the caves can be otherwise explained.[3] As a further proof, the fact is adduced that in the alluvial deposits of many of the river valleys in France, human implements and the bones of extinct animals have been found together, under conditions which do not admit of any doubt as to the simultaneous existence of men and these extinct animals. I must return to this point

---

[1] *Vorlesungen*, ii. 22.

[2] Pfaff, *Grundriss*, p. 375. *Die neuesten Forschungen*, p. 43. Fraas, *Vor der Sündfluth*, p. 449. Nadaillac, *L'ancienneté de l'homme*, p. 71.

[3] See the article on Lyell's book in the *Westminster Review*, Ap. 1863, p. 521.

and discuss it in more detail later, so I rest content here with merely alluding to it.

However convincing the proofs put together by Lyell, Vogt, and others are, taken as a whole, to me, —for there is much that is arbitrary in some of them, —yet the question as to the contemporary existence of man and the extinct animals cannot be regarded as settled, when we find such an esteemed geologist as Phillips declaring, when he was president of the British Association at Birmingham in September 1865, that further careful investigation was necessary before the matter could be definitely decided.[1] I only say therefore that it is probable, and according to the belief of most modern geologists, certain, that man existed in the Diluvial age. In addition to this, I may say that although men of science assert that man existed on earth even before the so-called Glacial period,[2] the greater number of savants, and these the most trustworthy, including Lyell and Vogt,[3] unanimously declare that, up to this time, proofs that man lived only after the Glacial period have been found, —or to speak more accurately, during the period which began with the advance of the glaciers; when doubtless the climate was much colder than it is

---

[1] *Athenæum*, 9th September 1865, p. 344.

[2] Perty, *Anthropol. Vorträge*, pp. 54, 57. Schleiden, *Das Alter des Menschengeschlechts*, p. 20. Büchner, *Die Stellung des Menschen*, p. 61. F. Unger, *Das Alter der Menschheit*, p. 45. "It is hardly credible that his (man's) *origin* should have coincided with the time at which such unfavourable conditions prevailed in *Europe;* on the contrary, one would rather be inclined to ascribe it to a time before the glacial period, when the conditions were more favourable, and a soil more fitted for his preservation and increase in numbers was provided." As if man's "origin" must necessarily have been in *Europe!*

[3] *Vorlesungen*, ii. 105. *Archiv für Anthropologie*, i. 19.

now, and when reindeer and northern mosses still existed in South Germany.[1]

Unless this theory, which as I have shown is the one now accepted by geologists, should be proved to be erroneous, the diluvial formations must be assigned to the present world; and we must consequently suppose that those species of animals which are now extinct, died out during the historical period, that is, after the creation of man; just as it has been proved that certain species of animals have died out in recent centuries, as the sea-cow of Steller, the dodo, the great auk, etc.,[2] only of course much earlier. And if we adopt the non-literal theory of the Hexæmeron, we may most safely assert that if man did exist in Europe at the same time as the above-mentioned extinct species of animals, it by no means follows that he was created at the same time. These species may possibly have been in existence for thousands of years before man appeared on the earth, or in Europe; for the fact that human bones are found belonging to the same period as do the bones of the extinct species, only proves that man existed before these species became extinct: the first period of his existence may

---

[1] Heer, *Die Urwelt*, p. 550. Pfaff, *Grundriss*, p. 376. *Die neuesten Forschungen*, p. 65.

[2] Quenstedt, *Sonst und Jetzt*, p. 244. Vogt, *Vorlesungen*, i. 284. Fraas, *Vor der Sündfluth*, p. 51. Cf. Hochstetter, *Neuseeland*, Stuttgard 1863, p. 431 seq.: " Many kinds of birds, and these the most remarkable, which are peculiar to New Zealand are fast dying out, and are partly extinct. The enormous bird called the moa, which certainly belongs to the recent period, is quite extinct; but probably it was destroyed by man, a few generations ago. The dodo, and the solitaire, which are now quite extinct, still lived in great numbers on the Mascarene Islands in the 16th and 17th centuries. The sea-cow of Steller (Cuvier) was discovered in 1741, but was quite extinct in 1768."

have been the last of theirs, or, to employ Lyell's terminology, it is possible that man only appeared on the earth towards the end of the Post-pliocene period. The extinction of these species may be connected partly with the appearance of man, that is, they were probably partly destroyed, or driven out of their former abodes, by man.[1] I say, "partly," for other causes may have been at work also. No doubt we cannot say what they were, and how quickly they may have acted. Lyell thinks that a long time must have elapsed before the large number of wild animals which existed in the Post-pliocene period, but which are absent from the recent fauna, diminished and finally died out, seeing that even now, with the help of fire-arms, it is often very difficult for man to extirpate hurtful animals. He adds that probably more general and powerful causes than the action of man were also at work; changes in the climate and the consequent dispersion of plants and animals, in the geographical condition of the countries in question, and so on. But all these causes, however, could only have effected the total disappearance of these species in an "immense number of years." This may be true, but it is still possible that all these causes may have been at work before the appearance of man, and that man found

---

[1] Fraas, *Die alten Höhlen bewohner*, Berlin 1873, p. 21 : "Man and these large animals do not agree well together. This has been experienced in the course of the last thirty years in South Africa. For hundreds of miles in the Orange Free State and in the Vaal, no elephant is now to be seen ; these used, forty years ago, to be the richest regions for ivory hunts. The knell of the mammoth and unicorn sounded when man first took possession of Europe ; they could not defend themselves against human wisdom and cunning, although man, with his primitive weapons, could not vanquish these animals in open battle."

these species already very much diminished, and also, that other more sudden and radical causes may have been at work. I cannot prove that they existed; but if the Deluge destroyed the greater part of all the animals in the land of Noah, might not other similar catastrophes in other countries, which were perhaps connected with that event, have acted equally destructively?

But if, on the other hand, with the supporters of the Restitution theory, we believe in the literal interpretation of the six days, we should be forced to assume that these species were created at the same time as man, and that their extinction, together with the whole diluvial period, fell within the historical age. Now, as we shall see later on, this would place us in a very difficult position with reference to the geological calculations concerning the antiquity of man; it would hardly be possible to prove that all the geological events since the Glacial period, which we might in that case take to be the boundary, could be contained within the limits of the ordinary chronology. Nor is this the only, or indeed the most important, difficulty encountered by the Restitution theory. As I have before observed, the Glacial period does not form a boundary line dividing the primæval and the present world in the sense required by this theory. Nor can any such boundary be discovered before the Glacial period within the Tertiary or Cainozoic ages.

In distinguishing the boundaries between the Eocene, Miocene, and Pliocene periods, Lyell has relied principally on the comparison of shells. He calls those strata eocene in which, among every 100 shells, 1 to 17 are identical with still existing species; 17 to 35 per cent. characterize the miocene strata; 35 to 90 per cent. the pliocene. It is evident that this mode of proceeding is arbitrary, but it shows us that, even in the oldest tertiary strata, there are shells similar to those now existing. H. von Meyer classes the tertiary formations according to the different kinds of mammals found in them; but, even by this means, no definite line can be drawn between the tertiary and diluvial formations. "It cannot be denied," he says, "that there are places where the mammalia of the Molasse (Miocene period) are found intermixed with those of the diluvial formations, although usually these formations, and those of the Molasse, can be clearly distinguished."[1] Vogt also says: "The theory which tallies best with the present condition of our knowledge is this, that the older tertiary formations should be considered as a separate epoch, and that a new geological epoch should be supposed to begin with the Miocene period, which, through the gradual dying out of species, and the replacing of these extinct species by others which now exist, has been continued uninterruptedly down to our own time."[2] Thus the boundary line would be pushed back far into the Tertiary period. But even here it is not safe. "Up till the commencement of the Eocene ages, if even then," says Hugh Miller, "there was no such chaotic period, in at least what is now Britain and the European continent; the persistency from a high antiquity of some of the existing races, of not only plants and shells, but of even some of the mammiferous animals, such as the badger, the goat, and the wild cat, prove

[1] *Die Reptilien*, p. 73.   [2] *Natürliche Geschichte*, p. 109.

there was not."[1] And in the narrative of the Novara expedition we find: "Up to the present time, with the exception of some very unimportant and restricted tertiary deposits, only crystalline rocks and primary formations (palæozoic) are known in Australia, and these form the principal part of the continent. The entire series of secondary (mesozoic) formations appears to be wholly wanting. It follows from this fact, that Australia has been a continent since the end of the primary age, that it has never since been covered by the sea, so that, since the beginning of the secondary age, all through those long periods during which Europe was subject to the most mighty geological convulsions, it has remained at rest,—a country in which plants and animals could flourish without interruption till the present day, undisturbed in their development by any convulsions of nature. Thus the fauna and flora of Australia are the oldest and most primitive in the world."[2]

But I must now close this collection of geological statements, and shortly enumerate the conclusions which may be drawn from them. They are as follows:—

1. The belief that the so-called diluvium is a proof of the deluge, is erroneous.

2. The diluvium ought not to be connected with the chaotic condition of the earth described in Gen. i. 2.

3. It is most probable that the diluvium was not a simultaneous and general inundation of the whole earth; modern geologists believe that, instead of this, a series of geological events took place, which occurred partly in the human and partly in the pre-human period.

[1] *Testimony of the Rocks*, p. 130. [2] *Ausland*, 1862, p. 619.

4. There is no proof of a distinct separation between the primæval and the recent fauna and flora; on the contrary, it seems as if by degrees, long before the first appearance of man, many species of plants and animals had died out, and had been replaced by others; and that this took place in consequence of geological convulsions, changes of climate, and other causes, and occurred at different times, and in different countries.

Under these circumstances, the theory of Restitution must be regarded as untenable. The Scotch geologist, Hugh Miller, who has been so often quoted in these pages, rejects it in the following words: "I certainly did once believe with Chalmers and with Buckland, that the six days were simply natural days of 24 hours each,—that they had compressed the entire work of the existing creation,—and that the latest of the geologic ages was separated by a great chaotic gap from our own. My labours at the time, as a practical geologist, had been very much restricted to the palæozoic and secondary rocks, . . . and the long extinct organisms which I found in them certainly did not conflict with the view of Chalmers. All I found necessary at the time to the work of reconciliation was some scheme that would permit me to assign to the earth a high antiquity, and to regard it as the scene of many succeeding creations. During the last nine years, however, I have spent a few weeks every autumn in exploring the later formations, and acquainting myself with their peculiar organisms. . . . And the conclusion at which I have been compelled to arrive is, that for many long ages ere man was ushered into being, not a few of his humbler contemporaries of the fields and woods enjoyed life in their present haunts, and that for thousands of years anterior to even *their* appearance, many of the existing molluscs lived in our seas. That *day* during which the present creation came into being, and in which God, when He had made 'the beast of the earth after his kind, and the cattle after their kind,' at length terminated His work by moulding a creature in His own image, to whom He gave dominion over them all, was not a brief period of a few hours' duration, but extended over mayhap millenniums of centuries. No blank chaotic gap of death and darkness separated the creation to which man belongs from that of the old extinct elephant, hippopotamus, and hyæna; . . . and so I have been compelled to hold, that the days of creation were not natural, but prophetic days, and stretched far back into the bygone eternity. After, in some degree, committing myself to the other side, I have yielded to evidence which I found it impossible to resist; and such, in this matter, has been my *inconsistency*,—an inconsistency of which the world has furnished examples in all the sciences, and will, I trust, in its onward progress, continue to furnish many more."[1]

Here I close the discussion of the Biblical account of creation, and I turn to the narrative given in the Bible of a historical event, which has a certain relation to the geological history of the earth, and which has been repeatedly mentioned in this lecture. I mean the Deluge.

[1] *Testimony of the Rocks*, p. x.

XXI.

THE DELUGE.

The Mosaic account of the Deluge differs from that of the creation in one point, which is not quite immaterial. The creation and formation of the earth occurs in the pre-human age; Moses therefore could only give an account of it in consequence of a Divine Revelation, which either was vouchsafed to him, or, as we have seen is more likely, had already been vouchsafed to the first men, and was handed down by them to posterity. Such a revelation was not necessary in the case of the Deluge. Noah and his family were eye-witnesses of all its details, and, no doubt, handed on the narrative of their experiences to their descendants. Moses could therefore write down an account of the Deluge, simply by repeating the tradition which had come down to him from Noah, and without having received any divine revelation on the subject. Perhaps he may have discovered a manuscript already in existence, giving an account of this and some other events, and may have simply included this older writing in his narrative, without making any, or any important, alterations on it. The whole character of the description of the Flood, its circumstantiality and breadth, its picturesqueness and attention to detail, gives us the impression that it is, if not the description given by an eye-witness, at least the transcription of a narrative which had been carefully passed on by an eye-witness.[1] According to the chronological statements in Genesis, Abraham might have heard from Noah's lips the narrative of this great event. We may begin by supposing it probable that this narrative would be accurately handed down in the family of the patriarch, so that we may safely say that Moses could get the information for his narrative from a good source.

We are confirmed in this favourable opinion of the historical value of the Mosaic record by the legends of the Deluge among other nations, which stand in a similar relation to the Mosaic narrative as do their accounts of the creation to the Mosaic account. Although much which has been collected and affirmed about these Flood-legends, and about their relation to the Biblical narrative,[2] will not stand criticism,[3] yet there still remain several of such legends; and the fact that they exist, and agree with the narrative in Genesis, in the main points, and in peculiar details, can only be explained on the supposition that there was a common source for them all; and this can be no other than the tradition which the nations took with them when they departed from the home of their ancestors. But if all the records are compared, the Mosaic clearly gives us the impression of being rela-

---

[1] "The narrative of the Flood is like a carefully-kept diary."—Kurtz, *Geschichte des A. B.* i. § 26. Herder calls it "a journal out of the ark."

[2] Lüken, *Traditionen*, p. 170. Stiefelhagen, *Theologie*, p. 528. Zöckler, *Op. cit.* p. 321. For the Babylonian account of the Deluge, discovered by G. Smith, see Fr. Lenormant, *Le Déluge et l'Epopée Babylonienne*, Paris 1873. (*Correspondant*, 1873. *N. S. T.* 54, p. 324.) *Jahrb. für Deutsche Theologie*, 1873, 69.

[3] Cf. Dillmann, *Genesis*, p. 145. L. Diestel, *Die Sündfluth und die Flutsagen des Alterthums*, Berlin 1871.

tively the truest and most historical. "The legends of the Flood among various peoples," says Delitzsch with truth, "are corrected by the Biblical record, just as they, in their turn, afford proof of its historical truth. For the same foundation underlies the heathen legends of the Flood, only they are mythologically exaggerated, and thereby so transformed that the moral meaning of the event is lost; the locality is brought as near as possible to the home of the nation, the idea of a general Flood is more or less lost in that of a national and particular Flood, and the national manners and customs are carried back to the time before the Flood. But the Biblical record, with its freedom from all mythological and national elements, is the true and purely historical reflection of the great universal tradition."[1]

I will also quote an interesting observation of Humboldt's: "The ancient legends of the human race, which we find dispersed throughout the whole world like the fragments of a great shipwreck, are of the deepest interest to the philosophical inquirer into the history of mankind. Like certain families of plants which preserve the type of a common ancestry in spite of the influences of height and the differences of climate, the cosmogonic traditions of nations everywhere display a similarity of form and feature which moves us to admiration. The most various languages, apparently belonging to entirely isolated tribes, give us the same facts. The essential part of the record which treats of the destroyed peoples, and the renewal of nature, hardly varies at all; but each nation has given to it its own local colouring. On the largest

[1] *Genesis*, 3rd ed. p. 242 (4th ed. p. 199).

continents, and on the smallest islands, it is always the highest and nearest mountain on which the remains of the human race took refuge, and the event becomes more recent as the people are more uncivilised; so that what they know about themselves covers a shorter space of time. No one who has observed with care the Mexican antiquities, which existed before the discovery of the New World, who has visited the interior of the forests on the Orinoco, who knows how small and isolated are the European colonies, and is acquainted with the condition of the tribes who have remained independent, can possibly be tempted to ascribe the existing resemblances to the influence of the missionaries and of Christianity on the national traditions."[1]

This much, therefore, may be assumed as certain. In the narrative given in Genesis of the Deluge, a tradition has been transcribed which goes back to the accounts given of the event by eye-witnesses; and the form in which this tradition is given reproduces it more truly than do the traditions of other nations. We may even go so far as to say, that the tradition was handed down unaltered from the time of Noah to that of Moses, in the family of the patriarchs, and among the people of Israel, and that therefore the Mosaic record was a true reproduction of this tradition.[2] Let us now see

---

[1] *Reise in die Aequinoctial-gegenden*, iii. 408.

[2] I cannot enter here into a discussion of the theory that two or three different accounts of the flood have been amalgamated in the record in Genesis, of which one estimates the duration of the Flood to have been a year, another sixty-one days. (See Dillmann, *Genesis*, p. 137.) I think that, theologically speaking, we may consider as admissible the theory that the narrative in Genesis, although historical in all essential points, contains legendary elements with regard to details which are not of

whether, as has often been asserted, there are any sure scientific conclusions which would justify us in disputing the truth of what the Bible says about the Deluge.

I shall continue the subject which was treated of in my last lecture by first discussing the relation of scientific conclusions to the Biblical record; and for that purpose I must mention the points in chaps. vi. to ix. in Genesis which we have to consider.

1. God says that He will destroy man and the animals from the face of the earth. "And behold I, even I, do bring a flood of waters upon the earth, to destroy all flesh, wherein is the breath of life, from under heaven; and everything that is in the earth shall die." Noah is to take a pair of each kind of animal, and seven of the clean animals,—that is, the animals for sacrifice,[1]—with him into the ark, "to keep seed alive upon the face of all the earth." And then the narrative goes on: "And every living substance was destroyed which was upon the face of the ground, both man, and cattle, and the creeping things, and the fowl of the heaven; and they were destroyed from the earth: and Noah only remained alive, and they that were with him in the ark."[2]

2. The following is stated as to the duration and

religious importance—for instance, in the statements about the size of the ark, and such like. Then with respect to these details, we are not told how each actually took place, but what impression the men who lived at the time when Genesis was written gathered as to these details from the tradition. In the text, however, in comparing the Biblical record with the results of natural science, I have treated the former as being strictly historical.

[1] "Three pairs, with one extra seventh individual, which it is supposed was a male animal intended for sacrifice."—Delitzsch, *Genesis*, p. 213.
[2] Gen. vii. 23.

extent of the Flood: "In the six hundredth year of Noah's life, in the second month, the seventeenth day of the month, the same day were all the fountains of the great deep broken up, and the windows of heaven were opened. And the rain was upon the earth forty days and forty nights."[1] "And the waters prevailed exceedingly upon the earth; and all the high hills, that were under the whole heaven, were covered. Fifteen cubits upward the waters prevail; and the mountains were covered."[2] "And the waters prevailed upon the earth a hundred and fifty days."[3] After this time they began to diminish, "And the ark rested in the seventh month, on the seventeenth day of the month, upon the mountains of Ararat."[4] "In the tenth month, on the first day of the month, were the tops of the mountains seen."[5] After forty days, Noah lets fly the raven, afterwards the dove. When, after some days, the latter is sent out a second time, she returns with a fresh olive branch, and Noah knows that the waters have diminished. When, on the third day, she is sent out again, she does not return. On the first day of the six hundred and first year, Noah sees that the waters have gone down; and on the twenty-seventh day of the second month the earth is quite dry. So that, from the beginning of the rain to the drying up of the earth, the flood lasted a year and a few days; exegetes may calculate how many.[6]

---

[1] Gen. vii. 11, 12.   [2] Gen. vii. 19, 20.   [3] Gen. vii. 24.
[4] Gen. viii. 4.   [5] Gen. viii. 5.
[6] "The Flood lasted a year and ten days. In spite of this and other distinct statements, the calculation of time during the year of the Deluge involves many difficulties, which rest partly on the inaccuracy of reckoning a year by lunar months, and partly on the uncertainty as to whether

3. As after the Creation, God said after the Flood to the men and animals who have been saved, "Be fruitful and multiply," and He confirms man in his dominion over the animal world. He further declares that He will not again curse the ground for man's sake, and will not again smite every living thing as He had done. Thenceforward, seed-time and harvest, cold and heat, summer and winter, day and night, should succeed one another without interruption. The rainbow was to be a sign of the divine resolve that all flesh should never again be destroyed by the waters.

The first question which we have to answer here is this, Did Moses mean that the Flood was universal; and if so, in what sense did he mean it? If the Mosaic record rested on a divine revelation, the answer would be easy. Had God revealed to Moses that all the high mountains which are in the earth were covered with water, and that the water stood fifteen yards deep above the mountains, we should be obliged to assume that the water did literally cover all the mountains, and that therefore the Flood was a general one in the strictest meaning of the word; and the passage is thus understood by many commentators. But I do not think the words of Holy Writ necessitate such an assumption. In the narrative given in Genesis we have before us, as I have shown, primarily the narrative of Noah and his sons. If we bear that in mind, we need only suppose that the words, "the mountains were covered," were spoken from their point of view,

---

the forty days of rain are to be included in the hundred and fifty days during which the waters increased."—Kurtz, *Op. cit.* Cf. Delitzsch, *Genesis*, p. 219.

and that therefore they only referred to those mountains which lay within their horizon;[1] and this is quite compatible with the notice in Genesis, ch. viii. ver. 5, that the tops of the mountains became visible on the first day of the tenth month, of course to the people in the ark. So that it would not be necessary for us to assume that all the mountains without exception were covered, but only that those known to Noah were so covered. We are the less obliged to take the expression, "All the high hills that were under the whole heaven,". strictly literally, because similar expressions occur in Holy Writ elsewhere in a manner which does not allow of our pressing them. For instance, God says in Deut. ii. 25 to the people of Israel, "This day will I begin to put the dread of thee and the fear of thee upon the nations that are under the whole heaven, who shall hear report of thee, and shall tremble and be in anguish because of thee." Of course this does not mean all the peoples of the earth absolutely. In the same way, of course, only the countries with which the Egyptians came into contact are meant, when it is said in the history of Joseph (Gen. xli. 54, 57) that there was famine "in all

---

[1] "Contemporary man, left to the unassisted evidence of his senses, *must* of necessity have been ignorant of the extent of the Deluge. True, what man could never have known of himself, God could have told him, and in many cases has told him ; but then God's revelations have in most instances been made to effect exclusively moral purposes. . . . And in this matter of the Flood, though it be a fact of great moral significancy that God in an early period of the human history destroyed the whole race for their wickedness,—all save one just man and his family,—it is not in the least a matter of moral significancy whether or no the Deluge, by which the judgment was effected, covered not only the parts of the earth occupied by man at the time, but extended also to Terra del Fuego, Tahiti, and the Falkland Islands."—Hugh Miller, *Testimony of the Rocks*, pp. 285, 286.

lands," or "over all the face of the earth," and that "all countries" came to Egypt in order to buy corn. According to the account in the Book of Kings,[1] "King Solomon exceeded all the kings of the earth for riches and for wisdom. And all the earth sought to Solomon, to hear his wisdom, which God had put in his heart." We must not take this geographical statement any more literally than we must take the saying of our Saviour literally (Matt. xii. 42), that the Queen of Sheba came from the "uttermost parts of the earth" to hear the wisdom of Solomon. It is said in the Acts (ii. 5) that at the time of the descent of the Holy Ghost there were people "out of every nation under heaven" dwelling at Jerusalem. I know no exegete who would suppose that Chinese and New Zealanders were there also. In the same way we may here understand the expression, "All the high hills that were under the whole heaven," in such a manner as not to include the mountains which lay quite outside Noah's horizon, such as Chimborazo or Dawalagiri.[2]

[1] 1 Kings x. 23, 24.
[2] "The general statements, and the word 'col,' 'omnis,' which occurs repeatedly in the history of the Deluge, must not and cannot be taken quite literally in the language of the sacred writers, and especially of Moses. . . . We are not, I think, unjust to Noah and his sons, or to the deliverer of Israel, if we assume that, like their contemporaries and later generations, they knew nothing of the existence of America or Australia; that they had no knowledge and no idea of the species of animals peculiar to those lands, and to the distant parts of the Old World, for instance the Cape of Good Hope; and that they knew no more of geography and zoology generally than did Aristotle, Hipparchus, Ptolemy, and Pliny. If this is the fact, Noah and his family could speak in their narrative, and Moses in his record of this great event, of 'the *whole* earth, *all* the animals, the high hills which were under the *whole* heaven;' and yet we may perhaps understand these expressions to refer to those portions of the earth's surface, to the animals and mountains, which were more or less known to them. . . . We revere Moses as an inspired writer, but we find

But it is expressly said that the waters stood fifteen yards deep above the mountains. This statement also may be perfectly well explained, without its being necessary to assume that there was a divine revelation on this point. Let us suppose that the ark drew forty-five feet of water, Noah would thus know, from the fact that it landed on the mountain which was the highest round about, that the water must have stood forty-five feet higher.

You see that the account in Holy Writ does not oblige us to assume that the Flood was universal, in the sense that all the high mountains in the earth were covered with water. The Flood no doubt was universal, but in another sense. Genesis repeatedly and distinctly asserts that all mankind, with the exception of the eight who were in the ark, were destroyed. I shall speak more particularly of the animals later on. God points this out as the real object of the Flood, and it is repeatedly said that this object was attained; for the last time, at the end of the narrative, in these words: "These are the three sons of Noah; and of them was the whole earth

---

even in the inspired writers, hyperbolical statements, and words which must not be understood in their most obvious and comprehensive sense; and we believe that they were silent about many things, and did not know many other things, which were not necessary for the (religious) teaching of others. God left the Biblical writers in ignorance of much which it was interesting, but not necessary or useful, to know. He also allowed them to make use of expressions in their writings of which the most obvious sense is not always that which is confirmed by the context, or by a comparison of parallel passages, or by the progress of human knowledge, which last sometimes furnishes an appropriate and necessary commentary on the words of Holy Scripture, where the sense is not explained by the infallible exposition of revelation."—Pianciani, *Cosmogonia*, pp. 543, 545.

overspread."¹ "And by these were the nations divided in the earth after the flood."²

The universality of the Flood as a sentence of destruction is the only thing of importance in the Bible narrative; whether it was also universal as a natural event, as an inundation, is a matter of quite secondary importance. I think the following observation of Delitzsch's is quite correct, " The Scriptures assert that the Flood was universal only as regards the inhabitants of the earth, not as regards the earth itself; and they are not concerned with the universality of the Flood in itself, but only in the universality of the judgment which it brought on the Old World. The whole race of man, with the exception of one family, was destroyed, together with the animals which inhabited a large portion of the earth around man. This, and this only, is stated in Scripture."³

I do not disguise from myself that this theory is not as yet universally recognised by exegetes, and that nearly all the older ones believe that the Flood was universal in the strictest sense, even that it was simultaneous. It is true that in former ages exceptions have been made in favour of the mountains whose summits reach above the clouds; St. Augustine⁴ speaks

---

¹ Gen. ix. 19.   ² Gen. x. 32.

³ *Genesis*, p. 217. See also Pianciani, *Op. cit.* p. 542: "It does not necessarily follow from the fact that the Deluge was universal with regard to the sinful children of Adam, that it was universal also with regard to the whole surface of the earth, and to all species of guiltless animals."

⁴ *C. D.*, 15, 27. The theory that the Deluge only overflowed the portion of the earth which was inhabited by man, is mentioned as being held by "some," by the author of the *Quæstiones ad Orthod.* (q. 34, p. 412, ed. *Otto.* iii. 2, 48), incorrectly ascribed to St. Justinian; and also by an Irish theologian of the seventh century, the author of the writing *De mirabilibus S. Scripturæ*, which purported to be by St. Augustine. Cf. Zöckler, *Geschichte der Beziehungen*, i. 278.

of some who for this reason would have excepted the summit of Olympus; and in the sixteenth century Cardinal Cajetan sought to prove that when Genesis speaks of all the high hills "under the heaven," the mountains under the clouds were meant, so that those would not be included whose summits rose above the clouds. Exegetes had no difficulty in disposing of these arguments; but you will observe that the line of argument I have brought forward is of a different nature.

Delitzsch's limitation of the universality of the Flood has been approved by several modern Roman Catholic savants. Shortly after I had first expressed my views on this point, the learned Jesuit Pianciani brought forward exactly the same theory, and defended it with practically the same arguments as I did, in his last great work on the *Biblical Cosmogony*,— of course, without suspecting my existence. The number of those who support this theory has increased very much in recent years.[1] Indeed, some savants who decidedly

---

[1] According to Lyell (*Principles*, i. 44), the Italian Quirini (1676) was the first geologist who asserted that the Deluge was not universal. But before this, the famous geographer Serardus Mercator had brought forward this theory in his work *Atlas S. Cosmographicæ Meditationes de Fabrica Mundi*, fol. 27, which was printed in 1595. The first supporters of the theory among theologians seem to have been Abraham Milius (ob. 1637), the Anglican bishop Edward Stillingfleet (*Origines Sacræ*, London 1666, l. 3, c. 4), and Isaac Vossius (1659). Zöckler, *Geschichte der Beziehungen*, ii. 127. In 1685, by order of the Congregation of the Index, Mabillon wrote a judgment (printed in the *Opera Posthuma*, ed. Vinc. Thuillier, 1714, t. 2, p. 59) on Vossius' theory,—" Diluvio quidem totum humanum genus periisse, non tamen aquis cataclysmi universum terræ globum fuisse obrutum, sed tantum eam partem, quæ ab hominibus tum habitata erat." He expresses himself against any censure of this theory in these words: " Haec opinio nullum continet errorem capitalem, neque contra fidem neque contra bonos mores; itaque tolerari potest et criticorum disputationi permitti." Isaac Vossius' book was placed upon the Index, but I do not know whether it

believe in the Bible, have even gone further, and have adopted the view which Cuvier upheld,[1] namely, that the Deluge need not even be regarded as universal in the sense that all mankind excepting Noah and his family had perished in it; but only in the sense that all the inhabitants of the countries known to Noah and to his family had perished; so that the tribes which were already quite separated from the principal part of mankind inhabiting Asia, and who had become strangers to them, were not at all affected by the Deluge.[2] This theory depends on the belief that man-

was because of the theory which Mabillon defended. The Jesuit Alfons Nicolai does not hesitate to say (*Dissertazioni e Lezioni de S. Scrittura; Genesi*, tome iv. p. 149, Venice 1781), "I do not think that Holy Scripture means to assert that the waters stood 45 feet higher than such high mountains as the Peak of Teneriffe and the Cordilleras; it is enough to assume that the waters stood above the ordinary hills, in some places more, in others less, than 45 feet deep." The following modern Roman Catholic savants, besides Pianciani, have expressed similar views:—M. de Serres, *Cosmogonie*, p. 154; Godefroy, *Cosmogonie de la Révélation*, 1847, p. 293, in Debreyne, *Théorie Biblique*, p. 266; Sorignet, *Cosmogonie*, p. 59; Lambert, *Le Déluge*, p. 113; F. X. Schouppe, S.J., *Cursus Scripturæ Sacræ*, Brussels 1870, i. 178; Michelis, *Natur und Offenbarung*, v. 263; Veith, *Die Anfänge*, etc., pp. 369, 377; H. Zschokke, *Historia Sacra Antiqui Test.*, Vienna 1863, p. 20. The Protestant apologists of the Mosaic record who support this theory are Pfaff, Nägelsbach, Hitchcock, H. Miller, John Pye Smith (*Relation*, pp. 132, 276); also the English bishop Harold Browne, in the *Speaker's Bible*, i. 75. Cf. Zöckler, *Op. cit.* ii. 784.

[1] Cuvier thought that the ancestors of the Mongolian and Ethiopian races might also have survived the Deluge in other localities, just as Noah and his family did, whom he held to be the ancestors of the Caucasian race. Cf. H. Miller's *Testimony of the Rocks*, p. 311.

[2] Fr. Lenormant (*Manuel d'histoire ancienne de l'Orient*, Paris 1869, i. 75) mentions as supporters of this theory, besides Cuvier and A. de Quatrefages, Ch. Schœbel (*De l'universalité du Déluge*, Paris 1858), and d'Omalius d'Halloy (*Discours Prononcé à la Classe des Sciences de l'Académie de Belgique*, Brussels 1866), of whom he says that they are "fils respectueux et soumis de l'Eglise." The Jesuit, A. Bellynck, speaking of the latter in the *Etudes Religieuses*, etc., 13 Année (1868), 4 s. t. i. p. 578, says, "We are in some degree responsible for two of M. d'Omalius' hypotheses, as the famous geologist submitted them to us before he published them. The one concerns the epoch, the other the universality, of the Deluge.

kind had spread over a great portion of the earth in the time before the Deluge; while the theory that all men, except Noah and his family, were destroyed by the Deluge, presupposes that a part only of Asia was peopled. Genesis contains no information about the dispersion of mankind before the Deluge, and, as we shall see later, geological and historical investigations have produced no certain information on this point.

At any rate, we need not consider the Flood as an inundation of the whole earth. But still, according to the description in Genesis, it was not an ordinary local inundation. No doubt, it cannot be ascertained how great was its extent. If, by the statement that the ark landed on Ararat, we are to understand that the highest summit of the mountain of Ararat in Armenia was covered with water, the Flood must have been very great; for the summit of Ararat is 16,000 feet above the level of the sea, and there is no basin, surrounded by mountains of such height, in the neighbourhood. Even if, as some suppose,[1] any other lower mountain

... Was the Deluge universal? or, in other words, are all men descended from Noah? M. d'Omalius thinks that after Genesis has given us an account of the creation, it assumes the special character of a history of the chosen people; and that therefore it is possible that the Flood mentioned in Genesis only affected the nations known to the Hebrews. He thinks that the Biblical expressions which point to a universal flood may be explained to mean only a very extensive flood, and he quotes similar expressions. We do not propose to attempt the defence of this hypothesis, which we do not consider necessary in the present condition of science; but we should not like to censure those who believe that this hypothesis may one day become valid."

[1] J. P. Smith, *Op. cit.* pp. 147, 273, 456. Pianciani, p. 538: "It is not necessary to assume that the ark landed on the highest peak of Ararat. It may have rested in a valley between the peaks, and thus, writes Nicolai, it would be true, as the text says, that it rested on Ararat,—that is one part of it; and yet it would not be necessary to assume that the waters stood 45 feet above the highest part of the mountain."

in Armenia was the landing-place of the ark, a flood which spread over the Armenian highlands must have been of very great extent.[1] But we may well suppose that the interior of Asia, where Noah and probably the whole race of men then existing lived, was as it were the centre of the flood; possibly the rush of water from below into the region of Ararat was the most violent, the forty days' rain, which at all events we need not suppose to have fallen everywhere at the same time, was there heaviest; the water would then have spread itself out in all directions from this centre, but it need not have reached all countries, and at any rate need not have reached the same height everywhere at the same time. Speaking from an exegetical point of view, therefore, we have ascertained as a fact that there was a flood, which in parts rose to a height of several thousand feet above the level of the sea.

What does geology say to this? After what I said in my last lecture, we cannot appeal to the direct geological proofs of the reality of the Noachian Flood, formerly collected by Buckland and others. But we may say, that the possibility of a flood such as is described in Genesis is proved by the facts ascertained by geologists.

On an earlier page, I have mentioned the English geologist Sedgwick as one of those who had at first defended the theory of the identity of the Geological

---

[1] In the Old Testament, Ararat is not the name of a mountain or chain of mountains, but of a tract of country; but it corresponds to Armenia, or the eastern part of Armenia, not to Karduchia on the left bank of the upper Tigris; so that the mountain of Gudi, south-west of Lake Van, must be the one on which the ark rested. See Dillmann, *Genesis*, p. 158; Delitzsch, *Genesis*, p. 221.

Diluvium and the Noachian Deluge and then had given it up. In the speech, in which he openly expresses his change of opinion, he says very strikingly, after having given the reasons against his former theory : " Are then the facts of our science opposed to the sacred records? and do we deny the reality of a historic deluge ? I utterly reject such an inference. . . . In the narrative of a great fatal catastrophe handed down to us, not in our sacred books only, but in the traditions of all nations, there is not a word to justify us in looking to any mere physical monuments as the intelligible records of that event; such monuments, at least, have not yet been found, and it is not perhaps intended that they ever should be found. . . . But there is a general accordance between our historical traditions and the phenomena of geology. Both tell us in a language easily understood, though written in far different characters, that man is a recent sojourner on the face of the earth. Again, though we have not as yet found the certain traces of any great diluvian catastrophe which we can affirm to be within the human period, we have at least shown that paroxysms of internal energy, accompanied by the elevation of mountain chains, and followed by mighty waves desolating whole regions of the earth, were a part of the mechanism of nature. And what has happened, again and again, from the most ancient up to the most modern periods in the natural history of the earth, may have happened once during the few thousand years that man has been living on its surface. We have therefore taken away all anterior incredibility for the fact of a recent deluge ; and we have prepared the mind, doubting about the truth of things of which it knows neither the origin nor the end, for the adoption of this fact on the weight of historic testimony."

Pfaff also says, "If the Deluge is supposed to have been a partial flood, only affecting the regions which were inhabited in the earliest times, and not an universal flood, covering the whole earth, no single objection can be made to it on the part of natural science. Natural science knows of the possibility, and history tells us of the reality, of such floods in various ages."[1] Pfaff further explains the fact, that geology does not afford any positive confirmation of the Biblical record, in the following manner :—"A passing flood which only lasted for a short time, such as the Deluge is represented to have been, would not leave any traces which would not be wiped out again by the continued change produced by the influence of the atmosphere and of vegetation. The occurrence of a flood can only be proved by stratified deposits, and the period in which these were formed can only be ascertained by their organic contents. But we cannot possibly expect to find any deposits of that particular flood, however considerable it may have been, which could now, after thousands of years, be identified and distinguished from deposits produced by other causes."

The learned French savant, Abbé Moigno, expresses himself in the same manner. "If the deluge, as the Mosaic record supposes, did not destroy vegetation; if it did not tear up the surface of the soil; if, after the waters had gone down, the

[1] *Schöpfungsgeschichte*, p. 659.

plants appeared again, clearly geologists have no interest in the Deluge, we have no more right to ask them for traces of it, than they have to make the absence of such traces and diluvial deposits a ground of objection to us. The bodies of the men and animals who were destroyed in the Deluge were devoured by wild animals and birds, or decayed, and were dissolved by the action of the atmosphere, . . . and we should seek everywhere in vain for the antediluvian fossil man."[1] Besides, as Pfaff adds, it is precisely in those regions which most probably were the dwelling-place of the first man, and the principal scenes of the Deluge, that no rigorous search for possibly existing traces has been instituted.

We need demand from science no positive proofs of the reality of the Deluge, as I have said, natural science cannot dispute the truth of the Biblical record, so long as nothing occurs in it which either contradicts scientifically proven facts, or can be proved by natural science to be impossible. But geology gives us no scientifically proven facts of this kind; on the contrary, the traces of floods in various lands and of great height, discovered by geology, show at least that inundations took place which were comparatively general, and which are analogous to the Deluge, if not identical with it.

Still less can natural science prove the impossibility of that which is narrated in Genesis. Natural science is founded on experience, on the observation of facts which now present themselves. It can therefore take note of the present physical conditions of the surface

[1] Abbé Moigno, *Les Mondes*, xx. No. 1 (May 6, 1869), p. 24.

of the earth, and of its atmosphere, and, relying on these conditions, it may possibly assert that under these conditions, in the ordinary course of things, such an inundation as is described in Genesis would not be possible. But if natural science could prove this decisively, what would be gained? We may unhesitatingly admit that the inundation could not have taken place in the ordinary course of things. Genesis never asserts that it did, on the contrary it characterizes the judgment of the Deluge as a singular event, lying outside the natural course of things. After the Deluge God expressly declares that no other similar flood should take place, that the seasons and natural conditions should thenceforth suffer no interruption. So that Moses clearly recognises that the events which he records did not happen in the natural course of things. We are dealing, then, with an event *præter naturam*, and such an one must not be judged by the laws of nature which have been laid down by science, and derived from present events. Natural science may decide whether an event in the realm of nature is in harmony with the laws which she has discovered; but natural science cannot even discuss the question, whether at some time something at variance with the known laws of nature may not have taken place; for all means for such an investigation are wanting.

The question as to the possibility of miracles is no scientific one. Men of science may say of any event, that according to the laws of nature which are known to them, and by the forces known to them, this cannot have taken place; their observations show them nothing analogous to it, and they can find no sufficient explanation of it in anything which they have discovered by their investigations. And here the man of science comes to the end of his tether. His science does not justify him in assuming that the occurrence is fictitious, but only in concluding that it lies outside the region of his knowledge. If he wishes to add anything, it can only be this. "Two things are still possible; either the occurrence is natural, and there are forces and laws in nature which produced it, but which I do not know; or the occurrence has been caused by forces and laws which are outside nature, and of whose existence natural science consequently can know nothing."

The prudent man of science will not deny that the first alternative is not impossible. Only sixty years ago, savants considered the stories of stone showers to be legends entirely opposed to natural science. When, in 1790, descriptions of the great shower of stones in the Department of Lardes were sent to Paris, the physicist Bertholon, a man who had taken numerous prizes, pitied not only the men of science, but all reasoning people who believed such popular tales; the fact was false, he asserted, and the phenomenon physically impossible. Four years later, the great shower of stones at Siena took place, which was witnessed by nearly a whole province. There was no longer any doubt of the fact; but these meteoric stones were then said to have been thrown up by Vesuvius, fifty miles off, which by chance had undergone a tremendous eruption eighteen hours before. But in the next year, a block weighing fifty-six pounds fell in England, which could hardly have come 170 miles from Hecla. Since then, so many similar occurrences have been noted, that now-a-days no man of science denies the fact that stones do fall from the sky.[1] But if, as Quenstedt says, the history of natural science affords instances of a thing being declared to be a superstition by one generation, and then being raised above all doubt by the next, men of science have every reason to hesitate before pronouncing an event to be physically impossible.

In the case of the Deluge, however, we may admit the other alternative; it is not a natural event in the sense that it was produced entirely by natural forces, and according to the regular laws of nature; but it must be traced back to a supernatural intervention of the divine power. If, then, it cannot be explained by natural means, it shares this fate with a great number of events which the Bible records. The meal and oil of the widow of Sarepta did not fail; that other widow in the time of Elisha filled as many vessels as she had borrowed from her neighbours with the small quantity of oil which she had left; our Saviour satisfied several thousand people with a few loaves and fishes; these, likewise, are events which do not claim to be explained by natural causes. If God, therefore, wished to cause an inundation of the earth, He need not have wanted for the means to bring about His resolution. He might, if necessary, as has actually been supposed to be the case by former savants, have increased the quantity of water by the creation of fresh floods, and have swept them away again, after they had done their work; or, as more modern savants have suggested, He might have

[1] Quenstedt, *Sonst und Jetzt*, p. 244. Fraas, *Vor der Sündfluth*, p. 19.

combined great quantities of oxygen and hydrogen, so as to produce the water, and have separated them again afterwards.[1]

If, therefore, we would attempt to explain the Deluge physically, we need not endeavour to prove that everything took place according to the forces and laws of nature which we know to be at work now, but we must ask whether God could have made use of natural means in order to produce the Deluge, and what these means were. I shall discuss this question in my next lecture; let me close this one with a short recapitulation of the conclusions to which we have come.

1. The Biblical record of the Deluge is confirmed by the traditions and legends of the nations.

2. The Noachian Flood is, according to the description in the Bible, essentially a catastrophe, the object and end of which was the destruction of all men then existing, with the exception of Noah and his family.

3. We are not obliged to suppose that a general simultaneous inundation of the earth took place. The narrative in Genesis does not put us in a position to estimate accurately the real extent of the Flood. The only thing it obliges us to believe is, that the Flood was so great as to destroy all the then existing men, with the exception of Noah and his family; and that all the earth, within the knowledge of Noah, was covered with water.

4. It was formerly supposed that many geological phenomena had been caused by the Deluge, and these

[1] Ebrard, *Der Glaube an die heilige Schrift*, p. 82.

were, therefore, adduced as proofs of the Mosaic record. At the present time, most geologists are of opinion that these phenomena are the work of many floods, partly occurring in the prehistoric, partly in the historic age. But, at any rate, we may adduce these phenomena as a proof that inundations of vast tracts, reaching to a considerable height, are not unknown in the history of the earth.

XXII.

THE DELUGE—*continued*.

ACCORDING to the narrative in Holy Scripture, the Deluge was an event brought about by God for the destruction of all men then existing; and was in so far, therefore, analogous to the catastrophe by which, at a later time, Sodom and Gomorrha were destroyed. But this does not exclude the possibility of God's having employed natural means in order to carry out this sentence of destruction. Although, according to the expressions of ancient theologians, the Will of God was the primary cause of the Deluge, this does not prevent our recognising the secondary causes which may have produced it. In comparing the Biblical records with the results of scientific research, it is important for us to have some knowledge of these secondary causes. I shall, therefore, to-day inquire whether the Bible itself, or whether natural science, enables us to ascertain in what manner the inundation of the earth was brought about.

It is clear that we cannot expect any completely satisfactory solution of this question from the Bible. It is only concerned with the Flood considered as a divine judgment, not as a physical event. It is the task of natural science, not of Biblical history, to consider the Flood from the latter point of view. Moses was not, therefore, called upon to describe the causes of the Flood, so far as to satisfy the man of science. He consequently confines himself to the simple statement: "The same day were all the fountains of the great deep broken up, and the windows of heaven were opened. And the rain was upon the earth forty days and nights."[1] And similarly, when he is describing the going down of the Flood, he says, "The fountains of the deep, and the windows of heaven were stopped, and the rain from heaven was restrained."[2]

It is clear from this narrative that *one* cause of the Flood was the rain. It is specially mentioned at the end of both passages, and it is previously alluded to in the figurative and picturesque expression: "The floodgates of heaven." According to the popular belief and expression of the Hebrews, the rain comes from stores of water which are above the firmament. Moses alludes to this belief in the Hexæmeron. He there says that God divided the mass of waters, which in the beginning covered the earth, into the waters above and below the firmament; and made the Rakiah, the firmament, in order to separate these two masses of waters. According to this view, then, the rain is produced by partially removing this dividing barrier, so that, as it were, its floodgates are opened. But this expression itself points to rain pouring down in great floods.[3] Heavy continuous rain such as this could by itself produce a considerable flood. Only consider the effects of heavy rain accompanying a thunderstorm which we experienced in this country some years

---

[1] Gen. vii. 11, 12.   [2] Gen. viii. 2.
[3] In Mal. iii. 10 the expression is used for a beneficial, plentiful rain.

ago, on the day before Whitsunday. An eye-witness describes the effect of such rain as this in the neighbourhood of Heidelberg — it must have been on the same day — in these words:[1] "It rained uninterruptedly from three o'clock in the morning till mid-day. At six o'clock, the small brooks which flow into the Rhine valley, from the valleys of the Odenwald, and which generally can hardly turn a mill-wheel, rose to great streams which carried everything away with them with irresistible force. Most of the bridges and many houses fell in, rocks weighing from twelve to fifteen hundredweight were carried down a long distance, oak trees thirty or forty feet high, and two or three feet in diameter, were torn up, and carried away for miles; the most solid vaults, which had resisted all inundations with impunity for years, fell in; full barrels, weighing from twelve to twenty hundredweight, floated like light wood on the whirling stream, and in many places rubbish, sand, and shingle were deposited to a depth of four or five feet." And this was the effect of rain which only lasted eight hours, while the rain in Noah's time lasted for weeks.

It is true that men of science[2] say that a general atmospheric precipitation, occurring simultaneously over the whole earth, would be impossible under the present atmospheric conditions. But, first, the account in Genesis does not oblige us to assume that the rain took place at the same time over all the earth. If, as I have tried to show is probable, it is a fact that in the narrative of Genesis we have the narrative of

---

[1] Keerl, *Schöpfungsgeschichte*, p. 504.
[2] Pfaff, *Schöpfungsgeschichte*, p. 609.

Noah and his family, this rain need at first only have taken place where the ark was. Further, and this is the main point, we may unhesitatingly admit that according to the present atmospheric conditions such tremendous and continuous rain as Genesis describes is not possible, that under the present conditions the atmosphere cannot contain such a mass of water as is said to have precipitated itself in rain at that time. But if this can in reality be proved, it would only show that such rain was impossible in the time of Noah if it is established beyond doubt that just the same atmospheric conditions existed then as now. But we cannot admit this to be the fact. We may assume—I will endeavour to justify the hypothesis later—that the atmospheric conditions of the Antediluvian age were so constituted as to make such rain as is implied in Genesis possible. The present atmospheric conditions might, then, extend back to the time just after the Flood, and other conditions may have existed before the Flood. The Flood may thus have been the time at which a great change took place in the atmospheric conditions, and this change itself might have been connected with, and caused by, the Flood. It is true that Genesis says nothing of such a change, but it was not within its province to describe and explain the Flood as a physical event; the outward facts and their consequences are the only things which concern it.

But this change in the atmospheric conditions, which for the present I bring forward only as a hypothesis, may be alluded to in Genesis. God declares after the Flood, that this event should not take place again; and that the succession of the seasons should undergo no interruption. May we not, perhaps, see in this an intimation that the atmospheric conditions were now so constituted that, as men of science say, the natural conditions for such a catastrophe were henceforth wanting. The rainbow is proclaimed to be the sign of the divine promise: "I do set my bow in the cloud, and it shall be for a token of a covenant between me and the earth."[1] "And the waters shall no more become a flood to destroy all flesh."[2]

I do not assert that these words *oblige* us to assume that the rainbow appeared now for the first time.[3] But this idea is, at any rate, the most likely. We should then gather from this statement in Genesis, not exactly that it did not rain in the Antediluvian age,[4] but that that counter-action of air, water, and light in the atmosphere, which causes the rainbow, could not take place then; that in this respect, therefore, the physical laws and conditions then existing, were different from the present.

The fact that to this day, in the tropics, the rain is never fine enough to allow of the formation of a perfect

---

[1] Gen. ix. 13.   [2] Gen. ix. 15.

[3] Cornelius a Lapide and others, writing on this passage, assume that the rainbow had appeared before as a natural phenomenon, and was only new as the sign of a covenant.

[4] Moigno (see above, p. 420, note) assumes this on p. 35. He is wrong in his further opinion that, according to the narrative in Genesis, the alternation of seasons did not take place before the Deluge. The fact that there is no mention of the seasons in the Mosaic account of the Antediluvian age proves nothing, for Moses had no reason for mentioning them. When God says (Gen. viii. 22), "While the earth remaineth, seed-time and harvest, and cold and heat, and summer and winter, and day and night shall not cease," this does not mean, as Moigno thinks, that the regular alternation of the seasons, etc., shall *begin* now, after the Deluge, but that it shall not again be disturbed by such an event as the Flood.

rainbow, shows that atmospheric conditions under which the rainbow is not formed are possible.[1] The conditions and laws by which the appearance of the rainbow is affected, are no doubt connected with other physical laws of the earth, and we must therefore suppose that these also were different in the time of Noah.[2]

For the present I will only just allude to the fact that, amongst other things, the difference between the present conditions of the earth, and those which existed at that time, may explain the long duration of human life in the Antediluvian period. I return to the scientific side of the question. Let us for the present bear this in mind; Genesis does not forbid, but rather leads us to suppose, that the tremendous rain which it mentions as one cause of the Deluge was produced by physical conditions different from those which obtain now.

Genesis describes the second cause of the Flood in these words: "The fountains of the great deep were broken up." The word which is translated "deep," in

[1] Nicholas, *Philosoph. Studien*, i. 392.

[2] "It is evident that, in the opinion of the narrator, the rainbow, that is, the arch which is visible from afar on the clouds of heaven after they have poured forth rain, now appears for the first time. For the same phenomenon of refraction may be observed in a waterfall, and it is also seen sometimes in a falling fog. But it is only since the Flood that the natural conditions came into play which made the appearance of the rainbow, as a shining bow arching itself over the earth, possible. The fact that the rainbow is caused by a natural combination of air, water, and light, is no proof that it could not have had the origin and object which has been mentioned. The laws of nature are themselves divinely fixed, and it is its very conformity to the laws of nature which makes the rainbow a pledge of the future continuation of the earth according to these laws; for so long as the rainbow appears, so long will the reciprocal relations between air, water, and light, and colour, vapour, and gravity continue."—Delitzsch, *Genesis*, p. 229.

the Hebrew "Thehom," in the Vulgate "abyssus," means, in many places, simply the sea, in other places it signifies the waters which are under the surface of the earth, and which break forth in the springs. Thus Jacob when dying says, in blessing Joseph, "The Almighty shall bless thee with blessings of heaven above, blessings of the deep that lieth under;" that is, rain and dew from above, springs and damp from below, shall extend their fertilizing powers over the land of Joseph. The Hebrew means by this one word, therefore, the waters of the earth, in contrast to the waters of the sky or the clouds. The sentence, "The fountains of the great deep were broken up," must mean, translated into our prosaic mode of expression, that the water in the springs gushed forth with unusual force, the brooks, rivers, and lakes overflowed their banks, and the sea its shores.

Here, also, Genesis contents itself with recounting the outward fact, it gives us no more information concerning the causes of the outbreak of the waters from below, than concerning those of the tremendous rain. We can well imagine that greater quantities of water could break forth from the earth, than ordinarily bubbles up from the springs. Schubert[1] has put together a series of scientific observations, from which it appears that besides the seas, lakes, and rivers, etc., water exists to a greater or lesser amount in the interior of the earth, and forms subterranean rivers. On the one hand, we see in many places large quan-

---

[1] *Gesch. der Natur*, Erlangen 1835, i. 293. *Die Urwelt und die Fixsterne*, Dresden 1822, p. 207. Cf. Keerl, *Schöpfungsgeschichte*, p. 495. Vogt, *Lehrbuch der Geologie*, ii. 24. Greenough, *Anniversary Address*, p. 27.

tities of water bursting forth from rocks, which point to the existence of subterranean streams of water of more or less length; on the other hand, the borings which were made for Artesian wells, have, in many places, struck rapid and large streams of water at various depths. Other facts prove that these subterranean waters are often connected with each other at a considerable distance. Modern men of science say that it would be difficult to explain the progress of earthquakes in certain directions and for vast distances if the earth is considered to be a solid uniform mass, but that it is easy if we suppose that caverns exist which are filled with water, and connected with one another.

If, therefore, such subterranean waters existed also before the Deluge,—and it is possible that there may have been even more then than now,—we may suppose that, in consequence of partial upheavals and other convulsions of the earth's crust, these waters might have been pushed to the surface. Further, we can imagine that the waters of the Flood afterwards partly ran off into these subterranean receptacles. A modern savant, Parrot, in his theory of earthquakes, gives such a wonderful description of the spaciousness and great extent of these subterranean reservoirs, that, as Schubert observes, we may well believe that larger quantities of water exist in one mountainous district than were necessary to cause the Deluge. For a space which is hardly equal to a 260th part of the earth would contain ten million cubic miles of water. And such caverns bear about the same proportion to the whole earth, as do the small clefts and caverns of a chalk hill to the whole mass.

2 E

But it would only be necessary to postulate so many million cubic miles of water for the Deluge, if we wished to insist on its being simultaneous and universal in the strictest sense of the words. A mass of water about equal to the 270th part of the earth's surface would suffice to put the whole earth, including the highest mountains, under water.[1] And, as I have shown, we need not imagine that this happened during the Deluge. A far smaller quantity of water would suffice to produce the results which, according to my explanation of the narrative in Genesis, we must necessarily assume. I cannot, of course, say how much, because Genesis does not put us in a position to judge in detail of the extent and course of the Flood, considered as a natural phenomenon.

Of course the sea must have borne a great part in the inundation of the earth. But we cannot explain any considerable overflow of the sea except by supposing that the sea-bed was partly raised, and the land partly depressed ; that is to say, by supposing that convulsions similar to those which, as we have said, caused the subterranean waters to burst forth, took place.

[1] "Dana calculates the mean depth of the sea at 15–20,000 feet. Humboldt reckons the mean height of the land to be 1000 feet. If, therefore, we wished to fill up the sea with all the land, and equalize all the unevennesses of the globe of the earth, the sea would not lose more than about 375 feet of its mean depth, all continents would have disappeared, and besides this, the water would stand about 15,000 feet high over all the earth."—Frans; *Vor der Sündfluth*, p. 89. "In the North Atlantic Ocean, the soundings have reached in recent years a depth of from 25-28,000 feet, in some cases the lead has not touched the bottom at 32,000 feet. The Himalaya mountains, the highest in the world, could lie buried at the bottom of the sea in this depth, and our largest ships could float over their highest peaks without touching them."—Haeckel, *Das Leben in den grössten Meerestiefen*. Berlin 1870, p. 8.

It seems to me that if we ascribe the Deluge to the causes which have been enumerated, we are not driven to assume that God created the waters, or formed them by combining oxygen and hydrogen, in order to produce it;[1] that is to say, if we assume that it was connected with a catastrophe by which the atmospheric conditions of the earth were modified, and partial changes with regard to the division of land and sea and the level of the land occurred in the surface and crust of the earth.

Of course, as I have already observed, these changes are only hypothetical. Genesis gives no account of them, because they do not come within the bounds of its narrative;[2] nor can I prove scientifically that

[1] "If we accept the theory that no country, island, or mountain was left untouched by the Flood, and that the water stood 45 feet deep not only on all the mountains of Armenia, but also on all the great heights of Asia and America, it is very difficult to find a satisfactory answer to the question, 'Whence did so much water come?' We may unhesitatingly admit that subterranean waters burst forth; but will that suffice? May we assume that enormous stores of water existed in subterranean caverns, when we know that the mean specific gravity of the centre of the earth is much greater than that of the portion of the earth's crust which is known to us, and perhaps seven times greater than that of water? It is of course possible to assume that more water was created by God, and was afterwards destroyed again, or that the water came from regions beyond our atmosphere, and returned thither again. These things certainly do not exceed the almighty power of the Creator, but I do not know how far they are in harmony with His wisdom, and with His usual mode of working; and these assumptions would involve a risk of exposing the Word of God to the ridicule of men of science, which, as St. Augustine and St. Thomas have observed, should be avoided as much as possible."—Pianciani, p. 551.

[2] "Moses mentions neither volcanoes, upheavals of mountains, nor settlements of the land, nor any other phenomena which may have preceded, accompanied, or followed the Deluge; but he does not exclude the possibility of any of these phenomena, and we may therefore admit that they might have occurred, without in any way contradicting his narrative. Perhaps these events took place in regions far from the dwelling-place of Noah's family. If, at that time, the great chain of the Andes was

they really took place. But, on the one hand, these hypotheses must be welcome to exegetes in so far as they are calculated to make the narrative of Genesis more plausible, and they may endure before the judgment-seat of natural science if it can be proved that they do not go beyond anything which men of science have themselves admitted to be possible. We will therefore ascertain whether these hypotheses can be reconciled with the teaching of geologists on the former conditions and events in the history of the earth, which is based on their scientific observations and conjectures.

An English[1] geologist thinks it probable that the earth was originally a ball, and attained to its present spheroidal shape by a sudden upheaval under the equator. By this means a change in the distribution of land and sea was likewise produced,—for instance, what had long been the bed of the sea in the tropics became a continent, as the Desert of Sahara, and, on the other hand, in the polar regions dry land became the bed of the sea; a considerable change in the climatic conditions also took place in consequence of this. At any rate, such a catastrophe, if it occurred, as the author supposes, in the time of Noah, might have produced a flood like the Deluge. Other men of science, both ancient and modern,[2] think it probable

---

upheaved in America, Noah would hardly have known about it, and there is no apparent reason why God should have revealed physical events of this kind to Moses; but even if we suppose that the sacred historian did know them, there is still no reason why he should have recounted them."
—Pianciani, p. 519.

[1] C. B., *Geology*, etc., p. 321.

[2] Fr. Klee, *Der Urzustand der Erde, und die Hypothese von einer Aenderung der Pole. Eine geologisch-historische Untersuchung über die sogenannte Sündfluth-katastrophe.* Stuttgard 1843.

that the inclination of the earth's axis to its plane was not always the same as it is now. If the axis round which the earth revolves daily were at right angles to the plane in which it revolves round the sun, there would be no alternation of the seasons; all parts of the earth would have equally long days and nights. The change of the seasons and the difference between the zones as they exist, is caused by the fact that the axis of the earth varies $23\frac{1}{2}$ degrees from a horizontal position. If the axis had formerly stood upright, or more upright than at present on the plane, the climatic conditions would then have been materially different from what they are now; and if the change in the position of the axis had taken place suddenly, it might have sufficed to produce catastrophes as considerable as the Deluge.

But both hypotheses are probably too bold. As regards the last, Burmeister no doubt only says that no decisive grounds could be found for supposing that a change took place in the position of the earth with reference to the sun, and that therefore this hypothesis has lately been given up.[1] This, as you see, is a very mild condemnation. But others, and especially Sir J. Herschel, express themselves more strongly against it.[2]

Let us therefore put aside these hypotheses. It is asserted by nearly all modern geologists as a fact which is almost certainly established, that other climatic and atmospheric conditions did exist formerly

[1] *Geschichte der Schöpfung.* p. 269.
[2] "The least alteration in the earth's axis would cause the sea to overflow the land. But there has never been, and for astronomical reasons there never could be, any change in the axis of our planet."—Herschel, *Physicalische Geographie. Ausland,* 1863, p. 985.

on the earth; and this in most cases without any reference to the Deluge. Burmeister says, "A comparison of the primæval with the present organisms, leaves no doubt that the present age is markedly different from the most recent preceding epochs. Even in the Tertiary or Cainozoic period, that is, in the last geological period before the recent period, the temperate zone seems to have been rather warmer than it is now; this is proved by many of its animal inhabitants, which in our days have chosen out the tropics as a home."[1] "All countries inhabited by organic beings," he says in another place, "might well have had a higher even temperature, and a tropical character."[2] "One of the most remarkable inferences," says Quenstedt, "from the nature of the buried fauna and flora of the Tertiary age, is that of the greater mean temperature. Not only do single plants or animals bear out this conclusion, but the variety of form in whole classes of animals, as, for instance, shells, sufficiently proves it. We may certainly assume that, in this comparatively late age, a subtropical climate existed in our latitudes."[3]

Geologists have made various conjectures as to the causes of the change in the climatic conditions. Lyell brings forward the hypothesis, which Quenstedt calls a happy expedient,[4] that the greater warmth in former ages was connected with a more favourable distribution of the land. If there had formerly been more land, or if the present land had gathered round the equator instead of the north pole, it must have

[1] *Gesch. der Schöpfung.* pp. 269, 451.   [2] P. 271.
[3] *Sonst und Jetzt*, p. 151.   [4] P. 152.

had a great influence on the quantity of warmth; because the land is more heated by the sun's rays than water is, and because the intensity of the sun's rays increases from the pole to the equator. Here you see we have a parallel to the hypothesis that a change in the distribution of land and water may have been connected with, and have caused, the Deluge.

If the Deluge was connected with a change in the atmospheric and climatic conditions, this change must have been a sudden and not a gradual one. For this assumption also, I find analogies in the hypothesis formulated by geologists, without reference to the Deluge or to the Bible. According to the opinion of many men of science, says Burmeister,[1] many geological facts point to the conclusion that "the last great catastrophe" in the history of the earth "occurred both very suddenly and violently." Many think that "the transition from the preceding to the present period was heralded by a remarkable and sudden sinking of the temperature in the Northern Hemisphere,"[2] and the Glacier theory mentioned above is connected with this. Thus, whatever we may think of the hypothesis, we see that geologists do not look upon great and sudden changes in the conditions of the earth as being *a priori* impossible.

If, in order to explain the overflowing of the sea, we suppose that upheavals and depressions of separate parts of the earth's surface occurred, geologists are the last people who can make any objection; for such upheavals and depressions play an important part in every system of geology. "We have many proofs," says an

---

[1] *Gesch. der Schopfung.* p. 246.   [2] Burmeister, pp. 246, 272.

English geologist, "that important sinkings of the land took place at a comparatively recent epoch."[1] According to Vogt,[2] a settlement of the land followed the Glacial period, which I have just mentioned, in the north of Europe and of America, and the land subsequently rose again. In the theory of the elevation of mountains, which Elie de Beaumont first brought forward, and which has been supported by many modern geologists, it is assumed that the biggest and highest mountains are the most recent; the Cordilleras, one of the most extensive and highest mountain ranges, being perhaps the most recent of all.[3] Burmeister[4] places the most violent and tremendous of these convulsions in the period immediately preceding the historical age. Even if they occurred singly, and were of small extent, could not such settlements and upheavals have taken place in the historical epoch, and have caused inundations? The circumstance that in the year 1822, 1000 miles of the coast of Chili were raised four feet in one night by an earthquake,[5] and that in 1819 more than ninety geographical square miles of the delta of the Indus were turned into a lake by a settlement of the land following on an earthquake, show that this is not impossible, and that tolerably important upheavals and settlements can occur.[6]

We can say nothing about the manner in which the Deluge was connected with such settlements and

[1] De la Beche, *Manual of Geology*, p. 172.
[2] *Lehr. der Geol.* i. 622.   [3] Burmeister, p. 265.   [4] *Ibid.* p. 272.
[5] *Natürliche Gesch. der Schöpfung.* p. 127.   Mantell, *Wonders*, i. 81. Pfaff, *Grundriss*, p. 133.
[6] H. Miller, *Testimony*, p. 298.   Pfaff, *Grundriss*, p. 138.

upheavals, because the Biblical narrative never hints at it, but the following quotations will show you what the connection *may* have been.

Leonhard says : " If we assume that the Deluge was general, or at least that it was spread over many lands, this event was very probably connected with the formation of a great mountain range, perhaps the range of the Andes. Why should not that which has taken place so repeatedly in the earth's history have happened once since man has inhabited the surface of the planet? .... We need entertain no doubts as to things which would now perhaps be considered almost incredible displays of powerful agencies, and which to our imagination appear monstrous, such that mountains were lifted up even to the clouds. Such phenomena as these only appear to be gigantic when estimated by the measure of our power ; but when compared with the greatness of the whole earth, these upheavals lose not a little of their importance." [1]

Hugh Miller gives us the following description :—
" There is a remarkable portion of the globe, chiefly in the Asiatic continent, though it extends into Europe, and which is nearly equal to all Europe in area, whose rivers (some of them such as the Volga, the Oural, the Sihon, the Kour, and the Amoo, of great size) do not fall into the ocean, or into any of the many seas which communicate with it. They are, on the contrary, all *turned inwards*, if I may so express myself; losing themselves in the eastern parts of the tract, in the lakes of a rainless district, in which they supply but the waste of evaporation, and falling, in the western parts,

[1] *Geologie*, ii. 120, 123.

into seas such as the Caspian and the Aral. In this region there are extensive districts still under the level of the ocean. The shore-line of the Caspian, for instance, is rather more than 83 feet beneath that of the Black Sea; and some of the great flat steppes which spread out around it, such as what is known as the steppe of Astracan, have a mean level of about 30 feet beneath that of the Baltic. Were there a trench-like strip of country that communicated between the Caspian and the Gulf of Finland to be depressed beneath the level of the latter sea, it would *so open up the fountains of the great deep*, as to lay under water an extensive and populous region. . . . Vast plains, white with salt, and charged with sea-shells, show that the Caspian Sea was at no distant period greatly more extensive than it is now. . . . It is quite possible, that this great depressed area—the region covered of old by a Tertiary sea, which we know united the Sea of Aral with the Caspian, and rolled over many a wide steppe and vast plain—may have been covered for a brief period (after ages of upheaval) by the breaking in of the great deep during that season of judgment when, with the exception of one family, the whole human race was destroyed."

"Let us suppose that the human family . . . were congregated in that tract of country which, extending eastwards from the modern Ararat to far beyond the Sea of Aral, includes the original Caucasian centre of the race; let us suppose that, the hour of judgment having at length arrived, the land began gradually to sink; . . . further, let us suppose that the depression took place slowly and equably for forty days together, at the rate of about 400 feet per day,—a rate not twice greater than that at which the tide rises in the Straits of Magellan, and which would have rendered itself apparent as but a persistent inward flowing of the sea; let us yet further suppose, that from mayhap some volcanic outburst coincident with the depression, and an effect of the same deep-seated cause, the atmosphere was so affected that heavy drenching rains continued to descend during the whole time, and that though they could contribute but little to the actual volume of the flood—at most only some five or six inches per day—they at least *seemed* to constitute one of its main causes, and added greatly to its terrors, by swelling the rivers, and rushing downwards in torrents from the hills. The depression, which, by extending to the Euxine Sea and the Persian Gulf on the one hand, and to the Gulf of Finland on the other, would open up by three separate channels the fountains of the great deep, and which included, let us suppose, an area of about 2000 miles each way, would, at the end of the fortieth day, be sunk in its centre to a depth of 16,000 feet—a depth sufficiently profound to bury the loftiest mountains in the district. . . . And when, after 150 days had come and gone, the depressed hollow would have begun slowly to rise,—and when, after the fifth month had passed, the ark would have grounded on the summit of Mount Ararat—all that could have been seen from the upper window of the vessel would be simply a boundless sea, roughened by tides, now flowing outwards, with a reversed course, towards the distant ocean, by the three great outlets which during the period of depression had given access to the waters."

"Let me further remark, that in one important sense a partial flood, such as the one which I have conceived as adequate to the destruction, in an early age, of the whole human family, could scarce be regarded as miraculous. Several of our first geologists hold that some of the formidable cataclysms of the remote past may have been occasioned by the sudden upheaval of vast continents. . . . And these cataclysms they regard as perfectly natural, though of course very unusual events. Nor would the gradual depression of a continent, or, as in the supposed case, of a portion of a continent, be in any degree less natural than the sudden upheaval of a continent. It would, on the contrary, be much more according to experience. Nay, were such a depression and elevation of the Asiatic basin to take place during the coming twelvemonth, as that of which I have conceived as the probable cause of the Deluge, though the geologists would have to describe it as beyond comparison the most remarkable oscillation of level which had taken place within the historic period, they would certainly regard it as no more miraculous than the great earthquake of Lisbon, or than that exhibition of the volcanic forces which elevated the mountain of Jorullo in a single night 1600 feet over the plains. . . . The revelation to Noah, which warned him of a coming flood, and taught him how to prepare for it, was evidently miraculous; the flood itself may have been purely providential."[1]

[1] H. Miller, *Testimony*, p. 344 seq.

XXIII.

THE DELUGE—*Conclusion.*

WE have seen that the Deluge must be considered as universal, in so far as it was a divine judgment for the destruction of mankind. All the men then existing, with the exception of the eight who were in the ark, were destroyed. But what happened to the animal world? This is one of the most difficult questions which could here be raised.

Genesis does not speak expressly of the vegetable world. But the dove brings back an olive leaf, and according to this it seems as if we ought to believe that vegetation was not destroyed, that it at least partially outlived the Flood, and that from those places in which it had survived, it spread to those where it had been destroyed.[1] Genesis says nothing of any new creation of vegetation after the Flood. But I should not like to assert that it is exegetically inadmissible to assume either that such a new creation occurred, or that the remaining vegetation was increased by a later creation. The silence of Genesis does not militate against it, and when it is said in the 2nd chapter that "God rested from His work," that is, that He left off creating, this

[1] The statement that the olive can bring forth leaves under water is probably only founded on an expression of Pliny's. (Lambert, *Le Déluge*, p. 120.) The leaf which the dove brought back had probably come out after the Flood; but the tree had been covered by the water, and had remained alive. (*Les Mondes*, t. 20, 24, Juin 1869, pp. 318, 325.)

refers primarily only to the conclusion of the six days of creation, and does not exactly exclude a later repeated creation, especially a re-creation of destroyed organisms. By the divine command Noah takes measures for the preservation of the animal world by the building of the ark, "to keep seed alive upon the face of the earth," as it is said in Gen. vii. 3. Noah is to take a pair of all the beasts into the ark with him—that is, the animals so taken in and saved by Noah are, as it is said when they are leaving the ark, meant to multiply and to repeople the earth. Are we to understand by this that all animals spring from the animals in the ark, as all men spring from Noah and his family? It is expressly said, in chap. ix. 19, that all men are descended from the sons of Noah. It is true that we find no such statement with reference to the animals, but it seems as if Genesis wished to imply that something similar should be understood in their case. It is said in chap. vii. ver. 21, "And all flesh died that moved upon the earth, both of fowl, and of cattle, and of beast, and of every creeping thing that creepeth upon the earth, and every man." But the very next sentence points to an exception. The Vulgate no doubt goes on, "Everything died in which was the breath of life *in terra*;" but, according to the Hebrew, "in terra" must not be translated "on the earth," but "on the dry land," for whereas in the preceding verse the more uncertain expression Haarez is employed, which may mean either earth or dry land, here the word Hecharabah is chosen, that is, the dry land. Of course, too, it is understood that only those animals were taken up into the ark which could not be saved in any other way. So that besides the aquatic animals, of which Genesis does not speak, other kinds of animals may also have survived the Flood, *e.g.*, the eggs or larvæ of insects may have been preserved, etc. If we may assume that the Flood was not a universal inundation—*i.e.*, that all the land was not overflowed at the same time, and that the results of the Flood were not everywhere, at any rate, so great as in the region in which Noah and his family witnessed it—we may believe that the preservation of many land animals also was quite possible. Of course we cannot go into the details, or calculate what kinds of animals, or how many of them, might have remained alive outside the ark, because, as I have shown above, we cannot arrive at any exact idea as to the real extent of the Flood. But if we may admit such exceptions, we gain two things. It has been declared impossible that all the animals could find room in the ark, and it has been said that it is inconceivable that the animals could have spread themselves over all the continents and islands from the ark. Both these difficulties are, at least, substantially diminished if we may assume that the words in chap. vii. 23, "And every living substance was destroyed which was upon the face of the ground, . . . and Noah only remained alive, and they that were with him in the ark," need not be taken literally.[1]

---

[1] "It does not necessarily follow, from the fact that human sinfulness was the moral cause of the Deluge, that that portion of the animal world which inhabited the countries still unknown to man must have been spared by the Deluge. But we may gather from that fact that it is impossible to argue from animals to man, and *vice versa;* and also that because all men died who were not in the ark, it does not necessarily follow that all the animals died likewise ; while on the other hand, if it were proved that certain kinds of animals had survived the Deluge, it

I shall return to this last question presently, but I will first discuss a few other points. May not many species of animals have really been destroyed at that time? There is no mention of aquatic animals in the ark; now several of these live only in salt water, several only in sweet water. Many of them, therefore, must have been destroyed in the Flood when the salt water was too much diluted with sweet water, or *vice versa*. Whole species may have been destroyed in this manner. We may assume that some species of land animals also were destroyed, if the command to Noah to take with him a pair of all the animals is not to be understood literally.

The difficulty of explaining the fact that the animals spread themselves from the ark over all the earth has induced many savants to assume that a new creation of animals took place after the Flood.[1] According to Delitzsch this assumption is altogether inadmissible, "for," he says, "between the completed creation (the six days) and the history which then begins stands the divine Sabbath, which excludes all after creation."[2] I have already observed, when speaking of a possible re-creation of plants, that this objection is not final, neither does the silence of Genesis about such a re-creation militate against its possibility. Ebrard[3] has recently found traces of such a re-creation in the

---

would not follow that any man had been saved. Lastly, it must be noted that in the ten chapters of Genesis which follow the first, Moses is telling the history of mankind, and not of the animal world; and that he nowhere says that all the existing kinds of animals had spread themselves over all the earth from the animals which came out of the ark."—Pianciani, p. 547.

[1] Prichard, *Researches into the Physical History of Mankind*, i. 101.
[2] *Genesis*, p. 210.   [3] *Der Glaube an die heilige Schrift*, p. 83.

Mosaic record itself. Three classes of animals were distinguished in the Hexæmeron—(1) *chajjath haarez*, beasts of the field, *i.e.* the wild larger animals; (2) *behemah*, cattle, the domestic animals; (3) *remes*, the small creeping animals. But when Noah receives the command to take the pairs of animals with him into the ark, it is specified that he should take (1) birds, (2) *behemah*, that is, domestic animals, (3) *remes*, that is, small animals. In this specification there is no mention of *chajjath haarez*, the larger wild animals. But when the animals are mentioned which remained outside the ark, and were drowned,[1] the beasts of the field are expressly spoken of, besides the three classes first mentioned; on the other hand, these are missing, and only the other three classes are mentioned when the animals go out of the ark.[2] Ebrard thinks that this circumstance justifies us in concluding that Noah was not commanded to put *all* animals, including the wild beasts, into the ark, and that, therefore, these last were destroyed, and were created anew after the Flood. He finds a confirmation of this theory in Gen. ix. 10, when God says: "I establish my covenant . . . with every living creature that is with you, of the fowl, of the cattle, and of every beast of the earth with you, from all that go out of the ark to every beast of the earth," that is, according to Ebrard's interpretation, both with the animals that went out of the ark, and also with the beasts of the field; which latter, therefore, did not go out of the ark, and are set in opposition to the animals which went out of the ark, as a second main class.

[1] Gen. vi. 19; vii. 2, 3, 8.   [2] Gen. vii. 21; viii. 17.

These exegetical observations are, no doubt, still open to objection. I do not think that the meaning of the words used to denote the separate `classes of animals is so sharply defined as Ebrard believes. Compared to beasts of the field, *behemah* may mean domestic animals; compared to *remes*, the smaller animals, it may mean the large animals. The account of the Flood is not quite consistent in the enumerations of the animals, sometimes one set of names, and sometimes another is used; and they are placed side by side in one passage chap. viii. 1, which Ebrard passes over too lightly, where the animals in the ark are called *chajjath* and *behemah*. The only object of all these lists is to give a particular description of the general notion, all classes of animals. But I should not like to say with Delitzsch, that it is entirely inadmissible to assume that a new creation of animals took place.

Let us now look a little more closely at the words themselves, which speak of the collecting together of the animals in the ark. God says to Noah : " And of every living thing of all flesh, two of every sort shalt thou bring into the ark, to keep them alive with thee."[1] " Two of every sort shall come unto thee, to keep them alive."[2] And again we find : " And Noah went in . . . into the ark, because of the waters of the flood. Of clean beasts, and of beasts that are not clean, and of fowls, and of everything that creepeth upon the earth, there went in two and two unto Noah into the ark, . . . as God had commanded Noah."[3]

[1] Gen. vi. 19.   [2] Gen. vi. 20.   [3] Gen. vii. 7, 8, 9.

How did Noah collect all these animals together? The difficulty is very slightly diminished if we say that probably the presentiment of the approaching catastrophe, which filled the animal world, drove them to him;[1] and if we point to the instinct of animals, which causes them to gather round man, of their own accord, when some great catastrophe of nature is at hand.[2] Nor can we get rid of the difficulty that Noah must have undertaken long journeys in order to collect the animals indigenous to different climates, by saying that the differences between the zones were probably not so great at that time, and the regions inhabited by the animals not so wide apart as they are now. And, further, how could Noah have gathered together all the animals, without exception, unless he possessed a knowledge of zoology wonderfully in advance of the culture of ancient times?[3]

I hold that, while there are two suppositions which these objections force us to accept, yet they can be brought into perfect harmony with the Biblical narrative. The first is even alluded to by S. Augustine—namely, that the gathering together of the animals was brought about less by the agency of man, than by the miraculous interposition of God; that God did not give Noah a command to gather together the animals, and to bring them into the ark, but rather imparted to him His desire to save the animals as well as Noah, and commanded him to prepare for their shelter and preservation in the ark.[4] The por-

[1] Delitzsch, *Genesis*, p. 209.
[2] Kurtz, *Gesch. des A. B.* i. § 26.
[3] Wagner, *Gesch. der Urwelt*, i. 528. Delitzsch, *Genesis*, p. 209.
[4] Augustine, *C. D.* 15, 17: " Non enim ea Noe capta intromittebat, sed

tion of the narrative in which it is said, "two of every sort shall come unto thee," does not oblige us to adopt this theory, but it is quite compatible with it. At any rate, it is easier to suppose that such a miraculous interposition of the divine power occurred in a catastrophe which even without it would be marvellous, than otherwise to remove the objections which by this means can be so easily disposed of.

The second supposition is this, that the admission into the ark of pairs " of all flesh " may, to a certain extent, have a relative meaning. If you remember that there is much in favour of the theory that the Mosaic account of the Deluge was an account written from the point of view of Noah and his family, you will not be surprised at my saying that the statement that two of every sort of animal were taken into the ark, is no more to be understood literally than the statement that all the high mountains under the whole heaven were covered with water. We have seen that in this last statement we are to understand primarily the mountains within Noah's horizon. Shall we be going too far if we assume that in the first statement we should understand primarily those animals "which had come into actual contact with man, and had attracted his attention and sympathy"?[1] To Noah these were " all the animals," those he did not know of did not exist for him; and although we cannot exactly say that God could not have informed Noah of the existence of strange animals, and have com-

venientia et intrantia permittebat. Ad hoc enim valet, quod dictum est: *Intrabunt ad te,* non scilicet hominis actu, sed Dei nutu."

[1] Delitzsch, *Genesis*, p. 210.

manded him to assemble them, or that God could not have brought to Noah pairs of these animals that were unknown to him, yet there is no reason for heaping up miracles in this manner, when the words of Holy Scripture do not oblige us to do so.[1]

God had other ways of preserving the animals besides the ark. As the Flood was brought about for the sake of man, so the ark was mainly built on account of man. Because of the sinfulness which had become universal, God repents of having created man. He therefore to a great extent, as it were, undoes His work of creation; He brings about a condition of the earth similar to that in the middle of the six days; the waters again cover the earth. After the judgment has been carried out, the land again emerges from the waters, as on the third day. God, however, does not intend to make a new creation, but only to remodel the existing one, and to bring it back to its original condition, as it existed before the universal corruption; for this reason He preserved those of the race of man who had remained untouched by the corruption; for

[1] "Noah was not commanded to do anything impossible, and he did no more than he could. If such a command had been given to some one who possessed much greater resources than Noah, for instance, to Alexander the Great, or Augustus, they would no doubt have collected together the most comprehensive menagerie that had ever been seen; and yet all the animals then unknown in Europe, and indigenous only in America and Australia, would have been wanting. Is Noah's zoological collection likely to have been more complete?" — Pianciani, p. 552. "It has been asserted quite seriously, even by men of science, that after the Deluge all living things went out from Ararat, and peopled the whole world. In the time of Moses this assertion was quite justifiable (although Moses does not make it), and we do not in the least dispute its truth according to the knowledge of that age. All the animals which were then known to the Jews, and in which they were interested, may quite well have spread themselves abroad from Ararat."—Giebel, *Tagesfragen*, p. 72.

this reason the old vegetation remains; and the animal world, to rule over which man had been established in the beginning, is brought safely from the old time into the new in the same way as man.

This is the historical and religious meaning of the Deluge. You see that it is not the preservation of the whole animal world as it is known to zoology, but the preservation of the animal world as it was known to the men who then existed, that is meant, and that therefore the account which Holy Scripture gives of the Flood regarded as an important event in sacred history, is not in the least affected, even should the preservation of all flesh in the ark be taken as having a relative meaning.

I have shown that such expressions as "everything in the whole earth" occur elsewhere in the Old Testament, and are not to be understood literally; and that the narrative of the Flood itself, while in some places it speaks of the destruction of all living things on the earth with the exception of those in the ark, in others alludes to the fact that many animals, especially the aquatic animals, were not included in that destruction. It is true that it is more difficult to decide with certainty how far the expression "all flesh" is to be understood literally, than to estimate the real extent of the Flood apart from its being a judgment of destruction on all mankind. We must at any rate assume that the animal world, in so far as it was known to Noah and his family, was completely represented in the ark. On the other hand, God may have made use of many natural and casual expedients in order to preserve, without the ark, many of the animals which lay quite beyond Noah's horizon. There is no more difficulty in assuming that species of land animals were preserved outside the ark,—especially if we need not suppose the inundation to have been simultaneous and universal,—than there is in supposing that species of aquatic animals were entirely destroyed by the Flood through the mixture of salt with fresh water, although Genesis is silent about both.[1] Further, species of land animals may have died out then, and lastly, the theory that a later creation filled up the gaps which had been caused in the animal world by the Flood cannot be called quite unbiblical.

Regarding the dissemination of the animal world after the Flood, it has been said that observations made in the present day also show us that in several ways, some of them very strange, animals are transported to distant places,—by icebergs in the north, by driftwood in large rivers and in the sea, etc.[2] It is also said that it is not unlikely that continents now separated were formerly connected by strips of land which are now destroyed, or broken through.[3] But we cannot explain how all the animals sprang from one ancestral pair in this way, nor can it be done in any way without supposing that many miracles occurred, which is another reason for not considering the Flood to be universal.[4]

[1] Delitzsch, *Genesis*, p. 210.   [2] Lyell, *Principles*, iii. 54.
[3] Kurtz, *Gesch. des A. B.* i. § 26.
[4] "It is not likely that whole species of land animals would have crossed the Atlantic, or any other ocean, for the pleasure of settling in America. And certainly the small bands who first peopled America and Australia, and did not take with them cattle and horses, would not take to the new continent a fauna which is quite different from that of our continent. Neither is it likely that so many animals, whose species is not found in

- If it is not necessary to assume that all the land animals were represented in the ark, we may spare ourselves the examination of the very detailed calculations as to the space in the ark, which have been entered into by the opposers and by the defenders of the Biblical narrative. A modern commentator on Genesis[1] calculates the space to be $3\frac{1}{2}$ million cubic feet, puts aside nine-tenths of the space for the provisions, and proves that in the remaining space, if an average of 54 cubic feet is reserved for every animal, nearly 7000 pairs could be housed. Space then was not wanting in the ark to house representatives of a great part of the whole animal world, besides their necessary food. A French naval officer, Vice-Admiral Thevenard, even calculates that the ark was one-third too big.[2] As regards other difficulties, a Berlin official, (Oberbaurath) Johann Esaias Silberschlag, writing in the year 1780, laboured diligently in the second part of his *Geogony* to be beforehand with them. He drew out a complete plan of the ark, which goes into the

---

the Old World, would have travelled on icebergs to the warmer regions of the New World; although it is true that in the North the reindeer and the polar bear, etc., could have passed in this way from one country to another."—Pianciani, p. 556. "Why did the animals who are the slowest movers, as for instance sloths, *all* travel the farthest distances, and this without even leaving some few representatives on the way? And why did those who can move fastest from place to place, as for instance horses, remain behind on the old continent? . . . It matters not from what point of view we contemplate the theory that *all* kinds of animals on the earth, those created for the coldest as for the warmest climates, have come from *one* pair, and from *one* place, its impossibility only becomes more and more apparent."—Pfaff, *Schöpfungsgeschichte*, p. 658. Hugh Miller discusses this question at length: see *Testimony*, p. 320 seq.

[1] Tiele; see Kurtz, *Op. cit.*
[2] Nicolas, *Philosophische Studien*, i. 380. C. G. Zöckler, *Geschichte der Beziehungen*, ii. 124.

minutest detail, and in which all necessary arrangements are provided for. He finds room for all the animals in the Linnean system which are not aquatic. The larger animals are housed in the lowest storey, together with the storehouses necessary for them, —partly so that it should not be necessary to bring their food from any other place, partly so that the lowest space should be heavy enough to preserve the ark from swaying, and especially from upsetting. The smaller kinds of animals and the men inhabit the middle storey; the birds are kept in safety, and separate, in the third. Further, Silberschlag has so arranged the division, that, as he says, animals which do not like each other are not put together, so that there should be no fights and disorders within the ark. At first he goes on to say, I had thought of putting all the animals useful to man next to Noah, but it seemed to me unseemly that the donkey's unbearable bray, the grunting of the pig, the lowing of cows and oxen, the nocturnal stamping of the horses should take place so near the habitation of the monarch of the whole globe. I have therefore placed their quarters in the lowest storey, and have only brought up those which either serve for man's amusement, or are not troublesome or annoying to them. This arrangement is explained, down to its minutest details, by means of numbers, plans of the ark and lists of the animals. Silberschlag has also sketched a detailed plan for the feeding and tending of the animals, and has divided the day's work suitably between the eight men.

I do not doubt that there may be many objections

to the details of this plan; but any one who looks at it with an unprejudiced mind, and is proof against the ludicrousness of parts of the exposition, will be impressed with the belief that the housing and feeding of an enormous number of animals in the ark cannot be proved to be impossible. As I have said, I think it neither necessary nor advisable to go into details in defending the Biblical narrative. In the description given of the Deluge in the Bible, it is considered only as a great divine judgment of destruction, and the ark as the means chosen by God for preserving part of the living beings in this judgment of destruction. At any rate, we must suppose that there was divine agency in it. But with God nothing is impossible,—not even an inundation of the earth in its widest sense, not even the preservation of all kinds of animals, and the dissemination of those saved in the ark over the whole earth. In the seventh chapter of Genesis, we stand at the beginning of a history, in the course of which not only natural and human powers are seen at work, but the Godhead often interferes in a great and striking manner. It would be a senseless undertaking to attempt to explain everything which the Bible narrates, in a natural manner. We cannot discuss separate events in the sacred history with any one who starts with the asssumption that nothing can ever have happened which is not compatible with the laws of nature as we know them; in such case it would be necessary to begin with those fundamental questions concerning the conception and possibility of miracle which belong properly to apologetics and not to exegesis.

But although we ought not to place the Deluge, and all that is connected with it, in the category of purely natural events, yet there is no reason why we should not assume that God made use of natural expedients in realizing His designs; and further, there is nothing to prevent our endeavouring, with careful reference to what Holy Scripture says, and to what we know about the forces and laws of nature, to ascertain what were these natural expedients of which God may have made use. As the narrative in Genesis is not complete and definite enough to give us a clear idea of the Flood considered as a physical event, it naturally follows that we can only conjecture as to the manner in which the event may have occurred, but that we cannot say with certainty how, with the co-operation of natural and supernatural causes, it did actually occur. Genesis, no doubt, does not assert that there was an inundation of the whole earth; but neither does it tell us what was the extent of the flood,—and, as we have seen, many things depend on this.[1]

[1] "The true question is, not whether or no Moses is to be believed in the matter, but whether or no we in reality understand Moses. The question is, whether we are to regard the passages in which he describes the Flood as universal, as belonging to the very numerous metonymic texts of Scripture, in which a part—sometimes a not very large part—is described as the whole, or to regard them as strictly and severely literal. Or, in other words, whether we are, with learned and solid divines of the olden time, such as Poole and Stillingfleet, and with many ingenious and accomplished divines of the passing age, such as the late Dr. Pye Smith and the Rev. Professor Hitchcock, to regard these passages as merely metonymic; or, with Drs. Hamilton and Kitto, to regard them as strictly literal, and to call up in support of the literal reading an amount of supposititious miracle, compared with which all the recorded miracles of the Old and New Testaments sink into insignificance. The controversy does not lie between Moses and the naturalists, but between the *readings* of theologians such as Matthew Poole and Stillingfleet on the one hand, and the *readings* of theologians such as Drs. Hamilton and Kitto on the

In conclusion, I must make a short observation about the Ark. Its size cannot be given accurately, because we do not know exactly how long the yard is which is mentioned in Genesis. If we suppose the yard to have measured about two feet—this, however, is the most that can be assumed—the ark must have been rather longer than Cologne Cathedral, but not half so broad, and only about one-third as high. (If the yard is reckoned at 21 English inches, the ark would have been 525 feet long, 87½ broad, 52½ high; the *Great Eastern* is 680 feet long, 83 broad, 58 high.) Celsus long ago ridiculed these enormous measurements, but it is well known that the most gigantic structures are those which belong to the earliest antiquity.

The proportions and the construction of the ark have also been objected to, and it has been asserted to be nautically useless. But in the year 1604, a Dutch Anabaptist, Peter Jensen, built a ship according to these proportions;[1] that is, 120 feet long, 20 broad, and 12 high. It was little suited for navigation, but could take a very large cargo. The ark was not intended to be a ship in the strict sense of the word; neither masts, nor sails, nor rudder are mentioned.

other. And finding all natural science arrayed against the conclusions of the one class, and in favour of those of the other, and believing, further, that there has always been a marked economy shown in the exercise of miraculous powers, that there has never been more of miracle employed in any one of the dispensations than was needed, I must hold that the theologians who believe that the Deluge was but co-extensive with the moral purpose which it served are more in the right, and may be more safely followed, than the theologians who hold that it extended greatly further than was necessary. It is not with Moses or the truth of revelation that our controversy lies, but with the opponents of Stillingfleet and Poole."—H. Miller, *Testimony*, pp. 340, 341.

[1] Cf. J. D. Michaelis, *Orient. und exeget. Bibliothek* (Frankf. 1782), xviii. 28.

It was a four-sided house, fit for floating and bearing weight; its floor was probably a raft well bound together. "It was not meant to steer or to sail, but only to float without being upset. It was not meant to make a voyage round the earth in the space of a year, but to remain close to the ancestral home of man."[1]

[1] Delitzsch, *Genesis*, p. 208.

END OF VOLUME I.

www.ingramcontent.com/pod-product-compliance
Lightning Source LLC
Chambersburg PA
CBHW022107300426
44117CB00007B/616